D1387884

Peter Bell

The Cornell Wordsworth

General Editor: Stephen Parrish
Associate Editor: Mark L. Reed
Assistant Editor: James A. Butler

Advisory Editors: M. H. Abrams, Geoffrey Hartman, Jonathan Wordsworth

---

An Evening Walk, edited by James Averill
Descriptive Sketches, edited by Eric Birdsall
The Salisbury Plain Poems, edited by Stephen Gill
The Borderers, edited by Robert Osborn
The Ruined Cottage and *The Pedlar,* edited by James Butler
Peter Bell, edited by John E. Jordan
The Prelude, 1798–1799, edited by Stephen Parrish
Home at Grasmere, edited by Beth Darlington
Benjamin the Waggoner, edited by Paul F. Betz
Poems, in Two Volumes, and Other Poems, 1800–1807, edited by Jared Curtis

CENTER FOR
SCHOLARLY EDITIONS
AN APPROVED EDITION
MODERN LANGUAGE
ASSOCIATION OF AMERICA

Peter Bell

by William Wordsworth

Edited by

JOHN E. JORDAN

WITHDRAWN

CORNELL UNIVERSITY PRESS

ITHACA AND LONDON

PUBLICATION OF THIS BOOK WAS ASSISTED BY GRANTS FROM THE PROGRAM FOR EDITIONS AND THE PUBLICATIONS PROGRAM OF THE NATIONAL ENDOWMENT FOR THE HUMANITIES, AN INDEPENDENT FEDERAL AGENCY.

Copyright © 1985 by Cornell University Press

All rights reserved. Except for brief quotations in a review, this book, or parts thereof, must not be reproduced in any form without permission in writing from the publisher. For information address Cornell University Press, 124 Roberts Place, Ithaca, New York 14850.

First published 1985 by Cornell University Press.

Published in the United Kingdom by Cornell University Press Ltd., London

Printed in the United States of America

Library of Congress Cataloging in Publication Data

Wordsworth, William, 1770–1850.
Peter Bell.

(Cornell Wordsworth)
I. Jordan, John E. II. Title. III. Series: Wordsworth, William. 1770–1850. Selections. 1981.
PR5869.P39 1984 821'.7 83-21042
ISBN 0-8014-1620-5

The paper in this book is acid-free and meets the guidelines for permanence and durability of the Committee on Production Guidelines for Book Longevity of the Council on Library Resources.

The Cornell Wordsworth

The individual volumes of the Cornell Wordsworth series, some devoted to long poems, some to collections of shorter poems, have two common aims. The first is to bring the early Wordsworth into view. Wordsworth's practice of leaving his poems unpublished for years after their completion, and his lifelong habit of revision—Ernest de Selincourt called it "obsessive"—have obscured the original, often the best, versions of his work. These original versions are here presented in the form of clean, continuous "reading texts" from which all layers of later revision have been stripped away. The second aim of the series is to provide, for the first time, a complete and accurate record of variant readings, from Wordsworth's earliest drafts down to the final lifetime or first posthumous publication. The most important manuscripts are shown in full transcription; on pages facing the transcriptions of the most complex and interesting of these manuscripts, photographs of the manuscript pages are also provided. Besides the transcriptions and the photographs, on which draft revisions may be seen, and an *apparatus criticus* in which printed variants are collected, a third device for the study of revisions is adopted: when two versions of a work match sufficiently well, they are arrayed on facing pages so that the steps by which one was converted into the other become visible.

Volumes in the series are unnumbered, but upon publication their titles are inserted into the list of volumes in print in the order in which the works were written. A more detailed introduction to the series may be found in the first volume published, *The Salisbury Plain Poems,* edited by Stephen Gill.

S. M. Parrish

Ithaca, New York

Contents

Preface

Wordsworth always regarded *Peter Bell* ("justly," said Ernest de Selincourt) as one of his great imaginative achievements. If critics have not commonly agreed with this assessment—the poem may seem to have drawn more scorn and parody than sympathetic appreciation—some further justification for this full edition of it can be found in the fact that Wordsworth worked over the poem so long that it has much of him in it, and that the five distinct manuscript versions that survive, along with the eight separate editions, afford us an unparalleled opportunity to observe the poet at work. De Selincourt's edition, in Volume II of *Poetical Works,* presents the final version—the 1849–50 text—and provides in an *apparatus* many early variants, but the variants are not complete and it is impossible for the reader to reconstruct the state of the poem at any given time. This edition tries to present *all* variants, in manuscript and in the lifetime printed editions, and to preserve the integrity of various versions of the poem, while separating an early and a late *Peter Bell.* Accordingly, it presents in parallel form an early reading text, dating from 1799, facing the first published edition, 1819, with later published variants and extant manuscript revisions to published texts appearing in an *apparatus.* There are also photographs and full transcriptions of the two earliest manuscripts, MSS. 1 and 2 (with variants in MSS. 3 and 4 in an *apparatus*), and a full transcription of MS. 5, accompanied by photographs through Part I and selected photographs from MS. 6 (with variants found in MS. 6 and in the surviving scrap of MS. 7 in an *apparatus*). The Introduction treats the history of the writing of the poem, describes the manuscripts, and speculates about the line of development as revision progressed.

I would like to express my gratitude to those who have helped in this long undertaking. First, this book is a genuine team effort: the supervising editors of the Cornell Wordsworth, together with the editors of other volumes in the series, have contributed significantly. I am indebted in particular to Stephen Gill, Jonathan Wordsworth, Mark Reed, James Butler, Paul Betz, Karen Green, Beth Darlington, and Carl Ketcham. Stephen Parrish has done more than could reasonably be expected of a general editor. Support furnished him by the National Endowment for the Humanities and by Cornell University also made possible the editorial assistance of Timothy

Bent, Linda Eisen, Ellen Jones, Veronica Kelly, Joseph Kishel, Evan Radcliffe, and William Thickstun. Other Wordsworthians and Dove Cottage people, including Phoebe Johnson, Nesta Clutterbuck, Sidney Cockerell, Mary Moorman, and Robert Woof, have been unfailingly cooperative. Richard Wordsworth's annual Summer Conference has played a role in helping me get to Grasmere. Of course I owe much to colleagues—notably Josephine Miles, Ulrich Knoepflmacher, and Alan Dundes—and to the Research Committee of the University of California at Berkeley for funding and for the research assistants that funding supported, especially Patricia Pelfrey and Robin Joly. I am also grateful to the many librarians and library authorities who made this work possible, especially the Trustees of Dove Cottage, the British Library, the Wellesley College Library, the Cornell University Library, and the Bancroft Library of the University of California, and for the gracious permission of Her Majesty Queen Elizabeth II for access to the Queen's Archives at Windsor Castle. Mention should also be made of the encouragement and assistance given my *Peter Bell* work by Carroll Camden, formerly editor of *Studies in English Literature,* and Marilyn Gaull, editor of *The Wordsworth Circle.* And finally, and always, of my manifold indebtedness to Marie.

JOHN E. JORDAN

Berkeley, California

Abbreviations

BL	British Library, London.
Chronology: EY	Mark L. Reed, *Wordsworth: The Chronology of the Early Years, 1770–1799* (Cambridge, Mass., 1967).
Chronology: MY	Mark L. Reed, *Wordsworth: The Chronology of the Middle Years, 1800–1815* (Cambridge, Mass., 1975).
DC MS.	Dove Cottage Manuscript (revised numbering).
De Q to W	John E. Jordan, *De Quincey to Wordsworth: A Biography of a Relationship, with the Letters of Thomas De Quincey to the Wordsworth Family* (Berkeley, 1963).
DW	Dorothy Wordsworth.
EY	*The Letters of William and Dorothy Wordsworth: The Early Years, 1787–1805,* ed. Ernest de Selincourt (2d ed.; rev. Chester L. Shaver; Oxford, 1967).
HCR	*Henry Crabb Robinson on Books and Their Writers,* ed. Edith J. Morley (3 vols.; London, 1938).
JC	John Carter, Wordsworth's secretary at Rydal Mount.
Journals	*Journals of Dorothy Wordsworth,* ed. Mary Moorman (Oxford, 1971).
Ketcham	*The Letters of John Wordsworth,* ed. Carl H. Ketcham (Ithaca, 1969).
Lucas	E. V. Lucas, *The Life of Charles Lamb* (London, 1914).
LY, I, II, III	*The Letters of William and Dorothy Wordsworth: The Later Years, 1821–1850,* ed. Ernest de Selincourt; (2d ed.; rev., arranged, and ed. Alan G. Hill; Oxford, 1978, 1979, 1982).
MH	Mary Hutchinson, later Mary Wordsworth.
MS. 1	MS. 1 of *Peter Bell,* DC MS. 18.
MS. 2	MS. 2 of *Peter Bell,* DC MS. 33.
MS. 3	MS. 3 of *Peter Bell,* DC MS. 34.
MS. 4	MS. 4 of *Peter Bell,* DC MS. 44.
MS. 5	MS. 5 of *Peter Bell,* DC MS. 60.
MS. 6	MS. 6 of *Peter Bell,* DC MS. 72.
MS. 7	MS. 7 of *Peter Bell,* DC MS. 105.
MS. 1819a/20	*Peter Bell,* second edition, containing Wordsworth's revisions, DC MS. 87.
MS. 1832/36	William Wordsworth, *Poetical Works* (4 vols., 1832), in the English Poetry Collection, Wellesley College Library, revised and used as printer's copy for the edition of 1836.
MS. 1836/45	William Wordsworth, *Poetical Works* (6 vols., 1836), in the Royal Library at Windsor Castle, in a proof state with revisions adopted 1836–1845.

MW	Mary Wordsworth.
MY, I, II	*Letters of William and Dorothy Wordsworth: The Middle Years, 1806–1820*, ed. Ernest de Selincourt (2 vols.; 2d ed.; Part I, 1806–1811, rev. Mary Moorman [Oxford, 1969]; Part II, 1812–1820, rev. Mary Moorman and Alan G. Hill [Oxford, 1970]).
Prose	*The Prose Works of William Wordsworth*, ed. W. J. B. Owen and J. W. Smyser (3 vols.; Oxford, 1974).
PW	*The Poetical Works of William Wordsworth*, ed. Ernest de Selincourt and Helen Darbishire (5 vols.; Oxford, 1940–1949; rev. 1952–1959).
SH	Sara Hutchinson.
SHL	*The Letters of Sara Hutchinson*, ed. Kathleen Coburn (London, 1954).
STCL	*Collected Letters of Samuel Taylor Coleridge*, ed. Earl Leslie Griggs (6 vols.; Oxford, 1956–1971).
STCNB	*Notebooks of Samuel Taylor Coleridge*, ed. Kathleen Coburn; vol. 2, 1804–1808, Text (London, 1962).
Stillinger	*William Wordsworth: Selected Poems and Prefaces*, ed. Jack Stillinger (Boston, 1965).
Waggoner	*Benjamin the Waggoner by William Wordsworth*, ed. Paul F. Betz (Ithaca, 1981).
WL	The Wordsworth Library, Grasmere.
WW	William Wordsworth.

Peter Bell

Introduction

I

Wordsworth lived with *Peter Bell* a long time. When he finally published it in 1819, he joked to Robert Southey in a dedicatory letter that the poem had "nearly survived its *minority*:—for it first saw the light in the summer of 1798." Its conception seems, in fact, to date from the spring of that year; Dorothy recorded in her Alfoxden journal for April 20: "William all the morning engaged in wearisome composition. The moon crescent. Peter Bell begun" (*Journals,* p. 14). Floyd Stoddard has suggested that Dorothy's comment is an oddly familiar way to refer to a poem *just* begun, and that perhaps *Peter* already had substantial existence; Dorothy may even have been talking of making a copy.[1] As Mark Reed points out, however, Dorothy often wrote up her journal entries some time after the events, and she could have been looking back at a poem that had a clear identity at the time she wrote, but was indeed "begun" on April 20. Reed even suggests that the reference to the crescent moon indicates that *Peter Bell* was begun after William and Dorothy returned from their evening walk (see *Chronology: EY,* pp. 32n, 233n). That is, of course, possible, and is suggested by the order of Dorothy's entry, although Dorothy's journal frequently mentions the moon—the "horned" moon, for example, on March 21 and 23, 1798 (*Journals,* p. 11). The horned or crescent moon, which is importantly related to the "little Boat" in the Prologue of *Peter Bell,* was probably in Wordworth's mind, and could have been the subject of a morning of "wearisome composition." At any rate, by about April 20, 1798, *Peter Bell* was under way.

Like much of Wordsworth's poetry, *Peter Bell* is retrospective, gathering up experiences and materials from his past, as the poet makes clear from his unusually circumstantial remarks about the poem to Isabella Fenwick:

> Founded upon an anecdote, which I read in a newspaper, of an ass being found hanging his head over a canal in a wretched posture. Upon examination a dead body was found in the water and proved to be the body of its master. The countenance, gait, and figure of Peter, were taken from a wild rover with whom I walked from Builth, on the river Wye, downwards nearly as far as the town of Hay. He told me strange stories. It has always been a pleasure to me through life to catch at every opportunity that has occurred in my rambles of becoming acquainted with this class of people. The number of Peter's wives was taken from the trespasses in this way of a

[1]Stoddard's suggestion appears in "Peter Bell: A Critical Edition," Ph.D. dissertation, Cornell University, 1965.

lawless creature who lived in the county of Durham, and used to be attended by many women, sometimes not less than half a dozen, as disorderly as himself, and a story went in the country that he had been heard to say while they were quarrelling, "Why can't you be quiet? there's none so many of you". Benoni, or the child of sorrow, I knew when I was a school-boy. His mother had been deserted by a gentleman in the neighbourhood, she herself being a gentlewoman by birth. The circumstances of her story were told me by my dear old Dame, Anne Tyson, who was her confidante. The lady died broken-hearted.—In the woods of Alfoxden I used to take great delight in noticing the habits, tricks, and physiognomy of asses; and I have no doubt that I was thus put upon writing the poem out of liking for the creature that is so often dreadfully abused. The crescent-moon, which makes such a figure in the prologue, assumed this character one evening while I was watching its beauty in front of Alfoxden House. I intended this poem for the volume before spoken of, but it was not published for more than 20 years afterwards.—The worship of the Methodists or Ranters is often heard during the stillness of the summer evening in the country with affecting accompaniments of rural beauty. In both the psalmody and the voice of the preacher there is, not unfrequently, much solemnity likely to impress the feelings of the rudest characters under favourable circumstances. [DC MS. 153, quoted in *PW*, II, 527]

The earliest of the events Wordsworth draws upon for *Peter Bell* is probably one that he owes to his Hawkshead School days (1779–1787), when Anne Tyson told him the history of Benoni (see the early reading text, ll. 1158–1160).[2] His account of meeting with the "wild rover" who told him "strange stories" on his way from Builth to Hay does not survive in the published *Peter Bell,* but is present in drafts in MS. 2 of 1799 (see transcription, ll. 941–965). The experience probably goes back to his 1793 trip to visit Robert Jones in Wales, which took him along the banks of the Wye (*Chronology: EY,* p. 145). The other pieces of the raw material of the poem are closer to the composition date, especially the observation of the "physiognomy of asses" in the Alfoxden woods. It is an oversimplification to suggest, as did the critic for the *Edinburgh Monthly Review* (II [1819], 657), that the ass is the hero of *Peter Bell*; nor does Wordsworth follow Coleridge in hailing the ass as "*Brother*" (*To a Young Ass, Its Mother Being Tethered Near It*), but obviously the ass is central to the genesis of the poem.

Apparently Wordsworth finished one version of *Peter Bell* more or less to his satisfaction fairly soon, for Hazlitt in his famous essay "My First Acquaintance with Poets," which describes a visit to the Wordsworths and Coleridge in the spring of 1798, reports having heard Wordsworth read the poem:

Wordsworth read us the story of Peter Bell in the open air; and the comment made upon it by his face and voice was very different from that of some later critics!

---

[2] If, as local stories have it, Peter Bell was the name of one of Wordsworth's schoolmates, the point cannot be verified. T. W. Thompson mentions no Peter Bell at Hawkshead School, though there were Bells in the Hawkshead neighborhood (*Wordsworth's Hawkshead,* ed. Robert Woof [London, 1970], pp. 60, 106). The benches in Hawkshead School are carved with several "R. B.'s," one "T. Bell," and one "J. T. Bell," but no "P. B.'s" or "Peter Bells" are now visible.

Whatever might be thought of the poem, "his face was as a book where men might read strange matters," and he announced the fate of his hero in prophetic tones.[3]

This reading probably took place between May 23 and June 12 (*Chronology: EY,* p. 238). It is hard to judge the nuances of Hazlitt's account, written some twenty-five years after the event, and after the personal relations of the participants had soured.[4] Certainly to quote Lady Macbeth's interpretation of her husband's expression when they were contemplating murder does not make Wordsworth's attitude toward *Peter Bell* entirely clear, but the implication is that he took the poem seriously; there appears to be no suggestion that the poet was displeased with his work, or considered it to be incomplete.

When next we hear of *Peter Bell,* however, Wordsworth does not seem to approve entirely of the 1798 version. In 1798–99, when he and Dorothy were in Goslar, Germany, he spent some of the bitter winter working on the poem with an eye to publishing it. He wrote Coleridge on February 27, 1799:

Wishing not to be in debt when I return to England I have lately been employ'd in hewing down Peter Bell, with another dressing I think he will do. He has risen in my esteem. Heaven knows there was need. The third part I think *interesting* a praise which I give myself with more pleasure as I know that in general I can lay little claim to it. [*EY,* p. 256]

"Hewing down" and "dressing" suggest that he was not making major structural changes, but reducing and polishing a work that was substantially intact. It is noteworthy that it is the third part, the redemptive finale, that he thinks "*interesting,*" and that he does not mention the Prologue or the "little boat / In shape just like a crescent moon."

Wordsworth did not push through his plans to depend on *Peter Bell* for funds when he and Dorothy returned to England in late April or early May 1799 (*Chronology: EY,* p. 267). Although the Fenwick note suggests that Wordsworth began *Peter Bell* with the idea that it would form a part of *Lyrical Ballads,* the poem did not get into the first edition of that work, perhaps because (as his Goslar opinion indicates) he did not think well enough of it, perhaps because his early contributions to *Lyrical Ballads* fitted into a pattern that was less narrative than was *Peter Bell,* and more statically descriptive.[5] Even when Wordsworth was thinking of a second edition of *Lyrical Ballads* and considered dropping *The Rime of the Ancyent Marinere,* which had attracted much criticism, he planned to "put in its place some little things which would be more likely to suit the common taste" (*EY,* p.

[3]P. P. Howe, ed., *The Complete Works of William Hazlitt* (21 vols.; London, 1930), XVII, 118.
[4]See Ralph M. Wardle, *Hazlitt* (Lincoln, Nebr., 1971), pp. 59n, 78–80, 85n.
[5]See my *Why the Lyrical Ballads?* (Berkeley, 1976), pp. 155–171.

264); he still did not, apparently, think of putting in *Peter Bell.* Nor was it included in *Lyrical Ballads* when that collection grew to two volumes, and possibly fulfilled Wordsworth's purpose of publishing to get himself out of debt—he was to receive £80 for two editions (*EY,* p. 310). Especially at this time Wordsworth was not disposed to publish more than was necessary to meet his financial needs. He told Joseph Cottle on July 27, 1799: "My aversion from publication increases every day, so much so, that no motives whatever, nothing but pecuniary necessity, will, I think, ever prevail upon me to commit myself to the press again" (*EY,* p. 267).

In any event, *Peter Bell* (like so many other long poems throughout Wordsworth's career) continued to languish unpublished—whatever Wordsworth may have meant by writing to Coleridge on December 24, 1799: "As to the Tragedy and Peter Bell, D. will do all in her power to put them forward" (*EY,* p. 277). It sounds as if Wordsworth considered that he had done, himself, about all he expected to do to *Peter*; Dorothy's chore may have been to complete a fair copy, and it is possible that she did just that in preparing MS.2 (see sec. II, below). But Wordsworth seems to have been looking at *Peter Bell* still in 1800. Dorothy's journal for August 23 records: "We had intended going by Rydale woods, but it was cold—I was not well, and tired. Got tea immediately and had a fire. Did not reach home till 7 o'clock—mended stockings—and W. read Peter Bell. He read us the Poem of Joanna beside the Rothay by the roadside" (*Journals,* p. 35). Dorothy's back-and-forth chronicle does not make clear whether Wordsworth read *Peter Bell* to himself in working it over or read it to "us" (presumably Dorothy and John) as a completed work—probably the latter, for John remembered the poem favorably. From aboard the *Earl of Abergavenny* at Portsmouth he wrote to Dorothy on April 22, 1801: "I always liked the preface to Peter Bell & would be obliged if you could send it to me—" (Ketcham, p. 119). When Dorothy obliged by sending, presumably, the Prologue—Reed suggests on April 29 (*Chronology: MY,* p. 119)—John thanked her for "the beginning of Peter Bell" and added, "I will be much obliged to you if you would let me have as much of the poem as possible" (Ketcham, p. 123). What the limitations of "possible" might be is not clear. John may only have been considerate of Dorothy's scrivener chores, but his phrase could suggest that he did not believe the poem to be yet finished.

Peter Bell seems to be finished, however, in a fair copy—the most nearly complete early copy to have survived (MS. 3)—that bears the inscription "Mary Hutchinson—Gallow-hill," and is partly in Mary's hand. The copy cannot be dated precisely; we cannot even be certain that Mary's maiden name was not put in the notebook earlier than the transcription of *Peter Bell.* But we have at least the intriguing possibility that Peter—he of twelve wives—assisted in 1800–1801 in Wordsworth's courtship of his future wife.

In 1802 there was more activity over *Peter,* some of it very precisely dated. Dorothy recorded in her journal for February 17 that she "copied the 2nd part of Peter Bell" (*Journals,* p. 92). The next day, in William's "absence," she copied the "third part of Peter Bell." Then on February 20 "After Tea" she "wrote the first part of Peter Bell," and on February 21 wrote "the 2nd prologue to Peter Bell" and "After dinner" added "the 1st Prologue." The curious order of Dorothy's transcription may owe something to the condition of the manuscript she was following, which would affect what it was feasible for her to attempt in Wordsworth's "absence." Obviously, not all of the contemporary activity over *Peter* consisted of Dorothy's copying, because on February 22, according again to Dorothy's record, Mr. Simpson came in and William "began to read Peter Bell to him" (*Journals,* p. 94). Wordsworth may have wearied—perhaps he ran out of voice—for he called Dorothy, who had returned to the kitchen fire to write to Coleridge, to come "to read the 3rd part." There may be some connection with the fact that she had copied that part on her own, or possibly Wordsworth still thought the third part "interesting" and wanted to hear it, possibly to observe Mr. Simpson's reaction to it. Less than a month later (March 10, 1802) Dorothy recorded that "William has since Tea been talking about publishing the Yorkshire Wolds poem with the Pedlar" (*Journals,* p. 99). The "Yorkshire Wolds poem" may have been *Peter Bell,* as de Selincourt and Reed suggest (*PW,* V, 366 and *Chronology: MY,* p. 152, which refers to *Journals,* p. 99). The identification is plausible, though it is puzzling that Dorothy should suddenly change the title she had been using for the poem. If she was talking about *Peter Bell,* her designation suggests a different way of thinking about it, shifting the emphasis from the character or the tale to the supposed setting. In any event, nothing came of the talk of publication.

The Wordsworths valued *Peter Bell* enough to include it in the collection of William's poems put together for Coleridge to take abroad, to Malta, in April 1804—the present DC MS. 44 (*Chronology: MY,* p. 636). Coleridge had doubtless known *Peter Bell* since 1798. That he had it in mind in Malta is clear from his notebook entry dated May 12, 1805. He had been making what he considered an "important" observation about the physiological/psychological bases of illusions that may "occasion in the highest degree the Wraith," and he cites an example from "Wordsworth's most wonderful as well as admirable Poem, Peter Bell, where he sees his own Figure" (*STCNB,* II, no. 2583). Coleridge even called the poem to the attention of his superior, Sir Alexander Ball, governor of Malta; in *The Friend* (no. 21, January, 25, 1810) Coleridge reports Sir Alexander's reaction:

> the only poetical Composition, of which I have ever heard him speak, was a Manuscript Poem written by one of my Friends, which I read to his Lady in his presence.

To my surprize, he afterwards spoke of this with warm interest; but it was evident to me, that it was not so much the poetic merit of the Composition that interested him, as the Truth and psychological insight with which it represented the practicability of reforming the most hardened minds, and the various accidents which may awaken the most brutalized Person to a recognition of his nobler Being.[6]

In a footnote to his 1818 edition of *The Friend,* Coleridge makes positive the identification of the poem: "I cannot resist the temptation of recording that it was Mr. Wordsworth's PETER BELL."[7] Although Wordsworth believed on August 1, 1806, that Coleridge had lost "*all* his papers" (*MY,* I, 64), he was misinformed, for Coleridge still had a manuscript copy of *Peter Bell,* perhaps the Malta notebook, which De Quincey reports Coleridge allowed him to read in 1807 (*De Q to W,* p. 326).

By this time Wordsworth had been reading and working over *Peter Bell* some more. The only hard evidence we have is in the form of references in letters of Dorothy and Sara Hutchinson. Dorothy wrote Lady Beaumont on January 3, 1808, nostalgically recollecting "the happy evening we spent together at the reading of *Peter Bell*" (*MY,* I, 188). This "happy evening" is not precisely datable; it could have occurred during the Wordsworths' visits with the Beaumonts at Coleorton, October 30–November 2, 1806, or June 3–10, 1807, or more probably when the Beaumonts were visiting at Grasmere, September 5–12, 1807 (*Chronology: MY,* pp. 339, 355, 362). If this is the occasion on which Lady Beaumont objected to the "party in a parlour" passage (*PW,* II, 529–530), Dorothy's tone suggests that her protests were amiable enough. Sara's letter, dated March 29, 1812, reports: "I have been transcribing the *Peter Bell* which is now completely finished and improved—and I intend to make another copy for myself when William has done with my Pen—" (*SHL,* p. 46). Two fair copies of *Peter Bell* exist in Sara's hand, but they are considerably different, and if one is the 1812 version, the other is probably earlier (see sec. II, below)—it may even be the copy read to the Beaumonts. Sara's "completely finished and improved" makes clear both that Wordsworth had been revising the poem and that she, at least, and probably he also, was more or less satisfied with it. But *Peter Bell* was not yet "finished." The second of the two copies in Sara's hand has been much revised by Wordsworth, and although the modified version is close to the published state of 1819, it is not identical with it. Perhaps "hewing" might now be better thought of as "honing," but the process went on; it continued even after the poem appeared in print. Since, however, we have been seeing *Peter Bell* through its "*minority*" largely on the basis of such external evidence

---

[6]*The Friend,* ed. Barbara E. Rooke, in *The Collected Works of Samuel Taylor Coleridge* (2 vols.; Princeton, 1969), II, 290.

[7]Ibid., I, 543.

as journals and letters, it is time now to go back and look at the manuscript evidence.

II

The earliest extant manuscript is DC MS. 18 (formerly Verse 34), which de Selincourt has labeled MS. 1 (for his designations, which I follow, see *PW*, II, 528–529). This manuscript is written on unlined laid paper, measuring 12.5 by 20.5 centimeters, watermarked with a small fleur-de-lys and countermarked B over the date 1795; the chain lines are approximately 2.6 centimeters apart. MS. 1 is apparently a much-worked-over fair copy made by Dorothy with the intention of writing on recto pages only; she ran over to the verso twice, once for one stanza, once for two. Some of the blank versos have been used by Wordsworth for revisions of *Peter Bell*; some were taken up later by drafts of blank verse that are identifiable as versions of *St. Paul's*, *To the Clouds*, and *The Tuft of Primroses* (*PW*, IV, 374; II, 316; and V, 348). This manuscript may be the copy of *Peter Bell* from which Hazlitt heard Wordsworth read in 1798. In its present state the two most notable characteristics of this version of *Peter Bell* are its fragmentary condition and the number of stanzas that have been canceled and do not appear in any other version (see headnote to transcription of MS. 1, below). There is no title page or heading; at least the first page is missing, and perhaps six pages are. The text begins at the equivalent of line 91 of the early reading text. The end of the manuscript has apparently been lost; *Peter Bell* stops in the vicinity of line 670 of the reading text. There are also internal gaps; stubs reveal that at least four pages bearing text have been cut out, and the top of one page and the bottom of another have been torn off. Since some of the missing pages may have contained cancellations—some of the stubs show the marks—we cannot be certain how much of MS. 1 was struck out, but it seems likely that at least 38 stanzas were—a high proportion of the extant manuscript. The cancellations are variously made—some in ink, some in pencil, some by scratching through lines, some by different systems of crossing out—suggesting that they occurred at various times and under a variety of impulses. Possibly some of these cancellations were effected in the "hewing" at Goslar; their vigor suits that term.

The next two manuscripts (de Selincourt's MSS. 2 and 3) are so similar that they are generally recognized to be nearly contemporary fair copies. MS. 2 is written largely in Dorothy's hand (William copied the end of Part II and began Part III) in a notebook bound in marble boards (DC MS. 33, formerly Verse 36), having unlined pages 9.8 by 15 centimeters. The paper is laid, showing chain lines about 2.8 centimeters apart, and an elaborate watermark, probably Britannia with a trident, and the legend PRO PATRIA. *Peter Bell* is written on 143 pages of this notebook, including the rear pasted-down endpaper; it begins on the recto of the first free leaf, and regularly uses rectos and versos for the text, three stanzas to the page. The verso of leaf 17 however, was used for an insertion to be made earlier in the text, and from that point on, versos were left blank in the transcription, though some were later used for additions and revisions. The binding is now loose, and some leaves have apparently come out, containing probably the equivalent of lines 171–400 and 546–560 of the early reading text. A leaf is torn out at the beginning of Part II.

An important clue to the date of MS. 2 is the fact that there is a section of 18 leaves (all but 6 are now stubs) between Part II and Part III of *Peter Bell* in which appear, among other things, some lines from *The Brothers* and a prose note to *To Joanna* entered, according to Reed, "shortly prior to 23 August 1800" (*Chronology: MY,* pp. 127–128n). Conceivably this note could have been entered in the notebook first and *Peter Bell* written in around it, but it seems curious that the Wordsworths should have picked up the notebook and, leaving the beginning and end blank, begun in the middle to use it for a variety of small entries; they would have been more likely, one might think, to turn the notebook upside down (as they did with other manuscripts) and enter the miscellaneous material at the back. It is more plausible to suppose that something interrupted the transcription of *Peter Bell,* and that the materials that now appear between Parts II and III were entered as a result of that interruption. There appear to be two possibilities. One is that the text of *Peter Bell* was stopped after Part II until Wordsworth could himself make some sense of the drafts of his "interesting" Part III; that this may have seemed necessary to Dorothy could be indicated by the fact that Part III is a fairly clean copy largely in Wordsworth's hand. Perhaps, however, Wordsworth did not promptly get around to deciphering Part III, or possibly did not then think it necessary, with the result that the notebook was treated as free for other use, until a change of plans called for the addition of Part III. The other possibility is that Part III was entered in the notebook before Part II, with a generous space (too generous, as it turned out) left for the omitted material. It is worth observing that Part III was recognized here as separate enough from the rest of the poem to require special identification: while the other manuscripts label this section "Part Third" or "Third Part," MS. 2 heads it "Peter Bell / Part 3^{d}," and there is no indication of squeezing to suggest that this heading was an afterthought. Moreover, the punctuation, especially toward the beginning of Part III in MS. 2, is especially full and careful, as though transcription were just starting. It thus seems to follow that either Part III was written into MS. 2 after the interpolated material or it was begun after a space had been left in the notebook. Dorothy's report of the way she jumped around in copying MS. 4 suggests that Part III of MS. 2 could have been transcribed before Part II, the copyist leaving room for the second part, or the first and second parts—what turned out to be too much room; the interpolated material could then have been written afterward in space that would otherwise have been wasted.

MS. 2 thus appears to be the first fair copy of *Peter Bell* made after the Goslar "hewing" of the poem. Evidence that the copy was itself made in Goslar lies in the presence of some German financial accounts scrawled on one of the leaves in the middle of the notebook, along with the later scraps of verse and prose datable 1800.

MS. 3 (DC MS. 34, formerly Verse 37) is noteworthy because it has special early connections with Mary Wordsworth, and because it does not appear to have been as much used for later revision as were other manuscripts. It is a neat fair copy, written, for the most part, four stanzas to the page on pages measuring 10.5 by 17.7 centimeters of laid paper having chain lines about 2.5 centimeters apart, undated, watermarked with a heraldic figure in a crowned wreath flanked by the initials I and B. The notebook is hand-sewn and there is no proper cover, but a folded half sheet now loose probably served as cover. On it Mary wrote: "Mary Hutchinson— / Gallow-hill, / Galu-hill"; this inscription stands on what must have been the top right-hand corner of the sheet. Mary also began transcription of the poem; she copied the Prologue, most of the first part, and some of the second. Dorothy wrote most of the second part, William taking over from time to time, and two other hands appear in the transcription; one of them entered most of the third part. The odd position of the "Gallow-hill" inscription (it now appears upside down at the bottom of the second page of the wrapper) makes its relation to the *Peter Bell* text uncertain, but the possibility exists that this version of the poem was made for and partly by Mary before she married William on October 4, 1802; she had moved to the farm called Gallow Hill in Yorkshire, near Scarborough, on May 21, 1800. A fascinating possibility is that Mary and Dorothy began copying MS. 3 when Mary visited Dove Cottage from late February to early April 1800 (*Chronology: MY*, p. 59), and that Mary, William, and unidentified helpers (perhaps more explicable in the Gallow Hill setting) worked on it and possibly finished it during Wordsworth's visit to Gallow Hill in late May to early June 1800. Mary and her family may have been involved even earlier, for Mark Reed's recent identification of one of the hands in MS. 3 as that of George Hutchinson, Mary's youngest brother, strongly suggests that this copy was written at least in part at Sockburn between May and November 1799. It seems clear in any case that wherever MS. 3 was copied, the underlying texts of the poem in MSS. 2 and 3, which are the basis of the early reading text, can be dated 1799.

The relation between MSS. 2 and 3 is tantalizing; they are close but different. The same blanks, for instance, are left following lines 117 and 164 and in line 833. Of the stanzas in MS. 3 that do not appear in MS. 2, three are canceled in MS. 3, and we might suppose that they were canceled tentatively or ambiguously in the source copy, and perhaps mistakenly recorded in MS. 3. Yet it seems clear that the earliest state of MS. 2 antedates the earliest state of MS. 3. An interesting small example is seen in the line that appeared in 1819 (l. 888) as "'Twas by a troop of miners made." The word that became "troop" was first "group" in MS. 2, revised there to "band," then to "crew" before becoming "troop." In MS. 3, however, the word started as "crew" and went to "troop," which suggests that MS. 3 came into the evolutionary process somewhat later than did MS. 2. It is hard to suppose that *all* of MS. 3 was simply copied from MS. 2. Some of the textual differences, such as "barge" for "boat," might be attributable to a careless copyist; an extra stanza in MS. 3 adjacent to three stanzas missing in MS. 2 where a leaf is lost might possibly have stood on the verso of the missing leaf. But a greater difficulty arises from an inserted passage of two stanzas in MS. 2 (on 17^v) canceled as a unit by one large X: one of these stanzas appears in regular sequence in MS. 3 and the other does not, which suggests that at this point the copyist of MS. 3 was referring to something other than MS. 2.

Nonetheless, clear evidence shows that substantial parts of MS. 3 derive from MS. 2. A scattering of obvious copyists' errors in the latter are reproduced in MS. 3 and then corrected there ("asse's," for example, altered to "ass's"). Even more convincing evidence shows up where for obvious reasons MS. 2 was misread by the copyist of MS. 3. At line 129 "bower" in MS. 2 is written carelessly so that it resembles "tower," which is the reading of MS. 3. At line 486 the upper loop of an imperfectly erased letter survives in MS. 2, resembling an "s" at the end of "side," and the reading of MS. 3 is "sides." At line 776 MS. 2 reads, in error, "Peter's" (for "Peter"), and the error copied into MS. 3 is corrected there; similarly, in lines 1147 and 1436 MS. 2 omits a word that had to be supplied by insertion in MS. 3. While the matter cannot be settled with entire precision, it does seem reasonably certain that much of MS. 3 is based on MS. 2.

The many corrections and revisions entered in MS. 2 can be separated into three layers: some were made in the process of transcription, some were made later but before MS. 3 was transcribed, and some were made after transcription of MS. 3 and adopted in subsequent manuscripts. MS. 2, that is, was used as a working copy after MS. 3 had been separated from it and given to Mary Hutchinson.

The next manuscript, MS. 4, is the one that Dorothy records in her Grasmere journal as having copied in February 1802; it bears on the title page her notation: "Grasmere Sunday 1/2 past 5 o'clock by the Gold watch, now hanging above the fire—a rainy coldish day—Snow on the ground—but there is a thrush singing February 21st 1802." The manuscript is included in the vellum-bound MS. M (DC MS. 44; for a description of its contents see *Chronology: MY*, Appendix III). This collection was put together for Coleridge to take to Malta and Italy, but with regard to *Peter Bell* Dorothy's remarks to Coleridge on March 6, 1804, are likely to be misleading. She wrote:

We have transcribed all William's smaller Poems for you, and have begun the Poem on his Life and the Pedlar, but before we send them off we mean to take another Copy for ourselves, for they are scattered about here and there in this book and in that, one Stanza on one leaf, another on another which makes the transcribing more than twice the trouble. . . . [*EY*, p. 448]

The implication of Dorothy's statement is that special transcriptions were being made for Coleridge, but this was not true of *Peter Bell* MS. 4. There is no doubt that this copy of the poem was among the poems given to Coleridge, for it bears on its title page in Coleridge's autograph the notation "Fra 6 e 7," which Reed suggests (*Chronology: MY*, p. 636) constitutes directions to Italian binders to place this manuscript between sections 6 and 7 of the other materials, which are numbered in blocks. Dorothy's headnote, however, indicates that this copy of *Peter Bell* was made two years before 1804, and its form shows clearly that it is not of a piece with the other poems in MS. M; its pages, measuring 11 by 18.5–19 centimeters, are longer than the other pages in MS. M by about two centimeters and they had to be folded up from the bottom. Moreover, the paper used for the text (the title page is a separate sheet)—laid paper having chain lines about 2.5 centimeters apart, watermarked by an oval flanked by the initials L and G—shows faint signs of having gilt on the edges,[8] suggesting that the pages were once part of a notebook from which they were cut, either by the Wordsworths before the manuscript was sent to Coleridge, or by Coleridge, or by his binders before the pages were bound up with the other poems in MS. M. One suspects the latter because there are blank pages (rectos and versos) at inexplicable places in the text, blanks that would hardly be present were a loose sheaf of papers being forwarded, especially since there is also evidence of leaves having been cut from the gathering for cause: no stubs show, no gaps in the text appear, but one page is cut out in the context of a long, crowded insertion on the preceding verso, suggesting replacement of canceled material. The blank pages may even have been put by the binders in the wrong place (see MS. 3, 8ʳ, ll. 281–285, and MS. 2, 68ʳ, ll. 1102–1103).

MS. 4 is the most formally set up of all the manuscripts of *Peter Bell,* having both a full title page and a half-title (see *apparatus criticus* to the transcription of MS. 2). Dorothy took advantage of the long pages to copy regularly five stanzas to the recto (one recto has an extra stanza inserted at the bottom, making a total of six): there are 51 rectos used for the text. Versos are blank except those used for insertions, usually in Dorothy's hand, and revisions or variants in William's; some of the latter are in pencil. Some

---

[8] I owe this observation to Sidney Cockerell, who restored MS. M.

of the revisions were put in fairly late, and appear to have influenced MS. 6 (see *apparatus criticus* to transcription of MS. 2, 36r, and MS. 5, 37r), suggesting that after Coleridge returned to England he gave the manuscript back to Wordsworth and that it continued in use for work on *Peter Bell.*

Although MS. 4 succeeds MS. 3, it probably does not derive directly from it; most likely MS. 3 was still at Gallow Hill when Dorothy made the copy that became MS. 4. This assumption fits the following facts: a long insertion on a verso adds eight stanzas to MS. 4, only five of which are in MS. 3; on another verso of MS. 4 is inserted a stanza that is not in MS. 3, but the first line of which is inserted there followed by "&" (suggesting that the stanza belongs in the text but is derived from another copy); a stanza canceled in MS. 3 but not canceled in MS. 2 appears in MS. 4; and two stanzas in the original MS. 3 are not in the base text of MS. 4 but have been inserted there on versos. Dorothy left four blanks in the last section of *Peter Bell* in MS. 4: one of the pertinent passages is corrected in MSS. 2 and 3; one is corrected in MS. 2 and clean in MS. 3; one is corrected in MS. 3 and clean in MS. 2—all suggesting that MS. 4 is derived from some manuscript other than MS. 2 or 3.

There are, however, signs of a close relationship between MSS. 3 and 4. Except for two stanzas that are also canceled in MS. 2 and do not appear in MS. 4, stanzas canceled in MS. 3 do not appear in MS. 4. Three of these stanzas may have been canceled in MS. 2 also; we cannot say, since these sections of MS. 2 are missing. We know that at least six stanzas canceled in MS. 3 are also canceled in MS. 2 and do not appear in MS. 4, and that three stanzas canceled in MS. 3 are not present in either MS. 2 or MS. 4. But two stanzas present in MS. 2 are canceled in MS. 3 and omitted from MS. 4; another stanza canceled in MS. 2 is also canceled in MS. 3 but marked there "in" and "in by all means" and is inserted in MS. 4, as if in response to the MS. 3 instruction.

MS. 5 (DC MS. 60, formerly Verse 35) is a neat fair copy in the hand of Sara Hutchinson on pages measuring 11.5 by 18.8–9 centimeters, numbered 1 through 68 (apparently by Sara, who skipped 43 and did not number a page at the end, used for a draft of ll. 156–165). Sara normally wrote on rectos, usually four stanzas to the page, but sometimes running a stanza over. Some material erased and rewritten in Mary's hand is present; there are some further insertions and revisions on rectos in William's hand. The date of MS. 5 is uncertain. As we have seen, Sara reported making a copy of *Peter Bell* in March 1812, and intending to make another. It is tempting to suppose that MS. 5 is one of those copies, but other indications point to an earlier date. Casually bound in a piece of vellum that was part of a conveyance of Allanby Manor, MS. 5 is written on laid paper having chain lines about 2.5 centimeters apart; the watermark is a crowned horn-in-shield and the countermark is 1798. This paper is used in many Wordsworth documents, including DC MSS. 56 and 57 and *Benjamin the Waggoner* MS. 2

(Ashley 4637 in the British Library; see *Chronology: MY*, pp. 312, 698, and *Waggoner*, p. 141). Although it could, of course, have been on hand as early as 1798, it is not known to have been used in the Wordsworth circle before 1805, and rarely after 1808. More than a third of the family letters written in 1806 use the paper,[9] and Reed, following Paul Betz, dates MS. 5 between October 30, 1806, and mid-April 1807 (*Chronology: MY*, p. 21).

MS. 5 is clearly a transitional manuscript; its original readings are close to those of MS. 4, usually following revisions in MS. 4, and its revised state is close to the original MS. 6. Often MS. 5 is so close to MS. 4 as to invite the belief that it was copied from MS. 4; and since MS. 4 was at one time in Malta and MS. 5 follows revisions in MS. 4 that seem to have been made after Coleridge returned the manuscript to Wordsworth, we would therefore have a date *ab quo* of sometime after late 1806. There are, however, differences between MS. 4 and the original text of MS. 5. Some of them could well have been introduced intentionally or carelessly by the copyist: expansion of ampersands, more formal capitalization and punctuation, changes of "from" to "through" and "doleful" to "dolorous," perhaps even changes from "scenes" to "sights" and "Come" to "Haste." Such differences, however, as that between "On me it cannot easy sit" and "Aw'd am I when I think of it" or that between "The meagre beast lay still as death" and "With legs stretched out and still he lay" indicate different sources, as does the presence in the base text of MS. 5 of stanzas not in MS. 4. It is possible to explain some of the latter on the basis of erasures in MS. 4 or pages cut out, but at least two stanzas in original MS. 5 cannot be so accounted for.

In short, the differences between MS. 4 and original MS. 5 are significant enough to make it improbable that Sara simply copied MS. 5 from MS. 4. We remember that Dorothy spoke of making "another Copy" for themselves before they sent William's poems off to Coleridge (*EY*, p. 448), and that when the Wordsworths believed that Coleridge had lost all his papers, William felt no alarm about his own poems because, as he wrote on August 1, 1806, "of all these I have copies" (*MY*, I, 64). Of course, as far as *Peter Bell* is concerned, Wordsworth may have been thinking of MSS. 2 and 3, but the possibility remains that there was another manuscript very close to MS. 4 which stayed in Westmorland and, having been worked over a little, served as Sara's copy source for MS. 5. Since MS. 5 generally incorporates the revisions in MS. 4, we may suppose that they were also in the postulated parallel to MS. 4 used by Sara. We cannot be sure when the revisions were entered in MS. 4—they could even have been inserted after MS. 5 was made—but the differences in ink and in the style of the revisions suggest that they were made over a period of time, not simply copied in from another manuscript. Probably, therefore, MS. 5 still postdates the revised MS. 4 and was written sometime after Coleridge's return. If MS. 4 remained

[9] I owe this information about paper use by the Wordsworth family to Paul Betz.

in Coleridge's hands so that he could allow De Quincey to read it in 1807 (see *De Q to W*, p. 326), and Wordsworth did not make his revisions until after he got it back, MS. 5 may date from 1807–8 or later.

The revised form of MS. 5 is almost certainly later; it is most probably the source of another transcription of *Peter Bell* by Sara Hutchinson, MS. 6, which may be one of those she talked of making in 1812, although de Selincourt dates it later (*PW*, II, 529). MS. 6 is DC MS. 72 (formerly Verse 52A), a marbled notebook quarter-bound in red calf which also contains *Benjamin the Waggoner* and *Artigal* [sic] *and Elidure* (see *Waggoner*, p. 282). The paper shows no chain lines; it is watermarked "Holland and Co" and countermarked with a date whose third digit always falls in the binding. All that is clearly visible of this date in the *Peter Bell* section of the manuscript is "18 8"; in the *Waggoner* section what looks like a bit of "0" shows. The pages are 11.5 by 18.6 centimeters; *Peter Bell* is entered on rectos and versos, normally three stanzas to the page; the pages are unnumbered. This manuscript began as a handsome fair copy, but it was later much revised; some of the revisions were made in pencil by William and written over in ink by Mary.

Although the revised version of MS. 6 is close to the first published edition of 1819, MS. 6 was clearly not the printer's copy. A single sheet that has come to light (in DC MS. 73, but now transferred to DC MS. 105) and been called MS. 7 was once part of that copy. MS. 7 consists of one sheet folded into two pages 18.2–18.3 by 22.5–22.6 centimeters, numbered "40" and "41" in upper right corners. The paper shows no chain lines and is watermarked 1816; it is the paper used in family letters from early December 1818 to mid-January 1819. The sheet seems to have been used first for *Peter Bell* and blank spaces later filled in with other verse. There are three stanzas of *Peter Bell* to the page: the last three stanzas of Part II and the first three of Part III (ll. 771–800 of the 1819 text). Although there are a few corrections, the copy is clean; punctuation looks as if it had been added after the text was copied. Readings of MS. 7 are given, along with those of MS. 6, in the *apparatus criticus* to the transcription of MS. 5.

III

What finally spurred Wordsworth to publish *Peter Bell* in 1819 is not known. He dedicated the poem to Southey, who only the year before had handsomely associated himself with Wordsworth, whom he recognized as his superior and whom he ranked with Milton.[10] It may be that Wordsworth thought some public response called for, and took the occasion to recognize part of his difference from the Romantic "epic" poet with whom he had been lumped in the "Lake School" by presenting a sort of mock epic told ostensibly by an inept village Milton.

---

[10] "A Letter to Henry Brougham, Esquire," BL Add. MS. 47890, f. 17.

In any event, Wordsworth did finally issue *Peter Bell* in April 1819, through his regular publisher, Longman, Hurst, Rees, Orme, and Brown. The reception was mixed: some reviewers praised the moral tone, others ridiculed the ludicrous machinery. Even before Wordsworth's poem was published there appeared what John Hamilton Reynolds called "an *Anticipated Parody*";[11] his *Peter Bell, A Lyrical Ballad* was published anonymously on April 15. As Sara Hutchinson put it, "a spurious Peter . . . made his appearance a week before the true one" (*SHL,* p. 154). Coleridge was sufficiently exercised by what he considered a breach of decorum to protest to Reynolds' publishers, Taylor and Hessey. The publishers replied that their author was a "true lover of Mr W's poetry" who had been moved to write this burlesque by "the Announcement of a new Poem with so untimely a Title as that of Peter Bell" and who had "never heard a line of the original poem" (*STCL,* IV, 934–935n). The parody contains suspicious echoes, however, which suggest some knowledge of the original. Sara thought Hazlitt was the parodist, but reported that Wordsworth insisted "H. could *not* write anything so foolish."

The whole episode had two significant effects on Wordsworth and on *Peter Bell.* First, the attack on the "untimely" title no doubt moved Wordsworth to use as an epigraph for *The Waggoner* (first announced as *Benjamin the Waggoner*), published in June 1819, a quotation from *Julius Caesar*: "What's in a Name? Brutus will start a Spirit as soon as Caesar!"—an epigraph that he transferred to *Peter Bell* in the 1827 edition of his *Poetical Works* and thereafter. Second, the parody probably increased demand for the real article. As Sara, who thought the false *Peter* "very stupid," explained, "I have no doubt that it has helped the sale of the true one—which has nearly all been sold in about a week" (*SHL,* p. 154). Thus, ironically, *Peter Bell* became Wordsworth's best-selling poem; a second edition came out within two weeks of the first. Sara thought the second edition had "no corrections except in printing," but she was not entirely accurate. Although there are indeed very few alterations, a note was added near the beginning of Part I defining "Potter."

Wordsworth answered his critics defensively in a sonnet, *On the Detraction which followed the Publication of a Certain Poem,* which he pointedly compared to Milton's "A Book was writ of late called 'Tetrachordon'" and published in the 1820 *River Duddon* volume (and thereafter among the "Miscellaneous Sonnets"):

> A Book came forth of late called, "Peter Bell;"
> Not negligent the style;—the matter?—good
> As aught that song records of Robin Hood;
> Or Roy, renowned through many a Scottish dell;
> But some (who brook those hacknied themes full well,

[11]*The Letters of John Hamilton Reynolds,* ed. L. M. Jones (Lincoln, Nebr., 1973), p. 65.

Nor heat, at Tam o'Shanter's name, their blood)
Waxed wrath, and with foul claws, a harpy brood—
On Bard and Hero clamorously fell.
Heed not, wild Rover once through heath and glen
Who mad'st at length the better life thy choice,
Heed not such onset! nay, if praise of men
To thee appear not an unmeaning voice,
Lift up that grey-haired forehead, and rejoice
In the just tribute of thy Poet's pen!

Nevertheless, when (also in 1820) Longman brought out *The Miscellaneous Poems of William Wordsworth* in four volumes, the poet took special trouble to make Peter more presentable. Henry Crabb Robinson described his perception of the poet's mood:

We talked of our expected journey. . . . He was, however, more occupied about the new edition of *Peter Bell.* He has resolved to make some concessions to public taste, and has resolved to strike out several offensive passages, such as "Is it a party in a parlour, etc.," which I had implored him to leave out before the book first appeared. So the over-coarse expressions: "But I will bang your bones," etc. I never before saw Wordsworth so little opinionated. [*HCR,* I, 241]

The poet was not, however, really "little opinionated." On May 22, 1819, he wrote Lord Lonsdale: "Peter Bell has furnished abundant employment to the Witlings and the small critics, who have been warring with me for more than 20 years, and seem more bitter than ever. Somebody, however, must have been pleased, for the Edition was sold in a few days" (*MY,* II, 542–543).

He still thought the witlings were wrong, but he was enjoying the sale and wanted it to continue. *The Examiner* as well as Lady Beaumont had joined Crabb Robinson in objecting to the "party in a parlour" passage, and Wordsworth later told Barron Field that he dropped the stanza, "though one of the most imaginative in the whole piece," in order "not to offend the pious" (*LY,* I, 646). Similarly, the *British Critic* and the *Eclectic Review* had objected to the "*bang* your bones" passage.[12] Therefore the unpersuaded but amenable Wordsworth did indeed drop from the 1820 edition the stanzas Robinson mentions, as well as four others; he also rewrote twenty-seven lines and made seven other single-word revisions. He or the printer in this edition spelled out the "ed" endings in most forms that had used the apostrophe in 1819. In the next edition, of 1827, another five stanzas were dropped (although two were reinstated in 1832), twenty-six lines were rewritten, and sixteen verbal changes were made.

Peter Bell next appeared in *Selections from the Poems of William Wordsworth, Esq. Chiefly for the Use of Schools and Young Persons* (1st ed. 1831, 2d 1834). Wordsworth allowed Joseph Hine, a Brixton schoolmaster, to choose the

[12]*British Critic,* 11 (June 1819), 594–595; *Eclectic Review,* 12 (July 1819), 64.

selections, but the poet considered the choices "judiciously made" (*LY*, II, 396). The text, which seems to derive from the 1827 edition, contains some bizarre errors, and does not appear to have any independent authority. The 1832 *Poetical Works,* however, continues to show revisions of *Peter Bell,* although at a slowed rate: it omitted no further stanzas, rewrote only three lines, and made five additional verbal changes. This edition did restore two stanzas dropped in 1827, but not an accompanying footnote.

In 1836, for the first collected edition to appear since the death of Coleridge, Wordsworth undertook substantial revision of nearly all his poems. Much of this revision was carried out in the copy of the 1832 edition now at Wellesley College (here designated MS. 1832/36). In *Peter Bell* only two stanzas were dropped, but fifty-one lines were rewritten and twenty-seven words were changed. A typographical innovation was the elimination of repeated quotation marks at the beginning of lines in quotations extending over several lines. A copy of the 1836 edition now at Windsor Castle contains further autograph revisions (here designated MS. 1836/45), some of them related to revisions Wordsworth had also made in a copy of the second edition of 1819, but relatively few further changes got into print. The 1840 edition has only one rewritten line and two verbal alterations; in the 1845 edition two lines are rewritten and one word is changed. Very few differences appear in the final lifetime edition, of 1849–50, and none is important enough to suggest that the poet had anything to do with it. For better or for worse, *Peter* was finished.

IV

As we look back over the long course of *Peter Bell*'s hewing and polishing, one simple fact becomes clear: the poem grew steadily shorter. MS. 1 is too fragmentary to consider; the 1799 reading text, derived from the base texts of MSS. 2 and 3, contains 1380 lines; what appears to be a later tabulation entered in MS. 2 lists 1265 lines. Revisions in MS. 6 show cancellation and telescoping of verses to lead to the first edition's 1185 lines; the final published version of 1849–50 has 1135. This whittling, however, was quite disproportionate; most of the cuts came in the central narrative of the discovery of the corpse and the beginning of the homeward journey. The third part, the ministrations of the spirits of the mind which brought about Peter's redemption (the part Wordsworth thought "interesting"), was cut only about 10 percent, while the biographical sketch of Peter, what one tabulation in MS. 2 calls the Second Prologue, was cut very little, and drafts in MS. 2 suggest that at one time Wordsworth even thought of expanding it. The Prologue—the characterization of the narrator and the description of the fairy boat and its fantastic explorations—was actually expanded by seven or eight stanzas. Most of these additions were in the dismissal of the barge that appeared as insertions in MS. 5 (6^v, 7^v; ll. 131–160 of 1819), but one elaboration of the barge's experience (1819, ll. 36–40) was added in revision of MS. 4 and one (1819, ll. 46–50) in revisions in MS. 6.

This obsessive playing with the fairy craft illustrates one of the problems—perhaps the most interesting—with which Wordsworth struggled in working over *Peter Bell*: the place of the supernatural in the poem.[13] Wordsworth had told himself and Coleridge, and ultimately would tell his readers, in the 1805 *Prelude,* that

> The hemisphere
> Of magic fiction, verse of mine perhaps
> May never tread. [VI, 102–104]

He seemed to adopt this position in *Peter Bell* when he added to the Prologue on a verso in MS. 5 (6^v) the oft-quoted

> The common growth of mother earth
> Suffices me—her tears, her mirth,
> Her humblest mirth and tears [1819, ll. 138–140]

and went on to elaborate in what looks like a still later addition:

> The dragon's wing, the magic ring,
> I need not covet for my dower. [1819, ll. 141–142]

He seemed to formalize this view by his dedication of the poem to Southey:

> The Poem of Peter Bell, as the Prologue will show, was composed under a belief that the Imagination not only does not require for its exercise the intervention of supernatural agency, but that, though such agency be excluded, the faculty may be called forth as imperiously, and for kindred results of pleasure, by incidents, within the compass of poetic probability, in the humblest department of daily life.

The manuscript history of *Peter Bell,* however, shows that the poem was composed under a regime of modifying, not eschewing, the supernatural, even if the dedication is interpreted as saying the latter—which it does not do. Some contemporary reviewers indeed complained that they did not understand the dedication because there *were* supernatural elements in *Peter Bell.*[14] In fact, Wordsworth in the dedication is engaged in an elaborate compliment to Southey's supernatural romances, and even then he says that *Peter Bell,* "whether from contrast or congruity, is not an unappropriate offering." Surely *Peter Bell* demonstrates both contrast and congruity with respect to use of the supernatural. Disavowal of the "magic ring"—which is,

[13]The following comments inevitably repeat, supplement, or correct observations I have made in "The Hewing of *Peter Bell,*" *Studies in English Literature,* 7 (Autumn 1967), 559–603, and "Wordsworth's Most Wonderful as Well as Admirable Poem" *Wordsworth Circle,* 10 (Winter 1979), 49–58.

[14]*Edinburgh Monthly Review,* 2 (1819), 655; *Theatrical Inquisitor,* 14 (1819), 375.

after all, the narrator-poet's, not Wordsworth's—came very late in the revision of MS. 5, probably as late as 1808–1812. Even then "experience forces" the narrator to dismiss the fairy barge. He had been still more reluctant in earlier versions, admitting that it grieved him "to the heart" to leave his "sweet and beautiful Canoe" (MS. 5, 6r). There was, we might remember, the saving "perhaps" in Wordsworth's *Prelude* dismissal of "magic fiction," and it is apparent that he continued to feel the pull of

> something loftier, more adorn'd
> Than is the common aspect, daily garb
> Of human life. [*Prelude* (1805), V, 599–601]

As we have seen, Wordsworth said that he intended *Peter Bell* for the *Lyrical Ballads,* and its closest affinities seem to be with *The Thorn, The Idiot Boy,* and the poem that Wordsworth began in partnership with Coleridge, *The Rime of the Ancyent Marinere.* In the first published version Peter believes that "Some ugly witchcraft must be here!" (l. 452), an idea that had persisted from the earliest manuscripts. The "must be" is a correction made to the base text of MS. 6; MS. 1 had "here is witch-craft"; MSS. 2 (revised), 3, 4, and 5, along with base 6, "There is some ugly witchcraft" (see Transcriptions, MS. 1, 20r, and MS. 5, *apparatus criticus* to 23r). Some changes of tone and emphasis, of course, appear. In MS. 1 (26r) the narrator speculates whether Peter

> felt a wicked chain
> Twined round him like a magic spell
> Upon my faith I cannot tell.

A revision in MS. 2 changes his expression to "Is more in truth than I can tell" (19r); MSS. 4 and 5 have "In honest truth I cannot tell" (MS. 5, 25r), as does one version in MS. 6, which also tries, as variants, "To drag him on" and "And force him on" with "demoniac sway" before settling on the version essentially adopted in the 1819 edition (ll. 513–514) and retained thereafter:

> In this serene and solemn hour
> Twin'd round him by demoniac power,

It is apparent that the acceptance of some supernatural possession persists; what changes is the elevation of the narrator. A similar change is evident in a passage that shows up first in MS. 2 (72r):

> Poor Peter by an ugly fiend
> Is troubled more & more,

The "ugly fiend" survives in MS. 3 and through the base text of MS. 4, where a revision internalizes it to "ugly thought"; MS. 5 reads "ugly fancy"—and the stanza is there canceled. But throughout its life, the final line had Peter saying that a devil was following him. What appears to change is thus not Peter's perception but the narrator's authentication of it. That is to say, the history of the manuscripts makes it clear that the supernatural—except for orthodox religious kinds, which the narrator and the audience are probably understood to share—is largely a matter of Peter's beliefs and fears: it is superstition.

To show this was probably Wordsworth's intention from the beginning. In his Preface to *The Borderers* he describes a proud character: "That influence which his pride makes him unwilling to allow to his fellow-men he has no reluctance to ascribe to invisible agents" (*Prose,* I, 78). Such a character is Peter, and the course of his reform in the poem is in the direction of recognizing the influence of his fellow-men.

Behind every revision lies, of course, a variety, sometimes a combination, of motives, and Wordsworth was persistently concerned not only with the role of the supernatural but also with the way in which Peter and the narrator were characterized. A stanza canceled in MS. 1 (22^r) had Peter cry, "The devil's in him," and another stanza in MS. 1 (31^r) and MS. 2 (19^v), canceled in MS. 2, has him declare "the devil in me wrought." Peter swore by the "devil's beard" in MS. 1 (19^r), in a stanza that appeared in MSS. 2 (17^v) and 3 but not in MS. 4. It was cut perhaps because Peter is here excessively crude, calling the ass a "mongrel hound" and clasping his arms round the beast's belly to pick him up, or perhaps because Wordsworth realized that he had written much the same thing in a stanza in which Peter called the beast a "little mulish dog" and threatened to fling it "like a log / Head fore-most down the river"—a stanza that remained virtually unchanged from MS. 1 (24^r) through the edition of 1849–50 (ll. 456–460). A stanza inserted on a verso in MS. 2 (45^v) has Peter sitting on the ass

> With doubt and reverential fear
> Oft deeming him as you will guess
> A supernatural beast—no less—
> An ass without compeer—

The stanza is canceled, however, and appears in no other text, probably not because of the "supernatural" beast, since at this point in the narrative Peter still harbored such a belief, but because of the unhappy rhyme and the homely style of the narrator in involving his hearers: "as you will guess."

Wordsworth's concern with the protagonist of a poem is well summarized in his comment on the *Ancient Mariner* which he attached as a note in the 1800 edition of *Lyrical Ballads* but did not thereafter reprint. He is itemizing the "defects" of Coleridge's poem:

> first, that the principal person has no distinct character, either in his profession of Mariner, or as a human being who having been long under the controul of super-

natural impressions might be supposed himself to partake of something supernatural: secondly, that he does not act, but is continually acted upon: thirdly, that the events having no necessary connection do not produce each other; and lastly, that the imagery is somewhat too laboriously accumulated.

We can only speculate whether or not *Peter Bell,* begun as we saw by April 1798, in some association with the "crescent moon," had in Wordsworth's mind any parallel to the *Ancient Mariner,* which was to have been written cooperatively, and which on March 23, 1798, a night marked by a "horned moon," Coleridge brought to the Wordsworths finished. But there are obvious similarities between the basic redemptive plots of the two poems and the roles of the potter and the mariner. At any rate, Wordsworth could be expected, feeling as he did about Coleridge's poem, to give his own "principal person" a markedly "distinct character" and show him acting in a causally related sequence of events. He begins the process by putting into the poem some hearers who not only, like Coleridge's Wedding Guest, react to the tale, but demand to know more about the central character: little Bess asks, "O dear Sir! but who is Peter?" (1819, l. 204), and revisions show Wordsworth developing Peter's character. Since parts of MSS. 1 and 2 are missing in this area, we cannot be sure when the elaboration began, but it is substantial in MS. 3, and MS. 5 expands the account of Peter's career, extending his wanderings to Caernarvon, to the Lake District, and to Sherwood Forest, where like a good fellow he drank to Robin Hood. Some vacillation appears in the stanza (1819, ll. 291–295) that tells us of Peter that "To see him was to fear him": the stanza was canceled in MS. 3 and omitted from MS. 4, but was written over an erased stanza in MS. 5 (14^r). The temporary dropping of the stanza might, of course, have been owing to its homely revelation of the narrator ("Upon my faith I cannot tell"), which is toned down in the final version—the cautiously fearsome character of the unregenerate Peter probably was supposed to be one of the poem's constants.

Once the narrator gets into his tale proper, Wordsworth keeps on trying to make the character of Peter consistent and active. The charge that Peter was a "lazy soul" is cut out of MS. 1 (8^r); his "savage elf" of a dog is canceled in MS. 3 (8^v). His advancing "chearfully," whistling as he goes along, is a revision in MS. 5 (17^r) of a picture of him cursing in MSS. 3 and 4; a subsequent "downright fury" and wrath are finally recognized and explained as a change of mood. Later versions contain nothing comparable to the inconsistently abject picture of Peter in a canceled stanza in MS. 1 (27^r):

His staff is in the grass, and look
With fainting heart and trembling knees
And visagė pale while both his hands
Hang loose against his thighs he stands
Beneath the moonlight trees.

It is of this Peter that the narrator asks plaintively in another stanza canceled in MS. 1 (23^{r}):

> How could it be? how could it be
> That while the poor ass thus did lie
> On Peter's heart on Peter's brain
> Not one impression did remain
> Of his large and shining eye.

Other touching up of Peter's character includes dropping his assertion that he will "grapple with the devil," which appears in MS. 3 (9^{v})—whether earlier we cannot tell; it is cut from MS. 4, perhaps as too brave an utterance for the superstitious Peter. A "sudden sympathy" attributed to Peter in MS. 1 (12^{r}) is canceled in that manuscript. The almost jocular conception of Peter is reinforced when his address to the ass, "Upon my soul," in MS. 3 (10^{v}) is revised in MS. 4 to "My honest Friend." But the cruder humor of "Are you asleep or are you dead" is canceled in MS. 1 (15^{r}), perhaps in the hewing that resulted in MS. 2, as are the ridiculous or painful images of Peter's giving the beast "a jirk enough / To turn six horses in a team" (15^{r}), or being "tickled" to let "lusty" blows fall on the ass (16^{r}–17^{r}), or callously giving the animal a "thundering kick" (17^{r}). A too jocular or implausibly ironic wish that his "Wife Kate" were there, so that they could have a "royal battle" with the ass and make him "dance for joy," appears in an unfinished and canceled stanza in MS. 2 (15^{v}). Also canceled in MS. 1 are the similarly hyperbolical pictures of Peter beating the ass "most furiously" (20^{r}), with "fierce & furious blows" (22^{r}), letting fall a "thundering smack" (25^{r}) and blows "that might have reached the bone" (19^{r}), and desperately heaving at him, although

> He might as well have tried to stir
> The abbey huge of Westminster
> Or twice five hundred head of beeves.

Passages in MSS. 1 (31^{r}) and 2 (19^{v}) that have Peter getting so close to the ass that it seemed as if he were trying to creep inside the animal are canceled, as is the MS. 2 stanza in which he tells the ass it is "to blame" (18^{v}); and a passage in MS. 1 that questions whether Peter is motivated by "shame or tenderness / Or from his coward heart's distress" (27^{r}) does not appear in later versions. Similarly, Wordsworth canceled in MS. 1 stanzas that make Peter think he heard a "barking cur" or a "voice behind his back / From the old quarry cry 'Thief! Thief!" (25^{r}), and others that attribute to Peter "fears" and "tenderness," and suppose that were he "safe full ten miles off / He'd leap and skip & dance & scoff" (30^{r}). Wordsworth made considerable efforts to keep a consistent image of Peter as violent, selfish, and opportunistic—the idea that a "wondrous alteration" occurred in Peter's attitude appears in MS. 1 (27^r), is canceled in MS. 2 (20^r), appears again in MSS. 4, 5 (26^r), and 6, and is finally canceled in MS. 6—yet not to allow him to appear ridiculous.

The most remarkable evidence of Wordsworth's concern with the characterization of Peter also involves elaboration of that of the narrator. In his note to *The Thorn* of 1800, Wordsworth remarked that he had intended to include but never got around to writing a prefatory poem presenting the character of the narrator of that ballad tale. Presumably it would have demonstrated his view that "superstitious men are almost always men of slow faculties and deep feelings . . . they have a reasonable share of imagination" (*PW,* II, 512). Wordsworth has in *Peter Bell* a much more active central figure than in *The Thorn,* and he gives his hero some of the characteristics of the *Thorn* narrator; but he is obviously concerned to develop internally the personality of the teller of the tale. Accordingly, he maintains two clear voices in *Peter Bell,* making his hero credulous, superstitious, slow but vocal, and capable of feeling and imagination, and making his narrator into a sort of village Milton with some epic pretensions, increasingly superior to Peter, both more objective and more fanciful. In drafts in MS. 2 (42^v–45^v, 63^v, 64^r), Wordsworth actually toyed with describing a meeting between Peter and the narrator, a meeting that was evidently to be a sort of confrontation. The narrator in the earliest versions is relatively chatty and informal, as in the final form of MS. 2 (42^r):

In truth I should be much inclined
To tell what's passing in his mind
If it would suit my tale as well.

He jocularly calls his hero "friend" Peter, supposes he is addressing him directly in a passage that appears in MS. 2 (16^r) and MS. 3 (a page is torn out of MS. 1 in this area) but not in MS. 4:

There's nothing, Peter, far or near
There's nothing with your purpose jars.

Canceled stanzas in MS. 1 have the narrator admit that he "cannot say" whether Peter had left "that night or day / His wife or wives" and "wonder" (8^r) that lazy Peter walked instead of rode. Throughout the evolution of the poem the narrator retains, though in a dignified manner, a posture of denying omniscience: Peter's purpose in making his journey remains "never known." But as the poem develops, the storyteller tends to become more self-effacing, and to suppress his "how could it be's" and "whether's."

The manuscripts reveal, moreover, a gradual but uncertain elevation of the narrator's tone. "We left the dead man in the river" in MS. 2 (26^r) is there revised to "Beneath the alders near the river," the reading of MS. 3

and essentially thereafter, though a variant in MS. 2 (24^v) plays with the more folksy

It was, as you belike have guessed
A dead man lying in the river.

MS. 3 (7^r) heightens the narrator's role by giving the audience a vivid reaction to the reference to Peter's twelve wives, in a passage that survived through MS. 4 The elimination in MS. 4 of the lines

And o'er the stream he hangs his nose
And points his staff as you'd suppose

probably reflects the continuing effort to make Peter less ridiculous (by leaving out the image of his drooping nose) and the narrator less casual (by omitting his "as you'd suppose"; MS. 2, 28^r). Something of the same desire to elevate the narrator probably explains why after MS. 2 (28^v) nothing is seen of the gauche lines

The ass looks on as you will guess
And with encreasing tenderness
You'd think he'd almost shake to pieces.

MS. 4 contains a stanza that expands the narrator's role by letting him propose having tea and waiting for the auditors to gather, but the stanza is deleted in that manuscript (see Transcriptions, *apparatus criticus* to MS. 3, 8^v); perhaps Wordsworth came to consider the gesture too low. And as the narrator becomes more elevated, his account of the ass becomes less pathetic, emphasizing less the animal's near-human character. Not only did it have in MS. 1 a poignant "shining hazel eye" (23^r), as it does in a passage added in MS. 5 (23^v) and surviving in 1819 (l. 470), but in two stanzas canceled in MS. 1 (27^v) it "wept as men and women weep"—indeed,

The tears flowed down his cheeks amain
You would have thought that he was dying.

By MS. 5 Wordsworth was trying to raise the level of the auditors as well as that of the narrator: for instance, Parson Swan and his wife become "the Vicar, & his Dame" in a revision in MS. 5 (8^r). Revisions in MS. 5 also eliminate the parson's wife as a speaking character: a comment that had been given to her as early as MS. 1 (5^r), "You've [actually 'You're' in MS. 1] got at once into the middle," is by a correction in MS. 5 ascribed instead to "a voice"; and a revision in MS. 6 makes it "the Vicar's voice" (9^r), as though propriety demanded that the ranking member of the little society pronounce the reproach. By MS. 6 and thereafter the narrator talks solemnly and elegantly about the miraculous power of "Repentance" (1850, ll. 146–150); decorously says, "A mother's hope is hers" (1850, l. 906) instead of "a Child was in her womb" (MS. 5, 56r); reports that Peter uttered "An impious oath" (1850, l. 461), instead of recording his "By God I will" (MS. 5, 25r), and generally increases his epic pretensions. He had, to the consternation of his unsophisticated hearers, plunged *in medias res* from the beginning, but the elaborate epic simile in 1819, lines 896–900, was an interlinear revision in MS. 6 (see Transcriptions, *apparatus criticus* to MS. 5, 51r), and part of the general heightening of the poem.

Readers of the present edition will be able to judge for themselves whether Wordsworth's prolonged, persistent efforts to elevate the tone, the diction, and the characterizations in *Peter Bell*—to make his chief character, his narrator, and his auditors more respectable, more credible—resulted in a better poem. Two things, at least, should be clear. The first is that, so far as we can tell from the poem's fragmentary beginnings in MS. 1, there were no fundamental changes in its conception or structure over its long gestation, though since the surviving portion of MS. 1 contains none of the second or third parts of the poem, we cannot be sure that there were no different twists to the redemption theme at the outset. The earliest version contained the Prologue fantasy of a fairy boat that tempts the narrator to voyage to distant romantic strands—a temptation that he resists in order to fulfill his obligation to tell the story of Peter Bell the Potter to his friends assembling around his stone table in the garden. The earliest version also provided an *in medias res* beginning that was repudiated by the hardheaded auditors, so that the narrator was required to go into the brief biographical sketch of Peter which Mary later called the Second Prologue. Peter's accidental discovery of the ass as a result of his following a deceptive "short cut" also goes back to the earliest version.

This is not to say that there are no significant changes in the poem. Initially the narrator does not repudiate the blandishments of the little boat with any philosophical flourishes of dedication to "the common growth of mother earth"; it "grieves" him "to the heart" to leave the boat, but he must leave, apparently, because of his promise to his friends, who live on an earthly plane. The assertion that the "blessed days" of Fairyland are "over" does not appear until MS. 4, although it may seem to be implied earlier. In MS. 1 we get the impression that the narrator dismisses the fairy boat's call to a "romantic land" reluctantly, because of the demands of the occasion, and not necessarily permanently. The situation is closely analogous to Wordsworth's toying with various romantic themes at the beginning of *The Prelude*, then turning to a more down-to-earth autobiographical strain—which did not prevent him later from writing a *White Doe of Rylstone*.

The second thing that should be clear from this history is that the successive versions of the poem accurately reflect the successive stages of Wordsworth's developing style. The poem began as something like a lyrical ballad, with syntax and diction resembling those of the experimental poems in the volume of 1798. Revision cleared away obscurities and ambiguities and tightened up the action, but it also moved the poem toward the manner and the mode of Wordsworth's later years. The result is a series of versions that offer a uniquely comprehensive view of the growth, perhaps the decline, of a poet's taste, and embody as much of the poet himself as any other work he wrote.

Editorial Procedure

Like other volumes in this series, this edition of *Peter Bell* provides two kinds of texts: (1) reading texts, from which all textual complexities and variant readings are stripped away, and (2) transcriptions of manuscripts, usually facing photographic reproductions of the manuscripts. Editorial procedures have been adapted to the aims of these two styles of presentation.

One might wish for a single, composite, collated text showing at once the full history of *Peter Bell* from 1798 to 1849. But the textual history of the poem is very complex; we are embarrassed by riches. Seven manuscripts have survived—five substantial or complete versions (MSS. 2–6) and two fragments (MSS. 1 and 7)—containing among them hundreds of revisions and cancellations. In addition, there are eight separate editions, and on copies of three of them Wordsworth entered numerous revisions. All of these states make a single collated text impossibly complicated and cluttered; nobody would understand it except the editor, and even he would be uncertain after it cooled on him.

In the reading texts, the various versions that make up the poem are partly separated. To allow a comparison of the earlier form of the poem with the first published version and to provide a record of Wordsworth's revisions after publication, an early reading text (derived from MSS. 2 and 3) is presented in parallel with—that is, facing—the text of the 1819 first edition, the latter collated with all authorized versions published in Wordsworth's lifetime, as well as with his autograph revisions.

The transcriptions are less simple. The manuscript history of *Peter Bell* divides into three strands: the much-canceled and fragmentary MS. 1; the early MSS. 2, 3, and 4; and the later manuscripts closer to the published versions—MSS. 5 and 6 and the extant page of MS. 7. These three phases are shown by facing photographs and transcriptions of MS. 1, MS. 2 (gaps filled from MS. 3, collated with MSS. 3 and 4), and MS. 5 (collated with MSS. 6 and 7).

Since Wordsworth was not happy using a pen (*EY,* pp. 277, 353, 401, 407, 411, 436, 452–453, 503, 630) and apparently was incapable of consistently legible penmanship, it is fortunate that he was well provided with amanuenses. Fair copies of his poems were commonly made by Dorothy, Mary,

Sara Hutchinson, and others, and *Peter Bell* was one of the poems they worked on. In the transcriptions, passages in Wordsworth's hand are printed in roman type, those by other scribes in italic type. Identification of hands is, however, made with some diffidence and depends largely on the expertise of Stephen Parrish, Mark Reed, Paul Betz, and others. It is often very difficult to be sure of the writer, especially of an inserted word or so; Wordsworth's more careful hand sometimes looks much like Dorothy's, and some manuscripts long thought to have been written by Sara are now known to have been written by Mary.

The original version in any manuscript is presented in the transcriptions in larger type, revisions in smaller type, usually above or below the lines to which they refer. For ease of reference, line numbers are assigned to each independent line in the fair copies and shown in the left margins of the transcriptions. Duplicate or near-duplicate lines resulting from alternate versions, drafts, and revisions are numbered identically; such lines are usually numbered serially in the order of their first appearance in the manuscript; subsequent appearances of the lines carry the original numbers in parentheses. Incomplete variants or drafts that do not appear to have been integrated into the text are not numbered unless their identity is fairly clear; they are normally indented. Except when a passage is clearly marked to be inserted elsewhere, it is usually numbered to correspond with the position of its appearance; the intended order of stanzas added on verso pages is, however, often uncertain. Bracketed numbers indicate lines that, from such evidence as a torn page, may reasonably be supposed to have been in the text or to have been intended to be there, but are not now present. To facilitate cross-reference the numbering of what seem to be corresponding lines as given in the early reading text is shown in the right margins of transcriptions in italic type.

Because the primary purpose of the transcriptions is to provide easy reading of the manuscripts of *Peter Bell,* they do not show doodles, pen testing, lines from other poems present in the notebooks, or other irrelevant material, although such matters are usually treated in the notes. Nor do the transcriptions represent deletion of blocks of lines or whole stanzas by means of a vertical line drawn in the margin, large X's or circles, or other devices that may be visible in facing photographs. (Here the precedent set in Jared Curtis's edition of *Poems, in Two Volumes* in this series has been followed.) Where there are no facing photographs, as in the second portion of MS. 5, these large-scale cancellations are remarked in the notes. The transcriptions do, however, show horizontal cross-out lines and slashes that delete single letters, since clarifying these matters frequently helps the reader to follow the process of revision.

The following symbols are used, variously, in reading texts, notes, transcriptions, and collations:

[ ]	Gap or blank in the manuscript
[?dutyful]	Doubtful reading
[? ?]	Illegible passage, each question mark indicating one word
[———?———]	Illegible word deleted
{at {in	Overwriting; "at" has been written on top of "in"
still as death	Word or phrase written over an erasure
sti**ll** **as** d**ea**th	Boldface letters are those discernible in a speculative reading of a generally illegible passage
alt	Alternate: a second reading has been written in, apparently to replace the original, but the original has not been deleted
del to	Deleted to: reading changed
eras	Erased, erasure
rev to	Revised to: original reading changed to another reading by alteration of letters or overwriting

Reading Texts

Texts of MSS. 2 and 3 (1799)

facing pages of

The First Edition (1819),

with an *Apparatus Criticus* of Variants, 1819–1849

About February 20, 1808, William and Dorothy Wordsworth wrote to Sir George and Lady Beaumont expressing satisfaction at hearing that Sir George had painted a picture, apparently from a sketch they had seen, for *Peter Bell.* Dorothy tactfully observed that the "*painting* must gain very much by the change of time, from moonlight to early morning; and, as separating that scene entirely from the action contained in the poem, it is very judicious"—changes that, she must have noticed, somewhat reduced its illustrative value (*MY,* I, 194, 197). In his reply, February 25, Sir George offered to have the "very small" painting engraved—William had worried that his sales were not likely to cover the expense of engraving (WL Letters, Beaumont 25). This frontispiece, used in the first and second editions, is probably the picture Sir George refers to as a "tailpiece." It was engraved by William Alexander and redone by J. C. Bromley (Reed, *Chronology: MY*, pp. 555n, 584n).

MSS. 2 and 3 (1799) and the First Edition (1819)

Since MS. 1 is fragmentary, the earliest possible full version of the poem must come from MSS. 2 and 3, which are nearly contemporary fair copies. Neither manuscript is complete, leaves having been torn out of both, but the missing portions do not coincide, so that it is possible to put together a full text. MS. 2, however, is primary, for it seems probable that at least part of MS. 3 was copied from a slightly revised state of MS. 2 (see Introduction); hence the numbered reading text here on the left-hand pages follows the reconstructed original base text of MS. 2, supplemented by seven fair-copy stanzas entered on facing versos (as explained below), drawing on MS. 3 only where MS. 2 is defective. At the same time, second and third early versions of the poem have been made available in footnotes that show the ways in which the underlying original texts of MS. 2 and MS. 3 differ from the numbered text. Where, as occasionally happens, blanks have been left in both manuscripts, the missing material is supplied in a note and the source indicated.

The base text of MS. 2, which is entirely in the hands of William and Dorothy, may date from Goslar, where William reported on February 27, 1799, that he had "lately been employ'd in hewing down Peter Bell"; MS. 3, which is in five different hands (those of William, Dorothy, Mary Hutchinson, and two others, one of them probably George Hutchinson), may have been transcribed at Sockburn, and therefore may be dated between May and November 1799.

Over the base fair-copy text of MS. 2 there are at least three levels of revision. The first was carried out by careful erasure, some but not all of it done in the course of transcription, and therefore marks a stage when the manuscript was being maintained as a clean final copy. The second, more casual, was carried out before MS. 3 was transcribed, and shows up in the base text of MS. 3. The third, by far the most extensive, apparently went on over a space of several years, much of it in preparation for transcription of MS. 4 (in early 1802), but some even later. A number of interpolations in MS. 2, especially those elaborating on the narrator's encounter with Peter, remain in draft state, and were never included in later versions of the poem.

Inside the back cover of MS. 2, at the end of the fair-copy text, is a tabulation in Mary Hutchinson's hand:

First Pro.	31 Stanzas
Second do	28

First Part	58
Sec. do	68
Third.	91
Total	276 Stanzas
	5
	1380 lines

The "First Pro." is certainly the Prologue, the "Second do [ditto]" the biography of Peter provided when the auditors objected to the *in media res* beginning of the tale; the three parts are clearly discernible, although the "First Part" is not so designated until MS. 4. We cannot be sure when this tabulation was entered, although it appears to antedate another tabulation, partly at the end and partly at the beginning of MS. 2 in William's hand, which lists only 1265 lines but also calculates the number of pages and is probably related to one of the plans to publish the poem. But we can at least suppose that the 1380-line tabulation represents an early finished state of *Peter Bell* to be found in MS. 2, and the numbered reading text has therefore been constructed so that the various sections correspond in length to the indicated number of stanzas. For the first two sections—the two prologues—the correspondence is exact, and no deviations from the base text of MS. 2 (supplemented by MS. 3 where leaves of MS. 2 are missing) are necessary. With the three parts of the poem, however, the correspondence is close but not exact (see Table 1).

Table 1. Number of stanzas of *Peter Bell* indicated in Mary Hutchinson's tabulation and found in base MSS. 2 and 3, by part

Part	Tabulation	Base MS. 2	Base MS. 3
I	58	56	57
II	68	66	67*
III	91	88	89

*Counting 8 from a missing leaf.

To bring the stanza counts of MS. 2 up to the counts in the tabulation, it is necessary to add stanzas transcribed in careful fair copy on blank versos of the manuscript. Some of these stanzas show up in the base text of MS. 3; some do not. The choice of stanzas to include can be fairly easily limited. In Part III only three such stanzas are entered on versos, and all three are required (although only one was taken into the base text of MS. 3). In Part II there are five, possibly seven, fair-copy verso stanzas, but only two that appear in the base text of MS. 3; hence those two have been included. With Part I the problem is more complicated. Alternate ways of arriving at the specified number of stanzas can be devised, since the base text of MS. 3

includes one stanza not in MS. 2 (although it could have been on the verso of a torn-out leaf) and three stanzas entered on the surviving versos of MS 2. We might thus include these four stanzas and omit the two stanzas in base MS. 2 which were deleted before MS. 3 was transcribed, and come out with the required 58. The simpler way is to assume that the tabulation was entered at an earlier stage than transcription of MS. 3, and to add to the original base text of MS. 2 only the two fair-copy verso stanzas in William's hand which were entered just at the point where the transcription ceases to use versos and moves to rectos only (perhaps because those two stanzas had been entered); both are in the base text of MS. 1. The simpler way has been adopted, but the other is made clear by inclusion or identification of the pertinent stanzas in footnotes.

In the early reading text, original spellings have been preserved, but what appear to be copyists' errors or idiosyncrasies (such as William's "asse's") have been mended; corrections and revisions made carefully in ink over erasure have been adopted, as have corrections apparently made in the course of transcription. Capitals and original punctuation in MS. 2 have been preserved, but punctuation has been sparingly added where modern standards seem to require it. Apostrophes have also been added when necessary, but verbal endings have been kept as they stand (rather inconsistently) in the manuscripts (William favored "'d" where Dorothy preferred "ed").

Facing the early reading text, on the right-hand pages, is the text of the first edition of *Peter Bell,* 1819, with line numbers added; bracketed line numbers are those of the final text of 1849, reproduced by de Selincourt. Underneath the 1819 text is an *apparatus criticus* of variants introduced into lifetime authorized editions of the poem, as follows:

1819a *Peter Bell,* 2d ed. (London, 1819).

1820 *The Miscellaneous Poems of William Wordsworth* (4 vols.; London, 1820).

1827 *The Poetical Works of William Wordsworth* (5 vols.; London, 1827).

1831 *Selections from the Poems of William Wordsworth, Esq.,* ed. Joseph Hine (London, 1831).

1832 *The Poetical Works of William Wordsworth* (4 vols.; London, 1832).

1834 *Selections from the Poems of William Wordsworth, Esq.,* ed. Joseph Hine (London, 1834).

1836 *The Poetical Works of William Wordsworth* (6 vols.; London, 1836–1837).

1840 *The Poetical Works of William Wordsworth* (6 vols.; London, 1840). A stereotyped reissue of the volumes of 1836 with various alterations; again reissued, with a few alterations, in 1841 and 1843.

1845 *The Poems of William Wordsworth* (London, 1845). Reissued in stereotype, 1847 and 1849.

1846 *The Poetical Works of William Wordsworth* (7 vols.; London, 1846). Another stereotyped reissue of the six volumes of 1836, incorporating further alterations, with an additional volume incorporating *Poems, Chiefly of Early and Late Years,* 1842; reissued, again with a few alterations, 1849.

1849 *The Poetical Works of William Wordsworth* (6 vols.; London, 1849–1850).

In the *apparatus criticus,* a citation of each volume in the list above implies its stereotyped reissues as well, unless otherwise noted, as follows:

1840 implies 1841, 1843
1841 implies 1843
1845 implies 1847, 1849 (1 volume)
1846 implies 1849 (7 volumes)
1847 implies 1849 (1 volume)

The *apparatus* also includes variants written into three printed copies of *Peter Bell:*

MS. 1819a/20 Unbound gatherings of the second edition, 1819, at Dove Cottage.
MS. 1832/36 WW's copy of *Poetical Works,* 1832, now at Wellesley College, containing revisions and drafts in the portions used as printer's copy for the edition of 1836.
MS. 1836/45 WW's copy of *Poetical Works,* 1836, now at Windsor Castle, containing revisions and drafts, used to prepare the editions of 1840 and 1845.

Variant readings for Wordsworth's manuscript corrections in MS. 1832/36 are given where such corrections differ from the readings printed in 1836. Wordsworth's revisions of wording here are in ink unless otherwise noted; most revisions of punctuation are in pencil. Up to line 915, the *apparatus* also notes when changes not made in the 1832 revision appear in the 1836 text. After line 915, there are no revisions of any kind in the Wellesley volume.

PETER BELL,

A

Tale in Verse,

BY

WILLIAM WORDSWORTH.

LONDON:

Printed by Strahan and Spottiswoode, Printers-Street;

FOR LONGMAN, HURST, REES, ORME, AND BROWN,

PATERNOSTER-ROW.

1819.

---

1 Bell. *1831–*

2–5 *omitted 1831, 1834*

2–3 A / Tale in Verse,] A TALE. *1820–*

3/4 What's in a *Name?*

* * * * * * *

Brutus will start a Spirit as soon as Caesar! *1827– epigraph appears opposite title page without asterisks and in quotation marks 1819a*

4–10 *omitted 1820–*

6/7 SECOND EDITION. *1819a*

[*1831 and 1834 have no separate title pages; 1845 and 1849 do not have separate title pages, but carry at the top of the first page of the poem the same matter as 1827–*]

TO

ROBERT SOUTHEY, Esq. P.L.

&c. &c.

MY DEAR FRIEND,

The Tale of Peter Bell, which I now introduce to your notice, and to that of the Public, has, in its Manuscript state, nearly survived its *minority;*—for it first saw the light in the summer of 1798. During this long interval, pains have been taken at different times to make the production less unworthy of a favourable reception; or, rather, to fit it for filling *permanently* a station, however humble, in the Literature of my Country. This has, indeed, been the aim of all my endeavours in Poetry, which, you know, have been sufficiently laborious to prove that I deem the Art not lightly to be approached; and that the attainment of excellence in it, may laudably be made the principal object of intellectual pursuit by any man, who, with reasonable consideration of circumstances, has faith in his own impulses.

The Poem of Peter Bell, as the Prologue will shew, was composed under a belief that the Imagination not only does not require for its exercise the intervention of supernatural agency, but that, though such agency be excluded, the faculty may be called forth as imperiously, and for kindred results of pleasure, by incidents, within the compass of poetic probability, in the humblest departments of daily life. Since that Prologue was written, *you* have exhibited most splendid effects of judicious daring, in the opposite and usual course. Let

---

dedication omitted 1831, 1834
Title &c here *in pencil top of page MS. 1832/36*
2–3 Esq. P.L. *&c. &c.*] *no italics 1832, 1836* ESQ., P.L., ETC. ETC. *1845, 1849*
7 *minority: 1832–*
11 my] our *1836– but not MS. 1832/36*
18 show *1832–*
21 imperiously,] imperiously *1840–*

this acknowledgment make my peace with the lovers of the supernatural; and I am persuaded it will be admitted, that to you as a Master in that province of the art, the following Tale, whether from contrast or congruity, is a not unappropriate offering. Accept it then as a public testimony of affectionate admiration from one with whose name your's has been often coupled (to use your own words) for evil and for good; and believe me to be, with earnest wishes that life and health may be granted you to complete the many important works in which you are engaged, and with high respect,

Most faithfully your's,
WILLIAM WORDSWORTH.

Rydal Mount,
April 7. 1819.

---

27 you, *1827–*
29 a not] not an *1820–*
29–30 it, then, *1827–*
31 yours *1820–*
35 yours *1820–*
36 WILLIAM WORDSWORTH. *1820–*
37 *Rydal Mount*] RYDAL MOUNT *1820–*
38 April] *April 1820–*

Peter Bell, a Tale

Prologue

There's something in a flying horse,
There's something in a huge balloon,
But through the clouds I'll never float
Untill I have a little boat
In shape just like the crescent moon.

And now I have a little boat
In shape just like the crescent moon;
Fast through the clouds my boat can sail
But if perchance your faith should fail
Look up and you shall see me soon.

The woods, my friends, are round you roaring,
The woods are roaring like a sea;
The noise of danger's in your ears
And you have all a thousand fears
Both for my little boat and me.

Meanwhile I from the helm admire
The pointed horns of my canoe;
And did not pity touch my breast
To see how you are all distress'd,
Till my ribs ached I'd laugh at you.

Away we go, my boat and I,
Sure never man had such another;

5, 7 WW told Miss Fenwick, "The crescent-moon, which makes such a figure in the prologue, assumed this character one evening while I was watching its beauty in front of Alfoxden House" (see Introduction, p. 3, and *Journals*, 20 April 1798). The moon reappears in a canceled insertion in MS. 2 (see ll. 1096–1100 of the transcription, below).

11 The "friends" and "woods" indicated here are not further accounted for; the narrator's audience has not yet assembled (see ll. 141–150).

PROLOGUE.

THERE'S something in a flying horse,
And something in a huge balloon;
But through the clouds I'll never float
Until I have a little Boat,
Whose shape is like the crescent-moon.

And now I *have* a little Boat,
In shape a very crescent-moon:—
Fast through the clouds my Boat can sail;
But if perchance your faith should fail,
Look up—and you shall see me soon!

The woods, my Friends, are round you roaring,
Rocking and roaring like a sea;
The noise of danger fills your ears,
And ye have all a thousand fears
Both for my little Boat and me!

Meanwhile I from the helm admire
The pointed horns of my canoe;
And, did not pity touch my breast,
To see how ye are all distrest,
Till my ribs ach'd, I'd laugh at you!

Away we go, my Boat and I—
Frail man ne'er sate in such another;

---

5 stanzas on page 3 first page *in pencil top of page MS. 1832/36*
2 And] There's *1827–*
5 Whose shape is] For shape just *1845, 1846* Shaped *1849*
7 *dash omitted 1836–*
8 boat *1832, 1836–*
11 roaring,] roaring *1827*
13 danger fills] danger's in *1845–*
16 I from the helm] untroubled I *1827– but* untroubled *del to* soberly *MS. 1836/45 (WW)*
20 ached *1820–*

Whether among the winds we strive
Or deep into the heavens we dive
We're both contented with each other.

Away we go, and what care we
For treasons, tumults, and for wars;
We are as calm in our delight
As is the crescent moon so bright
Among the scattered stars.

Up goes my boat between the stars
Through many a breathless field of light,
Through many a long blue field of ether
Leaving ten thousand stars beneath her,
Up goes my little boat so bright.

The towns in Saturn are ill built
But Jove has very pretty bowers;
The evening star is not amiss
But what are all of them to this,
This little earth of ours.

---

25 The boat's speech soon belies that they are "contented with each other"; see ll. 66–110.

Whether among the winds we strive,
Or deep into the heavens we dive,
Each is contented with the other.

Away we go—and what care we
For treasons, tumults, and for wars?
We are as calm in our delight
As is the crescent-moon so bright
Among the scattered stars.

Up goes my Boat between the stars
Through many a breathless field of light,
Through many a long blue field of ether,
Leaving ten thousand stars beneath her,
Up goes my little Boat so bright!

The Crab—the Scorpion—and the Bull—
We pry among them all—have shot
High o'er the red-hair'd race of Mars
Cover'd from top to toe with scars;
Such company I like it not!

The towns in Saturn are ill-built,
But proud let *him* be who has seen them;
The Pleiads, that appear to kiss
Each other in the vast abyss,
With joy I sail between them!

Swift Mercury resounds with mirth,
Great Jove is full of stately bowers;
But these, and all that they contain,
What are they to that tiny grain,
That darling speck of ours!

---

24 deep into the heavens] into massy clouds *1820* deep into the clouds *1827–*
31 between] among *1820–*
34 her. *1827–1834* her: *1836–*
36 Crab, the Scorpion, *1836–*
37 all; *1836–*
38 red-haired *1820–* Mars, *1827–*
39 Covered *1820–*
41 ill-built] decayed *1827–*
42 And melancholy Spectres throng them; *1827– but* them;— *1836– but not MS. 1832/36*
45 between] among *1827–* them!] them *1840* them. *1845–*
47 bowers! *1831, 1834*
49 grain,] grain *1819a, 1820*
50 darling speck] little Earth *1827–* ours? *1819a–*

Then back again to our green earth;
What business had I here to roam?
The world for my remarks and me
Will not a whit the better be;
I've left my heart at home.

And that is then the dear green earth
And that's the dear Pacific ocean
And that is Caucasus so dear;
To think that I again am here,
Oh! my poor heart's commotion!

And there is little Tartary
And there's the famous river Dnieper
And there, amid the ocean green,
Is that sweet isle of isles the queen;
Ye Fairies! from all evil keep her!

And there's the town where I was born
And that's the house of Parson Swan.
My heart is touched, I must avow;
Consider where I've been, and now
I feel I am a man.

Never did fifty things at once
Appear so lovely, never never;
The woods, how sweetly do they ring.
To hear the earth's sweet murmuring
Thus could I hang for ever.

Then back to Earth, the dear green Earth;
Whole ages if I here should roam,
The world for my remarks and me
Would not a whit the better be;
I've left my heart at home.

And there it is, the matchless Earth!
There spreads the fam'd Pacific Ocean!
Old Andes thrusts yon craggy spear
Through the grey clouds—the Alps are here
Like waters in commotion!

Yon tawny slip is Lybia's sands—
That silver thread the river Dnieper—
And look, where cloth'd in brightest green
Is a sweet Isle, of isles the queen;
Ye fairies from all evil keep her!

And see the town where I was born!
Around those happy fields we span
In boyish gambols—I was lost
Where I have been, but on this coast
I feel I am a man.

Never did fifty things at once
Appear so lovely, never, never,—
How tunefully the forests ring!
To hear the earth's soft murmuring
Thus could I hang for ever!

---

51 Earth;] Earth: *MS. 1832/36* Earth:— *1836–*
56 And] *And underscored; alt.* See! *MS. 1832/36 adopted 1836–* it] she *1836– but not MS. 1832/36* earth *1820*
57 famed *1820–*
59 clouds; *1836–* here, *1819a–*
61 Libya's *1827–* sands; *1836–*
62 Dnieper; *1836–*
63 clothed *1820–*
64 Queen *1827–*
65 fairies, *1827, 1832–*
68 gambols;— *1836–*
72 never,—] never;— *1836–*
73 ring!] ring *1820*

"Oh shame upon you! cruel shame!
Was ever such a heartless loon?
In such a lovely boat to sit
And make no better use of it,
A boat that's like the crescent moon.

Out, out and like a brooding hen
Beside your sooty hearth-stone cower;
Go creep along the dirt, and pick
Your way with your good walking-stick
Just three good miles an hour.

Sure in the breast of full-grown poet
So faint a heart was ne'er before.
Come to the poets' wild delights;
I have ten thousand lovely sights,
Ten thousand sights in store.

I am a pretty little barge,
Then come, I pray you, come with me;
I want a comrade, and for you
There's nothing which I would not do,
There's nothing which you shall not see.

Come, and above the land of snow
We'll sport amid the boreal morning
Where thousand forms of light are riding,
Among the stars, the stars now hiding
And now the stars adorning.

"Shame on you," cried my little Boat,
"Was ever such a heartless loon,
Within a living Boat to sit,
And make no better use of it,
A Boat twin-sister of the crescent-moon!

Out—out—and, like a brooding hen,
Beside your sooty hearth-stone cower;
Go, creep along the dirt, and pick
Your way with your good walking-stick,
Just three good miles an hour!

Ne'er in the breast of full-grown Poet
Flutter'd so faint a heart before—
Was it the music of the spheres
That overpower'd your mortal ears?
—Such din shall trouble them no more.

These nether precincts do not lack
Charms of their own;—then come with me—
I want a comrade, and for you
There's nothing that I would not do;
Nought is there that you shall not see.

Haste! and above Siberian snows
We'll sport amid the boreal morning,
Will mingle with her lustres gliding
Among the stars, the stars now hiding
And now the stars adorning.

---

76 you! *1827–*
77 heartless] homesick *1827–* Loon *1832, 1836–*
78 sit,] sit *1820*
79 it,— *1827–1834* it; *1836–*
80 crescent moon *1827–1832*
81–85 *omitted 1827–*
87 Fluttered *1820–* before;— *1827–*
89 overpowered *1820–*
92 me—] me; *1836–1846* me *1849*
93 Comrade *1832*
97 morning; *1836–*
98 mingle] mangle *1831 (corrected in errata)* lustres, *1827–1834*
99 hiding, *1827–*

I know a deep romantic land,
A land that's deep and far away;
And fair it is as evening skies
And in the farthest heart it lies
Of deepest Àfrica.

Or we'll into the world of fairy
Among the lovely shades of things,
The shadowy forms of mountains bare
And streams and bowers and ladies fair,
The shades of palaces and kings."

"My pretty little form of light,
My sweet and beautiful canoe,
Now though it grieves me to the heart
I feel, I feel that we must part;
I must take leave of you.

You are a pretty little barge
But while your pleasure you're pursuing
Without impediment or let,
My little Barge! you quite forget
What in the world is doing.

Suppose now in the land of Fairy
That we should play our sportive pranks
Above those shadowy streams, and there
Should make discoveries rich and rare;
The world would count us little thanks.

There was a time, a time indeed,
A time when poets lived in clover
[

]

118–120 Left blank in MSS. 2 and 3; MS. 4 reads:
—What boots it now to keep the key
Of Fairyland? for woe is me!
Those blessed days are over.

I know the secrets of a land
Where human foot did never stray;
Fair is the land as evening skies,
And cool,—though in the depth it lies
Of burning Africa.

Or we'll into the realm of Faery,
Among the lovely shades of things;
The shadowy forms of mountains bare,
And streams, and bowers, and ladies fair;
The shades of palaces and kings!

Or, if you thirst with hardy zeal
Less quiet regions to explore,
Prompt voyage shall to you reveal
How earth and heaven are taught to feel
The might of magic lore!"

"My little vagrant Form of light,
My gay and beautiful Canoe,
Well have you play'd your friendly part;
As kindly take what from my heart
Experience forces—then adieu!

Temptation lurks among your words;
But, while these pleasures you're pursuing
Without impediment or let,
My radiant Pinnace, you forget
What on the earth is doing.

There was a time when all mankind
Did listen with a faith sincere
To tuneful tongues in mystery vers'd;
Then Poets fearlessly rehears'd
The wonders of a wild career.

---

103 the] that *1827–*
104 cool,—] cool, *1836–*
108 mountains] fountains *1834*
109 fair;] fai *1819a* fair *1820* fair, *1827–*
118 played *1820–*
124 Pinnace! *1836–1840 but not MS. 1832/36* No wonder if you quite forget *1845–*
128 versed *1820–*
129 rehearsed *1820–*

Go—but the world's a sleepy world
And 'tis, I fear, an age too late;
Take with you some ambitious Youth,
For I myself, in very truth,
Am all unfit to be your mate.

Long have I lov'd what I behold,
The night that calms, the day that cheers:
The common growth of mother earth
Suffices me—her tears, her mirth,
Her humblest mirth and tears.

The dragon's wing, the magic ring,
I shall not covet for my dower,
If I along that lowly way
With sympathetic heart may stray
And with a soul of power.

These given, what more need I desire,
To stir—to sooth—or elevate?
What nobler marvels than the mind
May in life's daily prospect find,
May find or there create?

A potent wand doth Sorrow wield;
What spell so strong as guilty Fear!
Repentance is a tender sprite;
If aught on earth have heavenly might,
'Tis lodg'd within her silent tear.

---

131 (but *1827–* world, *1820–*
132 late:) *1827–1831, 1834* late) *1832, 1836–*
133 Youth; *1827–1834* Youth! *1836– but not MS. 1832/36*
134 For, restless Wanderer! I, in truth, *1827–*
136 loved *1820–*
137 cheers; *1832, 1836–*
138 mother earth] mother Earth *1832* mother-earth *1836–*
144 stray, *1827– but* stray. *1846*
146 desire,] desire *1827–*
147 stir, *1836–* soothe— *1819a–1834* soothe, *1836–*
152 fear *1832*
153 Sprite; *1827–*
155 lodged *1820–* tear.] tear *1840*

There is a party in the Bower
Round the stone table in my garden;
The Squire is there, and, as I guess,
His pretty little daughter Bess
With Harry the church-warden.

They were to come this very evening,
They know not I have been so far;
I see them there, in number nine,
All in the bower of Weymouth pine,
I see them, there they are.

And there's the wife of Parson Swan
And there's my good friend Stephen Otter;
And ere the light of evening fail
To them I must relate the tale
Of Peter Bell the Potter."

Off flew my pretty little boat
All in a trance of indignation;
And I, as well as I was able
On two poor legs to my stone table
Limped on with some vexation.

128 The nine visitors include the Squire, the Parson (later Vicar) and his wife, Harry the Churchwarden, Stephen Otter, and little Bess; the others are never identified.

But grant my wishes,—let us now
Descend from this ethereal height;
Then take thy way, adventurous Skiff,
More daring far than Hippogriff,
And be thy own delight!

To the stone-table in my garden,
Lov'd haunt of many a summer hour,
The Squire is come;—his daughter Bess
Beside him in the cool recess
Sits blooming like a flower.

With these are many more convened;
They know not I have been so far—
I see them there in number nine
Beneath the spreading Weymouth pine—
I see them—there they are!

There sits the Vicar, and his Dame;
And there my good friend, Stephen Otter;
And, ere the light of evening fail,
To them I must relate the Tale
Of Peter Bell the Potter."

Off flew my sparkling Boat in scorn,
Yea in a trance of indignation!
And I, as well as I was able,
On two poor legs, to my stone-table
Limp'd on with some vexation.

---

162 Loved *1820–*
163 come;—] come: *1836–*
167 far;— *1832, 1836–*
168 there, *1820–* nine, *1820–*
169 Weymouth-pine! *1836– but* Weymouth-pine; *MS. 1832/36*
171 Vicar,] Vicar *1827–*
176 Off flew the Boat—away she flees, *1845–*
177 Spurning her freight with indignation! *1820–*
179 to] tow'rd *1827–1834*, toward *1836–*
180 Limped *1820–* some] sore *1845–*

"Oh here he is!" cried little Bess;
She saw me at the garden door.
"O here he is!" cried Mistress Swan,
And all at once around me ran
Full nine of them or more.

"Sit down, I beg you would be seated,"
Said I, no doubt with visage pale;
"And if, my friends, it pleases you
This instant without more ado
We'll have the promised tale."

And so, though somewhat out of breath,
With lips, no doubt, and visage pale,
And sore too from a slight contusion
Did I to cover my confusion
Begin the promised tale.

Tale of Peter Bell

All by the moonlight river side
It gave three miserable groans;
" 'Tis come then to a pretty pass,"
Said Peter to the groaning ass,
"But I will bang your bones."

146–155 The verbal repetitions in these two stanzas are marks of WW's *Lyrical Ballads* style; they survived in *Peter Bell* through the original version of MS. 6.

155/156 In MS. 2 a blank half page was left (in MS. 3 a quarter page) so that the Tale begins at the top of a new page.

156–160 The tale begins with ll. 476–480. In later versions the objection is raised by the Vicar. There is some suggestion that WW did not at first consider that the Vicar (or earlier, Parson) was present at the beginning of the narration. A canceled insertion in MS. 4 suggests that Mr. Swan arrived after the description of Peter (see *apparatus criticus* to ll. 295/296 of the MS. 2 transcription, below).

"O, here he is!" cried little Bess—
She saw me at the garden door,
"We've waited anxiously and long,"
They cried, and all around me throng,
Full nine of them, or more!

Reproach me not—your fears be still—
Be thankful we again have met;—
Resume, my Friends! within the shade
Your seats, and promptly shall be paid
The well-remembered debt.

Breath fail'd me as I spake—but soon
With lips, no doubt, and visage pale,
And sore too from a slight contusion,
Did I, to cover my confusion,
Begin the *promised* Tale.

PART FIRST.

ALL by the moonlight river side
It gave three miserable groans;
" 'Tis come then to a pretty pass,"
Said Peter to the groaning Ass,
"But I will *bang* your bones!"

---

181 O,] O *1831, 1834*
182 garden-door, *1836–1840, 1846 but not MS. 1832/36* garden-door; *1845, 1849*
185 them,] them *1827–*
186 "Reproach *1819a–*
187 "Be *1819a*
188 "Resume *1819a*
189 "Your *1819a* promptly] quickly *1827–*
190 "The *1819a* debt." *1819a–*
191 failed *1820*
191–193 I spake with faltering voice, like one
Not wholly rescued from the pale
Of a wild dream, or worse illusion; *1827– but* Pale *1832; return to lowercase not indicated MS. 1832/36*
194 Did I] But, straight *1827– but* But straight *1834*
195 Begin] Began *1827–* *no italics 1827–* Tale] tale *1834*
197–200 Groaned the poor Beast—alas! in vain;
The staff was raised to loftier height,
And the blows fell with heavier weight
As Peter struck—and struck again. *1820–*

"My dearest Sir," cried Mistress Swan,
"You're got at once into the middle";
And little Bess with accents sweeter
Cried "Oh! dear Sir! but who is Peter?"
[ ]

The Squire cried "Sure as Paradise
Was lost to us by Adam's sinning
We all are wandering in a wood,
And therefore, Sir, I wish you would
Begin at the beginning."

A Potter, Sir, he was by trade,
Cried I, becoming quite collected,
And wheresoever he appeared
Full twenty times was Peter feared
For once that Peter was respected.

He two and thirty years or more
Had been a wild and woodland rover,
Had been in farthest Pembroke, Sir,
And he had been at Exeter,
In Kent, Sir, and in Dover.

---

163 MS. 2 first read "accent" with the "s" apparently added in transcription; MS. 3 reads "accents."

165 Left blank in MSS. 2 and 3; MS. 4 reads:

> Said Harry, "tis a downright riddle"

170 MS. 2 breaks off here and resumes at l. 401.

171 In the North of England a "potter" was not only, as WW's 1819 note affirms, a seller of earthenware; the term was sometimes the equivalent of "tinker." At any rate, potters were wanderers, the indigenous gypsies of the North; the name may also be related to "pattering" or begging (J. Sullivan, *Cumberland and Westmorland, Ancient and Modern: The People, Dialect, Superstitions, and Customs* [London, 1857], pp. 56–57).

176–200 The account of Peter's travels appears to make him crisscross Britain in a wandering fashion. It takes him across England from west to east and about halfway up into western Scotland, then back to northeast England.

"Good Sir!"—the Vicar's voice exclaim'd,
"You rush at once into the middle;"
And little Bess, with accent sweeter,
Cried, "O dear Sir! but who is Peter?"
Said Stephen,—" 'Tis a downright riddle!"

The Squire said, "Sure as paradise
"Was lost to man by Adam's sinning,
"This leap is for us all too bold;
"Who Peter was, let that be told,
"And start from the beginning."

——A potter, Sir, he was by trade,
Said I, becoming quite collected;
And, wheresoever he appeared,
Full twenty times was Peter feared
For once that Peter was respected.

He two and thirty years or more
Had been a wild and woodland rover;
Had heard the Atlantic surges roar
On farthest Cornwall's rocky shore,
And trod the cliffs of Dover.

201–205 *omitted 1820–*

206–207 Like winds that lash the waves, or smite
The woods, the autumnal foliage thinning— *1820–1834 but* the autumnal] autumnal *1827–1834*
Hold, cried the Squire, "against the rules
Of common sense you're surely sinning; *MS. 1832/36, adopted 1836– but* Hold,] "Hold!"

208 "Hold!" said the Squire, "I pray you, hold! *1820–1834 but* you,] you *1832* Are [? ?] young and [?] *in pencil then* This leap is for us all, too bold; *in ink MS. 1832/36, adopted 1836– but* all,] all

209 "Who] Who *1820–* was,] was *1820–1834 but comma not restored MS. 1832/36* told,] told *1820*

210 "And] And *1820–*

211 A potter] "A potter* *footnote added* *In the dialect of the North, a hawker of earthenware is thus designated. *1819a– but* Potter *1820–* earthenware *1834– but not MS. 1832/36* trade," *1819a–*

213 And,] "And, *1819a* "And *1820–*

214 "Full *1819a*

215 "For . . . respected." *1819a*

216 He, two-and-thirty years or more, *1820– but* He two *1849*

And he had been at Nottingham
And well he knew the spire of Sarum,
And he had been where Lincoln's Bell
To Shepherds in the distant dell
Rings out his loud alarum.

At York and at the hill of Brough
And merry Carlisle had he been,
And all along the lowlands fair
All through the bonny shire of Ayr
As far as Aberdeen.

And he had been at Inverness,
And Peter by the moonlight rills
Had danced his round with Highland lasses,
And he had lain beside his asses
On lofty Cheviot hills.

And he had trudged through Yorkshire dales
Among the rocks and winding scars
Where deep and low the hamlets lie
Beneath their little patch of sky
And little lot of stars.

And all along the winding coast
Where the sea dashed its whitening foam,
Where'er a knot of houses lay
On headland or in hollow bay,
Sure never man like him did roam.

183 The "Lincoln's" of MS. 3 may be a miswriting, as MS. 4 and later texts have "Lincoln."

And he had seen Caernarvon's towers,
And well he knew the spire of Sarum;
And he had been where Lincoln bell
Flings o'er the fen its ponderous knell,
Its far-renowned alarum!

At Doncaster, at York, and Leeds,
And merry Carlisle had he been;
And all along the Lowlands fair,
All through the bonny shire of Ayr—
And far as Aberdeen.

And he had been at Inverness;
And Peter, by the mountain rills,
Had danced his round with Highland lasses;
And he had lain beside his asses
On lofty Cheviot Hills:

And he had trudg'd through Yorkshire dales,
Among the rocks and winding *scars*;
Where deep and low the hamlets lie
Beneath their little patch of sky
And little lot of stars:

And all along the indented coast,
Bespattered with the salt-sea foam;
Where'er a knot of houses lay,
On headland, or in hollow bay;—
Sure never man like him did roam!

---

222 Spire *1831, 1834*
224 Fen *1831, 1834* its] his *1836 del to* that *MS. 1836/45 (WW) adopted 1840–* knell— *1836– but not MS. 1832/36*
225 Its] A *1836, 1845– but* A *del to* His *del to* A *MS. 1836/45 (JC)* His *1840* alarum. *1849*. *1849*.
226 Leeds,] Leeds *1827–1831, 1834*
229 Ayr; *1836–*
231–240 X *and vertical line in margin, in pencil, MS. 1836/45*
232 mountain-rills *1836–*
236 trudged *1820–*
240 stars; *1831, 1834*
243 lay,] lay *1827–*

As well might Peter in the fleet
Have been fast bound, a begging debtor;
He travelled here, he travelled there,
But Peter never was a hair
In heart or head the better.

He roved among the vales and streams,
In the green wood and hollow dell;
They were his dwellings night and day,
But Nature ne'er could find the way
Into the heart of Peter Bell.

In vain through every changeful year
Did Nature lead him as before;
A primrose by a river's brim
A yellow primrose was to him
And it was nothing more.

Small change it made in Peter's heart
To see his gentle panniered train
With more than vernal pleasure feeding
Where'er the tender grass was leading
Its earliest green along the lane.

In vain through water, earth, and air
The soul of happy sound was spread
When Peter on some April morn
Beneath the broom or budding thorn
Made the warm earth his lazy bed.

At noon when by the forest's edge
He lay beneath the branches high,
The soft blue sky did never melt
Into his heart, he never felt
The witchery of the soft blue sky.

---

206 The Fleet was a London prison, used for debtors.

218–219 The primrose (*Primulacaea vulgaris*) was a common plant that Peter may have been expected to come across frequently; WW may also have intended an allusion to Hamlet's "primrose path of dalliance" (I.iii.50).

220 To a sensitive observer, of course, the "meanest flower" could give thoughts that "lie too deep for tears" (*Ode. Intimations of Immortality*, ll. 203–204).

As well might Peter, in the Fleet,
Have been fast bound, a begging debtor;—
He travelled here, he travelled there;—
But not the value of a hair
Was heart or head the better.

He rov'd among the vales and streams,
In the green wood and hollow dell;
They were his dwellings night and day,—
But Nature ne'er could find the way
Into the heart of Peter Bell.

In vain, through every changeful year,
Did Nature lead him as before;
A primrose by a river's brim
A yellow primrose was to him,
And it was nothing more.

Small change it made in Peter's heart
To see his gentle pannier'd train
With more than vernal pleasure feeding,
Where'er the tender grass was leading
Its earliest green along the lane.

In vain, through water, earth, and air,
The soul of happy sound was spread,
When Peter, on some April morn,
Beneath the broom or budding thorn,
Made the warm earth his lazy bed.

At noon, when by the forest's edge
He lay beneath the branches high,
The soft blue sky did never melt
Into his heart,—he never felt
The witchery of the soft blue sky!

---

246 Peter,] Peter *1831, 1834*
247 Debtor *1832*
248 travell'd here *1819a*
251 roved *1820–*
254 nature *1836– but not MS. 1832/36*
257 nature *1831, 1834*
262 panniered *1820–*
268 Peter,] Peter *1836– but not MS. 1832/36*
271 when, *1827–* edge, *1819a–1834*
274 heart,—] heart; *1836–*

On a fair prospect some have looked
And felt, as I have heard them say,
As if the moving time had been
A thing as stedfast as the scene
On which they gazed themselves away.

With Peter Bell I need not tell
That this had never been the case;
He was a carl as wild and rude
As ever hue and cry pursued,
As ever ran a felon's race.

Of all that lead a lawless life,
Of all that *love* their lawless lives,
In city or in village small
He was the wildest far of all:
He had a dozen wedded wives.

"Oh monster!" cried the Parson's Lady;
"Poor fellow!" echoed Stephen Otter;
"Poor fellow! say you?" Mistress Swan,
I do assure you such a man
Was Peter Bell the Potter.

He had a dozen wedded wives
But how *one* wife could e'er come near him
Upon my faith I cannot tell,
For I can say of Peter Bell
To see him was to fear him.

Though Nature ne'er could touch his heart
By lovely forms and silent weather
And tender sounds, yet you could see
At once that Peter Bell and she
Had often been together.

---

258 Stillinger (pp. 513–514) calls attention to the parallel lack of information professed by the narrator of *The Thorn* (ll. 89, 203, 232). WW repeats l. 258 as l. 509, where one cannot suspect the attraction of a rhyme with "Bell"; his narrator makes no claim to omniscience (see also ll. 308–309).

On a fair prospect some have look'd
And felt, as I have heard them say,
As if the moving time had been
A thing as stedfast as the scene
On which they gaz'd themselves away.

With Peter Bell, I need not tell
That this had never been the case;—
He was a Carl as wild and rude
As ever hue-and-cry pursued,
As ever ran a felon's race.

Of all that lead a lawless life,
Of all that love their lawless lives,
In city or in village small,
He was the wildest far of all;—
He had a dozen wedded wives.——

Nay start not!—wedded wives—and twelve!
But how one wife could e'er come near him,
In simple truth I cannot tell;
For be it said of Peter Bell
To see him was to fear him.

Though Nature could not touch his heart
By lovely forms and silent weather,
And tender sounds, yet you might see
At once that Peter Bell and she
Had often been together.

---

276 looked *1820–*
279 steadfast *1827–*
280 gazed *1820–*
281–282 Within the breast of Peter Bell
These silent raptures found no place; *1820–*
286 lawless] lawful *1831, corrected in errata*
289 all;—] all; *1827–1834*
290 wives.———] wives. *1827–*
291 Nay, *1827–*
294 For, . . . Bell, *1820–*
297 forms, *1832, 1836–* silent] placid *1820*
299 once, *1820–*

A savage wildness round him hung
As of a dweller out of doors;
In his whole figure and his mien
A savage character was seen
Of mountains and of dreary moors.

To all the unshaped half human thoughts
Which solitary Nature feeds
'Mid summer's storms or winter's ice
Had Peter joined whatever vice
The cruel city breeds.

His face was keen as is the wind
That cuts along the hawthorn fence;
Of courage you saw little there
But in its stead a medley air
Of cunning and of impudence.

He had a dark and sidelong walk
And long and slouching was his gait;
Between his looks so bare and bold
You might perceive his spirit cold
Was playing with some inward bait.

His forehead wrinkled was and furred,
A work one half of which was done
By thinking of his whens and hows
And half by wrinkling of his brows
Beneath the glaring sun.

There was a hardness in his cheek,
There was a hardness in his eye,
As if the man had fixed his face
In many a solitary place
Against the wind that sweeps the sky.

A savage wildness round him hung
As of a dweller out of doors;
In his whole figure and his mien
A savage character was seen,
Of mountains and of dreary moors.

To all the unshap'd half human thoughts
Which solitary Nature feeds
'Mid summer storms or winter's ice,
Had Peter join'd whatever vice
The cruel city breeds.

His face was keen as is the wind
That cuts along the hawthorn fence;
Of courage you saw little there,
But, in its stead, a medley air
Of cunning and of impudence.

He had a dark and sidelong walk,
And long and slouching was his gait;
Beneath his looks so bare and bold,
You might perceive, his spirit cold
Was playing with some inward bait.

His forehead wrinkled was and furr'd;
A work one half of which was done
By thinking of his *whens* and *hows*;
And half by knitting of his brows
Beneath the glaring sun.

There was a hardness in his cheek,
There was a hardness in his eye,
As if the man had fix'd his face,
In many a solitary place,
Against the wind and open sky!

---

304 seen,] seen *1832, 1836–*
306 unshaped half-human *1820–*
309 joined *1820–*
312 hawthorn-fence *1836– but not MS. 1832/36*
321 furred *1820–*
322 work, *1820–*
323 '*whens*' and '*hows;*' *1836– but quotation marks del in pencil MS. 1836/45*
324 half, *1820–*
328 fixed *1820–*
330 sky!" *1845–*

[Part First]

One night, and now my little Bess
I'm coming to the promised tale,
One beautiful November night
When the full moon was shining bright
Upon the rapid river Swale,

Close by the river's winding banks
Was Peter travelling all alone,
Whether to buy or sell, or led
By pleasure running in his head,
To me was never known.

Along the turf and through the fern
And in the mire he travelled on;
If he had left that night or day
His wife or wives I cannot say,
But wife or comrade he had none.

Some chuse to travel with a dog
And Peter had a savage elf,
A lurcher, and he loved him well;
But sure it is that Peter Bell
That evening travelled by himself.

He trudged along through copse and brake,
He trudged along o'er hill and dale;
Nor for the moon cared he a tittle
And for the stars he cared as little
And for the murmuring river Swale.

Quoth Peter, "here's a nearer cut;
'Twill save a mile, as sure as day."
He took the path, the path did lead
Across a smooth and grassy mead
And a tall wood before him lay.

296–300 This stanza falls at the top of a page in MS. 3; there is no break to indicate the beginning of the "promised tale" until MS. 4, which starts a new page with a heading: "Tale of Peter Bell / First Part."

One night, (and now, my little Bess!
We've reach'd at last the promis'd Tale;)
One beautiful November night,
When the full moon was shining bright
Upon the rapid river Swale,

Along the river's winding banks
Peter was travelling all alone;—
Whether to buy or sell, or led
By pleasure running in his head,
To me was never known.

He trudg'd along through copse and brake,
He trudg'd along o'er hill and dale;
Nor for the moon car'd he a tittle,
And for the stars he car'd as little,
And for the murmuring river Swale.

But chancing to espy a path
That promis'd to cut short the way;
As many a wiser man hath done,
He left a trusty guide for one
That might his steps betray.

---

331 now,] now *1831–*
332 reached . . . promised *1820–*
341 trudged *1820–*
342 trudged *1820–*
343 cared *1820–*
344 cared *1820–*
346 But, *1820–*
347 promised *1827–* way, *1820–1834*

And now he to a wood is come
And Peter there in whole cart loads
Is heaping curses on them all,
Commissioners both great and small,
Who made the zig-zag roads.

For while he drives among the boughs
With head and hands and cheeks that burn
With downright fury and with wrath,
There's little sign that Peter's path
Will to the road return.

The path grows dim and dimmer still;
Now up, now down his way he wends
With all the sail that he can carry
Till he is brought to an old quarry
And there the path-way ends.

"What back again, old grim-face? No!
I'll grapple with the devil first;
Stretch like a yawning wolf your paws
But dam'me if by any laws
Of yours I'll ever be coerced."

And so where on the huge rough stones
The black and massy shadows lay
And through the dark and through the cold
And through the yawning fissures old
Did Peter boldly press his way.

---

341 The identity of "old grim-face" may seem unclear; a revision in MS. 5 toys with substituting "my Antient." But from MS. 5 on, "grizly Den" suggests that WW meant that Peter was only talking to the cul-de-sac in which he found himself, and which is telling him he must retrace his steps.

To a thick wood he soon is brought
Where cheerfully his course he weaves,
And whistling loud may yet be heard,
Though often buried, like a bird
Darkling among the boughs and leaves.

But quickly Peter's mood is chang'd,
And on he drives with cheeks that burn
In downright fury and in wrath—
There's little sign the treacherous path
Will to the road return!

The path grows dim, and dimmer still;
Now up—now down—the rover wends
With all the sail that he can carry;
Till he is brought to an old quarry,
And there the pathway ends.

"What! would'st thou daunt me grisly den?
"Back must I, having come so far?
"Stretch as thou wilt thy gloomy jaws,
"I'll on, nor would I give two straws
"For lantern or for star!"

And so, where on the huge rough stones
The black and massy shadows lay,
And through the dark, and through the cold,
And through the yawning fissures old,
Did Peter boldly press his way

---

352 cheerfully] cheerily *1836–*
354 bird, *1832 but comma not del MS. 1832/36*
355 Darkling, *1836– but not MS. 1832/36*
356 changed *1820–*
358 wrath;— *1836–*
362 up, now down, *1836–* Rover wends, *1832, 1836–*
363 carry;] carry, *1827– but* carry *1832*
364 Till brought to a deserted quarry; *1827– but* quarry— *1832, 1836–*
366–370 *omitted 1820–*
371–372 He paused—for shadows of strange shape,
Massy and black, before him lay; *1820–*
373 And] But *1820–*

And in a moment opened out
A scene of soft and lovely hue
Where blue and grey and tender green
Together made as sweet a scene
As ever human eye did view.

Beneath the clear blue sky you saw
A little plot of meadow ground.
But oh! far rather name it not;
Call it of earth a small green plot
With rocks encompass'd round.

The Swale flowed under the green rocks
But he flowed quiet and unseen;
You need a strong and stormy gale
To bring the noises of the Swale
To that green spot so calm and green.

Now you'll suppose that Peter Bell
Had some temptation here to tarry,
And so it was, but I must add
His heart was not a little glad
That he was out of the old quarry.

And is there no one dwelling here,
No hermit with his beads and glass?
And does no little cottage look
Upon this green and silent nook?
Does no one live near this green grass?

Across that deep and quiet spot
Is Peter driving through the grass,
And now he is among the trees

---

361 The Swale River takes its rise in the rugged moorland of northwest Yorkshire and flows southeast, joining the Ouse above York. Edmund Gosse pointed out, however, that the landscape of the poem is "pure Somerset in character," reflecting its Alfoxden origins (*Gossip in a Library* [London, 1913], p. 256).

367 By revising "some temptation" to "small temptation" in MS. 4 WW upset the logic of the stanza, never to correct it.

Right through the quarry;—and behold
A scene of soft and lovely hue!
Where blue, and grey, and tender green,
Together made as sweet a scene
As ever human eye did view.

Beneath the clear blue sky he saw
A little field of meadow ground;
But field or meadow name it not;
Call it of earth a small green plot,
With rocks encompass'd round.

The Swale flow'd under the grey rocks,
But he flow'd quiet and unseen;—
You need a strong and stormy gale
To bring the noises of the Swale
To that green spot, so calm and green!

Now you'll suppose that Peter Bell
Felt small temptation here to tarry,
And so it was,—but I must add,
His heart was not a little glad
When he was out of the old quarry.

And is there no one dwelling here,
No hermit with his beads and glass?
And does no little cottage look
Upon this soft and fertile nook?
Does no one live near this green grass?

Across that deep and quiet spot
Is Peter driving through the grass—
And now he is among the trees;

---

378 blue,] blue *1827–*
379 made] make *1827–*
385 encompassed *1820–*
386 flowed *1820–*
387 flowed *1820–*
391–395 *omitted 1820–*
401 that] the *1827–*
403 And now has reached the skirting trees; *1836– but* trees *MS. 1832/36*

And turning round his head he sees
The solitary ass.

"No doubt I'm foundered in these woods.
For once," quoth he, "I will be wise;
Upon my faith, I'll back again,
And not to make my journey vain
I'll take the ass likewise."

So off he goes, as you'll suppose,
With thoughts as blithe as any dream
To where the ass beside the bed
Of that green meadow hung his head
Over the silent stream.

"A pretty beast! though we'll allow
Not quite so fat as he might be;
Upon my soul, with such a platter
You should have been a little fatter;
But come, Sir, come with me."

But first friend Peter deems it fit
To spy about him far and near;
There's not a single house in sight,
No woodman's hut, no cottage light—
Peter you need not fear.

There's nothing to be seen but woods
And rocks that spread a hoary gleam,
And this poor ass which near the bed
Of the green meadow hangs his head
Over the silent stream.

---

401 MS. 2 resumes here.

When, turning round his head, he sees
A solitary Ass.

"No doubt I'm founder'd in these woods—
"For once," quoth he, "I will be wise,
"With better speed I'll back again—
"And, lest the journey should prove vain,
"Will take yon Ass, my lawful prize!"

Off Peter hied,—"A comely beast!
"Though not so plump as he might be;
"My honest friend, with such a platter,
"You should have been a little fatter,
"But come, Sir, come with me!"

But first doth Peter deem it fit
To spy about him far and near;
There's not a single house in sight,
No woodman's hut, no cottage light—
Peter you need not fear!

There's nothing to be seen but woods
And rocks that spread a hoary gleam,
And this one beast that from the bed
Of the green meadow hangs his head
Over the silent stream.

405/416 *illegible line erased between stanzas MS. 1832/36*
405/416 "I've lost [?my] way among these woods," thought he
Thought he I will
But [?I'll] for once ^ [?be] wise
With better speed I'll back again
And not to make the journey vain
Yon Ass shall be my prize. *foot of page, del MS. 1832/36*
406 foundered *1820*
406–410 *omitted 1827–*
407 "For] For *1820*
408 "With] With *1820*
409 "And] And *1820*
410 "Will] Will *1820*
411–415 *omitted 1820–*
416 "A prize," cried Peter, stepping back *1827–1834* "A prize!" cries Peter—but he first *1836–*
417 To] Must *1836–* near: *1836–*
419 cottage-light *1836 but not MS. 1832/36* cottag light *1840*
420 Peter, *1827–*
421 woods, *1820–*
423 beast, *1827–1840* Beast, *1845–*

Close to the river's brink he stands,
His head is with a halter bound;
Now Peter's purpose did not alter
And so at once he seized the halter
And would have turned him round.

He pulled, the creature did not move;
Upon his back then Peter leapt
And with his staff and heels he plied
The little ass on either side
But still the ass his station kept.

Quoth Peter, "you're a beast of mettle;
I see you'll suit me to an ace."
And now the ass through his left eye
On Peter turned most quietly
Looked quietly in his face.

"What's this?" cries Peter, brandishing
A new peeled sapling white as cream;
The ass knew well what Peter said
But as before hung down his head
Over the silent stream.

"[ ] would that my Wife Kate
Were here, my pretty rough haired boy!
She would have at you with a rattle
And we should have a royal battle;
We'd make you dance for joy!"

Then Peter gave another jirk,
A jirk that from a dungeon floor
Would have pulled up an iron ring;
But still the heavy headed thing
Stood just as he had stood before.

406–407 The tenses appear to have been altered by erasure, probably in transcription, in MS. 2 from "stood" to "stands" and from "was" to "is"; MS. 3 has the revised readings.

426 The line was left incomplete in MS. 2, and the stanza, carefully deleted with wavy horizontal lines, does not appear in MS. 3, or anywhere else.

His head is with a halter bound;
The halter seizing, Peter leapt
Upon the Ass's back, and plied
With ready heel the creature's side;
But still the Ass his station kept.

"What's this!" cried Peter, brandishing
A new-peel'd sapling white as cream;
The Ass knew well what Peter said,
But, as before, hung down his head
Over the silent stream.

Then Peter gave a sudden jirk,
A jirk that from a dungeon floor
Would have pulled up an iron ring;
But still the heavy-headed thing
Stood just as he had stood before!

---

428 Ass's] Creature's *1827–* plied, *1820*
429 heel, *1820* heels *1836– but not MS. 1832/36* the creature's] his shaggy *1827–*
431–435 out *in margin, stanza del MS. 1832/36, omitted 1836–*
432 A new-peeled sapling;—though, I deem, *1820–1834 but* though *1827–1834* deem *1832*
433 This threat was understood full well, *1827–1834*
434 But] He *1820* Firm *1827–1834* hung down his head] the Sentinel *1827–1834*
435 Over] Stood by *1827–1834*
436 jirk] jerk *1832, 1836–*
437 jirk] jerk *1832, 1836–* dungeon-floor *1836–*
439 Thing *1827–*

Quoth Peter, leaping from the ass,
"There is some plot against me laid."
Once more the little meadow-ground
And all the hoary cliffs around
He cautiously surveyed.

There's nothing, Peter, far or near,
There's nothing with your purpose jars;
Only the full moon's in the sky
And with her a fair company,
The fairest of the stars.

All, all is silent, rocks and woods,
All, all is silent far and near;
Only the ass with motion dull
Upon the pivot of his skull
Turns round his long left ear.

Quoth Peter, "what can mean all this?
In faith there is some witchcraft here."
Once more the ass with motion dull
Upon the pivot of his skull
Turned round his long left ear.

---

438 The line began "At this" in MS. 2, but appears to have been revised in transcription, first in the line, then above it; MS. 3 has "Once more."

451–452 The base text of MS. 3 incorporates revisions in MS. 2:

Thought Peter what can mean all this
There is some ugly witchcraft here

Quoth Peter, leaping from his seat,
"There is some plot against me laid;"
Once more the little meadow ground
And all the hoary cliffs around
He cautiously survey'd.

All, all is silent, rocks and woods,
All still and silent—far and near;
Only the Ass, with motion dull,
Upon the pivot of his skull
Turns round his long left ear.

Thought Peter, What can mean all this?
Some ugly witchcraft must be here!
Once more the Ass, with motion dull,
Upon the pivot of his skull
Turn'd round his long left ear.

"I'll cure you of these desperate tricks"—
And, with deliberate action slow,
His staff high-raising, in the pride
Of skill, upon the Ass's hide
He dealt a sturdy blow.

What followed?—yielding to the shock
The Ass, as if to take his ease,
In quiet uncomplaining mood

---

442 *open quote missing 1846*
443 meadow-ground *1836– but not MS. 1832/36*
445 cautioulsy *1834* surveyed *1820–*
446 silent— *1827–*
447 near;] near *1819a* near! *1820–*
450 Turns] Turned *1834*
451 this?— *1819a–1834 but dash not del MS 1832/36*
453 —Once *1836– but not MS. 1832/36*
455 Turned *1820–*
456 Suspicion ripened into dread; *1827– but del to original with no apos, no dash MS. 1836/45 (WW)*
457 And,] Yet *1827–*
458 high-raising,] high-raising *1831, 1834*
459 Ass's hide] sounding hide, *1827–*
461 shock, *1827–1834* The poor Ass staggered with the shock; *1836– but* shock, *MS. 1832/36*
462 The Ass *del to* [?Dropped],—yet *del to* And then, *MS. 1832/36, adopted 1836–*
463 mood, *1820–*

Quoth Peter, "by the devil's beard,
I'll make you stir, you mongrel hound!"
And both his arms did Peter pass
Beneath the belly of the ass;
With both his arms he clasp'd him round.

"Now for it, now, you sturdy rogue,"
And desperately friend Peter heaves;
He might as well have tried to stir
The abbey huge of Westminster
Or twice five hundred head [?of beeves].

Cried Peter, "you'll be wise, I hope,
Before we're both five minutes older!"
Upon the ass the sapling rings;
Each blow the arm of Peter stings
Up to the elbow and the shoulder.

At last, poor patient thing, at last
His sides they heaved, his belly stirr'd;
He gave a groan and then another,
Of that which went before the brother,
And then he gave a third.

All by the moonlight river side
He gave three miserable groans.
" 'Tis come then to a pretty pass,"
Said Peter to the groaning ass,
"But I will bang your bones."

456–465 These stanzas are entered by WW in fair copy on a verso in MS. 2 and marked for insertion here; only the first was taken into the base text of MS. 3, but both are in the base text of MS. 1.

465 The last two words were erased in MS. 2 when subsequent revisions were made on the page; they are confirmed by MS. 1.

Upon the spot where he had stood
Dropt gently down upon his knees.

And then upon his side he fell
And by the river's brink did lie
And, as he lay like one that mourn'd,
The patient beast on Peter turn'd
His shining hazel eye.

'Twas but one mild, reproachful look,
A look more tender than severe;
And straight in sorrow, not in dread,
He turn'd the eye-ball in his head
Towards the river deep and clear.

Upon the beast the sapling rings,—
Heav'd his lank sides, his limbs they stirr'd;
He gave a groan—and then another,
Of that which went before the brother,
And then he gave a third:

All by the moonlight river side
He gave three miserable groans,
"'Tis come then to a pretty pass,"
Said Peter to the groaning ass,
"But I will *bang* your bones!"

---

464 stood, *1820–*
465 Dropped *1827–* gently *del, deletion line erased MS. 1832/36* knees; *1836– but not MS. 1832/36*
466 And then upon] As gently on *1836–* fell, *1827–1834* fell; *1836– but not MS. 1832/36*
467 lie; *1819a–*
468 as *del in pencil to* while *MS. 1836/45, adopted 1840–* lay, *1834* mourned *1820–*
469 patient beast on Peter] Beast on his tormentor *1827–1834* patient Beast on Peter *1836–* turned *1820–*
470 His] A *1827–1831, 1834*
474 turned *1820–*
475 the river] the smooth river *1836–*
476 Beast *1845, 1849* rings,—] rings; *1836–*
477 Heaved *1820–1831, 1834* Heav'd his lank sides] His lank sides heaved, *1832, 1836–* stirred *1820–*
478 groan, *1836–*
480 third. *1820–*
481–485 *omitted 1820–1834, coalesced with ll. 486–490 1836–*
484 Ass *1819a*

And now the little harmless beast
Gently, as if to take his ease,
The ass whom Peter thus had bruised,
Whom he so cruelly had used,
Dropped gently down upon his knees.

And then upon his side he fell,
His countenance it shewed no fear;
He lay upon the meadow-bed
And as before hung down his head
Over the stream so deep and clear.

For Peter's merriment is flown,
His lips with rage and fury quiver;
Quoth he, "you little mulish dog!"
Quoth he, "I'll fling you like a log
Headforemost down the river,

By God I will!" When this was said
As stretched upon his side he lay,
To all the echoes south and north

486–490 The base text of MS. 3 omits this stanza, but includes another with the same first line, crowded onto a facing verso by WW in MS. 2 (where the upper loop of a partially erased letter looks like an "s" after "side"):

And then upon his sides he fell
And now to Peter's eye was shown
What till this time he had not seen
That the poor Ass was guant & lean
And almost wasted to the bone.

The base text of MS. 1 (28[r]) contains the same stanza, with a different first line and a variant in the second line.

490/491 The base text of MS. 3 includes a stanza taken from a crowded verso addition in WW's hand in MS. 2 (17[v]):

The meagre beast lay still as death
No word of kind commiseration
Fell at the sight from Peters tongue
With hard contempt his heart was wrung
With hatred and with new vexation.

491 A blank appears to have been left by DW in her fair copy of MS. 2 for WW to write in the line.

And Peter halts to gather breath,
And now full clearly was it shown
(What he before in part had seen)
How gaunt was the poor Ass and lean,
Yea wasted to a skeleton!

With legs stretched out and stiff he lay:—
No word of kind commiseration
Fell at the sight from Peter's tongue;
With hard contempt his heart was wrung,
With hatred and vexation.

The meagre beast lay still as death—
And Peter's lips with fury quiver—
Quoth he, "You little mulish dog,
"I'll fling your carcase like a log
"Head foremost down the river!"

An impious oath confirmed the threat—
But, while upon the ground he lay,
To all the echoes, south and north,

486–488 *del to, interlined:*
All by the moonlight river side
He gave three miserable groans
And now [?befo] Peter's eye is seen *MS. 1832/36*

486–490 All by the moonlight river side
He gave three miserable groans;
And not till now hath Peter seen
How gaunt the Creature is,—how lean
{A / and sharp his} {staring bones! / bones} ~~How lean~~ *(with dash in pencil) at foot of page MS. 1832/36, adopted as revised 1836–, in effect coalescing ll. 481–490*

487 And, while he halts, was clearly shown *1827–1834*

489 was the poor Ass] the Creature was, *1827–1834*, was, and *del to* is, how *MS. 1832/36* lean,] lean *MS. 1832/36*

490 Yea] Yea, *1827–1834* skeleton!] skeleton. *1832* *del to*
His sides, {A / and sharp his} ^staring bones! *interlined MS. 1832/36*

496 lay *del to* [?is] *del, then restored with* stet *in margin MS. 1832/36* death; *1836–*

497 quiver; *1836–*

499 "I'll] I'll *1820–* carcass *1827–*

500 "Head foremost] Head-foremost *1820–*

501 threat: *1832*

502 That instant, while outstretched he lay, *1827–1834 del to* [?Then] ^And from the ground whereon he lay *interlined, then del to* Whereat from the earth on which he lay *first interlined MS. 1832/36, then rewritten at foot of page; adopted 1836–*

And east and west the ass sent forth
A loud and horrible bray.

This outcry on the heart of Peter
Seems like a note of joy to strike;
Joy on the heart of Peter knocks,
But in the echo of the rocks
Was something Peter did not like.

Whether to chear his coward heart
Or that he felt a wicked chain
Twined round him like a magic spell,
Upon my faith I cannot tell,
But to the work he fell again.

Among the rocks and winding crags,
Among the mountains far away,
Once more the ass did lengthen out
Just like a sounding trumpet's shout
The long dry see-saw of his horrible bray.

What is there now in Peter's heart,
Or what's the power of that strange sound?
The moon uneasy look'd and dimmer,
The broad blue heavens appear'd to glimmer,
And the rocks stagger'd all around.

And east and west, the Ass sent forth
A loud and piteous bray!

This outcry, on the heart of Peter,
Seems like a note of joy to strike,—
Joy on the heart of Peter knocks;—
But in the echo of the rocks
Was something Peter did not like.

Whether to cheer his coward breast,
Or that he could not break the chain,
In this serene and solemn hour,
Twin'd round him by demoniac power,
To the blind work he turn'd again.—

Among the rocks and winding crags—
Among the mountains far away—
Once more the Ass did lengthen out
More ruefully an endless shout,
The long dry see-saw of his horrible bray!

What is there now in Peter's heart?
Or whence the might of this strange sound?
The moon uneasy look'd and dimmer,
The broad blue heavens appear'd to glimmer
And the rocks stagger'd all around.

---

505 loud and piteous] long and clamorous *1836–*
508 on] at *1820–* knocks;—] knocks; *1832, 1836–*
514 Twined *1820–*
515 turned *1820–* again.—] again. *1836–*
515/516 looked over/—WW *in pencil across top of page MS. 1836/45 (WW)*
516 crags; *1836–*
517 away; *1836–*
519 an endless] a deep-drawn *1836–*
520 long] hard *1836–*
521 heart! *1832, 1836–*
523 looked *1820–*
524 appeared *1820–* glimmer, *1819a–*
525 staggered *1820–* around— *1836– but not MS. 1832/36*

From Peter's hand the sapling dropp'd;
'Twas plain that he felt small temptation
To play again the ruffian's part
For by this time in Peter's heart
There was a wondrous alteration.

Yet in a fit of dastard rage
He stoops the ass's neck to seize
And in the clear deep stream below
He spies an ugly sight, I trow,
Among the shadows of the trees.

Is it the shadow of the moon?
Is it the shadow of a cloud?
Is it a gallows there pourtrayed?
Is Peter of himself afraid?
Is it a coffin or a shroud?

521–525 Carefully deleted in MS. 2 with wavy horizontal lines and omitted from the base text of MS. 3.

From Peter's hand the sapling dropp'd!
Threat has he none to execute—
"If any one should come and see
"That I am here, they'll think," quoth he,
"I'm helping this poor dying brute."

He scans the Ass from limb to limb;
And Peter now uplifts his eyes;—
Steady the moon doth look and clear,
And like themselves the rocks appear,
And tranquil are the skies.

Whereat, in resolute mood, once more
He stoops the Ass's neck to seize—
Foul purpose, quickly put to flight!
For in the pool a startling sight
Meets him, beneath the shadowy trees.

Is it the moon's distorted face?
The ghost-like image of a cloud?
Is it a gallows there pourtray'd?
Is Peter of himself afraid?
Is it a coffin,—or a shroud?

---

526 dropped! *1820–*
527 execute; *1836–*
529 "That] That *1820–*
531–535 *canceled and rewritten at foot of page:*
He scans the Ass from limb to limb,
And ventures now to lift his eyes;
More steady looks the moon, and clear,
More like themselves the rocks appear,
And touch more quiet skies. *MS. 1832/36, adopted 1836– but* lift] uplift *and* appear,] appear
532 Peter *del to* ventures *and* uplifts *del to* to lift *interlined in pencil, MS. 1832/36* eyes;—] eyes; *1832, 1836–*
533 look, *1832*
535 touch more *inserted after* And *in pencil,* are the *del MS. 1832/36* tranquil] quiet *1820–1834*
535–541 *on interleaf:*
And touch more quiet skies.
His scorn returns {—, his hate re[?]s; (revives interlined)
He stoops the Ass's neck to seize
With malice—that again takes flight;
For in the pool a startling sight
Meets him, among the inverted trees.
Is [?] it the moon's [?] *MS. 1832/36, ll. 535–540 adopted as revised 1836–*
536–543 *apparatus continues, p. 91*

Is it a fiend that to a stake
Of red hot fire himself is tethering?
Some solitary ward or cell
Where lies a damned soul in hell
Ten thousand miles from all his brethren?

Is it some party in a parlour,
Crammed just as they on earth were cramm'd—
Some sipping punch, some sipping tea,
But as you by their faces see
All silent, and all damn'd?

'Tis no such thing, I do assure you,
Which Peter sees in the clear flood;
It is no ugly apprehension
Of eyes and ears, 'tis no invention;
It is a thing of flesh and blood.

It cannot be a water-rat—
No, Peter is not such a noddy;
The flesh and blood which Peter sees
Among the shadows of the trees,
It is a dead man's body.

And Peter looks, and looks again
Just like a man whose brain is haunted;
He looks, he cannot chuse but look,
Like one that's reading in a book,
A book that is enchanted.

---

537 Miswritten in MS. 2 ("That to a stake of red hot fire him-") and corrected in transcription; MS. 3 has the corrected reading.

541–545 De Selincourt notes (*PW*, II, 529–530) that WW wrote Barron Field that he omitted this stanza, "though one of the most imaginative in the whole piece," in order "not to offend the pious" (October 24, 1828). Crabb Robinson was offended, calling it "the only stanza I wish to have taken out," and reported that WW said Lady Beaumont also objected to it (*HCR*, I, 98). Charles Lamb is supposed to have shouted at a house in which festivities were under way: "You damned party in a parlour!" (Lucas, p. 410). Shelley (who would not have regarded himself as one of the pious) used the stanza as an epigraph to his satiric *Peter Bell the Third.* De Selincourt doubts that the scene was suggested to WW by Mrs. Basil Montagu as she claimed, since her anecdote of a party of ladies sitting frozen in near-asphyxiation is unnecessary to explain the situation, and she was not likely to have been able to tell it to WW before her marriage to Montagu in 1808.

546–560 A leaf is missing from MS. 2; these three stanzas are supplied from MS. 3.

A grisly idol hewn in stone?
Or imp from witch's lap let fall?
Or a gay ring of shining fairies,
Such as pursue their brisk vagaries
In sylvan bower, or haunted hall?

It is a fiend that to a stake
Of fire his desperate self is tethering?
Or stubborn spirit doom'd to yell
In solitary ward or cell,
Ten thousand miles from all his brethren?

Is it a party in a parlour?
Cramm'd just as they on earth were cramm'd—
Some sipping punch, some sipping tea,
But, as you by their faces see,
All silent and all damn'd!

A throbbing pulse the Gazer hath—
Puzzled he was, and now is daunted;
He looks, he cannot choose but look;
Like one intent upon a book—
A book that is enchanted.

---

536 once more] once more, *1832, del to* again *MS. 1832/36*
538–539 *del to*
When in the pool, by gloom {and / [?or]} light
Halff shaped—half shown a startling sight *interlined MS. 1832/36*
538–540 *horizontally from top to bottom of page across right margin, then deleted:*
When in the pool by gloom and light
[?part] shaped—part shown a startling sight
Meets him between the downward trees. *MS. 1832/36*
540 shadowy *del to* downward *del MS. 1832/36*
543 a] the *1832* poutrayed? *1820–1831, 1834* portrayed? *1832, 1836–*
548 Perhaps a ring of shining fairies? *1836–*
549 brisk] feared *1836–*
551 It is] Is it *1819a–*
553 doomed *1820–*
556–560 *omitted 1820–*
561–562 Never did pulse so quickly throb,
And never heart so loudly panted; *1827–*
563 He looks like one who reads a book *interlined, erased MS. 1832/36*
563–565 He looks like one who reads a book.
On which he cannot choose but look—
A book *bottom of page, deleted in ink and partially erased, MS. 1832/36*
564 *del to* Like some one reading in a book— *MS. 1832/36 with dash in pencil; adopted 1836–*
565 *dash in ink before line, deleted in pencil MS. 1832/36*

He grasps the poor ass by the jaws,
His hands and body shake and shiver;
And up and down, and to and fro,
The ass's head and mouth they go,
Dimpling the surface of the river.

Ah! well a day for Peter Bell;
He will be turned to iron soon,
Flesh, sinew, fibre, bone and gristle;
His hat is up, his hairs they bristle,
Bristle and whiten in the moon.

And see him now fast bound like iron—
Head, joints and hands, and lips and teeth;
You'd think that he was looking at you,
But no, this uncouth iron statue
Is looking at the stream beneath.

And now poor Peter is convinced
While still he holds the ass's head
That 'tis a fiend with visage wan,
A live man fiend, a living man,
That's lying in the river bed.

He looks, he looks, he looks again,
He sees a motion, hears a groan;
His eyes will burst, his heart will break,
He gives a loud and frightful shriek
And back he falls just like a stone.

End of Part first

565/566 The base text of MS. 3 includes this stanza:

Sure uglier sights were never seen
By good or bad by sad or simple
Than Peter while he holds the Ass
Saw clearly in that watry glass
Where the still moonlight waters dimple.

There is no room for the stanza in the base text of MS. 2 unless it was inserted on the verso of the missing leaf, which seems to have held ll. 546–560.

580 Both MS. 2 and MS. 3 originally read "river bed" and were altered by DW to "river's bed."

585/586 MS. 3 has a heading, "Second Part"; MS. 2 begins the second part at the top of a page, with no heading, following a stub where a leaf (possibly bearing the heading) was cut out. One five-line stanza stood about the middle of the missing recto, but the visible initial letters do not match any other stanza in the poem.

Ah, well-a-day for Peter Bell!—
He will be turned to iron soon,
Meet Statue for the court of Fear!
His hat is up—and every hair
Bristles—and whitens in the moon!

He looks—he ponders—looks again;
He sees a motion—hears a groan;—
His eyes will burst—his heart will break—
He gives a loud and frightful shriek,
And drops, a senseless weight, as if his life were flown!

566 Bell!—] Bell! *1836–*
570 Bristles, *1836–*
571 looks, he ponders *1836–*
572 groan;—] groan; *1836–*
575 drops, a senseless weight] back he falls *1836–*
575/576 *illegible erasure (2–3 lines) below stanza MS. 1832/36*

[Part Second]

We left poor Peter in a trance,
We left the dead man in the river;
The ass is by the river side
And where the feeble breezes glide
Upon the stream the moon beams quiver.

And Peter wakes, he wakes at last,
He feels the glimmerings of the moon,
And to stretch forth his hand he's trying;
Sure, when he knows where he is lying
He'll sink into a second swoon.

He lifts his head—he sees his staff,
He touches—'tis to him a treasure;
To find that he is not in hell,
As you'll suppose, to Peter Bell
Doth give a sweet and languid pleasure.

And while upon his side he lies,
His head upon his elbow raised
Almost, you'd say, as in a dream
His eyes are settling on the stream
Where he before had gazed.

---

604 In MS. 2 "they settle" was revised by erasure to "are settling" (which is the reading of MS. 3). The original phrase was an example of the simplistic syntax characteristic of *Lyrical Ballads* (cf. *Expostulation and Reply*, l. 7).

PART SECOND.

WE left our Hero in a trance,
Beneath the alders, near the river;
The Ass is by the river side,
And, where the feeble breezes glide,
Upon the stream the moon-beams quiver.

A happy respite!—but he wakes;—
And feels the glimmering of the moon—
And to stretch forth his hands is trying;—
Sure, when he knows where he is lying,
He'll sink into a second swoon.

He lifts his head—he sees his staff;
He touches—'tis to him a treasure!
Faint recollection seems to tell
That he is yet where mortals dwell—
A thought receiv'd with languid pleasure!

His head upon his elbow propp'd,
Becoming less and less perplex'd
Sky-ward he looks—to rock and wood—
And then—upon the placid flood
His wandering eye is fix'd.

---

578 river-side *1836–*
580 moonbeams *1827–*
581 respite!—] respite! *1836–* but he wakes;—] but at length *1827–*
582 And] He *1827–* glimmmering *1820* moon; *1827–*
583 trying;—] trying; *1819a, 1820* Wakes with glazed eye, and feebly sighing— *1827–*
584 Sure, when he knows] To sink perhaps, *1827– but* sink, *1832, 1836–*
585 Into a second swoon! *1827–*
586 head, *1836–*
590 received *1820–*
591 propped *1820–*
592 perplexed, *1820–*
594 placid] glassy *1827–*
595 fixed *1820–*

No dimple now disturbs the stream,
In Peter's brain there is no riot;
His eye upon the stream he fixes
And with the sight no terror mixes;
His heart is calm and quiet.

Quoth he, "that is a dead man's face
Among the shadows of the trees;
Those are, no doubt, a dead man's knuckles
And there you see his brass shoe-buckles
And there his breeches' knees."

At last he rises from his side
And sits upright upon the ground
And o'er the stream he hangs his nose
And points his staff, as you'd suppose,
The river's depth to sound.

This sees the ass while on the grass
Close by the river's brink he lies,
And strait with a transition tragic
That seems just like the touch of magic
Up from the ground the ass doth rise.

At this friend Peter round him looks
And sees the poor and patient creature
Close to him, in his uncouth way
Expressing all the joy he may
In every limb and every feature.—

His meagre bones all shake with joy
And close by Peter's side he stands;
While Peter o'er the river bends
The little ass his neck extends
And fondly licks his hands.

Such life is in the ass's eyes,
Such life is in his limbs and ears,
That Peter Bell, if he had been
The veriest coward ever seen,
Must now have thrown aside his fears.

626–630 Inserted in fair copy on facing verso by WW in MS. 2 and marked to go in here; included in the base text of MS. 3.

Thought he, that is the face of one
In his last sleep securely bound!
So, faltering not in *this* intent,
He makes his staff an instrument
The river's depth to sound—

Now—like a tempest-shatter'd bark
That overwhelm'd and prostrate lies
And in a moment to the verge
Is lifted of a foaming surge—
Full suddenly the Ass doth rise!

His staring bones all shake with joy—
And close by Peter's side he stands:
While Peter o'er the river bends,
The little Ass his neck extends,
And fondly licks his hands.

Such life is in the Ass's eyes—
Such life is in his limbs and ears—
That Peter Bell, if he had been
The veriest coward ever seen,
Must now have thrown aside his fears.

598–599 So toward the stream his head he bent,
And downward thrust his staff, intent *1820– but* bent *1834*

600 sound—] sound.— *1819a* sound. *1827–* To reach the Man who lay there drowned.— *1820*

601 tempest-shattered bark, *1820–*

602 overwhelmed *1820–* lies, *1820–*

606 joy, *1836–*

611 eyes, *1836–*

612 ears; *1836–*

With caution Peter eyes the stream;
His sapling deep and deeper goes;
"The body is, no doubt," quoth he,
"The thing which it appears to be—
It moves not, neither limbs nor clothes."

The ass looks on and to his work
Is Peter quietly resigned;
He touches here, he touches there,
And now among the dead man's hair
His sapling Peter has entwined.

He pulls, he pulls, and pulls again,
And he whom the poor ass had lost,
The man who had been four days dead,
Head-foremost from the river's bed
Uprises like a ghost.

And Peter draws him to dry land
And lays him strait upon the grass,
And Peter feels some ugly pains
Across his liver, heart, and reins
Just like a weaver's shuttle pass.

He sees the poor man's blue swoln face
And through the brain of Peter pass
Those ugly twitches fast and faster;
"No doubt," quoth he, "he is the master
Of this poor miserable ass."

Then on the ass did Peter look
And to his eye was clearly shewn
What to that time he had not seen,

---

654 MS. 2 originally had "river-bed" and revision seems to have taken place during transcription; MS. 3 has "river's bed."

660 Revised in MS. 2 to "As quick as lightning pass" but the base text of MS. 3 has "In quick succession pass."

666–670 Carefully deleted in MS. 2 with wavy horizontal lines and followed by a signal to insert a stanza copied by DW onto the facing verso:

An ass so lean was never seen
By road or shed or out-door penthouse
If you should meet in wood or lane
As ass so lean 'twould give you pain
The sight would almost seem portentous.

(Note continues, p. 100.)

The Ass looks on—and to his work
Is Peter quietly resign'd;
He touches here—he touches there—
And now among the dead man's hair
His sapling Peter has entwin'd.

He pulls—and looks—and pulls again,
And he whom the poor Ass had lost,
The man who had been four days dead,
Head foremost from the river's bed
Uprises—like a ghost!

And Peter draws him to dry land;
And through the brain of Peter pass
Some poignant twitches, fast and faster,
"No doubt," quoth he, "he is the master
"Of this poor miserable Ass!"

---

617 resigned; *1820– but* resigned: *1834*
620 entwined *1820–*
621 again; *1819a–*
623 man] Man *1827–1834*
624 Head-foremost *1836– but not MS. 1832/36*
625 Uprises—] Uprises *1836–*
628 faster; *1836– but* faster: *1846*
629 master] Master *1827–1832, 1836–*
630 "Of] Of *1820–*

That the poor ass was gaunt and lean
And almost wasted to the bone.

And scanning him from limb to limb,
"I've played with you an ugly game,"
Quoth Peter to the ass, "but still
I did not mean to use you ill;
You must allow you were to blame."

But the poor shadow all this while,
The little ass, what is he doing?
His joy is passed, his joy is flown,
He on his knees has laid him down
As if he were his grief renewing.

That Peter on his back should mount
He's shewing all the wish he can.
"I'll go, I'll go if life forsake me;
No doubt he to his home will take me,
The cottage of this drowned man."

The same stanza was (probably earlier) crowded onto a facing verso by WW, probably to follow the stanza that replaced ll. 486–490. The base text of MS. 3 contains neither the inserted stanza nor the one it follows (both of which were moved in revision to the First Part of the poem in MS. 2—see 17v of the transcription, below), but does contain a revised version of the latter, entered by WW in MS. 2, on the facing verso (30v):

Then on the ass did Peter look
And all those ugly pains encreas'd
To see him wasted to the bone
To see the meagre skeleton
Of that poor faithful beast.

671 First three words written over illegible erasure in MS. 2, possibly "He scanned the ass"; MS. 3 has "And scanning him."

671–675 On a verso in MS. 2 (18v) this stanza is expanded to two stanzas:

He scans the ass from limb to limb
And Peter now uplifts his eyes
Steady the moon doth look, & clear
And like themselves the rocks appear
And quiet are the skies

He sees the ass's sad condition
I've played with you an ugly game
Quoth Peter to the ass but still
I did not mean to use you ill
You must allow you were to blame

676 In MS. 2 "shadow" (the reading of MS. 3) is written over "creature" (erased).

678 In MS. 2 "his joy" was left out in transcription, with no gap; it is supplied from MS. 3.

The meagre Shadow all this while—
What aim is his? what is he doing?
His sudden fit of joy is flown,—
He on his knees hath laid him down,
As if he were his grief renewing.

That Peter on his back should mount
He shows a wish, well as he can,
"I'll go, I'll go, whate'er betide—
"He to his home my way will guide,
"The cottage of the drowned man."

---

631 shadow *1849* all this while] that looks on *1836– but not MS. 1832/36*
632 aim is his] would he now *1836–*
635 renewing; *1836–*
636–637 But no—that Peter on his back
Must mount, he shows well as he can *right margin, MS. 1832/36*
636–640 But no—his purpose and his wish
The Suppliant shews, well as he can;
Thought Peter whatsoe'er betide [3]
I'll go, and he my way will guide
To the cottage of the drowned man. *1820–1834* but [2] shews] shows *and* [3] Peter, whatsoe'er betide, *1827–1834, then revisions interlined MS. 1832/36:* [1] his purpose and his wish *del to* that Peter on his back [2] The Suppliant shows *del to* Must mount he shows [3] whatsoe'er betide *del to* then come weal or woe [4] go, and he my way will guide *del to* mount, and take him for my guide *del* [5] cottage *del to* dwelling
But no—that Peter on his back
Must mount, he shews well as he can:
Thought Peter then, come weal or woe, [3]
I'll do what he would have me do,
In pity to this poor drowned man. *1836– but* [2] shews] shows *1849*
637–640 ~~To the dwelling of the poor drowned~~
man
Must mount he shows well as he can
Thought Peter then, come weal or woe
I'll do what he would have me do,
In pity to this poor drowned Man. *bottom of page MS. 1832/36*

This said, friend Peter mounts forthwith
Upon that good and faithful ass
And strait without a moment's stay
The ass turns quietly away,
Leaving the body in the grass.

The little ass is strong at heart
And firm he walks and bolt upright,
But well may the poor beast be wasted—
For four long days he has not tasted
Of food a single bite.

Amid that green and quiet spot
He four long days and nights had pass'd;
A sweeter meadow ne'er was seen
And there the ass four days had been
And never once had broke his fast.

Across the meadow they are gone
And now are at the quarry's mouth;
The little ass who is the guide
Into a thicket turns aside
And takes his way towards the south.

But hark! among the rocks they hear
A cry of lamentable sort;
Though there is nothing he should stick at
Yet in the middle of the thicket
The little ass stops short.

And Peter hears the doleful sound
And he in honest truth may say
The like came never to his ears
Though he has been full thirty years
A rover night and day.

'Tis not a plover of the moors,
'Tis not a bittern of the fen
Nor is it like a barking fox

687 In MS. 2 "beast," is revised to "Ass" (as required by the rhyme), which is the reading of base MS. 3.

This utter'd, Peter mounts forthwith
Upon the pleas'd and thankful Ass;
And then, without a moment's stay,
The earnest creature turn'd away,
Leaving the body on the grass.

Intent upon his faithful watch
The beast four days and nights had pass'd;
A sweeter meadow ne'er was seen,
And there the Ass four days had been,
Nor ever once did break his fast!

Yet firm his step, and stout his heart;
The mead is cross'd—the quarry's mouth
Is reach'd—but there the trusty guide
Into a thicket turns aside,
And takes his way towards the south.

When hark, a burst of doleful sound!
And Peter honestly might say,
The like came never to his ears
Though he has been full thirty years
A rover night and day!

'Tis not a plover of the moors,
'Tis not a bittern of the fen;
Nor can it be a barking fox—

---

641 utter'd] hoping *1820* Encouraged by this hope, he mounts *1827–1831, 1834* This hoping, Peter boldly mounts *1832– but* This hoping, Peter *del to* With that resolve he *MS. 1832/36, adopted 1836–*
642 pleased *1820–*
644 The] That *1827–* Creature *1827–* turned *1820–*
646 watch, *1827–*
647 Beast *1827–* passed; *1820* past; *1827–*
649 there] here *1831, 1834*
650 fast. *1832* fast: *1836–*
651 heart: *1846*
652 crossed *1820–*
653 reach'd—] reached— *1820–1834* reached; *1836– but not MS. 1832/36*
655 takes his way] deftly ambles *1836–*
656 hark,] hark *1827–*
658 ears, *1820–*
659 been, . . . years, *1820–*
660 rover— *1820– but* Rover— *1832 but return to lowercase not indicated MS. 1832/36*
663 fox, *1836–*

Nor like a night-bird of the rocks
Or wild-cat in a woody glen.

It does not die—'tis louder still.
—The little ass, who meant to climb
That lofty mountain which you see,
Beneath the shadow of a tree
Is listening all this time.

And Peter's on the ass's back,
Is in the middle of the thicket,
And though he's used to whistle loud
Whether alone or in a croud
He's silent as a silent cricket.

Now should it be a crazy ghost,
One who must sing in doleful pain
Through a long vision, to be broken
When Time shall snap the true love token
To which she sings her doleful strain—

What ails you now my pretty Bess?
What is't that makes you look so grave?
The cry which sets your heart a throbbing,
It is a little boy that's sobbing
Beside the entrance of a cave.

A blooming wood-boy of the woods,
And Bess I will be bold to say
If once you knew but where he is
Your heart would be as sad as his
Till you had kiss'd his tears away.

A cavern high among the hills,
A rough, it is, a dismal place,
With trees, with rocks, with ivy dark
Yet by the moonlight I can mark
The tears upon his ruddy face.

---

721 The base text of MS. 3 has a revised version of MS. 2: "The cry grows loud & louder still."

726 Correction of "Peter's" to "Peter" in MS. 3 may have restored WW's original intention.

741–745 In MS. 2 this stanza (which is in the base text of MS. 3) is entered in fair copy on the facing verso and marked to go here.

747 The stanza does not appear in MS. 3; in MS. 2 "rough" is written over "wild" (erased).

Nor night-bird chamber'd in the rocks—
Nor wild-cat in a woody glen!

The Ass is startled—and stops short
Right in the middle of the thicket;
And Peter, wont to whistle loud
Whether alone or in a crowd,
Is silent as a silent cricket.

What ails you now, my little Bess?
Well may you tremble and look grave!
This cry—that rings along the wood,
This cry—that floats adown the flood,
Comes from the entrance of a cave:

I see a blooming Wood-boy there,
And, if I had the power to say
How sorrowful the wanderer is,
Your heart would be as sad as his
Till you had kiss'd his tears away!

---

664 chambered *1820–* rocks, *1836–*
668 Peter,] Peter *1820*
677 And,] And *1836– but not MS. 1832/36*
680 kissed *1820–*

A branch of hawthorn's in his hand,
The haws they are both ripe and red,
And now towards the cave he creeps
And now into its mouth he peeps
And then draws back in fear and dread.

His eye is fix'd upon the cave
He shews a wondrous self-command,
Yet though his heart be bold and staunch
The berries on the hawthorn branch
All rattle in his hand.

And now he's close beneath the ivy
And hidden there quite out of view
With voice as plaintive as can be
He sobs aloud, "come, come to me,
I cannot come to you."

Ah well, my pretty little Bess,
To hear that miserable sound
The tears into your eyes may gather;
The boy is seeking his dead Father,
His father dead and drowned.

Poor Robin loved his Father well,
For often by the hand he led
Sweet Robin to the [   ], and he
Gave Robin many a halfpenny
And many a crust of bread.

---

756 The base text of MS. 3 has the line as revised in MS. 2: "He is bewitch'd by some strange hope."

762–763 Most of both lines is entered in MS. 2 over illegible erasures. The base text of MS. 3 contains a revised version of the stanza (developed from a version entered on the verso of MS. 2):

Beneath the ivy now he creeps
Upon his hands and knees, and then
Like swans when pinch'd by hunger make
Their moan beside a frozen lake,
He sobs and sobs and sobs again.

767 In MS. 2 "miserable" is entered over an illegible erasure of several words, possibly ending with "doleful."

769 First three words over illegible erasure, MS. 2.

773 Both MS. 2 and MS. 3 leave a gap; revision in MS. 3 supplied "wood."

Holding a hawthorn branch in hand,
All bright with berries ripe and red;
Into the cavern's mouth he peeps—
Thence back into the moon-light creeps;
What seeks the boy?—the silent dead!

---

681 Holding *alt* Grasping *MS. 1819a/20 (WW)* Holding *del in pencil to* Q Grasping *(WW) del in pencil and* stet *entered in opposite margin (WW) in pencil, then del once more to* Grasping *MS. 1836/45 (pencil), adopted 1840–*

682 red! *1820* red, *1827–*

683 peeps; *1836–*

684 moonlight *1820–* creeps, *1836*

685 What seeks the boy] Seeking for whom *1836* Whom seeks he—what or whom? *pencil alt interlined (WW), then* what or *del and* —the silent dead: *added to line in pencil* Whom seeks he —whom?— *pencil alt, del, at foot of page (WW) MS. 1836/45, adopted 1840–* What seeks the Boy *ink alt entered in margin (WW) MS. 1836/45* dead— *1827–1834* dead: *1836–*

Since five oclock hath Robin sought
O'er heath and hill, through copse and lane,
Through gipsey-scenes of rocks and woods
Sooth'd day and night by murmuring floods
And wild as any place in Spain.

And hither is he come at last,
When he through such a day has gone,
By this dark cave to be distress'd
Where like a bird about its nest
He flutters off and on.

At last both in despair and fear
Along the wood his road he takes,
And like a little child that's lost
And thinks he's follow'd by a ghost
A wild and doleful cry he makes.

The ass, when first he caught the noise,
Stopp'd short and soon he knew it well;
And since, directed by the sobbing,
Along the path of little Robin
He has been carrying Peter Bell.

And soon as Peter saw the ass
His road all on a sudden change
And turn right upwards from the hollow
That lamentable noise to follow,
It wrought in him conviction strange.

A sober and a firm belief
Is in the heart of Peter Bell
That something will to him befall,
A visitation worse than all
Which ever till this night befell.

---

786 Entire line over illegible erasure in MS. 2

793–794 MS. 3 has a revised version of MS. 2:

And towards the cave whence Robin sent
All through the wood that sad lament.

805 Here transcription of MS. 3 was interrupted; three-fourths of a page are left blank, and the next stanza, beginning with l. 806, was entered overleaf, at the top of a new page.

His father!—Him doth he require,
Whom he hath sought with fruitless pains,
Among the rocks, behind the trees,
Now creeping on his hands and knees,
Now running o'er the open plains.

And hither is he come at last,
When he through such a day has gone,
By this dark cave to be distrest
Like a poor bird—her plunder'd nest
Hovering around with dolorous moan!

Of that intense and piercing cry
The listening Ass doth rightly spell;
Wild as it is he there can read
Some intermingl'd notes that plead
With touches irresistible;

But Peter, when he saw the Ass
Not only stop but turn, and change
The cherish'd tenor of his pace
That lamentable noise to chase,
It wrought in him conviction strange;

A faith that, for the dead man's sake
And this poor slave who lov'd him well,
Vengeance upon his head will fall,
Some visitation worse than all
Which ever till this night befel.

---

686 —Him] Him *1831, 1834* require— *1836–*
687 Whom he hath] Him hath he *1836–*
688 trees; *1836– but not MS. 1832/36*
694 plundered *1820–*
695 around] about *pencil alt in margin, del MS. 1836/45 (?WW)*
697 doth rightly spell;] conjectures well, *1820– but* well; *1827–*
698 is, *1827–*
699 intermingled *1820–*
700 irresistible. *1836– but not MS. 1832/36*
701 Peter— *1836– but not MS. 1832/36*
703 cherished *1820–*
704 noise] cry *1836–* chase— *1836– but not MS. 1832/36*
707 loved *1820–*

Meanwhile the ass in Robin's track
Is following stoutly as he may,
But while he climbs the woody hill
The cry grows weak and weaker still
And now at last dies quite away.

Fain would he overtake the boy,
He loves him with a dear delight;
But finding 'tis an idle hope
Down the close pathway's rugged slope
He gently turns towards the right.

With Peter on his back he turns
Into a gloomy grove of beech,
Along the shade with footstep true
Descending slowly till the two
The open moonlight reach.

And there along a narrow dell
A fair smooth pathway you discern,
A verdant and an open road,
As any little river broad,
Winding away among the fern.

The rocks that tower on either side
Build up a wild fantastic scene—
Temples like those among the Hindoos,
And mosques and spires and abbey windows
And castles all with ivy green.

---

813 For "'tis an" MS. 2 originally read "still as an"; although revision seems not to have been immediate, it has been adopted to make grammatical sense; the revised version is in the base text of MS. 3.

823 First four words over illegible erasure beginning with "A" and ending with "and" in MS. 2.

826–865 The leaf that probably contained these eight stanzas has been torn out of MS. 3.

Meanwhile the Ass to gain his end
Is striving stoutly as he may;
But, while he climbs the woody hill,
The cry grows weak—and weaker still,
And now at last it dies away!

So with his freight the creature turns
Into a gloomy grove of beech,
Along the shade with footstep true
Descending slowly, till the two
The open moonlight reach.

And there, along a narrow dell,
A fair smooth pathway you discern,
A length of green and open road—
As if it from a fountain flowed—
Winding away between the fern.

The rocks that tower on either side
Build up a wild fantastic scene;
Temples like those among the Hindoos,
And mosques, and spires, and abbey windows,
And castles all with ivy green!

And, while the Ass pursues his way,
Along this solitary dell,
As pensively his steps advance,
The mosques and spires change countenance,
And look at Peter Bell!

That unintelligible cry
Hath left him high in preparation,—
Convinced that he, or soon or late,
This very night, will meet his fate—
And so he sits in expectation!

---

711 Ass to gain his end] Ass, to reach his home, *1820* Ass to reach his home, *1827–*
712 may. *1834*
714 still; *1836–*
715 away!] away *1832 (but some copies retain exclam point)* away. *1836– but not MS. 1832/36*
716 Creature *1820–*
718 footsteps *1845–*
721 a] the *1836– but not MS. 1832/36*
724 fountain] mountain *1831, 1834*
729 abbey-windows *1849*
739 night,] night *1836– but not MS. 1832/36*

This smooth-green path, you know not how,
Winds upwards like a straggling chain,
And when you two good miles have pass'd
Between the rocks you come at last
Unto a high and level plain.

While Peter now is travelling on
Along this solitary dell
In truth I should be much inclined
To tell what's passing in his mind
If it would suit my tale as well.

That unintelligible cry
Hath left him high in preparation,
Convinc'd that he, or soon or late,
This luckless night will meet his fate
And so he sits in expectation.

The little ass makes no complaint;
He feels not any want of strength
And slowly up the smooth-green track
He winds with Peter on his back
And to the top is come at length.

And while together now they go
Across the open moonlight down,
To say the truth, they seem a pair
Come from some region of the air,
Some unknown region of their own.

Right onward [walks] the little ass;
Over the down his way he bends
Where smooth and bare as any sea
Without a plant, without a tree,
The level plain extends.

And ever, where along the down
They go with smooth and steady pace,
You see driven onward by the wind
A dancing leaf that's close behind,
Following them o'er that lonely place.

---

856 For the blank left in MS. 2, "walks" was supplied from a verso version in MS. 2 (an alternate version reads "goes"); base MS. 4 has "walks," with "goes" as an alternate.

The verdant pathway, in and out,
Winds upwards like a straggling chain;
And, when two toilsome miles are past,
Up through the rocks it leads at last
Into a high and open plain.

The strenuous animal hath clomb
With the green path,—and now he wends
Where, shining like the smoothest sea,
In undisturbed immensity
The level plain extends.

How blank!—but whence this rustling sound
Which, all too long, the pair hath chased!
—A dancing leaf is close behind,
Light plaything for the sportive wind
Upon that solitary waste.

741–745 *omitted 1827–*
743 And,] And *1820*
746 Animal *1820–*
747 path,—] path; *1836–*
750 The] A *1827–*
751 But whence that faintly-rustling sound *1820–1834*
751–752 *rev to:*
But what can this faint rustling mean
This sound by which the pair are chased! *del and then rewritten at foot of page:*
But whence this faintly rustling sound
By which the journeying Pair are {chased? / [~~?cross'd~~]} *MS. 1832/36 (WW), adopted as revised but* faintly-rustling *and* pair *1836–* By which *del to* that long *and* journeying pair are *del to* pair have long been *MS. 1836/45 (WW)*
752 Which, *del to* That *then* That all too long *del to* By which the pair [?have] *MS. 1819a/20*
753 dancing] withered *1836–*

And Peter hears the rustling leaf
And many a time he turns his face
Both here and there ere he can find
What 'tis which follows close behind
Along that lonely place.

At last he spies the wither'd leaf
And Peter is in sore distress.
"Where there is not a bush or tree
The very leaves they follow me,
So huge hath been my wickedness."

Along the [ ] down they go
And to a broad high-way are come;
They quit the turf and on the gravel
Upon the broad high-way they travel,
A pair both sad and dumb.

For Peter Bell, he looks, I vow,
With his dull face of ashy white,
Just like a creature that pertains
To some strange world of silent pains,
A creature of a moonlight-night.

And now they to a lane are come
And still the little meagre ass
Moves on without a moment's stop,
Nor once turns round his head to crop
A bramble leaf or blade of grass.

Between the hedges on they go,
The dusty road is white as bone,
And Peter casting down his eyes
Towards the moonlight road espies
A drop of blood upon a stone.

Peter has little power to move;
Upon the ass remain he must.
He travels on and now and then
He sees that drop of blood again
Upon a stone or in the dust.

---

876 The blank was left in both MS. 2 and MS. 3, and the stanza does not appear in later texts.

When Peter spies the withered leaf,
It yields no cure to his distress—
"Where there is not a bush or tree,
"The very leaves they follow me—
"So huge hath been my wickedness!"

To a close lane they now are come,
Where, as before, the enduring Ass
Moves on without a moment's stop,
Nor once turns round his head to crop
A bramble leaf or blade of grass.

Between the hedges as they go
The white dust sleeps upon the lane;
And Peter, ever and anon
Back-looking, sees upon a stone
Or in the dust, a crimson stain.

---

756 spies the withered leaf] spied the moving thing *1836–*
757 yields no cure to] only doubled *1836–* distress, *1820* distress; *1827–*
759 "The] The *1820–*
760 "So] So *1820–*
765 bramble-leaf *1836–*
766 go, *1827–*
769 Back *del to* [?] *eras to* Back *MS. 1832/36* sees, *1827–* stone. *1840* stone, *1845, 1849*

Did Peter e'er with club or stone
Smite some poor traveller on the head,
Or beat his father in a rage
And spill the blood of his old age,
Or kick a child till he was dead?

Did Peter ever kill his man
With fist or staff in single duel,
Or stab with some inhuman wound
A soldier bleeding on the ground?
No—Peter never was so cruel.

Then why to see this drop of blood
Doth Peter look so pale and wan?
Why is he in this sad despair?
He knows not how the blood comes there,
And Peter is a wicked man.

At length he spies a bleeding wound
Where he had struck the ass's head;
He sees the blood, sees what it is—
A glimpse of sudden joy was his,
But then it quickly fled.

He thought—he could not help but think—
Of that poor beast, that faithful ass,
And once again those ugly pains
Across his liver, heart and reins
Just like a weaver's shuttle pass.

End of Part 2nd—

Part 3d

I've heard of one, a gentle soul,
Though giv'n to sadness and to gloom,
And, for the fact I'll vouch, one night
It chanc'd that by a taper's light
This man was reading in his room.

925/926 In MS. 2 the heading is "Peter Bell / Book 3rd"—perhaps because there is a variety of irrelevant material between Part II and Part III but more probably because Part III was transcribed here before Part II (see Introduction, above); in MS. 3 the heading is only "Part 3d"

A stain—as of a drop of blood
By moonlight made more faint and wan—
Ha! why this comfortless despair?
He knows not how the blood comes there,
And Peter is a wicked man.

At length he spies a bleeding wound,
Where he had struck the Ass's head;
He sees the blood, knows what it is,—
A glimpse of sudden joy was his,
But then it quickly fled;

Of him whom sudden death had seized
He thought,—of thee, O faithful Ass!
And once again those darting pains,
As meteors shoot through heaven's wide plains,
Pass through his bosom—and repass!

PART THIRD.

I've heard of one, a gentle soul,
Though given to sadness and to gloom,
And for the fact will vouch, one night
It chanc'd that by a taper's light
This man was reading in his room;

---

772 wan; *1836–*
773 this comfortless] these sinkings of *1836– but not MS. 1832/36*
774 there— *1836–*
777 Ass's] Creature's *1827–1834* creature's *1836–1840 but not MS. 1832/36*
781–782 *illeg single-word pencil alt in margin del MS. 1836/45*
782 thought— *1834*
783 darting] ghastly *1836–*
784–785 *del to:*
Shot to and fro through heart and reins,
And through his brain like lightening pass. *MS. 1832/36 adopted but* Shot] Shoot *and* lightening] lightning *1836– but* pass.] pass *1847*
786 Soul *1820–*
788 vouch,— *1819a–*
789 chanced *1820–*

Reading as you or I might read
At night in any pious book,
When sudden darkness overspread
The snow-white page in which he read
And made the good man round him look.

The chamber all was dark all round
And to his book he turn'd again;
The light had left the good man's taper
And form'd itself upon the paper
Into large letters bright and plain.

The godly book was in his hand
And on the page as black as coal
Those ghostly letters form'd a word
Which till his dying day, I've heard,
Perplex'd the good man's gentle soul.

The wondrous word which thus he saw
Did never from his lips depart;
But he has said, poor gentle wight!
It brought full many a sin to light
Out of the bottom of his heart.

—Dread Spirits! thus to vex the good
How can ye with your functions jar,
Disordering colour, form and stature?
Let good men feel the soul of Nature
And see things as they are.

---

932 In MS. 2 "pious" (the reading of MS. 3) is written over "godly" (erased).

933 In MS. 2 "darkness" was revised by overwriting to "blackness" (the reading of MS. 3), possibly in transcription.

943–950 There seems to be no indication as to what the "wondrous word" was; the meaning of l. 947 is apparently that the good man never uttered the word, not that he was constantly babbling it.

948 The "wight" is a rare example in *Peter Bell* of the archaisms found in the contemporary (at least at its conception) *Ancient Mariner*.

Reading, as you or I might read
At night in any pious book,
When sudden blackness overspread
The snow-white page on which he read,
And made the good man round him look.

The chamber walls were dark all round,—
And to his book he turn'd again;
—The light had left the good man's taper,
And form'd itself upon the paper,
Into large letters—bright and plain!

The godly book was in his hand—
And, on the page more black than coal,
Appeared, set forth in strange array,
A *word*—which to his dying day
Perplex'd the good man's gentle soul.

The ghostly word, which thus was fram'd,
Did never from his lips depart;
But he hath said, poor gentle wight!
It brought full many a sin to light
Out of the bottom of his heart.

Dread Spirits! to torment the good
Why wander from your course so far,
Disordering colour form and stature!
—Let good men feel the soul of Nature,
And see things as they are.

---

791 Reading . . . read] Bending . . . bend *1827–*
792 in] o'er *1827–*
795 look.] look *1820*
797 turned *1820–*
798 good man's] lonely *1836–* taper,] taper *1820*
799 formed *1820–* paper,] paper *1827–*
802 page, *1832, 1836–*
805 Perplexed *1820–*
806 framed *1820* which thus was fram'd] full plainly seen *1827– but* full] thus *1836–*
811 torment the good] confound the meek *1836–*
813 colour, form, *1820–*
814 nature *1836– but not MS. 1832/36*

I know you, potent Spirits! well,
How with the feeling and the sense
Ye play, both with your foes and friends,
Most fearful work for fearful ends,
And this I speak in reverence.

But might I give advice to you
Whom, in my fear, I love so well,
From men of pensive virtue go,
Dread Beings! and your empire show
On hearts like that of Peter Bell.

Your presence I have often felt
In darkness and the stormy night,
And well I know, if need there be,
Ye can put forth your agency
Beneath the sweet moonlight.

Then, coming from the wayward world,
That powerful world in which ye dwell,
Come, Spirits of the mind, and try,
Tonight, beneath the moonlight sky,
What may be done with Peter Bell.

---

956 Charles I. Patterson, Jr., has suggested that these Spirits ("Spirits of the Mind" in l. 973) may be related to "nonmalicious, pre-Christian Greek daemons," and that they function to remove "the taint of salvation through superstition" ("The Daemonic in *Peter Bell*," *Wordsworth Circle*, 8 (1977), 139–146). Patterson compares the tutelary spirit in *Ancient Mariner*, the forms and breathings of *Prelude* I, ll. 395–400 and 322–323, and the "tiny spirits" of "I love upon a stormy night" (unpublished by WW), which appears in the Alfoxden Notebook and employs the Peter Bell meter (see Appendix II). De Selincourt suggested that the "stormy night" lines were an overflow from the Prologue, but it seems more likely that they relate to the beginning of Part III (see *PW*, II, 464–465, 531).

973 Stillinger (p. 514) suggests that this passage fits WW's comment concerning the poetic use of the supernatural in his dedicatory epistle. The dedication seems, actually, to have it both ways, and the force of these "spirits" depends on some belief in the supernatural.

I know you, potent Spirits! well,
How with the feeling and the sense
Playing, ye govern foes or friends,
Yok'd to your will, for fearful ends—
And this I speak in reverence!

But might I give advice to you,
Whom in my fear I love so well,
From men of pensive virtue go,
Dread Beings! and your empire show
On hearts like that of Peter Bell.

Your presence I have often felt
In darkness and the stormy night;
And well I know, if need there be,
Ye can put forth your agency
When earth is calm, and heaven is bright.

Then, coming from the wayward world,
That powerful world in which ye dwell,
Come, Spirits of the Mind! and try
To-night, beneath the moonlight sky,
What may be done with Peter Bell!

---

816 Yet, potent Spirits! well I know, *1836–*

817 How, *1819a–1834* How ye, that play with soul and sense, *1836– but not MS. 1832/36*

818 Playing *del to* Ye play *del and* ye govern foes or *del to* deluding both the *del MS. 1832/36*

818–819 Are not unused to trouble friends
Of goodness, for most gracious ends— *1836–*

818–820 P{ ing, ye trouble
~~Ye~~ p}lay ^ ~~deluding~~ both the friends
And foes of good, for gracious ends
And this I speak *at bottom of page MS. 1832/36*

819 Yoked *1820–1834* Yoked to your will *del to* And foes, of good *and* fearful *del to* gracious *MS. 1832/36*

822 well; *1836–*

826 I have often] often have I *1836–*

828 And well I know *del to illeg phrase, then del and* And well I know *restored MS. 1832/36,* And, with like force, *1836–*

829 Ye can *rev to* can ye *MS. 1832/36*

830/831 For have I not been taught how high
Ye soar, how humbly can descend;
How Life's most trivial incidents
Are made to further your intents,
{Her
{Or gravest to your wishes bend.
Then &c *in margin, del MS. 1832/36*

833 try, *1849*

834 To night *1819a*

Oh! would that any, friend or foe,
My further labour would prevent!
On me it cannot easy sit,
I feel that I am all unfit
For such high argument.

I've play'd, I've danc'd with my narration,
A happy and a thoughtless man;
I've mov'd to many a giddy measure,
But now, my Friends, for your good pleasure
I'll do the best I can.—

The ass, as you remember well,
Is travelling now along a lane
And Peter many tricks is trying
And many anodynes applying
To ease his stomach of its pain.

By this his heart is lighter far,
For finding that he can account
So snugly for this crimson stain
His evil spirit up again
Does like an empty bucket mount.

Quoth Peter, "wounds will bleed, we know,
And blood is blood, and fools have fears,"
But yet the leaf, he can't deny,
It dogg'd him, and that doleful cry
Is ringing in his ears.

But Peter is a deep logician
And hath no lack of wit mercurial.
"Why after all 'tis plain," quoth he,
"This poor man never but for me
Could have had christian burial.

991–995, 1006–1010 Entered in fair copy in MS. 2 on the facing verso for insertion here (the first by WW, the second by DW), but not in MS. 3; both stanzas are required to bring the number in Part III up to the 91 cited in the tabulation at the end of the text (see headnote).

—O, would that some more skilful voice,
My further labour might prevent!
Kind listeners, that around me sit,
I feel that I am all unfit
For such high argument.

I've play'd and danc'd with my narration—
I loiter'd long ere I began;
Ye waited then on my good pleasure,—
Pour out indulgence still, in measure
As liberal as ye can!

Our travellers, ye remember well,
Are thridding a sequester'd lane;
And Peter many tricks is trying,
And many anodynes applying,
To ease his conscience of its pain.

By this his heart is lighter far;
And, finding that he can account
So clearly for that crimson stain,
His evil spirit up again
Does like an empty bucket mount.

And Peter is a deep logician
Who hath no lack of wit mercurial;
"Blood drops—leaves rustle—yet," quoth he,
"This poor man never, but for me,
"Could have had Christian burial.

---

836 voice,] voice *1827–*
838 Listeners, *1820–*
839 am] um *1820*
841 play'd and danc'd] played and danced *1820–1834* and *del to* I've *MS. 1832/36* played, I've danced, *1836–* narration; *1836–*
842 loitered *1820–* began: *1827–*
843 pleasure,—] pleasure; *1836–*
846 Travellers *1836–*
847 sequestered *1820–*
853 clearly] snugly *1836– but not MS. 1832/36*
858 yet,"] yet, *1836–1840 but not MS. 1832/36*
859 "This] This *1836–1840 but not MS. 1832/36*
860 "Could] Could *1836– but not MS. 1832/36*

And say the best you can, 'tis plain
That here has been some wicked dealing;
No doubt the devil in me wrought;
I'm not the man that could have thought
An ass like this was worth the stealing."

So from his pocket Peter takes
His shining horn tobacco-box
And in a careless way, as you
Or I, good Mr. Swan, might do
Upon the lid he knocks.

There's some of you, my Friends, perhaps,
There's some of you in yawning weather
Who may have seen an ass's grin;
'Tis uglier far than death and sin
And all the devils together.

And just as Peter struck the box—
—It might be to recruit his wind,
Or for some more important cause—
The quiet creature made a pause,
Turn'd round his head and grinn'd.

You know that Peter is resolved
His drooping spirits to repair,
And though, no doubt, a sight like this
To others might have come amiss,
It suited Peter to a hair.

And Peter, grinning with a joke,
His teeth in approbation shewed
When, cruel blow to Peter's mirth,
He heard a murmur in the earth,
In the dead earth beneath the road.

1023 WW's suggestion that the ass paused to relieve itself anticipates the central action of "Barnham Downs; or Goody Grizzle and her Ass. A Lyrical Ballad, in the present Fashionable Stile," published in the *European Magazine* in September 1801.

"And, say the best you can, 'tis plain
"That here hath been some wicked dealing;
"No doubt the devil in me wrought;—
"I'm not the man who could have thought
"An Ass like this was worth the stealing!"

So from his pocket Peter takes
His shining horn tobacco-box,
And, in a light and careless way
As men who with their purpose play,
Upon the lid he knocks.

Let them whose voice can stop the clouds—
Whose cunning eye can see the wind—
Tell to a curious world the cause
Why, making here a sudden pause,
The Ass turn'd round his head—and *grinn'd.*

Appalling process!—I have mark'd
The like on heath—in lonely wood,
And, verily, have seldom met
A spectacle more hideous—yet
It suited Peter's present mood.

And, grinning in his turn, his teeth
He in jocose defiance show'd—
When, to confound his spiteful mirth,
A murmur, pent within the earth,
In the dead earth beneath the road,

---

861 "And] And *1836– but not MS. 1832/36* plain, *1820–*
862 "That here hath] That here has *1836– but not MS. 1832/36*
863 "No] No *1836– but not MS. 1832/36* wrought;—] wrought; *1819a–*
864 "I'm] I'm *1836– but not MS. 1832/36* could] would *1831, 1834*
865 "An] An *1836– but not MS. 1832/36*
867 tobacco-box; *1827–*
868 way, *1827–*
871 clouds, *1836–*
872 wind, *1836–*
875 turned *1820–* head, *1836–* *grinned (italics in text) 1820–*
876 process!—] process! *1836–* marked *1820–*
877 heath, *1836–* wood; *1836–*
879 hideous—] hideous; *MS. 1832/36*
882 showed— *1820–*
883 confound] upset *1836– but not MS. 1832/36*

Beneath the ass's feet it pass'd,
A murmur and a rumbling sound;
'Twas by a group of miners made
Who plied with gunpowder their trade
Some hundred fathoms under-ground.

And I will venture to affirm
If ever any, king or cotter,
Did think as sure as five is five
That he'd be swallowed up alive
'Twas Peter Bell the Potter.

And while the little silent ass
Requiring neither rein nor goad
Moves on beneath the moonlight skies,
And the grey dust in silence lies
Upon the moonlight road,

Poor Peter by an ugly fiend
Is troubled more and more; quoth he,
"I know the truth, I know it well,
Through meadow-ground and rock and dell
A devil is following me."

At this poor Peter gave a groan
And straightway from a cottage-door
A little cur came barking out,
Barking and making such a rout
As never cur had made before.

This barking cur, as you suppose,
Must needs have been a joyful sight;
You think, no doubt, it must have cut
The thread of Peter's trance and put
The subterraneous devil to flight.

The barking cur, he might have been
A roaring lion just as well
For any good that he has wrought,
For any comfort he has brought
To poor unhappy Peter Bell.

1036–1040 Entered in fair copy on the facing verso of MS. 2 for insertion here; the stanza also appears in the base text of MS. 3, with "crew" (revised to "Troop") for "group" in l. 1038.

Roll'd audibly!—it swept along—
A muffled noise—a rumbling sound!
'Twas by a troop of miners made,
Plying with gunpowder their trade,
Some twenty fathoms under ground.

Small cause of dire effect!—for, surely,
If ever mortal, King or Cotter,
Believed that earth was charg'd to quake
And yawn for his unworthy sake,
'Twas Peter Bell the Potter!

But, as an oak in breathless air
Will stand though to the centre hewn,
Or as the weakest things, if frost
Have stiffen'd them, maintain their post,
So he, beneath the gazing moon!—

886 Rolled *1820–* audibly!—] audibly! *1836–* along, *1836–*
887 sound!— *1836– but not MS. 1832/36*
890 underground. *1836– but not MS. 1832/36*
891 effect!—] effect! *1836–*
893 charged *1820–*
895 Potter. *1832, 1836–*
897 hewn; *1827–*
899 stiffened *1820–* post; *1827–*

Upon the ass's back he sits
Like one that's riding in a swoon,
Or as a ghost that cannot see,
Whose face, if any such there be,
Is like the eyeless moon.

And every twenty yards or less
Poor Peter, well may he look grim,
Whether on rising ground or level
Still feels the subterraneous devil
Heave up the little ass and him.

And now the patient ass is come
To where beneath a mountain cove
A little chapel stands alone
With greenest ivy overgrown
And tufted with an ivy grove.

A building dying half away
From human thoughts and purposes,
It seems, both wall, and roof and tower,
To bow to some transforming power
And blend with the surrounding trees.

Deep sighing as he passed along
Quoth Peter, "in the Shire of Fife
'Twas just in such a place as that,
Not knowing what I would be at,
I married my sixth wife."

Thus Peter communed with himself.
By this time he is somewhat wean'd,
I think, from his delirious notion
That the road's giddy with commotion
Made by a subterraneous fiend.

The little ass moves slowly on
And now is passing by an Inn
That's full of a carouzing crew,
Making with curses not a few
An uproar and a drunken din.

1097 In MS. 2 "is" (the reading of MS. 3) is written over "was" (erased).

But now the pair have reach'd a spot
Where, shelter'd by a rocky cove,
A little chapel stands alone,
With greenest ivy overgrown,
And tufted with an ivy grove.

Dying insensibly away
From human thoughts and purposes,
The building seems, wall, roof, and tower,
To bow to some transforming power,
And blend with the surrounding trees.

Deep sighing as he pass'd along,
Quoth Peter, "In the shire of Fife,
"'Mid such a ruin, following still
"From land to land a lawless will,
"I married my sixth wife!"

The unheeding Ass moves slowly on,
And now is passing by an inn
Brim-full of a carousing crew,
Making, with curses not a few,
An uproar and a drunken din.

---

901 But now] Meanwhile *1820–1834* reached *1820–1832*

901–902 *rev to* The Beast bestriding thus, he reached
A spot where, in a sheltering cove, *MS. 1832/36 adopted 1836–*

902 sheltered *1820–1834*

905 grove; *1836–*

908 tower,] tower *1820, 1831, 1834* *line rev to* It seemed—wall, window roof, and tower— *interlined, then* It seemed—wall, window, roof and tower— *in right margin MS. 1832/36, adopted 1836–*

911 Deep-sighing *1820–1834 del to* Quoth Peter *interlined, then del to* He saw, and *left margin, del and* as he passed along, *del to* sighing as he passed *interlined, del MS. 1832/36* passed *1819a–1834* As ruinous a place it was *interlined, followed by* thou *del MS. 1832/36*

912 Quoth del to Thought *del and* "In the shire of Fife, *del MS. 1832/36*

912/913 Thought Peter in the shire of Fife *interlined MS. 1832/36*

913 "'Mid such a ruin, *del to* Such was the place and *del, left margin MS. 1832/36*

913/914 {T / that served my turn when} *interlined MS. 1832/36*

914 lawless *del to* reckless *del right margin MS. 1832/36*

911–915 *stanza redrafted over illegible erasure:*
As ruinous a place it was,
Thought Peter, in the shire of Fife,
That served my turn, when following still [3]
From land to land a {reck / ~~law~~}less will
I married my sixth wife! *MS. 1832/36, adopted 1836– but with* [1] "As . . . was," *1836–1840,* [2] "in *1836–1840, 1846, and* Fife,] Fife *1836–* [5] wife!" *1836–1840, 1846*

916 *no further entries in MS. 1832/36*

919 Making] That make *1827–*

I cannot well express the thoughts
Which Peter in those noises found;
A stifling power compressed his frame,
'Twas just as if a darkness came
Over that dull and dreary sound.

—For well did Peter know the sound;
The language of those drunken joys
To him, a jovial soul, I ween,
But a few hours ago had been
A gladsome, and a welcome noise.

But now, 'tis plain that Peter's thoughts
Have taken a far different course;
Whate'er he sees, whate'er he hears,
Gives him new sorrow or new fears,
Deepens his anguish and remorse.

And passing by a twisted elm
Again poor Peter thus began,
"'Twas just by such another tree
I robbed of sixpence half-penny
A Boy that led a poor blind man.

And close by such a gate as that
Did I by a most heinous murther
Destroy my good dog, Ruffian, he
Who gladly would have gone for me
To the world's end and further—

A faithful beast like this poor ass
Whom I have bruised so cruelly,
Just such another animal,
Made by the God that made us all
And fitter far to live than I."

But more than all his heart is stung
To think of one, almost a child,
A sweet and playful Highland Girl
As light and beauteous as a squirrel,
As beauteous and as wild.

1123–1125 This passage seems to be related to *Andrew Jones* (see Appendix I).
1128 In MS. 2 "my good dog" (the reading of MS. 3) is written over an illegible erasure.
1134 Cf. *Ancient Mariner*, l. 617.

I cannot well express the thoughts
Which Peter in those noises found;—
A stifling power compressed his frame,
As if confusing darkness came
Over that dull and dreary sound.

For well did Peter know the sound;
The language of those drunken joys
To him, a jovial soul I ween,
But a few hours ago had been
A gladsome and a welcome noise.

Now, turn'd adrift into the past,
He finds no solace in his course;—
Like planet-stricken men of yore
He trembles, smitten to the core
By strong compunction and remorse.

But more than all, his heart is stung
To think of one, almost a child;
A sweet and playful Highland girl,
As light and beauteous as a squirrel,
As beauteous and as wild!

921–925 But how shall I express the change
Which Peter in those noises found?
A stifling power compress'd his frame
And clouds of swimming darkness came
Over a dull and dreary sound! *alt MS. 1819a/20 foot of page*

921 thoughts] *alt* change *MS. 1819a/20*

924 While clouds of swimming darkness came *alt MS. 1819a/20* As if confusing] And a confusing *1832* While-as a swimming *1836– but* -as a *del to* clouds of *MS. 1836/45 (WW)*

924–925 See the 2nd Edition *entered in margin (WW) and variants entered at foot of page (WW):*
And clouds of
~~While as a~~ swimming darkness came
Over his eyesight with the sound
[?Together], over sight & sound *MS. 1836/45*

925 that] a *MS. 1819a/20; line del to* Suddenly over sight & sound *MS. 1836/45 (WW)*

925/926 A [?primal] change as Peter felt *possible alt interlined MS. 1836/45 (WW)*

926 For] Full *MS. 1819a/20*

928 soul, *1827–*

929 ago, *1827–*

931 Now, turn'd] *Now,* turned (*italics in text*) *1820–*

932 course;—] course; *1820–*

933 yore, *1827–*

934 smitten to the core *del to* pierced to his hearts core *MS. 1819a/20, MS. 1836/45*

935 remorse, *1831, 1834*

936 But, *1820–*

937 Child *1834*

A lonely house her dwelling was,
A cottage in a heathy dell,
And she put on her gown of green
And left her mother at sixteen
And follow'd Peter Bell.

But many good and pious thoughts
Had she, and in the Kirk to pray
Two long Scotch miles through rain and snow
To Kirk she had been us'd to go
Twice every sabbath day.

And when she follow'd Peter Bell
It was to live an honest life,
For he with tongue not us'd to falter
Had pledg'd his troth before the altar
To love her as his wedded wife.

A child was in her womb, but soon
She droop'd and pin'd like one forlorn;
From scripture she a name did borrow,
Benoni, or the child of sorrow
She called her babe unborn.

For she had learn'd how Peter lived
And took it in most grievous part;
She to the very bone was worn
And ere that little child was born
Died of a broken heart.

1143 A woman supposedly got a gown of green by tumbling in the grass; hence the phrase became a euphemism for loss of virginity.

1158–1160 "Benoni" means "son of my sorrow"; it was the name Rachel gave to the child she died bearing, and whom Jacob renamed Benjamin (Genesis 35:18). WW told Isabella Fenwick: "Benoni, or the child of sorrow, I knew when a school-boy" (see Introduction). T. W. Thompson cites the Hawkshead parish registers, which record the baptism on June 17, 1759, of "David Benoni Bastard Child of Ms Mary Rigge of Colthouse David Kirkby the Supposed Father of Conistone" and the burial of Mary on May 16, 1760. The "supposed father" married a sixteen-year-old in 1762 and became a sideman, overseer, and churchwarden before he died in 1814, aged 84. Thompson further suggests that Mary was the heroine of Wordsworth's early poem published by de Selincourt as "A Ballad" in *PW*, I, 265–267; see *Wordsworth's Hawkshead*, ed. Robert Woof (London, 1970), pp. 65–69.

A lonely house her dwelling was,
A cottage in a heathy dell;
And she put on her gown of green,
And left her mother at sixteen,
And followed Peter Bell.

But many good and pious thoughts
Had she; and, in the kirk to pray,
Two long Scotch miles, through rain or snow,
To kirk she had been used to go,
Twice every sabbath-day.

And, when she follow'd Peter Bell,
It was to lead an honest life;
For he, with tongue not used to falter,
Had pledg'd his troth before the altar
To love her as his wedded wife.

A mother's hope is her's;—but soon
She droop'd and pin'd like one forlorn;—
From Scripture she a name did borrow;
Benoni, or the child of sorrow,
She call'd her babe unborn.

For she had learn'd how Peter liv'd,
And took it in most grievous part;
She to the very bone was worn,
And, ere that little child was born,
Died of a broken heart.

---

941 Her dwelling was a lonely house, *1836–*
943 And] As *1834*
944 sixteen. *1831, 1834*
950 Sabbath-day *1820–*
951 followed *1820–*
952 an] a *1831, corrected in errata*
954 pledged *1820–*
956 her's;] hers; *1820– but* hers! *1831, 1834*
957 drooped and pined *1820–*   forlorn;—] forlorn; *1832, 1836–*
958 a] her *1820*
960 called *1820–*
961 learned . . . lived *1820–*

And now the Spirits of the mind
Are busy with poor Peter Bell,
And from the ass's back he sees,
I think, as ugly images
As ever eye did see in hell.

Close by a brake of flowering furze
He sees himself as plain as day;
He sees himself, a man in figure
Just like himself, nor less nor bigger,
Not five yards from the broad high-way.

And stretch'd beneath the furze he sees
The highland girl—it is no other—
And hears her crying as she cried
The very moment that she died,
"My mother! oh! my mother!"

The sweat pours down from Peter's face
So grievous is his heart's contrition;
With agony his eye-balls ache
While he beholds by the furze-brake
This miserable vision.

The ass is pacing down a hill,
By this he has not far to go,
And now while down the slope he wends
A voice to Peter's ears ascends
From the deep woody dell below.

1166 For "Spirits of the mind" see the notes to ll. 956 and 973.

1168 In MS. 2 "from the ass's back" (the reading of MS. 3) is written over illegible erasure.

1172–1173 Peter's seeing himself outside of his body may presage his death—he dies a spiritual death and is reborn (see l. 1379 and note). But since he also sees his dead wife, it is possible that the Spirits of the mind are merely recreating a tableau of remorse to work upon him regeneratively. Coleridge cites this passage as an example of a "Wraith" (*STCNB*, 2:2583). Apparitions called "wraiths" or "fetches" or (in Cumberland) "swarths" were thought to appear, usually to friends or family but sometimes to the individual himself, to presage his death (John Brand, *Observations on Popular Antiquities: Chiefly Illustrating the Origin of Our Vulgar Customs, Ceremonies, and Superstitions* [London, 1813], II, 542n, 547n).

1188 In MS. 2 "now" (the reading of MS. 3) is written over an erasure, probably "hark!'

And now the Spirits of the Mind
Are busy with poor Peter Bell;
Distraction reigns in soul and sense,
And reason drops in impotence
From her deserted pinnacle!

Close by a brake of flowering furze
(Above it shivering aspins play)
He sees an unsubstantial creature,
His very self in form and feature,
Not four yards from the broad highway;

And stretch'd beneath the furze he sees
The Highland girl—it is no other;
And hears her crying, as she cried
The very moment that she died,
"My mother! oh my mother!"

The sweat pours down from Peter's face,
So grievous is his heart's contrition;
With agony his eye-balls ache
While he beholds by the furze-brake
This miserable vision!

Calm is the well-deserving brute,
His peace, hath no offence betray'd;—
But now, while down that slope he wends,
A voice to Peter's ears ascends,
Resounding from the woody glade:

---

966 spirits *1834*
968–970 Upon the rights of visual sense
Usurping, with a prevalence
More terrible than magic spell. *1820–*
972 aspens *1827–*
975 highway: *1820–*
976 stretched *1820–*
978 crying,] crying *1832, 1836–* cried, *1820–*
987 peace,] peace *1836–* betray'd;—] betrayed;— *1820–1831, 1834* betrayed; *1832, 1836–*
989 ear *1820–*

It is a voice just like a voice
Reecho'd from a naked rock;
It comes from that low chapel, list!
It is a pious Methodist
That's preaching to his pious flock.

"Repent, repent," he cries aloud,
"God is a God of mercy,—strive
To love him then with all your might;
Do that which lawful is and right
And save your souls alive.

My friends! my brethren, though you've gone
Through paths of wickedness and woe
After the Babylonian harlot,
And though your sins be red as scarlet
They shall be white as snow."

Just as he pass'd the door these words
Did plainly come to Peter's ears,
And they such joyful tidings were
The joy was more than he could bear;
He melted into tears.—

1194–1195 For discussion of contemporary Methodist exhortation to repentance, see Mary Jacobus, "*Peter Bell* the First," *Essays in Criticism,* 24 (July 1974), 219–242, and *Tradition and Experiment in Wordsworth's "Lyrical Ballads," 1798* (Oxford, 1976), pp. 262–272.

1203 The Babylonian harlot was the "great whore" of Rev. 17:1.

Though clamorous as a hunter's horn
Re-echoed from a naked rock,
'Tis from that tabernacle—List!
Within, a fervent Methodist
Is preaching to no heedless flock.

"Repent! repent!" he cries aloud,
"While yet ye may find mercy;—strive
"To love the Lord with all your might;
"Turn to him, seek him day and night,
"And save your souls alive!

"Repent! repent! though ye have gone
"Through paths of wickedness and woe
"After the Babylonian harlot,
"And though your sins be red as scarlet
"They shall be white as snow!"

Even as he pass'd the door, these words
Did plainly come to Peter's ears;
And they such joyful tidings were
The joy was more than he could bear—
He melted into tears.

---

991 The voice, though clamorous as a horn *1832, 1836–*
992 from] by *1832, 1836–*
993 'Tis] Is *1832* Comes *1836–*
994 fervent *del to* pious *MS. 1819a/20, MS. 1836/45 (WW)*
995 flock! *1819a–*
997 ye] he *1819a*
998 "To] To *1836–*
999 "Turn] Turn *1836–*
1000 "And] And *1836–*
1001 "Repent!] "Repent; *1831* Repent! *1836–* gone, *1827–*
1002 "Through] Through *1836–* woe, *1827–*
1003 "After] After *1836–* harlot; *1836–*
1004 "And] "And, *1827–1834* And, *1836–* scarlet, *1827–*
1005 "They] They *1836–*
1006 Even] [?So] *MS. 1819a/20* passed *1820–*
1007 ears;] ears *1819a*
1008 were, *1820–*
1009 bear!— *1820–*

Sweet tears of hope and tenderness!
And fast they fell, a plenteous shower;
His nerves, his sinews seem'd to melt,
Through all his iron frame was felt
A gentle, a relaxing power.

Each nerve, each fibre of his frame
And all the animal within
Was weak, perhaps, but it was mild
And gentle as an infant child,
An infant that has known no sin.

Sweet tears of hope and tenderness!
And fast they fell, a plenteous shower;
His nerves, his sinews seem'd to melt;
Through all his iron frame was felt
A gentle, a relaxing power!

Each fibre of his frame was weak,
Weak all the animal within,
But in its helplessness grew mild
And gentle as an infant child,
An infant that has known no sin.

'Tis said, that through prevailing grace
He not unmov'd did notice now
The cross* upon thy shoulders scored
Meek beast! in memory of the Lord
To whom all human-kind shall bow;

In memory of that solemn day
When Jesus humbly deign'd to ride
Entering the proud Jerusalem,
By an immeasurable stream
Of shouting people deified!

1012 shower;] shower *1819a* shower! *1820–*
1013 seemed *1820–*
1015 relaxing, *1845–*
1016 weak; *1820–*
1017 within; *1820–*
1018 But, in its helplessness, *1820–*
1021–1025 *omitted 1827–1831, 1834*
1021 that, . . . grace, *1832* 'Tis said, meek Beast! that, through Heaven's grace, *MS. 1819a/20, 1836–*
1022 He, *1820, 1832* unmoved, *1820, 1832* unmoved *1836–*
1023 *asterisk and footnote omitted 1832–* shoulder *1836–* scored, *1820, 1832–* upon thy shoulder scored *foot of page, MS. 1836/45 (WW)*
1024 Beast *1832* (Belief of Millions) by the Lord *MS. 1819a/20* For lasting impress, by the Lord *1836– but* For lasting impress, by] For blest memorial of *alt interlined* Firm faith of millions! *alt entered between stanzas and at foot of page, where* Firm faith *is del to* Belief *MS. 1836/45 (WW) with* millions! *over* millions,
1026–1030 *omitted 1827–1831, 1834*
1026 Memorial of his touch—that day *alt MS. 1819a/20 adopted 1836–*
1027 deigned . . . ride, *1820, 1832–*

---

*The notion is very general, that the Cross on the back and shoulders of this Animal has the origin here alluded to.

But now the little patient ass
Towards a gate that's full in view
Turn'd up a narrow lane; his chest
Against the yielding gate he press'd
And quietly pass'd through.

And up the stony lane he goes;
No ghost more softly ever trod.
Among the stones and pebbles he
Sets down his hoofs inaudibly
As if with felt his hoofs were shod.

Along the lane the little ass
Had gone two hundred yards, not more,
When to a lonely house he came;
He turn'd aside towards the same
And stopp'd before the door.

Thought Peter, 'tis the poor Man's house.
He listens—not a sound is heard
But ere you could count half a score
It chanced that at the cottage door
A little girl appear'd.—

Towards the chapel she was going
With hope that she some news might gather.
She saw the pair and with a scream
Cried out like one that's in a dream,
"My father! here's my father!"

1226–1230 The ass seems to be supernaturally quiet; perhaps the meaning is that the sensitive beast intuitively recognizes the appropriateness of muffled grief, in another example of sympathetic oneness (cf. l. 1134).

Meanwhile the persevering Ass,
Towards a gate in open view
Turns up a narrow lane; his chest
Against the yielding gate he press'd,
And quietly pass'd through.

And up the stony lane he goes;
No ghost more softly ever trod;
Among the stones and pebbles, he
Sets down his hoofs inaudibly,
As if with felt his hoofs were shod.

Along the lane the trusty Ass
Had gone two hundred yards, not more;
When to a lonely house he came;
He turn'd aside towards the same
And stopp'd before the door.

Thought Peter, 'tis the poor man's home!
He listens—not a sound is heard
Save from the trickling household rill;
But, stepping o'er the cottage-sill,
Forthwith a little girl appear'd.

She to the meeting-house was bound
In hope some tidings there to gather—
No glimpse it is—no doubtful gleam—
She saw—and utter'd with a scream,
"My father! here's my father!"

1032 view, *1820–1834* Turned towards a gate that hung in view *1836–*
1033 Turns up a narrow] Across a shady *1836–*
1034 pressed, *1820–1836* pressed *1840–*
1035 passed *1820–*
1042–1045 Went twice two hundred yards or more,
And no one could have guessed his aim,—
Till to a lonely house he came, *1836–*
1044 turned *1820–1834* same, *1827–1834*
1045 stopped *1820–* before] beside *1836–*
1048 rill;] rill *1831, 1834*
1050 Girl *1827–* appeared *1820–*
1051 Meeting-house *1820–*
1052 hopes *1831, 1834, 1836–* gather—] gather;— *1820–1834* gather; *1836–*
1053 is, *1836–* gleam; *1836–*
1054 uttered *1820–*

The very word was plainly heard,
Heard plainly by the wretched mother;
Her joy was like a deep affright
And forth she ran into the light
And saw it was another.

And instantly upon the earth
Beneath the full moon shining bright,
Just at the ass's feet she fell,
And from the ass poor Peter Bell
Dismounts in most unhappy plight.

What could he do? the woman lay
Dead, as it seemed, both breath and limb.
Poor Peter sadly was confused;
To scenes like these he was not used,
'Twas altogether new to him.

He raised her up and while he held
Her body propped against his knee
She waked, and when the woman spied
The poor ass standing by her side
She moan'd most bitterly.

"Oh God be prais'd! my heart's at ease,
For he is dead, I know it well!"
Of tears she poured a bitter flood
And in the best way that he could
His tale did Peter tell.

The very word was plainly heard,
Heard plainly by the wretched Mother—
Her joy was like a deep affright;
And forth she rush'd into the light,
And saw it was another!

And instantly, upon the earth
Beneath the full-moon shining bright,
Close at the Ass's feet she fell;
At the same moment Peter Bell
Dismounts in most unhappy plight.

What could he do?—The Woman lay
Breathless and motionless;—the mind
Of Peter sadly was confus'd;
But, though to such demands unus'd,
And helpless almost as the blind,

He rais'd her up; and, while he held
Her body propp'd against his knee,
The Woman wak'd—and when she spied
The poor Ass standing by her side,
She moaned most bitterly.

"Oh! God be prais'd!—my heart's at ease—
"For he is dead—I know it well!"
—At this she wept a bitter flood;
And, in the best way that he could,
His tale did Peter tell.

1058 affright: *1832*, *1836–*
1059 rushed *1820–*
1061 And, *1832*, *1836–* earth, *1827–*
1062 full moon *1820–*
1063 at] to *1827–*
1066 As he beheld the Woman lie *1832*, *1836–*
1067 motionless;—] motionless, *1832*, *1836–*
1068 confused *1820–*
1069 unus'd,] unused, *1820– but* unused *1832*
1071 raised *1820–*
1072 prop'd *1819a* propped *1820–*
1073 waked *1820–*
1075 moan'd *1819a*
1076 prais'd!—] prais'd— *1819a* praised— *1820–*
1077 "For] For *1836–*
1079 And,] And *1834*

He trembled, he was pale as death;
His voice is weak with perturbation.
He turns aside his head, he pauses;
Poor Peter from a thousand causes
Is crippled sore in his narration.

At last she learned how he espied
The ass in that small meadow-ground,
And that beside the river-bed
Her husband now was lying dead,
That he was dead and drowned.

The wretched mother looks and looks
Upon the ass that near her stands;
She sees 'tis he, that 'tis the same,
She calls the poor ass by his name
And wrings and wrings her hands.

"Oh woe is me! he was so stout—
If he had died upon his bed
—He knew no sickness, knew no pain,
He never will come home again—
He's dead, for ever dead!"

Beside the woman Peter stands,
His heart is opening more and more;
A holy sense is in his mind,
He feels what he for human kind
Had never felt before.

1286–1287 In MS. 2 a false start of two lines was erased at the top of a page; the "Oh" is supplied from revision in MS. 2 and the base text of MS. 3.

He trembles—he is pale as death—
His voice is weak with perturbation—
He turns aside his head—he pauses;
Poor Peter from a thousand causes
Is crippled sore in his narration.

At length she learn'd how he espied
The Ass in that small meadow ground;
And that her husband now lay dead,
Beside that luckless river's bed
In which he had been drown'd.

A piercing look the sufferer cast
Upon the beast that near her stands;
She sees 'tis he, that 'tis the same;
She calls the poor Ass by his name,
And wrings, and wrings her hands.

"O wretched loss!—untimely stroke!
"If he had died upon his bed!
"—He knew not one forewarning pain—
"He never will come home again—
"Is dead—for ever dead!"

Beside the Woman Peter stands;
His heart is opening more and more;
A holy sense pervades his mind;
He feels what he for human kind
Had never felt before.

1081 death; *1836–*
1082 perturbation; *1836–*
1083 head, *1836–*
1084 causes; *1832* causes, *1836–*
1086 learned *1820–*
1087 meadow-ground *1836–*
1088 Husband *1827–*
1090 drowned *1820–*
1091 sufferer] Sufferer *1820–1834* Widow *1836–*
1092 Beast *1820–* stands;] stands: *1834*
1096 loss!—] loss— *1820–*
1097 "If] If *1836–*
1098 "—He] He *1836–* pain; *1836–*
1099 "He] He *1836–*
1100 "Is dead—] Is dead, *1836–*
1103 holy sense] tenderness *del to* And tender thoughts *MS. 1819a/20*
1104 human-kind *1849*

At length by Peter's arm sustained
The woman rises from the ground;
"Oh mercy! something must be done;
My little Rachael, you must run
Across the meadow, by the pound.

Make haste, my little Rachael, do!
Bid Matthew Simpson hither come,
Ask him to lend his horse tonight,
And this good man, whom heaven requite,
Will help to bring the body home."

Away goes Rachael weeping loud;
An infant, waked by her distress,
Makes in the house a piteous cry
And Peter hears the mother sigh,
"Poor thing, 'tis fatherless!"

And now does Peter feel
The heart of man's a holy thing,
And Nature through a world of death
Breathes into him a second breath
Just like the breath of spring.

Upon a stone the woman sits
In agony of silent grief.
From his own thoughts does Peter start;
He longs to press her to his heart
From love that cannot give relief.

1311 The line was left incomplete in both MSS. 2 and 3; revision in MSS. 3 and 4 supplied "deeply" before "feel."

At length, by Peter's arm sustain'd,
The Woman rises from the ground—
"Oh, mercy! something must be done,—
"My little Rachael, you must run,
"Some willing neighbour must be found.

"Make haste—my little Rachael—do!
"The first you meet with bid him come,—
"Ask him to lend his horse to-night,—
"And this good man, whom Heaven requite,
"Will help to bring the body home."

Away goes Rachael weeping loud;—
An infant, waked by her distress,
Makes in the house a piteous cry,—
And Peter hears the Mother sigh,
"Seven are they, and all fatherless!"

And now is Peter taught to feel
That man's heart is a holy thing;
And Nature, through a world of death,
Breathes into him a second breath,
More searching than the breath of spring.

Upon a stone the Woman sits
In agony of silent grief—
From his own thoughts did Peter start;
He longs to press her to his heart,
From love that cannot find relief.

1106 sustained, *1820– but* sustained; *1834*
1108 done,—] done, *1836–*
1109 "My] My *1836–* run,— *1827–*
1110 "Some] Some *1836–*
1111 "Make] Make *1836–* do, *1827–*
1112 "The] The *1836–* with— *1827–* come,—] come, *1836–*
1113 "Ask] Ask *1836–* to-night,—] to-night— *1820–1834* to-night, *1836–*
1114 "And] And *1836–* Man *1827–*
1115 "Will] Will *1836–*
1116 Rachael, *1834*
1117 Infant *1820–*
1118 cry,—] cry; *1827–*

At last, upspringing from her seat
As with a sudden fear and dread,
The woman through the threshold flies
And up the cottage stairs she hies
And flings herself upon the bed.

And Peter turns his steps aside
Towards a shade of alder trees
And he sits down, he knows not how,
With his hands fix'd against his brow
And his head fix'd between his knees.

In silence there does Peter sit,
Not any sign of life he makes,
As if his mind were sinking deep
Through years that have been long asleep—
—At last as from a trance he wakes.

He turns his head and sees the ass
Yet standing in the clear moonshine:
"When shall I be as good as thou?
Oh would, poor beast, that I had now
A heart but half as good as thine!"

But hark! that doleful cry again,
'Tis travelling up the woody slope.
Once more while Peter hears the sound
With stifling pain his heart is bound;
He feels like one that has no hope.

'Tis little Robin, he who sought
His father with such grief and pain,
And after many perils past
Has found his way safe home at last
And now is coming up the lane.

1321 In MS. 2 "upspringing" (the reading of MS. 3) is written over "she springs up" (erased).

1323–1324 In MS. 2 these lines are inserted carefully by WW over two of DW's original fair-copy lines, erased and illegible.

1324–1325 Reversed in the base text of MS. 3, then restored to their proper places by writing numbers "5" and "4" above the lines.

1336 MS. 2, miswritten, reads "He turn he turns"; revision of "he turns" to "his head" subsequent to transcription of MS. 3 (which reads "He turns he turns") probably restored the intended original phrase.

But rous'd, as if through every limb
Had pass'd a sudden shock of dread,
The Mother o'er the threshold flies,
And up the cottage stairs she hies,
And to the pillow gives her burning head.

And Peter turns his steps aside
Into a shade of darksome trees,
Where he sits down, he knows not how,
With his hands press'd against his brow,
And resting on his tremulous knees.

There, self-involv'd, does Peter sit
Until no sign of life he makes,
As if his mind were sinking deep
Through years that have been long asleep!
The trance is past away—he wakes,—

He turns his head—and sees the Ass
Yet standing in the clear moonshine,
"When shall I be as good as thou?
"Oh! would, poor beast, that I had now
"A heart but half as good as thine!"

—But *He*—who deviously hath sought
His father through the lonesome woods,
Hath sought, proclaiming to the ear
Of night, his inward grief and fear—
He comes—escaped from fields and floods;—

1131 roused *1820–*
1132 past *1820–*
1134 stairs] stair *1819a–1820*
1135 to . . . gives] on . . . lays *1836–* head.] head *1820*
1139 hands] hand *1831, 1834* pressed *1820–*
1140 And resting] His elbows *1827–*
1141 self-involved, *1820–*
1145 past] passed *1836–* wakes,—] wakes; *1836–*
1146 turns] lifts *1827–*
1147 moonshine; *1832, 1836–*
1149 "Oh] Oh *1836–*
1150 "A] A *1836–*
1151 —But] But *1836–*
1152 Father *1827–*
1154 night,] night *1819a–* inward grief and fear—] sorrow and his fear *alt MS. 1819a/20* grief and sorrowful fear— *1836– but* sorrow and his *alt MS. 1836/45 (WW)*
1155 comes, *1836–*

He's coming tow'rds the door, and now
He sees the ass—and nothing living
Had ever such a fit of joy
As has this little orphan boy,
For he has no misgiving.

Towards the gentle ass he [?springs]
And up about his neck he climbs;
In loving words he talks to him,
He kisses, kisses face and limb,
He kisses him a thousand times.

This Peter sees where in the shade
He stood beside the cottage door,
And Peter, he the ruffian wild,
Sobs loud, he sobs just like a child,
"Oh God! I can endure no more!"

Here ends my tale, for in a trice
Came Matthew Simpson with his horse.
Peter set out with him strait-way,
And, two hours ere the break of day,
Together they brought back the corse.

And many years did this poor ass,
Whom once it was my luck to see
Not many miles from Leeming-lane,
Help by his labour to maintain
The widow and her family.

1356 In MS. 2 the original reading (possibly "springs") has been obscured by the overwriting of a word that may be "sprang"; above the word is written "springs"; above the line "springs" is restored, and it is the reading of MS. 3.

1371, 1374 In MS. 2 "did" is a correction written over an extra "this" (presumably a miswriting; a question mark was inserted following it), but "Help'd" was allowed to stand at the beginning of l. 1374. In MS. 3 the grammar was mended by altering "Help'd" to "Help" and that emendation has been adopted; it stands in later texts.

1373 Leeming Lane is the name given to the old Roman road between Cattrick and Boroughbridge, in Yorkshire. It roughly parallels and is about one to three miles west of the River Swale. The modern spelling is "Leeming," though Wordsworth or his copyists or editors changed it to "Leming" from MS. 4 on.

With weary pace is drawing nigh—
He sees the Ass—and nothing living
Had ever such a fit of joy
As had this little orphan Boy,
For he has no misgiving!

Towards the gentle Ass he springs,
And up about his neck he climbs;
In loving words he talks to him,
He kisses, kisses face and limb,—
He kisses him a thousand times!

This Peter sees, while in the shade
He stood beside the cottage door:
And Peter Bell, the ruffian wild,
Sobs loud, he sobs even like a child,
"Oh! God, I can endure no more!"

—Here ends my Tale:—for in a trice
Arrived a neighbour with his horse;
Peter went forth with him straightway;
And, with due care, ere break of day
Together they brought back the Corse.

And many years did this poor Ass,
Whom once it was my luck to see
Cropping the shrubs of Leming-Lane,
Help by his labour to maintain
The Widow and her family.

1156 nigh; *1836–*
1159 had] hath *1827–*
1161 Towards] Forth to *1836–*
1162 climbs, *1834*
1167 cottage door:] cottage door; *1832* cottage-door; *1836–*
1171 Tale:—] tale:— *1831, 1834* Tale: *1836–*
1174 day, *1832, 1836–*
1175 Corse.] Corse *1846*
1180 widow *1834*

And Peter Bell, who till that night
Had been the wildest of his clan,
Forsook his crimes, forsook his folly,
And after ten months' melancholy
Became a good and honest man.

1377 In MS. 2 the line is written into a blank left in the fair-copy text; it appears in the base text of MS. 3.

1379 Stillinger (p. 514) suggests that the reference is to ten lunar months, the human gestation period, and symbolizes Peter's spiritual rebirth.

And Peter Bell, who, till that night,
Had been the wildest of his clan,
Forsook his crimes, repressed his folly,
And, after ten months' melancholy,
Became a good and honest man.

1183 repressed] renounced *1832, 1836–*

Transcriptions

MS. 1 (1798), with Facing Photographs

MS. 2 (1799), with Facing Photographs
and Variant Readings of MS. 3 (1799) and
MS. 4 (1802) in an *Apparatus Criticus*

MS. 5 (1806–1808), with Facing Photographs
through Part I, Variant Readings of
MS. 6 (1812–1818) and MS. 7 (1819) in an
Apparatus Criticus, and Selected
Photographs of MS. 6, through Prologue

MS. 1 (1798)

MS. 1 (DC MS. 18), the earliest surviving manuscript of *Peter Bell*—perhaps going back to 1798—exists in a quite fragmentary state (see description in Introduction). Dorothy Wordsworth began, at least, to make a fair copy of the poem, writing three neat stanzas to the page. Either she did not finish the copy or—more probably—the end of the poem, as well as the beginning and some internal pages, are lost. She did not regularly number the pages; one page, however, is numbered 44 (26^r). This curious situation suggests that Dorothy may have made two more or less contemporary copies, numbered the pages in one and not the other, and here carried over the number from the numbered to the unnumbered version. If so, the numbered version seems not to have survived.

This fragmentary, loosely sewn manuscript is now coming to pieces. The order of three unnumbered loose pages (here labeled 8, 30, and 31) is therefore uncertain. The order used in this transcription is that which seems most plausible on the basis of such evidence as conjugate leaves and the context of lines judged by comparison with the order in other manuscripts (see textual notes).

Dorothy's neat copy was subjected to radical revision by William. Even with these cancellations and changes, the earliest version does not—at least in its present fragmentary condition—reveal any fundamental shifts in the conception of the poem, but it does give MS. 1 particular interest as a version in many ways different from the received text and even from the next surviving manuscript: 33 stanzas in this transcription do not appear in the early reading text.

The lines in the transcription are numbered sequentially in the left margins, beginning at number 1; although it is likely that lines have been lost from gaps in the manuscript, there is no way of knowing how many. To assist the reader's orientation, when there are approximate equivalent lines in the early reading text, their numbers are shown in the right margins of the transcriptions in italics.

I know a deep romantic land
A land that's deep and far away
And fair it is as evening skies
And in the farthest heart it lies
Of deepest Africa

DOVE COTTAGE TRUST

Or will into the ~~land~~ world of fairy
Among the lovely shades of things
The shadowy forms of mountains bare
And streams & bowers and ladies fair
The shades of palaces and kings

My pretty little form of light
My sweet and beautiful canoe
Now though it grieves me to the heart
I feel I feel that we must part
I must take leave of you

[1r]

1 *I know a deep romantic land* 91–95
2 *A land that's deep and far away*
3 *And fair it is as evening skies*
4 *And in the farthest heart it lies*
5 *Of deepest Africa*

world
6 *Or we'll into the ~~land~~ of fairy* 96–100
7 *Among the lovely shades of things*
8 *The shadowy forms of mountains bare*
9 *And streams & bowers and ladies fair*
10 *The shades of palaces and kings*

11 *My pretty little form of light* 101–105
12 *My sweet and beautiful canoe*
13 *Now though it grieves me to the heart*
14 *I feel I feel that {we / m} must part*
15 *I must take leave of you*

3

They were to come this very evening
They know not I have been so far
I see them there in number nine
All in the bower of Weymouth pine
I see them there they are

And there's the wife of Parson Swan
And there's my good friend, Stephen Otter
And ere the light of evening fail
To them I must relate the tale
Of Peter Bell the Potter

Off flew my pretty little boat
All in a trance of indignation
And I, as well as I was able
On two poor legs to my stone table
Limped on with some vexation

[3r]

21 *They were to come this very evening* 126–130
22 *They know not I have been so far*
23 *I see them there in number nine*
24 *All in the bower of Weymouth pine*
25 *I see them there they are*

26 *And there's the wife of Parson Swan* 131–135
27 *And there's my good friend, Stephen*
Otter
28 *And ere the light of evening fail*
29 *To them I must relate the tale*
30 *Of Peter Bell the Potter*

31 *Off flew my pretty little boat* 136–140
32 *All in a trance of indignation*
33 *And I, as well as I was able*
34 *On two poor legs to my stone table*
35 *Limped on with some vexation*

The preceding leaf has been torn out of MS. 1, leaving a bit of stub (conjugate with leaf 5) in the middle, containing the beginnings of three words: "Supp / Tha / Ab" (presumably ll. 111–113 of the early reading text, these are here taken to be ll. 16–18 followed by ll. [19–20] of MS. 1). It seems likely that the page once held three stanzas, possibly resembling MS. 2, ll. 106–115 and 121–125.

5

"O! here he is" cried little Bess
She saw me at the garden door
O! here he is "cried Mistress Swan
And all at once around me ran
Full nine of them or more

"Sit down – I beg you would be seated"
Said I, no doubt with visage pale
And if, my Friends it pleases you
This instant without more ado
We'll have the promised tale

[illegible]

And so though some what out of breath
With lips, no doubt and visage pale
And sore too from a slight contusion
Did I to cover my confusion
Begin the promised tale

[4r]

"O! here he is" cried little Bess 141–145
She saw me at the garden door
O! here he is" cried Mistress Swan
And all at once around me ran
Full nine of them or more

"Sit down—I beg you would be seated" 146–150
Said I, no doubt with visage pale
And if, my Friends it pleases you
This instant without more ado
We'll have the promised tale

~~*All by the moon*~~
And so though somewhat out of breath 151–155
With lips, no doubt and visage pale
An} s}or{e
Di}d I} {to too from a slight contusion
Did I to cover my confusion
Begin the promised tale

45/46 Apparently Dorothy, confused by the similar endings of ll. 45 and 50, started to copy l. 51 after l. 45, caught her mistake, and erased the first four words. A similar anticipation is corrected by overwriting in l. 48.

Tale 7

All by the moonlight river side
It gave three miserable groans
'Tis come then to a pretty pass
Said Peter to the groaning ass
But I will bang your bones

"My dearest Sir" cried Mistress Swan
"You're got at once into the middle"
And little Bess with accents sweeter
Cried "Oh dear Sir! but who is Peter

The Squire cried "Sure as paradise
Was lost to us by Adam's sinning
We all are wandering in a wood
And therefore Sir I wish you would
Begin at the beginning

[5^{r}]

Tale

All by the moonlight river side 156–160
It gave three miserable groans
'Tis come then to a pretty pass
Said Peter to the groaning ass
But I will bang your bones

"My dearest Sir" cried Mistress Swan 161–164
"You're got at once into the middle"
And little Bess with accents sweeter
Cried "Oh dear Sir! but who is Peter

The Squire cried "Sure as paradise 166–170
Was lost to us by Adam's sinning
We all are wandering in a wood
And therefore Sir I wish you would
Begin at the beginning

"Tale" is in pencil.

60 The line is left blank in MSS. 1, 2, and 3; MS. 4 supplies: Said Harry, "tis a downright riddle."

9

A Potter Sir he was by trade
Cried I becoming quite collected
And wheresoever he appeared
Full twenty times was Peter feared
For once that Peter was respected

He two and thirty years or more
Had been a wild and woodland rover
Had been in farthest Pembroke Sir
And he had been at Exeter
In Kent Sir and in Dover

And he had been at Nottingham
And well he knew the Spire of Sarum
And he had been where Lincoln ~~[illegible]~~ bell
To shepherds in the distant dell
Rings out his loud alarum

[6r]

66 *A Potter Sir he was by trade* 171–175
67 *Cried I becoming quite collected*
68 *And wheresoever he appeared*
69 *Full twenty times was Peter feared*
70 *For once that Peter was respected*

71 *He two and thirty years or more* 176–180
72 *Had been a wild and woodland rover*
73 *Had been in farthest Pembroke Sir*
74 *And he had been at Exeter*
75 *In Kent Sir and in Dover*

76 *And he had been at Nottingham* 181–185
77 *And well he knew the Spire of Sarum*
78 *And he had been where Lincoln* {*b* ~~*Bell*~~ *bell*
79 *To shepherds in the distant dell*
80 *Rings out his loud alarum*

Whe
In th
Sure

As w
Have
The tr
But
In hea

The rov
In

[7r]

201–205
W
Whe
[?On]
~~In~~ h
Sure

As w 206–210
Have
He tra
But
In hear

He rove 211–215
In

80/96 A leaf is torn out; the stub is conjugate with leaf 8. In a previous ordering of this loose page, it was placed after leaf 11 (see headnote, p. 157). Initial letters and words on the stub indicate that the three stanzas present were equivalent to ll. 201–215 of the early reading text. Ll. 186–200 presumably stood on another, earlier leaf pulled out of MS. 1 without leaving a stub.

84 The deletion and revision are in pencil.

Close by the rivers wandering banks
~~Beside the rapid river Swale~~ 17
Was Peter travelling all alone
Whether to buy or sell
~~If in the way of trade~~, or led
By pleasure running in his head
To me was never known

~~Along the turf & through the fern~~
~~And in the [illegible] he travelled on~~
~~When he had left that night or day~~
~~His wife or [illegible] I cannot say~~
~~But wife or comrade he had none~~

As Peter was a lazy soul
And seldom walked when he could ride
I wonder he should trudge alone
I wonder that he had not thrown
His legs o'er some poor asses hide

[8r]

Close by the river's winding banks
96 ~~*Beside the rapid river Swale*~~ *301–305*
97 *Was Peter travelling all alone*
Whether to buy or sell
98 ~~*If in the way of trade*~~*, or led*
99 *By pleasure running in his head*
100 *To me was never known*

101 ~~*Along the turf & through the fern*~~ *306–310*
102 ~~*And in the mire he travelled on*~~
If
103 ~~*Where he had left that night or day*~~
104 ~~*His wife or wives I cannot say*~~
105 ~~*But wife or comrade he had none*~~

106 *As Peter was a lazy soul*
107 *And seldom walked when he could ride*
108 *I wonder he should trudge alone*
109 *I wonder that he had not thrown*
110 *His legs o'er some poor asses hide*

100/101 The curious character between the stanzas may result from Dorothy's practicing German script, as she did in the Alfoxden Notebook, perhaps here (like the "amen" at ll. 101/102) as a means of testing a new or newly sharpened pen. This leaf has come loose from the sewing; in a previous ordering of the manuscript it was placed before 12 (see headnote).

106–110 Canceled by two X's in pencil and one in ink.

In
11

Some love to travel with a dog
And Peter had a savage elf
A butcher, and he loved him well
But sure it is that Peter Bell
That evening travelled by himself

He travelled on through copse & bri
He travelled on o'er hill and dale
Nor for the moon cared he a tittle
And for the stars he cared as little
And for the murmuring river Swa

Quoth Peter "here's a nearer cut
'Twill save a mile as sure as day
He took the path the path did lea
Across a smooth and grassy mead
And a tall wood before him lay

[9r]

In
chuse
Some love to travel with a dog 311–315
And Peter had a savage elf
A lurcher, and he loved him well
But sure it is that Peter Bell
That evening travelled by himself

He travelled on through copse & brak[ ] 316–320
He travelled on o'er hill and dale
Nor for the moon cared he a tittle
And for the stars he cared as little
And for the murmuring river Swale

Quoth Peter "here's a nearer cut 321–325
'Twill save a mile as sure as day
He took the path the path did lead
Across a smooth and grassy mead
And a tall wood before him lay

---

111 The alternate "chuse" is in pencil. The "In" at the top of the page is of the sort that usually indicates that a canceled passage is to be restored, but nothing seems to have been canceled on this page; ll. 111–115 are, however, canceled in MS. 3 and are not present in MS. 4 (this section of MS. 2 is missing).

116 The last word runs off the page; undoubtedly "brake" was intended.

now he to the
13
And ~~Peter to~~ the wood is come
through the wood
~~Betty there~~
And ~~Peter toss~~ in whole cart loads
Lets heaping curses on them all
Commissioners both great and small
Who made the zig-zag roads
As through
Awhile he drives along
And ~~Peter's driving through~~ the boughs
With head and hands & ~~his~~ cheeks the
With downright fury and with wrath
There's little sign that Peter's path
Will to the road return
And Peter's path grows dimmer still
Now up now down his way he wends
With all the sail that he can carry
Till he is brought to an old quarry
And there the pathway ends

[10r]

Now he to the
And ~~Peter to the~~ wood is come *326–330*
through the wood
Peter there
And ~~Peter now~~ in whole cart loads
He'
I}s heaping curses on them all
Commissioners both great and small
Who made the zig-zag roads

For while he drives along
~~And Peter's driving through~~ the boughs *331–335*
& that
With head and hands—~~his~~ cheeks ~~they~~
burn
With downright fury and with wrath
There's little sign that Peter's path
Will to the road return

The
{~~And~~
{Now dim & dimmer
~~And~~ ~~Peter's~~ path grows ^ dimmer still *336–340*
Now up now down his way he wends
With all the sail that he can carry
Till he is brought to an old quarry
And there the pathway ends

130/131 William's interpolated "As thick" is probably an abortive beginning on revision of a line in *To the Clouds* on the facing verso. He was working on this poem (reproduced in *PW*, II, 316–320) on the versos of this section of the notebook, and the material between ll. 135 and 136 and in the margin represents more of the spill-over.

15

And so where on the huge rough stones
The black and massy shadows lay
And through the dark, & through the cold
And through the yawning fissures old
Did Peter boldly press his way

And in a moment opened out
A scene of soft and lovely hue
Where blue and grey & tender green
Together made as sweet a scene
As ever human eye did view

[11r]

And so where on the huge rough stones 346–350
The black and massy shadows lay
And through the dark, & through the cold
And through the yawning fissures old
Did Peter boldly press his way

And in a moment opened out 351–355
A scene of soft and lovely hue
Where blue and grey & tender green
Together made as sweet a scene
As ever human eye did view

A space is left blank at the top of the page sufficient to contain a stanza and possibly intended for a version of a stanza that apparently gave Wordsworth much trouble (ll. 341–345 of the early reading text, ll. 366–370 of the 1819 text).

19

There is one lonely tenant here
By this small patch of greenest grass
Beneath these winding rocks so grey
And where the river steals its way
There is one solitary ass

Of [illegible]
Across that deep and quiet spot
Is Peter driving through the grass
And now he is among the trees
And turning round his head he sees
A solitary ass [illegible]
[illegible]

And Peter underneath the trees
Stops short as if against his will
He looks around [illegible]
What is there [illegible]
And why does Peter stand stock still

[12r]

~~*There is one lonely tenant here*~~
~~*By this small plot of greenest grass*~~
~~*Beneath these winding rocks so grey*~~
And where the river steals its way
~~*There is one solitary ass*~~

Across that deep and quiet spot *371–375*
Is Peter driving through the grass
And now he is among the trees
And turning round his head he sees
a ~~*The*~~ *solitary ass*

~~*And Peter underneath the trees*~~
~~*Stops short as if against his will*~~
~~*He looks around what can he see?*~~
~~*What means this sudden sympathy?*~~
~~*And why does Peter stand stock still*~~

155/156, 160/161 William's insertions between stanzas are variants of lines in *To the Clouds* on the facing verso.

21

"No doubt I'm foundered in these woods
For once" quoth he "Twill be wise
Upon my faith I'll back again
And not to make my journey vain
I'll take the ass likewise"

So off he goes; as you'll suppose
With thoughts as blithe as any dream
To where the ass beside the bed
Of that green meadow hung his head
Over the silent stream

"A pretty beast, though we'll allow
Not quite so fat as he might be
Upon my soul with such a platter
You should have been a little fatter
But come Sir, come with me"

[13r]

"No doubt I'm foundered in these woods 381–385
~~Peter Ill~~
For once" quoth he "I will be wise
Upon my faith I'll back again
And not to make my journey vain
I'll take the ass likewise"

So off he goes; as you'll suppose 386–390
With thoughts as blithe as any dream
To where the ass beside the bed
Of that green meadow hung his head
Over the silent stream

"A pretty beast, though we'll allow 391–395
Not quite so fat as he might be
Upon my soul with such a platter
You should have been a little fatter
But come Sir, come with me"

---

167 The correction was written in pencil and canceled in ink.

[illegible] [illegible] [illegible]
of the boldest mountain sheep and [illegible]
of the wild Goat, still bolder, nor more tame
[illegible] them to tread there stretching away [illegible]

He pulled the creature did not move
Upon his back then Peter leapt
And with his staff and heels he plied
The little ass on either side
But still the ass his station kept

[13v]

X

196 *He pulled the creature did not move* 411–415
197 *Upon his back then Peter leapt*
198 *And with his staff and heels he plied*
199 *The little ass on either side*
200 *But still the ass his station kept*

The top two-thirds of this page is taken up by some 20 lines of draft for *Tuft of Primroses* (*PW*, V, 348). The stanza of *Peter Bell* at the bottom is marked for insertion at the end of 14r, and it has been numbered accordingly.

23

But first friend Peter deems it fit
To spy about him far and near
There's not a single house in sight
No woodman's hut, no cottage light
Peter you need not fear

There's nothing to be seen but woods
And rocks that spread a hoary gleam
And this poor ass which near the bed
Of the green meadow hangs his head
Over the silent stream

Close to the river's breathless shore
Over the stream he hung his head
His head was with a halter bound
Now Peter's purpose did not alter
And so at once he seized the halter
And would have turned him round

×

[14r]

But first friend Peter deems it fit 396–400
To spy about him far and near
There's not a single house in sight
No woodman's hut, no cottage light
Peter you need not fear

There's nothing to be seen but woods 401–405
And rocks that spread a hoary gleam
And this poor ass which near the bed
Of the green meadow hangs his head
Over the silent stream

Close to the rivers brink he stood
~~*Over the stream he hung*~~ *his head* 406–410
His head was with a halter bound
Now Peter's purpose did not alter
And so at once he seized the halter
And would have turned him round
X

---

191 The original reading is canceled in pencil.
The X at the bottom of the page indicates that the stanza inserted at the bottom of 13r belongs here.

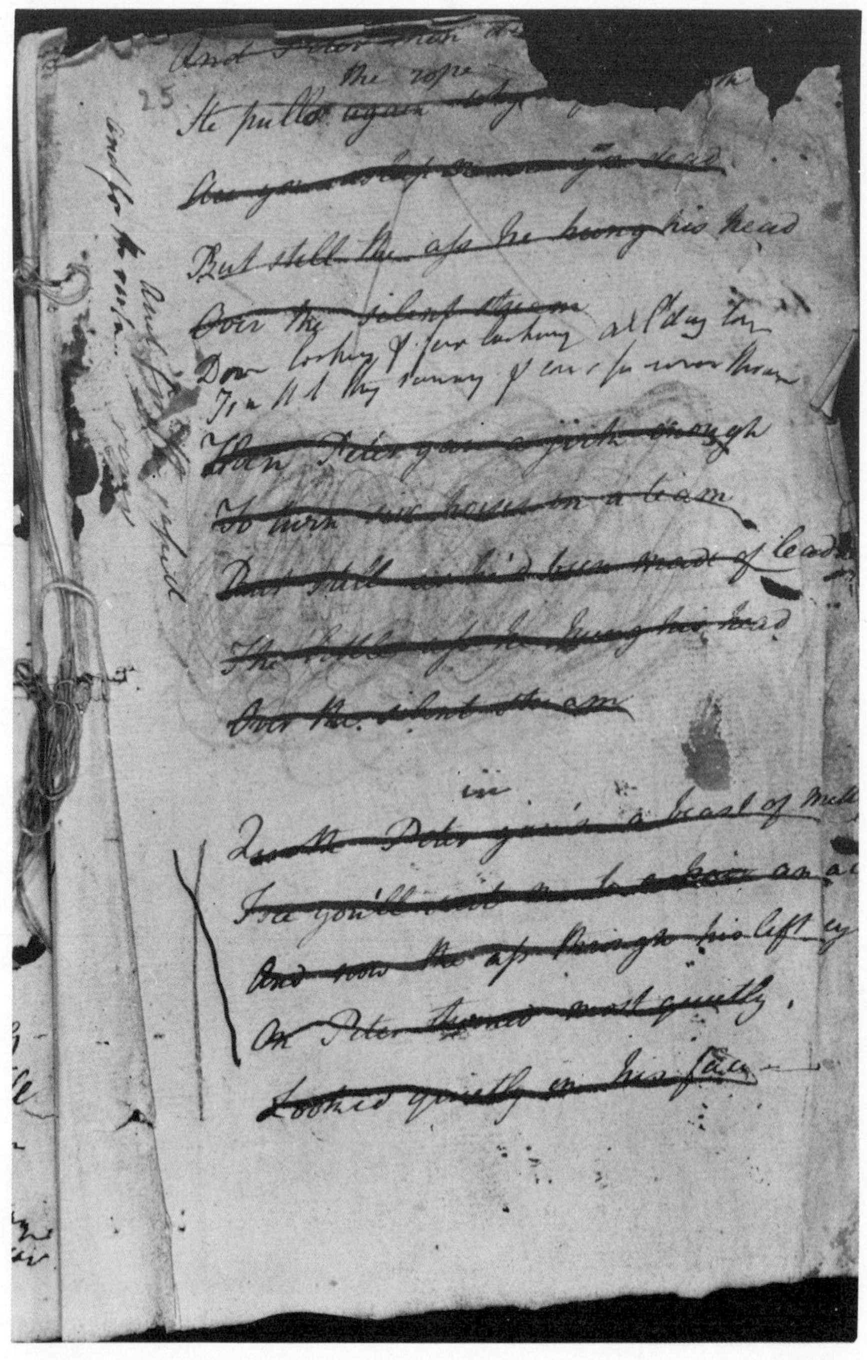

[15r]

~~And Peter then di~~

the rope

{s

~~He pull~~⎩*~~ed again why~~* *m*

~~Are you asleep or are you dead~~

~~But still the ass he hung~~ his head

~~Over the silent stream~~

~~Then Peter gave a jirk enough~~

~~To turn six horses in a team~~

~~But still as he'd been made of lead~~

~~The little ass he hung his head~~

~~Over the silent stream~~

in

~~Quoth Peter you're a beast of mettle~~ *416–420*

n⎫ an ace

~~I see you'll suit me to a~~ ⎭*~~hair~~*

~~And now the ass through his left eye,~~

~~On Peter turned most quietly,~~

~~Looked quietly in his face—~~

The top corner of the page is torn and the ends of these lines are lost. The first stanza is canceled by a penciled X and horizontal deletion lines in ink.

205/206 Wordsworth's interpolated lines here and in the margin relate to *Tuft of Primroses* (*PW*, V, 348–349) on the facing verso.

206–210 The entire stanza is canceled by pencil shadowing, with horizontal deletion lines in ink.

211–215 One vertical line down the margin is in pencil, one in ink.

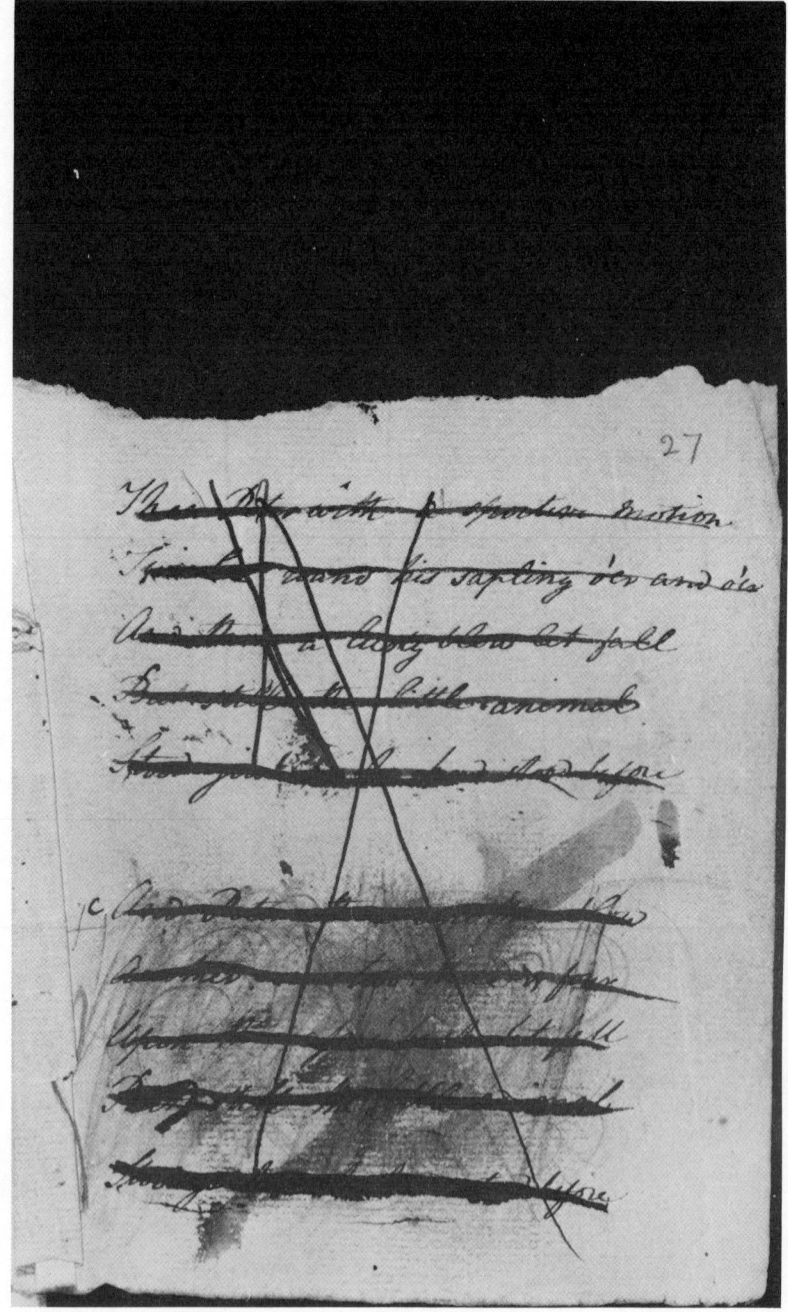

[16r]

~~*Then Peter with a sportive motion*~~
~~*Twirls round his sapling o'er and o'er*~~
~~*And then a lusty blow let fall*~~
~~*But still the little animal*~~
~~*Stood just as he had stood before*~~ *435*

~~*And Peter threw another blow*~~
~~*Another, one two three & four*~~
~~*Upon the asse's back let fall*~~
~~*But still the little animal*~~
~~*Stood just as he had stood before*~~ *435*

The top third of the page has been torn off. A stanza may have stood there, but no evidence survives: no stub remains, the verso is blank, and since the two stanzas on the page are canceled (the lower one by pencil shadowing before ink deletion lines were drawn) and do not appear in other manuscripts, no conclusions can be drawn from comparison of context.

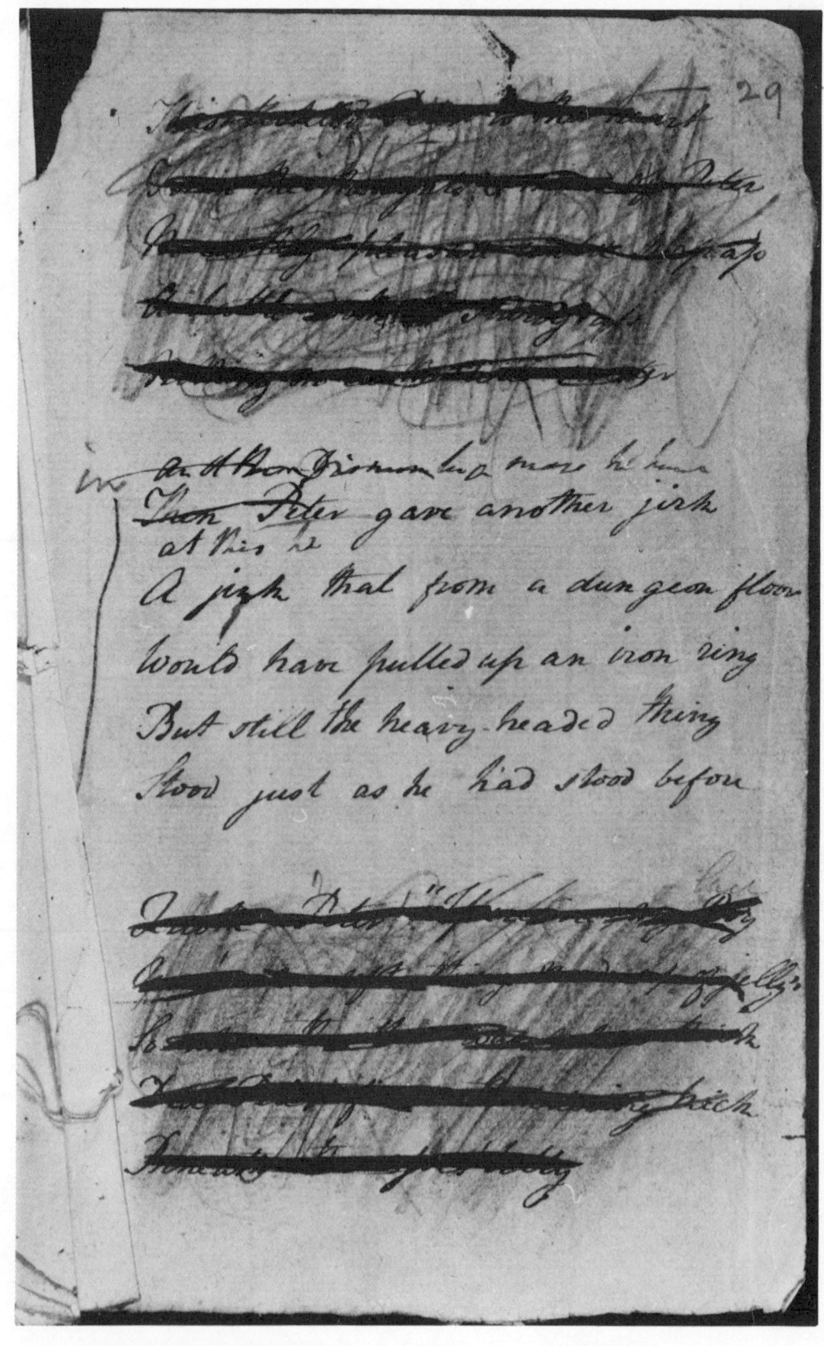
29

Then Peter gave another jirk
at this he
A jirk that from a dungeon floor
Would have pulled up an iron ring
But still the heavy-headed thing
Stood just as he had stood before

[17r]

226 *~~This tickled Peter to the heart~~*
227 *~~For in the thoughts & mind of Peter~~*
228 *~~No earthly pleasure could surpass~~*
229 *~~A battle with a sturdy ass~~*
230 *~~Nothing on earth was sweeter~~*

in ~~And then Dismount~~ing more he [?heaved]
231 *~~Then Peter~~ gave another jirk* *431–435*
at this he
232 *A jirk that from a dungeon floor*
233 *Would have pulled up an iron ring*
234 *But still the heavy-headed thing*
235 *Stood just as he had stood before*

lad
236 *~~Quoth Peter "I perceive, my Boy~~*
237 *~~You're no soft thing made up of jelly"~~*
238 *~~So where the skin was not so thick~~*
239 *~~Did Peter fix a thundering kick~~*
240 *~~Beneath the asses' belly~~*

The first and third stanzas are canceled by pencil shadowing and ink deletion lines; the middle stanza is marked "in" in pencil; the vertical lines alongside the two bottom stanzas are in pencil.

236 The word "lad" is a pencil addition.

Following this page, a leaf is torn out of MS. 1; the stub suggests that it held three stanzas (here assigned line numbers 241–255). Initial letters of only two lines are decipherable: "Ov" in the last line of the first stanza and "F" in the first line of the second. Only a fragment of an initial letter in a third stanza remains. At least the first two stanzas appear to have been canceled. The stub is conjugate with leaf 17.

31

And still did Peter [illegible] the ass
With blows that might have cracked the bone
The ass as if he felt it not
Beside the [illegible] stood stock still
As if he had been made of stone

Quoth Peter "by the devils' beard
I'll make you stir you mongrel hound
And both his arms did Peter pass
Beneath the belly of the ass
With both his arms he clasped him round
...

Now for it now you sturdy thief"
And desperately friend Peter heaves
He might as well have tried to stir
The abbey huge of Westminster
Or twice five hundred head of beeves

DOVE-COTTAGE-TRUST

[19r]

X

256 *And still did Peter   the ass*
257 *With blows that might have reached the*
bone
258 *The ass as if he felt no ill*
259 *Beside the river stood stock still*
260 *As if he had been made of stone*

261 *Quoth Peter, "by the devil's beard* 456–460
d}
262 *I'll make you stir you mongrel houng*}
263 *And both his arms did Peter pass*
264 *Beneath the belly of the ass*
265 *With both his arms he clasped him*
round

266 *Now for it now you sturdy thief"* 461–465
267 *And desperately friend Peter heaves*
268 *He might as well have tried to*
stir
269 *The abbey huge of Westminster*
270 *Or twice five hundred head of beeves*

The first stanza is canceled by pencil shadowing and an X in ink.
256 The small X in the margin is in pencil.

32.

And Peter halts to gather breath
He halts and to his eye was shewn
What till this time he had not seen
How gaunt was the Poor ass & lean
Yea wasted to a skeleton.

With legs stretched out & stiff he lay

[19^v]

And Peter halts to gather breath
He halts and to his eye was shewn
What till this time he had not seen
How gaunt was the Poor ass & lean
Yea wasted to a skeleton.

With legs stretched out & stiff he lay

The stanza inserted here is not numbered in sequence because it appears to be a late addition, probably an original version of ll. 486–490 of 1819. In this manuscript it may have been designed first to replace ll. 281–285 on 20^r, then to replace ll. 401–405 on 28^r. The last line on 19^v is l. 491 of 1819; it could also be a variant of the revised l. 401 on 28^r. What is probably another variant is found, in William's hand, entered on 21^v:

And thus while on his side he lay
To {P / [?]}eters eye was
And to the

33

Quoth Peter "here is witch-craft here
And damned tricks but what care I"
And so upon the asses hide
Making the hair and dust fly wide
He beat most furiously

Once [illegible]

At last the little harmless ass bears
and meek at length
Gently as if to take his ease
The ass whom Peter thus had bruised
Whom he so cruelly had used
Dropped gently down upon his knees

And then upon his side he fell
~~Upon [illegible] he [illegible] down~~
~~His [illegible] shewed no fear~~
~~He lay upon the meadow bed~~
~~[illegible]~~
~~And still the ass he hung his head~~
~~Over the [illegible] and clear~~

[20r]

Quoth Peter "here is witch-craft here
And damned tricks but what care I?
And so upon the asses hide
Making the hair and dust fly wide
He beat most furiously

Cried Peter you'll be wise
{*l* beast
At last the little harm{ *ess ass* 481–485
~~And now~~ at length
Gently as if to take his ease
The ass whom Peter thus had bruised
Whom he so cruelly had used
Dropped gently down upon his knees

And then upon his side he fell
~~*Upon his knees he laid him down*~~ 486–490
~~*His countenance it shewed no fear*~~
~~*He lay upon the meadow bed*~~
~~as befor hung down~~
~~*And still the ass he hung his head*~~
~~*Over the stream so deep and clear*~~

The first stanza is canceled by pencil shadowing.

275/276 The pencil insertion indicates that ll. 291–305 are to be moved to that point, as they are in MSS. 2 and 3.

284 Wordsworth sometimes did not bother to write the terminal letters of words; however, the end of "before" (obviously intended) may have been lost in the cancellation.

37

Quoth Peter "I shall have you now
Now I shall have you safe & sound
To Peter it was like a token
That some curst magic spell was broke

Cried Peter you'll be wise I hope
Before we're both five minutes older
Upon the ass his sapling rings
Each blow the arm of Peter stings
Up to the elbow & the shoulder

O mercy for the Beast! — at last
At last, poor patient thing! at last
His sides they heaved his belly stirr'd
He gave a groan, & then another
Of that which went before the broth
And then he gave a third

[21r]

Quoth Peter "I shall have you now
Now I shall have you safe & sound
To Peter it was like a token
That some curst magic spell was broken

*

Cried Peter you'll be wise I hope 466–470
Before we're both five minutes older
Upon the ass his sapling rings
Each blow the arm of Peter stings
Up to the elbow & the shoulder

O Mercy for the Beast—at last
Up up ye [?patient]
At last, poor patient thing! at last 471–475
His sides they heaved his belly stirre'd
He gave a groan, & then another
Of that which went before the brother
And then he gave a third

The incomplete first stanza is canceled with an ink X and pencil shadowing.

291 The asterisk, in pencil, probably indicates that ll. 291–295 are to be moved to a position before ll. 276–280; see 20r.

296 The entry underneath "O Mercy for the Beast—at last" is in very dim pencil.

39

All by the moonlight river side
He gave three miserable groans
"'Tis come then to a pretty pass"
Said Peter to the groaning ass
But I will bang your bones

~~And Peter [illegible]~~
~~For Peter's anger was increased~~
~~And with his heels and with his toes~~
~~And with more fierce & furious blows~~
~~He fell upon the heavy beast~~

~~Again the ass was still as death~~
~~"The devil's in him"~~ Peter cried
~~At length [illegible] the moonlight [illegible]~~
~~Once more he stirred, & from his knees~~
~~The ass~~
~~Fell down upon his side~~

[22r]

301 *All by the moonlight river side* 476–480
302 *He gave three miserable groans*
303 *"'Tis come then to a pretty pass"*
304 *Said Peter to the groaning ass*
305 *But I will bang your bones*

306 ~~*And Peter did as he had said*~~
307 ~~*For Peter's anger now encreased*~~
308 ~~*And with his heels and with his toes*~~
309 ~~*And with more fierce & furious blows*~~
310 ~~*He fell upon the harmless beast*~~

311 ~~*Again the ass was still as death*~~
312 ~~*"The devil's in him" Peter cried*~~
313 ~~*At length beneath the moonlight trees*~~
314 ~~*Once more he stirred, & from his knes*~~
~~The ass~~
315 ^ ~~*Fell down upon his side*~~

The second stanza is canceled in ink and pencil, the third in ink only.

Close by the moonlight river's brink
Upon his side the ass did lie
And as he lay like one that mourned
The patient ass on Peter turned
His shining hazel eye

'Twas but one look one patient lo[ok]
~~[illegible]~~
~~So strait as plainly did appear~~
~~[illegible]~~
~~Whether in sorrow or in dread~~
He turned again & hung his head
Over the silent stream so deep & clear

~~How could it be? how could it be~~
~~That while the poor ass there did lie~~
~~On Peter's heart or Peter's brain~~
~~Not one impression did remain~~
~~Of his large and shining eye~~

[23r]

Close by the moonlight river's brink
Upon his side the ass did lie
And as he lay like one that mourned
The patient ass on Peter turned
His shining hazel eye

in
'Twas but one look one patient look
{And straightway, silent, without fear
{F
~~*For straight as plainly did appear*~~
For twas in sorrow, not in dread,
~~*Whether in sorrow or*~~ *in dread*
He turned again & hung his head
Over the ~~*silent*~~ *stream so deep & clear*

~~*How could it be? how could it be*~~
~~*That while the poor ass thus did lie*~~
~~*On Peter's heart on Peters brain*~~
~~*Not one impression did remain*~~
~~*Of his large and shining eye*~~

All three stanzas are canceled by pencil shadowing. The "in" in ink may apply to the first stanza or the second or both.

321–325 The stanza is canceled in pencil and ink. On 22v, facing, are two lines of revision for ll. 324–325, in William's hand:

He turned the eyeball in his head
Towards the stream so deep & clear.

43

And Peter's more & more enraged
His lips with rage and fury quiver
~~And now his lips begin to quiver~~
Quoth he "you little mulish dog"
Quoth he "I'll fling you like a log
Head fore most down the river

By God I will.. When this was said
As stretched upon
~~The ass, as on~~ his side he lay
To all the echoes south and north
And east and west the ass sent forth
A loud and horrible bray

This outcry on the heart of Peter
Seems like a note of joy to strike
Joy on the heart of Peter knocks
But on the echo of the rocks
Was something Peter did not like

[24r]

331 *And Peter's more & more enraged* 491–495
His lips with rage and fury quiver
332 ~~*And now his lips begin to quiver*~~
333 *Quoth he "you little mulish dog"*
334 *Quoth he "I'll fling you like a log*
335 *Head fore-most down the river*

{*W*
336 *By God I will—* {*when this was said* 496–500
as stretched upon
337 ~~*The ass, as on*~~ *his side he lay*
338 *To all the echoes south and north*
339 *And east and west the ass sent forth*
340 *A loud and horrible bray*

341 *This outcry on the heart of Peter* 501–505
342 *Seems like a note of joy to strike*
343 *Joy on the heart of Peter knocks*
{*i*
344 *But* {*on the echo of the rocks*
345 *Was something Peter did not like*

---

336 "By God I will" is written with an unusual boldness, as it is in MS. 2 (l. 496 of the reading text).

45

"Up up" The ass brayed loud again
And Peter's heart far less rejoices
He's now beginning to demur
He thinks he hears a barking cur
And there's a sound of human voices

Quoth Peter "is it come to this
Then I shall ere sure we must be brief
So he let fall a thundering smack
And heard a voice behind his back
From the old quarry cry Thief! Thief!

As you'll suppose this ugly voice
His rage did not a little quell
But as he did not hear again
The voice which he had heard so plain
To work again he fell

[25^{r}]

"Up up" The ass brayed loud again
And Peter's heart far less rejoices
He's now beginning to demur
He thinks he hears a barking cur
And there's a sound of human voices

Q$^{\{u}$ooth Peter "is it come to this
Then kill or cure we must be brief
So he let fall a thundering smack
And heard a voice behind his back
From the old quarry cry "Thief! Thief!

As you'll suppose this ugly voice
His rage did not a little quell
But as he did not hear again
The voice which he had heard so plain
To work again he fell

346–350 Canceled in ink.
351–360 Canceled by pencil shadowing and with a large ink X.

44 47 44

Whether to chear his coward heart
Or that he felt a wicked chain
Twined round him like a magic spell
Upon my faith I cannot tell
But to the work he fell again

DOVE-COTTAGE-TRUST

Among the rocks and winding crags
Among the mountains far away
Once more the ass did lengthen out
Just like a sounding trumpets shout
The long dry see-saw of his horrible
bray

What is there now in Peter's heart
Or what's the power of that strange sound
The moon uneasy looked and dimmer
The broad blue heavens appeared to glimmer
And the rocks staggered all around

[26r]

44

44

Whether to chear his coward heart 506–510
Or that he felt a wicked chain
Twined round him like a magic spell
Upon my faith I cannot tell
But to the work he fell again

Among the rocks and winding crags 511–515
Among the mountains far away
Once more the ass did lengthen out
Just like a sounding trumpet's shout
The long dry see-saw of his horrible
bray

What is there now in Peter's heart 516–520
Or what's the power of that strange
sound
The moon uneasy looked and dimmer
The broad blue heavens appeared to glimmer
And the rocks staggered all around

The page number at the top is the only example among the surviving sheets of this manuscript.

371–372 On 25v, facing, are two lines of draft revision in William's hand:

d} t}
Now Peter had a dastar }heard}
And ~~such~~ [?&] with the power of that strange sound

49

From Peter's hand the sapling ~~fell~~ dropp'd
'With stutt'ring teeth and trembling
'Twas plain that he felt small temp=
=tation
To play again the ruffian's part
For by this time in Peter's heart
There was a wondrous alteration

~~His staff is in the grass and look~~
~~With fainting heart and trembling knees~~
~~And visage pale while both his hands~~
~~Hang down against his thighs he~~
~~stands~~
~~Beneath the moonlight trees~~

~~Shall Peter go or shall he stay~~
~~Or what is it that he must do~~
~~Whether from shame or tenderness~~
~~Or from his coward heart's distress~~
~~At length towards the ass he drew~~

[27r]

drops dropp'd
376 *From Peter's hand the sapling ~~fell~~* *521–525*
With chattering teeth and trembling
377 *'Twas plain that he felt small temp=*
=tation
378 *To play again the ruffian's part*
379 *For by this time in Peter's heart*
380 *There was a wondrous alteration*

381 *His staff is in the grass, and look*
382 *With fainting heart and trembling knees*
383 *And visage pale while both his hands*
384 *Hang loose against his thighs he*
stands
385 *Beneath the moonlight trees*

386 *Shall Peter go or shall he stay*
387 *Or what is it that he must do*
388 *Whether from shame or tenderness*
389 *Or from his coward heart's distress*
390 *At length towards the ass he drew*

376–377 Further revision appears on 26v, facing, in William's hand:
His sapling lay upon the ground
And Peter now felt small temptation
The entire stanza appears twice in MS. 2, canceled both times. The first time (on 18v) it stands as the first of four canceled stanzas; it is followed by the equivalent of ll. 401–405 of MS. 1, by a stanza the first two lines of which are inserted in MS. 1 on 28v, and by a stanza that does not now appear in MS. 1 but that may have been at the bottom of 28r. The second time (20r), where it follows the equivalent of ll. 371–375 of MS. 1, it seems to be marked "in."

381–390 Canceled by pencil shadowing.

50

1

The little ass still hung his head
Over the stream so clear & deep
Over the stream his head he kept
And like a human being wept
He wept as men and women weep

No doubt he was in piteous case
While on his side the ass was lying
From sorrow weakness or from pain
The tears flowed down his cheeks amain
You would have thought that he
was dying

[27v]

391 *The little ass still hung his head*
392 *Over the stream so clear & deep*
393 *Over the stream his head he kept*
394 *And like a human being wept*
395 *He wept as men and women weep*

396 *No doubt he was in piteous case*
397 *While on his side the ass was lying*
398 *From sorrow weakness or from pain*
399 *The tears flowed down his cheeks amain*
400 *You would have thought that he*
was dying

391–400 Canceled lightly in pencil. The ink X at the bottom of the page is blotted from the missing stanza on the facing recto.

395/396 There is a line of erased, and illegible, penciling here.

With trembling knees he stumps & now
And to the eye of Peter now
To Peter's eye was clearly shewn
What till this time he had not seen
That the poor ass was gaunt & lean
And almost wasted to the bone

You often meet a poor man's horse
Whose bones stare on you as you pass
Of such you will see many a one
But never such a skeleton
As this poor miserable ass

[28r]

With trembling knees he stood & now
401 *And to the eye of Peter now* *666–670*
402 *To Peter's eye was clearly shewn*
403 *What 'till this time he had not seen*
404 *That the poor ass was guant &*
lean
405 *And almost wasted to the bone*

406 *You often meet a poor man's horse*
407 *Whose bones stare on you as you pass*
408 *Of such you will see many a one*
409 *But never such a skeleton*
410 *As this poor miserable ass*

[411]
[412]
[413]
[414]
[415]

406–410 Canceled in pencil. The bottom third of the page, after the stanza it contained was canceled (the ink cancellation blotted over onto 27v), was torn off. The stanza may have been one entered on a verso (18v) in MS. 2 (see note to 27r, above):

He sees the ass's sad condition
I've played with you an ugly game
Quoth Peter to the ass but still
I did not mean to use you ill
You must allow you were to blame.

[28v]

He scans the ass from limb to limb
And Peter now uplifts his eyes

[?When]
[?at] last
And when he sees
And [?]
Poor peter is sore distress

So huge has been his wickedness.

The two lines at the top of the page may have been intended as variants of ll. 401–402, but on a canceled verso of MS. 2 (18v) they begin a stanza (MS. 2, ll. 541–545) which continues as follows:

Steady the moon doth look, & clear
And
~~Just~~ like themselves the rocks appear
And quiet are the skies

The inverted passage appears to be an early version of the following stanza from MS. 2 (ll. 871–875 of the early reading text; see ll. 756–760 of 1819):

At last he spies the withered leaf
And Peter's in a sore distress
Where there is not a bush or tree
The very leaves they follow me
So huge hath been my wickedness

The bottom (or the top, inverted) of the leaf has been torn off.

Following leaf 28 a leaf has been torn out in such a way as to leave a stub at the bottom only. This section reveals the initial letters of one stanza: "He / With / Pe / Bu / H." Two more stanzas could have stood at the top of the page. The indicated stanza cannot be identified by comparison of initial letters in other manuscripts; since it seems to have been canceled, it may not appear elsewhere. Because the pages are loose, the proper position of this stub in MS. 1 is uncertain; it is conjugate with leaf 30.

53.

Perhaps
~~You wonder he should loiter here~~
~~You wonder Peter here should tarry~~
~~But Peter by his fears is bound~~
~~To this small plot of meadow ground~~
~~He [illegible] the rocks and the old quarry~~

But
~~In spite of all his tenderness~~
~~[illegible]~~
~~Not long full surely would he linger~~
~~If he were safe full ten miles off~~
~~He'd leap and skip & dance & scoff~~
~~Though now he scarce dares stir a~~ finger

And down he sits beside the ass
Just under a tall alder root
"If any one should come and see
That I am here they'll think" quoth he
I'm helping this poor dying brute

[30r]

Perhaps
416 ~~*You wonder he should loiter here*~~
417 ~~*You wonder Peter here should tarry*~~
418 ~~*But Peter by his fears is bound*~~
419 ~~*To this small plot of meadow ground*~~
420 ~~*He dreads the rocks and the old quarry*~~

But
421 ~~*In spite of all his tenderness*~~
~~Tis peters fears that make him~~
422 ~~*Not long full surely would he linger*~~
{*es*
423 ~~*If he were safe full ten mi\{l off*~~
424 ~~*He'd leap and skip & dance & scoff*~~
425 ~~*Though now he scarce dares stir a*~~
finger

426 *And down he sits beside the ass*
427 *Just under a tall alder root*
428 *"If any one should come and see*
{*y'll*
429 *That I am here the\{l think" quoth he*
430 *I'm helping this poor dying brute*

The top stanza is canceled with pencil shadowings and in ink, the middle one in ink only.
426–430 This stanza corresponds to one added to MS. 2 at the top of 19v.

35

"'Tis plain" quoth he "as plain can be
That here has been some wicked dealing
No doubt the devil in me wrought
I'm not the man that could have thought
An ass like this was worth the stealing

But now while he
While ~~Peter~~ Bell is thus employed
The burthen of his soul relieving
Ten thousand ugly apprehensions
Of eyes and ears the black inventions
The soul of Peter are deceiving

And closer to the ass he draws
[illegible] his nut
As if into the ass he'd creep
The ass, no doubt in piteous case,
Just as before hangs down his face
Over the stream so clear & deep

[31^r]

"'Tis plain" quoth he "as plain can be
That here has been some wicked dealing
No doubt the devil in me wrought
I'm not the man that could have thought
An ass like this was worth the stealing

But now while he
While ~~Peter Bell~~ is thus employed
The burthen of his soul relieving
Ten thousand ugly apprehensions
Of eyes and ears the black inventions
The soul of Peter are deceiving

And closer to the ass he draws
~~behind~~ his neck
As if into ~~the~~ ass he'd creep
The ass, no doubt in piteous case,
Just as before hangs down his face
Over the stream so clear & deep

The proper position of this loose page is uncertain. It has recently been placed before leaf 30, but an earlier pencil pagination (which omitted stubs) put it between 20 and 21. Needle-hole patterns indicate that a position between 20 and 21 cannot be right; they make it equally probable that a location very near 30 is where the page belongs. Since ll. 431–435 follow ll. 426–430 on the same page in MS. 2 (19^v), it seems likely that this page in MS. 1, which begins with ll. 431–435, follows 30^r, which ends with ll. 426–430.

And Peter looks towards the stream
And there an ugly sight he ~~[illegible]~~ sees
An uncouth sight as [illegible] I trow

36

Blacksmith at his anvil
I see a weaver at his loom
I see a man that's threshing corn
A woman milking of a cow
A Wheelwright
A Blacksmith mending an old plough
A huntsman blowing loud his horn

I see a lady on a sofa
In muslin dress'd and netting lace
as you would swear
Breathing damnation in the air
And misery in the vacant space

[31v]

And Peter looks toward the stream
sees
And there an ugly sight he [—?—]
An uncouth sight it is, I trow

blacksmith at his anvil
Is it a weaver at his loom
Is it a man thats threshing corn
A woman milking of a cow
Wheelwright
A Blacksmith mending an old plough
A huntsman blowing loud his horn

{on
Is it a lady {in a sofa
In muslin dress'd and netting Case
as you would swear
Bawling damnation in the air
And misery in the vacant space

The three lines at the top of this page may belong to a stanza that appears in two versions in MS. 2 (the first is ll. 526–530 of the early reading text). The version closest to MS. 1 is on 20v:

While he upholds the ass's head
What sight is that which Peter sees
Some ugly sight it is I trow
Amid the deep clear stream below
Among the shadows of the trees

(see 1819, ll. 536–540).

The two stanzas at the bottom of the page appear in no other manuscript; they seem to be related to ll. 541–560 of 1819.

MS. 2 (1799)

MSS. 2 and 3, DC MSS. 33 and 34 (see descriptions in Introduction), are roughly contemporary fair copies dating from 1799–1800. MS. 2, however, is probably slightly earlier, and MS. 3 may in part derive from MS. 2. Therefore it seems appropriate to present here in its entirety MS. 2 and fill in the few gaps with leaves from MS. 3 (leaves 5^r–11^r, 14^v–15^r), so as to give an idea of the appearance of this manuscript. Lines are numbered sequentially in the left margins of the transcriptions in such a way as to show the intended final order; line numbers in parentheses indicate approximate duplicates, occasioned either by the overlapping of the two manuscripts or by alternate versions, usually written on versos. In the right margins in italics are the numbers of roughly equivalent lines in the early reading text. Because MS. 2 was much used for revision, it contains more lines than does any other version, including many tentative or canceled stanzas that are not incorporated in the reading text.

In the *apparatus criticus* the readings of MS. 2 are collated with those of MS. 3 and the next version, MS. 4 (see Introduction). All variants from the original numbered lines of MS. 2 are shown, and information concerning hands of transcription and revision is provided. By convention, italic type is used in the *apparatus* to distinguish editorial comment from citations from the text; however, line references given in italics are, of course, to the left-hand numbering in romans, not to the right-hand cross-references to the reading text, although these are printed in italics.

1

Peter Bell, a Tale

Prologue

There's something in a flying horse
There's something in a huge balloon
But through the clouds I'll never float
Untill I have a little boat
In shape just like the crescent moon.

And now I have a little boat
In shape just like the crescent moon
Fast through the clouds my boat can sail
But if perchance your faith should fail
Look up and you shall see me soon

[1r]

Broloque
Broad
Peter Bell, a Tale
Peter Bell
Peter Bell amen
Peter *Prologue* Peter Bell
Beter Bell amen

There's something in a flying horse *1–5*
There's something in a huge balloon
But through the clouds I'll never float
Untill I have a little boat
In shape just like a crescent moon

And now I have a little boat *6–10*
In shape just like the crescent moon.
oat
Fast through the clouds my b[?at]} can
sail
ce
But if perchan{g your faith should fail
Look up and you shall see me soon
Look up and

---

title Peter Bell—a Tale / Prologue *3. MS. 4 is the first to have a title page:* Peter Bell / a Tale / in Verse / by / William Wordsworth *at page foot is a note by DW:* Grasmere Sunday ½ past 5 o clock / by the Gold watch, now hanging above / the fire—a rainy coldish day—Snow / on the ground—but there is a thrush / singing February 21st 1802 *on the verso is a half-title:* Peter Bell / A Tale *on the facing recto the first stanzas of the poem are headed* Prologue

MS. 3 begins; MH's hand through l. 440

4 Until *4* Boat *3, 4*
5 In shape just] Whose shape is *4* *no period 3, 4*
6 Boat *4*
8 boat *3* Boat *4*
9 if perchance *3* if, perchance *4*
10 up, & *4*

The repetition of titles and the word "amen" are presumably doodles produced in trying out a new or resharpened pen. The three words at the bottom of the page are in pencil.

2
The woods. my friends are round you roaring
The woods are roaring like a sea
The noise of danger's in your ears
And you have all a thousand fears
Both for my little boat and me

Meanwhile I from the helm admire
The pointed horns of my canoe
And did not pity touch my breast
To see how you are all distress'd
Till my ribs ached I'd laugh at you

Away we go my boat and I
Were never man had such another
Whether among the winds we strive
Or deep into the heavens we dive
We're both contented with each other

[1v]

The woods, my friends are round you roaring 11–15
The woods are roaring like a sea
The noise of danger's in your ears
And you have all a thousand fears
Both for my little boat and me

Meanwhile I from the helm admire 16–20
The pointed horns of my canoe
And did not pity touch my breast
To see how you are all distress'd
Till my ribs ached I'd laugh at you

Away we go my boat and I 21–25
Sure never man had such another
Whether among the winds we strive
Or deep into the heavens we dive
We're both contented with each other

---

11 *no comma 3* Friends, *4*
15 Boat *3, 4*
17 Canoe *4*
20 ach'd *4* you— *4*
21 go, *4* Boat *4*
24 dive] drive *3*
25 both . . . each] each . . . the *4*

3

Away we go and what care we
For treasons tumults and for wars
We are as calm in our delight
As is the crescent moon so bright
Among the scattered stars

Up goes my boat between the stars
Through many a breathless field of light
Through many a long blue field of ether
Leaving ten thousand stars beneath her
Up goes my little boat so bright

The towns in Saturn are ill built
But Jove has very pretty bowers
The evening star is not amiss
But what are all of them to this
This little earth of ours

[2r]

Away we go and what care we 26–30
For treasons tumults, and for wars
We are as calm in our delight
As is the crescent moon so bright
Among the scattered stars

Up goes my boat between the stars 31–35
Through many a breathless field of light
Through many a long blue field of ether
Leaving ten thousand stars beneath her
Up goes my little boat so bright

The towns in Saturn are ill built 36–40
But Jove has very pretty bowers
The evening star is not amiss
But what are all of them to this
This little earth of ours

---

26 go, & *4*
27 *no comma 3* treasons, *4*
    as
28 as] [?so] *3*
30 scatter'd stars. *4*
31 Boat *4*
35 Boat *4*
35/36 *on facing verso, MS. 4, marked to go here, are pencil drafts in WW's hand:*
The honest folks in Charles's wain
Have a dull journey out [?Lyrawards]

God help the folks in Charles's Wain
these lines are followed by five mostly illegible pencil lines:
There's [?] & Charles's Wain
Da[?] war!
—They are a red-headed [?] in Mars
Cover'd from top to toe with scars
Such company I like it not·
over the pencil DW wrote fair copy in ink:
Those honest Folks in Charles's Wain
Jog forwards at a weary trot;
They are a red-headed race in Mars
Cover'd from top to toe with scars,
Such company I like it not.
36 Towns *4*
40 ours. *4*

4
Then back again to our green earth
What business had I here to roam
The world for my remarks & me
Will not a whit the better be
I've left my heart at home

there it is
And that is then the dear green earth
And that's the dear Pacific ocean
And that is Caucasus so dear
To think that I again am here
Oh! my poor hearts commotion!

And there is little Tartary
And there's the famous river Dnieper
And there amid the ocean green,
Of that sweet isle of isles the queen
Ye Fairies! from all evil keep her!

[2v]

o}
Then back again to }*ur green earth* *41–45*
What business had I here to roam
The world for my remarks & me
Will not a whit the better be
I've left my heart at home

there it is
And that is then the dear green earth *46–50*
And that's the dear Pacific ocean
And that is Caucasus so dear
To think that I again am here
Oh! my poor heart's commotion!

And there is little Tartary *51–55*
And there's the famous river Dnieper
And there, amid the ocean green,
Is that sweet isle of isles the queen
Ye Fairies! from all evil keep her!

---

41 our *3, 4* earth! *4*
43 &] and *3, 4*
46 that is then] there it is *4* earth! *4*
47 Ocean! *4*
48 dear! *4*
49 To *over* That *erased 3* here! *4*
50 *no exclamation points 4*
52 River *4*
53 there,] there *3* Ocean *4* green,] green *3, 4*
54 Isle . . . Isles . . . Queen *4*
55 her!] her *3, 4*

And there's the town where I was born 5

And that's the house of Parson Swan

My heart is touched I must avow

Consider where I've been; & now

I feel I am a man

Never did fifty things at once

Appear so lovely never never

The woods how sweetly do they ring

To hear the earth's sweet murmuring

Thus could I hang for ever.

A shame o you cruel any better

[illegible]

~~Oh shame upon you cruel~~ Shame

Was ever such a heartless loon

In such a lovely boat to sit

And make no better use of it

A boat that's like the crescent moon

[3^r]

56 *And there's the town where I was born* *56–60*
57 *And that's the house of Parson Swan*
58 *My heart is touched I must avow*
59 *Consider where I've been, & now*
60 *I feel I am a man*

61 *Never did fifty things at once* *61–65*
62 *Appear so lovely never never*
63 *The woods how sweetly do they ring*
64 *To hear the earth's sweet murmuring*
65 *Thus could I hang for ever.*

Shame on you cried my little
boat
Shame cried my [?magic ?boat ?at]
66 ~~*Oh shame upon you! cruel shame!*~~ *66–70*
67 *Was ever such a heartless loon*
68 *In such a lovely boat to sit*
69 *And make no better use of it*
70 *A boat that's like the crescent moon*

---

58 touch'd *4*
59 been, and *3* been and *4*
60 man. *4*
63 do] to *3* ring! *4*
65 *no period 3*
66 Shame on you! cried my little Boat *4*
68 Boat *4*
70 Boat *4* thats *3* moon. *4*
70/71 *two pages cut out of 4, no visible writing on stubs*

---

66 The first revised version and the deletion line are in pencil, now very faint; although the ink version written above presumably replaces it, the pencil version is not canceled.

O
Set out and like a brooding hen
Beside your sooty hearth-stone cower
Go creep along the dirt & pick
Your way with your good walking-stick
Just three good miles an hour

Sure in the breast of full-grown poet
So faint a heart was ne'er before
Come to the poets' wild delights
I have ten thousand lovely sights
Ten thousand sights in store

bark
I am a pretty little ~~barge~~
Then come I pray you, come with me
I want a comrade & for you
There's nothing which I would not do
There's nothing which you shall not see

[3^{v}]

Out, out and like a brooding hen 71–75
Besid your sooty hearth-stone cower
Go creep along the dirt, & pick
Your way with your good walking-stick
Just three good miles an hour

Sure in the breast of full-grown poet 76–80
So faint a heart was ne'er before
Come to the poets' wild delights
I have ten thousand lovely sights
Ten thousand sights in store

bark
I am a pretty little ~~barge~~ 81–85
Then come I pray you, come with me
I want a comrade & for you
There's nothing which I would not do
There's nothing which you shall not see

---

72 Beside *3, 4*
73 dirt and *3, 4*
74 walking stick *3*
76 full grown *3* Poet *4*
78 poets *3* Poets' *4*
81 Barge *4*
83 comrade and *3* comrade, and *4*
84 which] that *4*

---

81 The deletion and the revision are in pencil.

7

Come, & above the land of snow
We'll sport amid the boreal morning
Where thousand forms of light are riding
Among the stars, the stars now hiding
And now the stars adorning

I know a deep romantic land
A land that's deep & far away
And fair it is as evening skies
And in the farthest heart it lies
Of deepest Africa

Or we'll into the world of fairy
Among the lovely shades of things
The shadowy forms of mountains bare
And streams & bowers & ladies fair
The shades of palaces & kings

[4r]

86 *Come, & above the land of snow* *86–90*
87 *We'll sport amid the boreal morning*
88 *Where thousand forms of light are riding*
89 *Among the stars, the stars now hiding*
90 *And now the stars adorning*

91 *I know a deep romantic land* *91–95*
92 *A land that's deep & far away*
93 *And fair it is as evening skies*
94 *And in the farthest heart it lies*
95 *Of deepest Africa*

96 *Or we'll into the world of fairy* *96–100*
97 *Among the lovely shades of things*
98 *The shadowy forms of mountains bare*
99 *And streams & bowers & ladies fair*
100 *The shades of palaces & kings*

---

86 &] and *3, 4* Land *4*
88 {F / forms} *4*
90 adorning. *4*
92 &] and *3, 4*
95 Africa *3* Africa. *4*
96 Fairy *4*
99 and bowers & *3* and bowers and *4*
100 &] and *4*

8

Thy pretty little form of light
Thy sweet & beautiful canoe
Now though it grieves me to the heart
I feel, I feel that we must part
I must take leave of you

most delightful
You are a pretty little barge
But while your pleasure you're pursu-
=ing
Without impediment or let
My little Barge! you quite forget
What in the world is doing

Suppose now in the Land of Fairy
That we should play our sportive pranks
Above those shadowy streams & there
Should make discoveries rich & rare
The world would want us little thanks

[4ᵛ]

My pretty little form of light *101–105*
My sweet & beautiful canoe
Now though it grieves me to the heart
I feel, I feel that we must part
I must take leave of you

most [?delight]
You are a pretty little barge *106–110*
But while your pleasure you're pursu~~e~~
=ing
Without impediment or let
My little Barge! you quite forget
What in the world is doing

Suppose now in the land of Fairy *111–115*
That we should play our sportive pranks
Above those shadowy streams & there
Should make discoveries rich & rare
The world would count us little thanks

---

101 form] [?] *overwritten* form *then* Form *written above l. 4*
102 &] and *3, 4* bea‸[u]tiful {C canoe! *4*
104 feel,] feel *3*
105 you. *4*
106 You are a most delightful Barge *4*
107 pursuing *3, 4*
108 let, *4*
109 Barge!] barge *3*
110 What on the earth is doing. *4*
111–115 *omitted 4*

111–115 The cancellation is in pencil.

There was a time a time indeed 9
A time when poets lived in clover

There is a party in the Bower
Round the stone table in my garden
The Squire is there, &, as I guess
His pretty little daughter Bess
With Harry the church-warden

They were to come this very evening
They know not I have been so far
I see them there, in number nine
All in the bower of Weymouth pine
I see them, there they are

[5^{r}]

There was a time a time indeed 116–117
A time when poets lived in clover

There is a party in the Bower 121–125
Round the stone table in my garden
The Squire is there, &, as I guess
His pretty little daughter Bess
With Harry the church-warden

They were to come this very evening 126–130
They know not I have been so far
I see them there, in number nine
All in the bower of Weymouth pine
I see them, there they are

---

116 *second* a time *over* indeed *erased* *3* a time, a time *4*
117 Poets *3* liv'd *4*
118–120 *omitted 3*; *present in 4*:
——What boots it now to keep the key
Of Fairyland? for woe is me!
Those blessed days are over
121 {P / party} *4*
122 Garden *4*
123 there, &,] there & *3* there, & *4* guess, *4*
124–125 *no space before names 3, 4*
124 Daughter *4*
125 Harry, *4* church warden *3* Church-warden. *4*
128 there,] there *3, 4*
129 bower] tower *3* Bower *4*
130 them— *4* are. *4*

124–125 The spaces suggest that the names were entered into blanks left for them.

10 And there's the wife of Parson Swan
And there's my good friend Stephen Otter
And ere the light of evening fail
To them I must relate the tale
Of Peter Bell the Potter

Off flew my pretty little boat
All in a trance of indignation
And I, as well as I was able
On two poor legs to my stone table
Limped on with some vexation

"Oh here he is!" cried little Bess
She saw me at the garden door.
"O here he is" cried Mistress Swan
And all at once around me ran
Full nine of them or more.

[5v]

And there's the Wife of Parson Swan *131–135*
And there's my good friend Stephen Otter
And ere the light of evening fail
To them I must relate the tale
Of Peter Bell the Potter

Off flew my pretty little boat *136–140*
All in a trance of indignation
And I, as well as I was able
On two poor legs to my stone table
Limped on with some vexation

"Oh here he is!" cried little Bess *141–145*
She saw me at the garden door
"O here he is" cried Mistress Swan
And all at once around me ran
Full nine of them or more

---

131 wife *3*
132 Friend, *4*
133 'ere *3*
134 Tale *4*
136 boat] barge *3* Boat *4*
138 I,] I *3* able, *4*
140 Limp'd *4*
143 "Oh *4* is"] is"! *3*
145 more. *4*

"Sit down, I beg you would be seated" 11
Said I, no doubt with visage pale
And if my friends it pleases you
This instant without more ado
We'll have the promised tale

And so, though some what out of breath
With lips, no doubt & visage pale
And sore too from a slight contusion
Did I to cover my confusion
Begin the promised tale

[6r]

"Sit down, I beg you would be seated" *146–150*
Said I, no doubt with visage pale
And if my friends it pleases you
This instant without more ado
We'll have the promised tale

And so, though somewhat out of breath *151–155*
With lips, no doubt & visage pale
And sore too from a slight contusion
Did I to cover my confusion
Begin the promised tale

---

146 down,] down *3* down— *4* seated"] seated *4*
147 I,] I *4*
148 Friends, *4*
150 promis'd Tale *4*
151 so,] so *3*
152 &] and *4*
153 too, *4*
155 promis'd Tale. *4*
155/156 Peter Bell. *4*

The bottom half of this page was left blank, presumably so that the "Tale" could begin a new page, as it does in MSS. 3 and 4.

12

Tale of Peter Bell

All by the moonlight river side
It gave three miserable groans
Tis come then to a pretty pass
Said Peter to the groaning ass
But I will bang your bones

"My dearest Sir," cried Mistress Swan
You've got at once into the middle
And little Bess with accents sweeter
Cried "oh dear Sir"! but who is Peter

The Squire cried "Sure as Paradise
Was lost to us by Adam's sinning
We all are wandering in a wood
And therefore Sir, I wish you would
Begin at the beginning.

[6v]

Tale of Peter Bell
All by the moonlight river side *156–160*
It gave three miserable groans
'Tis come then to a pretty pass
Said Peter to the groaning ass
But I will bang your bones

"My dearest Sir" cried Mistress Swan *161–165*
You're got at once into the middle
And little Bess with accent{s sweeter
Cried "oh dear Sir! but who is Peter

The Squire cried "Sure as Paradise *166–170*
Was lost to us by Adam's sinning
We all are wandering in a wood
And therefore Sir, I wish you would
Begin at the beginning.

---

156 River *4*
157 It] He *4*
159 Ass *3, 4*
161 *no quotation marks 4*
163 accents *3, 4*
164 "oh dear] "Oh! dear *3* O dear *4* Peter? *4*
165 *omitted 3; present in 4*: Said Harry, "tis a downright riddle".
166 cried, Sure {a / is} {P / paradise} *4*
169 therefore Sir,] therefore Sir *3* therefore, Sir, *4*
170 *no period 3, 4*

Tale of Peter Bell

All by the moonlight river side
It gave three miserable groans
'Tis come then to a pretty pass
Said Peter to the groaning ass
But I will bang your bones

"My dearest Sir" cried Mistress Swan
You've got at once into the middle
And little Bess with accents sweeter
Cried "Oh! dear Sir! but who is Peter

The Squire cried "Sure as Paradise
Was lost to us by Adam's sinning
We all are wandering in a wood
And therefore Sir I wish you would
Begin at the beginning

A Potter Sir he was by trade
~~Cried~~ Said I becomming quite collected
And wheresoever he appeared
Full twenty times was Peter feared
For once that Peter was respected

[MS. 3: 5^r]

Tale of Peter Bell
All by the moonlight river side
It gave three miserable groans
'Tis come then to a pretty pass
Said Peter to the groaning ass
But I will bang your bones

"My dearest Sir" cried Mistress Swan
You're got at once into the middle
And little Bess with accents sweeter
Cried "Oh! dear Sir! but who is Peter

The Squire cried "Sure as Paradise
Was lost to us by Adam's sinning
We all are wandering in a wood
And therefore Sir I wish you would
Begin at the beginning

A Potter Sir he was by trade *171–175*
Said
~~*Cried*~~ ^ *I becomming quite collected*
And wheresoever he appeared
Full twenty times was Peter feared
For once that Peter was respected

---

171 Potter, Sir, *4*
172 Said I, becoming *4*
173 appear'd *4*
174 fear'd *4*

Here begins this Book
He two and thirty years or more
Had been a wild and woodland rover
Had been in farthest Pembrokeshire
And he had been at Exeter
In Kent, sir, and ~~at~~ Dover

And he had been at Nottingham
And well he knew the spire of Sarum
And he had been where Lincoln's bell
To Shepherds in the ~~distant~~ dell
Rings out his loud alarum

Doncaster, ~~at~~ at York, and Brough
~~At York and at the hill of Brough~~
And merry Carlisle had he been
And all along the lowlands fair
All through the bonny shire of Ayr
As far as Aberdeen

And he had been at Inverness
And Peter by the moonlight rills
Had danced his round with Highland lasses
And he had lain beside his asses
On lofty Cheviot hills

[MS. 3: 5ᵛ]

Here begins this Book
He two and thirty years or more *176–180*
Had been a wild and woodland rover
Had been in farthest Pembroke Sir
And he had been at Exeter
{at
In Kent, Sir, and {*in Dover*

And he had been at Nottingham *181–185*
And well he knew the spire of Sarum
And he had been where Lincoln's Bell
To Shepherds in the distant dell
Rings out his loud alarum

at
{*Y*
Doncaster, & {york, and Brough
~~*At York and at the hill of*~~*Brough* *186–190*
{*ad* {*e*
And merry Carlisle h{e h{as been
And all along the lowlands fair
All through the bonny shire of Ayr
As far as Aberdeen

And he had been at Inverness *191–195*
And Peter by the moonlight rills
Had danced his round with Highland lasses
And he had lain beside his asses
On lofty Cheviot hills

---

177 and] & *4*
178 Pembroke, *4*
180 *added in different ink 4, with* at Dover.
182 Spire *4*
183 Lincoln Bell *4*
185 alarum. *4*
186 At Doncaster at York and Brough *4*
187 had he *4*
188 Lowlands *4*
189 Shire *4*
190 As] And *4*
192 moonlight] mountain *4*
193 danc'd *4* Lasses *4*
195 Hills *4*

The instruction at the top of the page is probably a direction for the copying or revision of another manuscript; the "other book" (see MS. 3, 8ᵛ) was very likely MS. 2. Similar directions, generally limited to "in" or "out," appear periodically in MSS. 2 and 3.

And he had trudged through Yorkshire dales
Among the rocks and winding scars
Where deep and low the hamlets lie
Beneath their little patch of sky
And little lot of stars

And all along the winding coast
Bespattered by the salt sea foam
~~[illegible]~~
Where'er a knot of houses lay
On headland or in hollow bay
Sure never man like him did roam

As well might Peter in the Fleet
Have been fast bound a begging debtor
He travelled here he travelled there
But Peter never was a hair
In heart or head the better

He roved among the vales and streams
In the green wood & hollow dell
They were his dwellings night & day
But Nature ne'er could find the way
Into the heart of Peter Bell

[MS. 3: 6r]

And he had trudged through Yorkshire 196–200
dales
Among the rocks and winding scars
Where deep and low the hamlets lie
Beneath their little patch of sky
And little lot of stars

And all along the winding coast 201–205
Bespatter'd by the salt sea foam
~~*Where the sea dashed its whitening*~~ *foam*
Where'er a knot of houses lay
On headland or in hollow bay
Sure never man like him did roam

As well might Peter in the fleet 206–210
Have been fast bound a begging debtor
He travelled here he travelled there
But Peter never was a hair
In heart or head the better

He roved among the vales and streams 211–215
In the green wood & hollow dell
They were his dwellings night & day
But Nature ne'er could find the way
Into the heart of Peter Bell

---

196 trudg'd *4*
200 stars. *4*
202 *inserted in different ink:* bespatter'd by the salt sea foam, *4*
207 bound, *4*
208 travell'd . . . travell'd *4*
211 rov'd *4*
212 &] and *4*
215 Bell. *4*

In vain through every changeful year
Did Nature lead him as before
A primrose by a river's brim
A yellow primrose was to him
And it was nothing more

Small change it made in Peter's hea
To see his gentle panniered train
With more than vernal pleasure feedin
Where'er the tender grass was leading
Its earliest green along the lane

In vain through water earth & air
The soul of happy sound was spread
When Peter on some April morn
Beneath the broom or budding thorn
Made the warm earth his lazy bed

At noon when by the forest's edge
He lay beneath the branches high
The soft blue sky did never melt
Into his heart he never felt
The witchery of the soft blue sky

[MS. 3: 6v]

            through
In vain {*did every changeful year* 216–220
Did Nature lead him as before
A primrose by a river's brim
A Yellow primrose was to him
And it was nothing more

Small change it made in Peter's heart 221–225
To see his gentle panniered train
With more than vernal pleasure feeding
Where'er the tender grass was leading
Its earliest green along the lane

In vain through water earth & air 226–230
The soul of happy sound was spread
When Peter on some April morn
Beneath the broom or budding thorn
Made the warm earth his lazy bed

At noon when by the forest's edge 231–235
He lay beneath the branches high
The soft blue sky did never melt
Into his heart he never felt
The witchery of the soft blue sky

---

216 vain through *4*
216–217 *over two lines erased 4:*
From year to year from month to month
He walked with his load as before
on facing verso are 3 lines of WW's pencil, possibly variants of ll. 241–242:
But wherefore talk of this the soul
But what of that the very soul
Of Peter was in desperate case
219 yellow *4*
220 more. *4*
222 pannier'd *4*
226 water, *4* &] and *4*
230/231 *false start, erased, 4:* [?It st]

On a fair prospect some have looked
And felt as I have heard them say
As if the moving time had been
A thing as stedfast as the scene
On which they gazed themselves away

With Peter Bell I need not tell
That this had never been the case
He was a carl as wild and rude
As ever hue & cry pursued
As ever ran a felon's race

Of all that lead a lawless life
Of all that love their lawless lives
In city or in village small
He was the wildest far of all
He had a dozen wedded wives

"Oh monster!" cries the Parson's Lady
"Poor fellow!" echoes Stephen Otter
"Poor fellow! say you" Mistress Sal
I do assure you such a Man
Was Peter Bell the Potter

[MS. 3: 7r]

On a fair prospect some have looked 236–240
And felt as I have heard them say
As if the moving time had been
A thing as stedfast as the scene
On which they gazed themselves away

With Peter Bell I need not tell 241–245
That this had never been the case
He was a carl as wild and rude
As ever hue & cry pursued
As ever ran a felon's race

Of all that lead a lawless life 246–250
Of all that love their lawless lives
In city or in village small
He was the wildest far of all
He had a dozen wedded wives

"Oh monster!" cried the Parson's Lady 251–255
"Poor fellow!" echoed Stephen Otter
"Poor fellow! say you" "Mistress Swan
I do assure you such a Man
Was Peter Bell the Potter

---

236 looked] gaz'd *4*
240 gaz'd *4*
244 pursu'd *4*
250 wives. *4*
251 monster"! *4*
252 fellow"! echo'd *4*
253 you!" *4*
254 man *4*
255 Potter." *4*

~~He had a dozen wedded wives~~
~~But how one wife could e'er come near him~~
~~Upon my faith I cannot tell~~
~~For I can say of Peter Bell~~
~~To see him was to fear him~~

Though nature could not touch his heart
By lovely forms & silent weather
And tender sounds yet you could see
At once that Peter Bell & she
Had often been together

A savage wildness round him hung
As of a dweller out of doors
In his whole figure & his mien
A savage character was seen
Of mountains & of dreary moors

To all the unshaped half human thoughts
Which solitary nature feeds
Mid summer's storms or winter's ice
Had Peter joined whatever vice
The cruel city breeds.

[MS. 3: 7v]

He had a dozen wedded wives *256–260*
But how <u>one</u> wife could e'er come near
him
Upon my faith I cannot tell
For I can say of Peter Bell
To see him was to fear him

not
Though Nature ~~ne'er~~ could touch his *261–265*
^ heart
By lovely forms & silent weather
And tender sounds yet you could see
At once that Peter Bell & she
Had often been together

A savage wildness round him hung *266–270*
As of a dweller out of doors
In his Whole figuer & his mien
A savage character was seen
Of mountains & of dreary moors

To all the unshaped half human thoughts *271–275*
Which solitary Nature feeds
'Mid summer's storms or winter's ice
Had Peter joined whatever vice
The cruel city breeds

256–260 *omitted, 4*
261 Though Nature could not touch his heart *4*
262 &] and *4*
263 sounds, *4*
264 &] and *4*
268 whole figure and *4*
270 &] and *4*
271 unshap'd half-human *4*
273 Mid summer *4*
274 join'd *4*

His face was keen as is the wind
That cuts along the hawthorn fence
Of courage you saw little there
But in its stead a medley air
Of cunning & of impudence

He had a dark & sidelong walk
And long & slouching was his gait
Between his looks so bare & bold
You might perceive his spirit cold
Was playing with some inward bait

His forehead wrinkled was & furred
A work one half of which was done
By thinking of his whens & hows
And half by wrinkling of his brows
Beneath the glaring sun

There was a hardness in his cheek
There was a hardness in his eye
As if the man had fixed his face
In many a solitary place
Against the wind that sweeps
the sky

[MS. 3: 8r]

His face was keen as is the wind *276–280*
That cuts along the hawthorn fence
Of courage you saw little there
But in its stead a medley air
Of cunning & of impudence

He had a dark & sidelong walk *281–285*
And long & slouching was his gait
Between his looks so bare & bold
You might perceive his spirit cold
Was playing with some inward bait

His forehead wrinkled was & furred *286–290*
A work one half of which was done
By thinking of his whens & hows
And half by wrinkling of his brows
Beneath the glaring sun

There was a hardness in his cheek *291–295*
There was a hardness in his eye
As if the man had fixed his face
In many a solitary place
Against the wind that sweeps
the sky

---

280 &] and *4* impudence. *4*
281–285 *inserted on facing verso, 4, and marked to go here; a blank leaf has been bound between this verso and the recto containing ll. 286–*
281 &] and *4* walk, *4*
282 &] and *4* gait; *4*
283 &] and *4*
285 bait. *4*
286 wrinkl'd and furr'd *4*
290 sun. *4*
293 fix'd *4*
295 Against the wind and open sky. *4*

One night & now my little Bess
We have reached at last to
~~I'm coming to~~ the promised tale
One beautiful November night
When the full moon was shining bright
Upon the rapid river Swale
It chanced that by
~~Close by~~ the river's ~~winding~~ banks
~~[illegible]~~ Peter was travelling all alone
Whether to buy or sell, or led
By pleasure running in his head
To me was never known
Back to other Book
Along the turf & through the fern
And in the mire he travelled on
If he had left that night or day
His wife or wives I cannot say
But wife or comrade he had none

Some chuse to travel with a dog
And Peter had a savage elf
A lurcher & he loved him well
But sure it is that Peter Bell
That evening travelled by himself

[MS. 3: 8v]

One night, & now my little Bess 296–300
We have reachd at last the
~~I'm coming to~~ the promised tale
One beautiful November night
When the full moon was shining bright
Upon the rapid river Swale

It chanced that by
~~Close by~~ the river's ~~winding~~ banks 301–305
was
~~Was~~ Peter ^ travelling all alone
Whether to buy or sell, or led
By pleasure running in his head
To me was never known

Back to other Book
Along the turf & through the fern 306–310
And in the mire he travelled on
If he had left that night or day
His wife or wives I cannot say
But wife or comrade he had none

Some chuse to travel with a dog 311–315
And Peter had a savage elf
A lurcher & he loved him well
But sure it is that Peter Bell
That evening travelled by himself

295/296 *MS. 4 adds l. 296 (with* &] and *and* Bess,*) erased, followed by a deleted stanza:*
Let's wait here, there's Mr. Swan
Has [?leaped] across the fields before ye
He's [?wheeling] this way like a bee
——We'll wait for him & take our tea
And then we'll have the Story
on fresh recto MS. 4 adds title: Tale of Peter Bell / First Part
296 and now, *4* Bess, *4*
297 We've reach'd at last the promis'd Tale, *4*
300 River Swale. *4*
301 Beside the River's winding banks *del to* It chanc'd that by the River's Banks *4 (revised line possibly first entered in pencil)*
302 Was Peter *del to* Peter was *4*
306–315 *omitted, 4*

He trudged along through copse & brake
He trudged along oer hill and dale
Nor for the moon cared he a tittle
And for the stars he cared as little
And for the murmuring river Swale

DOVE COTTAGE TRUST

Quoth Peter "here's a nearer cut
'Twill save a mile at least a day
He took the path, the path did lead
Across a smooth and grassy mead
And a tall wood before him lay

And now he to a wood is come
And Peter there in whole cart loads
Is heaping curses on them all
Commissioners both great & small
Who made the zig-zag roads

For while he drives among the boughs
With head & hands & cheeks that burn
With downright fury & with wrath
There's little sign that Peter's path
Will to the road return

[MS. 3: 9ʳ]

316 *He trudged along through copse & brake* *316–320*
317 *He trudged along o'er hill and dale*
318 *Nor for the moon cared he a tittle*
319 *And for the stars he cared as little*
320 *And for the murmuring river Swale*

321 *Quoth Peter "heres a nearer cut* *321–325*
322 *'Twill save a mile as sure as day*
323 *He took the path, the path did lead*
324 *Across a smooth and grassy mead*
325 *And a tall wood before him lay*

326 *And now he to a wood is come* *326–330*
327 *And Peter there in whole cart loads*
328 *Is heaping curses on them all*
329 *Commissioners both great & small*
330 *Who made the zig-zag roads*

331 *For while he drives among the boughs* *331–335*
332 *With head & hands & cheeks that burn*
333 *With downright fury & with wrath*
n}
334 *There's little sigh*} *that Peter's path*
335 *Will to the road return*

---

316 trudg'd *4*
317 trudg'd *4*
318 car'd *4*
319 he cared] cared he *4*
320 River Swale. *4*
321 Peter, here's *4*
322 mile, *4*
324 smooth and grassy] green and open *4*
325 lay. *4*
326–330 And Peter to the wood is come
And there he is, in whole cart-loads
Upheaping curses on them all
Commissioners both great and small
Who made those elbows in the roads. *4*
332 & hands] and hands— *4*
334 sign *4*
335 return. *4*

The path grows dim & dimmer still
Now up now down his way he wends
With all the sail that he can carry
Till he is brought to an old quarry
And there the path-way ends

"What back again old grime face no
I'll grapple with the devil first
Stretch like a yawning wolf your paws
But dam'me if by any laws
Of yours I'll ever be coerced

And so where on the huge rough stones
The black & massy shadows lay
And through the dark & through the cold
And through the yawning fissures old
Did Peter boldly press his way

And in a moment opened out
A scene of soft and lovely hue
Where blue & grey & tender green
Together made as sweet a scene
As ever human eye did view

[MS. 3: 9v]

The path grows dim & dimmer still *336–340*
Now up now down his way he wends
With all the sail that he can carry
Till he is brought to an old quarry
And there the path-way ends

"What back again old grim-face—No *341–345*
I'll grapple with the devil first
Stretch like a yawning wolf your paws
But dam'me if by any laws
Of yours I'll ever be coerce'd

And so where on the huge rough stones *346–350*
The black & massy shadows lay
And through the dark & through the cold
And through the yawning fissures old
Did Peter boldly press his way

And in a moment opened out *351–355*
A scene of soft and lovely hue
Where blue & grey & tender green
Together made as sweet a scene
As ever human eye did view

---

337 up, *4*
340 pathway *4*
341–345 What back again, old Grimface? No
Back think you when I've come so far
You stretch a pair of gloomy jaws
But I'm your man, nor care two straws
For lantern or for star *4*
346 so, *4*
347 &] and *4*
351 *MS. 4 read as 3, then del to* Right through the quarry— and behold *in pencil (WW), overwritten in ink (DW) with* &] and *and* behold!
353 & grey] and grey, *4*

Beneath the clear blue sky you see
A little plot of meadow ground
But oh! far rather name it not
Call it of earth a small green plot
With rocks encompass'd round

The Swale flowed under the grey rocks
But he flowed quiet & unseen
You need a strong & stormy gale
To bring the noises of the Swale
To that green spot so calm & green

Now you'll suppose that Peter Bell
Had some temptation here to tarry
And so it was but I must add
His heart was not a little glad
That he was out of the old quarry

And is there no one dwelling here
No hermit with his beads & glass
And does no little cottage look
Upon this green & silent nook
Does no one live near this green grass

[MS. 3: 10r]

Beneath the clear blue sky you saw 356–360
A little plot of meadow ground
But oh! far rather name it not
Call it of earth a small green plot
With rocks encompass'd round

The } *Swale* }
And } [?] } *flowed under the green* 361–365
rocks
But he flowed quiet & unseen
You need a strong & stormy gale
To bring the noises of the Swale
To that green spot so calm & green

Now you'll suppose that Peter Bell 366–370
Had some temptation here to tarry
And so it was but I must add
His heart was not a little glad
That he was out of the old quarry

And is there no one dwelling here 371–375
No hermit with his beads & glass
And does no little cottage look
Upon this green & silent nook
Does no one live near this green grass

---

357 meadow-ground *4*
361 The Swale flow'd under the grey rocks *4*
362 flow'd *4* &] and *4*
363 &] and *4*
365 &] and *4*
367 Had some] Felt small *4*
368 was, *4*
371–375 *squeezed in at page foot in different ink, 4*
371 here, *4*
372 and glass? *4*
374 &] and *4* nook? *4*
375 grass? *4*

Across that deep & quiet spot
Is Peter driving through the grass
And now he is among the trees
And turning round his head he sees
The solitary ass

"No doubt I'm foundered in these wood
For once" quoth he "I will be wise
Upon my faith I'll back again
And not to make my journey vain
I'll take the ass likewise

So off he goes as you'll suppose
With thoughts as blithe as any dream
To where the ass beside the bed
Of that green meadow hung his head
Over the silent stream

"A pretty beast! though will allow
Not quite so fat as he might be
Upon my soul with such a platter
You should have been a little fatter
But come Sir come with me"

[MS. 3: 10ᵛ]

376 *Across that deep & quiet spot* *376–380*
377 *Is Peter driving through the grass*
378 *And now he is among the trees*
379 *And turning round his head he sees*
380 *The solitary ass*

381 *"No doubt I'm foundered in these woods* *381–385*
382 *For once" quoth he "I will be wise*
383 *Upon my faith I'll back again*
384 *And not to make my journey vain*
385 *I'll take the ass likewise*

386 *So off he goes as you'll suppose* *386–390*
387 *With thoughts as blithe as any dream*
388 *To where the ass beside the bed*
g}
389 *Of that d}reen meadow hung his head*
390 *Over the silent stream*

391 *"A pretty beast! though we'll allow* *391–395*
392 *Not quite so fat as he might be*
393 *Upon my soul with such a platter*
394 *You should have been a little fatter*
395 *But come Sir come with me"*

{at
376 th{e deep and *4*
379 And] When *4*
380 A solitary Ass. *4*
381 "No] No *4* founder'd *4*
382 For once, quoth he, I . . . *4*
383 faith, *4*
385 Ass *4*

—}
386–389 Off Peter hied, } and at his side
Behold beneath the bright moon-beam
The Ass is standing on the bed
Of that green meadow with his head *4*
391 beast!] beast *4*
393 Upon my soul *del to* My honest Friend, *4*
395 Sir, *4* me." *4*

But first friend Peter deems it fit
To spy about him far & near
There's not a single house in sight
No woodman's hut no cottage light
Peter you need not fear

There's nothing to be seen but woods
And rocks that spread a hoary gleam
And this poor ass which near the bed
Of the green meadow hangs his head
Over the silent stream

Close to the river's brink he stands
His head is with a halter bound
Now Peter's purpose did not alter
And so at once he seized the halter
And would have turned him round

He pulled, the creature did not move
Upon his back then Peter leapt
And with his staff & heels he plied
The little ass on either side
But still the ass his station kept

[MS. 3: 11r]

396 *But first friend Peter deems it fit* 396–400
397 *To spy about him far & near*
398 *There's not a single house in sight*
399 *No woodman's hut no cottage light*
400 *Peter you need not fear*

(401) *There's nothing to be seen but woods*
(402) *And rocks that spread a hoary gleam*
(403) *And this poor ass which near the bed*
(404) *Of the green meadow hangs his head*
(405) *Over the silent stream*

(406) *Close to the river's brink he stand* [ ]
(407) *His head is with a halter bound*
(408) *Now Peter's purpose did not alter*
(409) *And so at once he seized the halter*
(410) *And would have turned him round*

(411) *He pulled, the creature did not move*
(412) *Upon his back then Peter leapt*
(413) *And with his staff & heels he plied*
(414) *The little ass on either side*
(415) *But still the ass his station kept*

---

396 first, *4* Friend *del to* doth *4* deems *del to* deem *4*
397 &] and *4*
399 hut, *4*

13v

There's nothing to be seen but woods
And rocks that spread a hoary gleam
And this poor ass which near the bed
Of the green meadow hangs his head
Over the silent stream

Close to the river's brink he stands
His head is with a halter bound
Now Peter's purpose did not alter
And so at once he seized the halter
And would have turned him round

He pulled the creature did not move
Upon his back then Peter leapt
And with his staff and heels he plied
The little ass on either side
But still the ass his station kept

[15r]

There's nothing to be seen but woods *401–405*
And rocks that spread a hoary gleam
And this poor ass which near the bed
Of the green meadow hangs his head
Over the silent stream

{ *ands*
Close to the river's brink he st{[*?ood*] *406–410*
{ *is*
His head {[*?was*] *with a halter bound*
Now Peter's purpose did not alter
And so at once he seized the halter
And would have turned him round

He pulled the creature did not move *411–415*
Upon his back then Peter leapt
And with his staff and heels he plied
The little ass on either side
But still the ass his station kept

---

401 *MS. 2 resumes*
401–405 *omitted, 4*
406 stand[] *3* Close to the River stands the Ass *4*
407 is *3, 4*
409 seiz'd *4*
410 turn'd him round. *4*
411 pulled, *3* pull'd— *4*
413 staff and] staff & *3* Staff and *4*
414 Ass *4*
415 Ass his Station kept. *4*

14

Quoth Peter you're a beast of mettle
I see you'll suit me to an ace
And now the ass through his left eye
On Peter turned most quietly
Looked quietly in his face

"What's this?" cries Peter brandishing
A new peeled sapling white as cream
The ass knew well what Peter said
But as before hung down his head
Over the silent stream

[15v]

Quoth Peter you're *a beast of mettle* *416–420*
I see you'll suit me to an ace
And now the ass through his left eye
On Peter turned most quietly
Looked quietly in his face

{" ?"}
{ *What's this* } *cries Peter, brandishing* *421–425*
{*A*
{*a new peeled sapling white as cream*
k}
The ass }*new well what Peter said*
But as before hung down his head
Over the silent stream

~~*would that my Wife Kate*~~ *426–430*
~~*Were here my pretty rough-haired boy*~~
~~*She would have at you with a rattle*~~
~~*And we should have a royal battle*~~
~~*We'd make you dance for joy*~~

---

416 Peter, *4*
417 suit me to] suit to *4*
418 Ass *4*
419 turn'd *4*
420 Look'd . . . face. *4*
421 "What's this?" cries *3* What's this, cried *4* Peter,] Peter *3*
422 A *3, 4* new-peel'd Sapling *4* cream? *4*
423 Ass *4* knew *3, 4*
424 But, as before, *4*
426–430 *omitted 3, 4*

426–430 The wavy deletion lines seem to have been early, certainly before MS. 3 was transcribed; this stanza appears in no other manuscript.

Then Peter gave another jirk 15
A jirk that from a dungeon floor
Would have pulled up an iron ring
But still the heavy headed thing
Stood just as he had stood before

Quoth Peter, leaping from the ass,
There is some plot against me laid
~~[illegible]~~ Once more the little meadow-ground
And all the hoary cliffs around
He cautiously surveyed

There's nothing, Peter far or near
There's nothing with your purpose jars
Only the full moon's in the sky
And with her a fair company
The fairest of the stars

[16^r]

Then Peter gave anothe jirk *431–435*
A jirk that from a dungeon-floor
Would have pulled up an iron ring
But still the heavy headed thing
Stood just as he had stood before

Quoth Peter, leaping from the ass, *436–440*
There is some plot against me laid
Once more
~~At [?this more]~~ the little meadow-ground
And all the hoary cliffs around
He cautiously surveyed

There's nothing, Peter far or near *441–445*
There's nothing with your purpose jars
Only the full moon's in the sky
And with her a fair company
The fairest of the stars

---

431 another *3, 4*
432 dungeon floor *3, 4*
433 pull'd *4*
434 heavy-headed *4*
435 he] it *4* before. *4*
436 *no commas 3* Ass, *4*
438 Once more the *3, 4* meadow ground *3*
440 survey'd *4*
440/441 *page cut from MS. 3 at this point, with writing visible but not legible on the stub; ll. 441–450 in MS. 3 are in WW's hand*
441–445 *omitted 4*
441 There's nothing,] Theres nothing *3*
442 Theres *3*

16
All all is silent rocks & woods
All all is silent far & near
Only the ass with motion dull
Upon the pivot of his skull
Turns round his long left ear

~~Quoth he~~ Thought
Peter what can mean all this
~~In faith~~ There is some ugly witchcraft here
Once more the ass with motion dull
Upon the pivot of his skull
Turned round his long left ear
*

Cried Peter you'll be wise I hope
Before we're both five minutes older
Upon the ass the sapling rings
Each blow the arm of Peter stings
Up to the elbow and the shoulder

[16v]

446 *All all is silent, rocks & woods* *446–450*
447 *All all is silent far & near*
448 *Only the ass with motion dull*
449 *Upon the pivot of his skull*
450 *Turns round his long left ear*

Thought
Thought
451 ~~*Quoth*~~ *Peter what can mean all this* *451–455*
{T ugly
452 ~~*In faith*~~ {*there is some* ^ *witchcraft here*
453 *Once more the ass with motion dull*
454 *Upon the pivot of his skull*
455 *Turned round his long left ear*
*

466 *Cried Peter you'll be wise I hope* *466–470*
467 *Before we're both five minutes older*
468 *Upon the ass the sapling rings*
469 *Each blow the arm of Peter stings*
470 *Up to the elbow and the shoulder*

---

446 All, *4* silent,] silent *3* &] and *3*, *4*
447 &] and *3*, *4*
448 Ass *4*
450 ear. *4*
451 *in MS. 3 MH's hand resumes and runs through l. 515*
451 Thought *3*, *4* Peter, *4* this? *4*
452 There is some ugly witchcraft here *3*, *4*
453 Ass *3*, *4*
455 Turn'd *4* ear. *4*
466 Peter, *4*
468 Ass *3*, *4*
470 and] & *3*

455/466 The asterisk indicates that two fair-copy stanzas inserted on 17v (ll. 456–465) were intended to go here.

At last poor patient thing at last 17

His sides they heaved, his belly stirred

He gave a groan & then another

Of that which went before the brother

And then he gave a third

All by the moonlight river side

He gave three miserable groans

Tis come then to a pretty pass

Said Peter to the groaning ass

But I will bang your bones

And now the little harmless beast

Gently as if to take his ease

The ass whom Peter thus had bruised

Whom he so cruelly had used

Dropped gently down upon his knees

[17r]

471 *At last poor patient thing at last* 471–475
472 *His sides they heaved, his belly stirr'd*
473 *He gave a groan & then another*
474 *Of that which went before the brother*
475 *And then he gave a third*

476 *All by the moonlight river Side* 476–480
477 *He gave three miserable groans*
478 *T'is come then to a pretty pass*
479 *Said Peter to the groaning ass*
480 *But I will bang your bones*

481 *And now the little harmless beast* 481–485
482 *Gently as if to take his ease*
483 *The ass whom Peter thus had bruised*
484 *Whom he so cruelly had used*
485 *Dropped gently down upon his knees*

---

471 At last, *4* thing! *4*
472 they heaved,] they heav'd, *del to* did heave *4* (WW) stirr'd *4, del and rewritten*
474 before, *4*
476 river side *3* River-side *4*
478 'Tis *3, 4* come, then, *4*
479 Ass *3, 4*
480 bones. *4*
481 now, *4* {harmless / gentle *3*} Beast *4*
482 Gently, *4*
483 Ass *3, 4* bruis'd *4; then entire line del to* In quiet uncomplaining mood
484 us'd *4; then entire line del to* Upon the spot where he had stood
485 Dropp'd *4*

And then upon his sides he fell

18

And now to Peters eye was shown
What till this time he had not seen
That the poor ass was gaunt & lean
And almost wasted to the bone

An ass so lean was never seen
By road or shed or out door penthouse
If you should seek in wood or lane
An ass so lean tis only seen you see
Of the sight it would seem portentous

* quoth Peter by the devils beard
I'll root you up you mongrel hound

And both his arms did Peter pass
Beneath the belly of the ass
With both his arms he clasp'd him round

Now for it now you sturdy rogue
And desperately fierce Peter heaves
He might as well have tried to stir
The abbey huge of Westminster
Or two or five hundred head
Of the meagre beasts as dead

No word of kind commiseration
Fell at the sight from Peters tongue
With hard contempt his heart was wrung
With hatred and with vexation

[17^{v}]

(491) And then upon his side he fell
[~~?He lay ? ? ? ?~~]
(492) And now to Peters eye was s hown
(493) What till this time he had not seen
(494) That the poor ass was guant & lean
(495) And almost wasted to the bone

496 An ass so lean was never seen
497 By road or shed or out-door penthouse
498 If you should meet in wood or lane
499 An ass so lean twould give you pain
500 The sight would almost seem portentous

456 *Quoth Peter by the devils beard *456–460*
root you up
457 I'll ~~make you stir~~ you mongrel hound
458 And both his arms did Peter pass
459 Beneath the belly of the ass
460 With both his arms he clasp'd him
round

(491–495) *in base text 3, 4; for variants see 31^{r}, ll. 491–495*
496–500 *omitted 3, 4*
456–460 *omitted 4; follows ll. 451–455 in base text 3, DW's hand*
456 devil's *3*
457 I'll root you up *3*
458 did Peter pass] did pass *3*
459 Ass *3*
460 clasped *3*

Although to this point DW's practice was to use both rectos and versos for her running transcription, she moved here to rectos only, probably because WW had moved ahead and made an insertion here to go on 16^{v}, and it becomes increasingly difficult to ascertain the intended order of inserted stanzas. Leaf 17^{v} contains insertions by WW written at various times and with various intentions. The first stanza, ll. (491–495), apparently is intended to follow or replace the first stanza on 18^{r} (there is, however, a version of this stanza in the middle of 18^{v}, and another—the earliest—at the top of 31^{r}). The next stanza, ll. 496–500, also appears on 30^{v}, where it is likewise canceled. The two fair-copy stanzas are marked by an asterisk for insertion on 16^{v}; they are accordingly numbered as part of the base text.

(492) Underneath the erasure was probably "To Peter's eye was clearly s"; the two capital letters are still visible.

And then upon his sides he fell
5:
And now to Peter's eye was shown 18
What till this time he had not seen
That the poor ass was gaunt & lean
And almost wasted to the bone

An ass so lean was never seen
By road or [illegible] or out door pent house
If you should meet in wood or lane
An ass so lean [illegible] you pain
Of the sight would [illegible] portentous
* Quoth Peter by the devil's beard
root you up
I'll ~~make you~~ [illegible] you mongrel hound
And both his arms did Peter pass
Beneath the belly of the ass
With both his arms he clasp'd him
round

Now for it now you sturdy rogue
And desperately fierce Peter heaves
He might as well have tried to stir
The abbey huge of Westminster
Or twice five hundred head
in
The meagre beast lies still as death
No word of kind commiseration
Fell at the sight from Peter's tongue
With hard contempt his heart was wrung
With hatred and with vexation

[17v continued]

461 Now for it now you sturdy rogue *461–465*
462 And desperately friend Peter heaves
463 He might as well have tried to
stir
464 The abbey huge of Westminster
465 Or twice five hundred head
[?of beeves]

in
beast
501 The meagre ~~ass~~ lay still as death
502 No word of kind commiseration
l} in
503 Felt} at the sight from Peters tongue
504 With hard contempt his heart was wrung
505 With hatred and with new vexation.

461–465 *omitted 3, 4*
501–505 *in base text 3, 4, following l. (495)*
501 The meagre beast lay still as death *3, 4*
503 Fell *3, 4* sight, *3* Peter's *3, 4*
504 rung *rev to* wrung *4*
505 and with new vexation.] & with new vexation *3* and vexation. *4*

---

501 The last phrase was written over the erased "[?of beeves]" in the line above.

ant-

And then upon his side he fell 19
His countenanse it shewed no fear
He lay upon the meadow-bed
And as before hung down his head
Over the stream so deep & clear

The meagre beast lay still as death

~~For victory merriment~~ is flown
And the legs lift with ~~~~
His lips with rage & fury & quiver
Quoth he "you little mulish dog
Quoth he "I'll fling you like a log
Headforemost down the river

By God I will" When this was said
As stretched upon his side he lay
To all the echoes south & north
And east and west the ass sent forth
A loud & horrible bray

[18r]

out —
486 *And then upon his side he fell* *486–490*
487 *His countenance it shewed no fear*
488 *He lay upon the meadow-bed*
489 *And as before hung down his head*
490 *Over the stream so deep & clear*

The meagre beast lay still as death
506 ~~For Peters merriment is flown~~ *491–495*
And Peters lips with [?fury]
507 *His lips with rage & fury & quiver*
508 *Quothe he "you little mulish dog*
509 *Quoth he "I'll fling you like a log*
510 *Headforemost down the river*

" W
511 *By God I will* *when this was said* *496–500*
stre
512 *As [?he]tched upon his side he lay*
513 *To all the echoes south & north*
514 *And east and west the ass sent forth*
515 *A loud & horrible bray*

486–490 *omitted 3, 4, although 486 is identical with (491) on 17v*
506–507 For Peters merriment is flown
His lips with rage & fury quiver *3*

The meagre Beast lay still as death
And Peter's lips with fury quiver *4*
508 Quoth he "you *3* Quoth he, you *4* dog *over* [?beast] *erased 3*
509 he "I'll] he, Ill *4*
R
510 Head foremost *3* Head-foremost *4* river *4*
511–512 *squeezed in at bottom of page, MS. 4, in a different ink; text runs on in same ink to facing verso, where ll. 513–540, 551–555, and 541–545 are entered*
511 will. When this was said *3* will," the word scarce said *4*
512 stretched *over illeg eras 3* stretch'd *4*
S
513 north & south *rev to* south & north *3* south and North, *4*
W
514 east & west *3* East and west, *4* Ass *3, 4*
515 &] and *4* bray. *4*

---

506 The line appears to have been left blank for WW to fill in.

20

From Peter's hand the sapling dropp'd
'Twas plain that he felt small temp-
tation
To play again the ruffian's part
For by this time in Peter's heart
There was a wondrous alteration

And to the eye of Peter now
To Peter's eye was clearly shewn
What till this time he had not seen
That the poor ass was gaunt & lean
And almost wasted to the bone

He scans the ass from limb to limb
And Peter now uplifts his eyes
Steady the moon doth look, & clear
~~Just~~ now like themselves the rocks appear
And quiet are the skies
Stop. Here,
He sees the ass's sad condition
I've played with you an ugly game
Quoth Peter to the ass but still
I did not mean to use you ill
You must allow you were to blame

[18v]

(536) *From Peter's hand the sapling dropp'd*
(537) *T'was plain that he felt small temp=*
=tation
(538) *To play again the ruffian's part*
(539) *For by this time in Peter's heart*
(540) *There was a wondrous alteration*

(491–492) *And to the eye of Peter now*
(492) *To Peter's eye was clearly shewn*
(493) *What till this time he had not seen*
(494) *That the poor ass was guant & lean*
(495) *And almost wasted to the bone*

541 *He scans the ass from limb to limb* *671*
542 *And Peter now uplifts his eyes*
543 *Steady the moon doth look, & clear*
And
544 ~~*Just*~~ *like themselves the rocks appear*
545 *And quiet are the skies*
stop here

(546) *He sees the ass's sad condition*
(547) *I've played with you an ugly game*
(548) *Quoth Peter to the ass but still*
(549) *I did not mean to use you ill*
(550) *You must allow you were to blame*

541–545 *omitted 3; follows ll. 551–555 in 4*
541 Ass *4*
543 Steady] Stead *4* &] and *4*
544 And like *4* rocks] stars *over illeg erasure 4*
545 skies. *4*
(546–550) *appear in Part II, MSS. 3 and 4, following l. 725; for variants see 31r*

Particularly since 18v and 19v are entirely canceled and their stanzas do not appear in sequence in MS. 3, the proper order of the stanzas on 18v–20r is uncertain. A stanza on 20r, ll. 536–540, appears also at the top of 18v, and the sequence seems to be, curiously, 19r, top of 20r, 18v—except for a stanza, ll. (491–495), which also appears on 17v—19v, and the bottom of 20r. The italic line numbering generally shows where the stanzas earlier stood.

This outcry on the heart of Peter 21
Seems like a note of joy to strike
Joy on the heart of Peter knocks
But in the echo of the rocks
Was something Peter did not like

Whether to cheer his coward heart
Or ~~that~~ he felt a wicked chain
Twined round him like a magic spell
Upon my faith I cannot tell
But to the work he fell again

Among the rocks & winding crags
Among the mountains far away
Once more the ass did lengthen out
~~Just~~ [even] like a sounding trumpets' shout
The long dry see-saw of his horrible
bray

[19r]

This outcry on the heart of Peter *501–505*
Seems like a note of joy to strike
Joy on the heart of Peter knocks
But in the echo of the rocks
Was something Peter did not like

Whether to chear his coward heart *506–510*
Or that he felt a wicked chain
Twined round him like a magic spell
Is more in truth than
Upon my faith I cannot tell
But to the work he fell again

Among the rocks & winding crags *511–515*
Among the mountains far away
Once more the ass did lengthen out
even
~~Just~~ like a sounding trumpet's shout
The long dry see-saw of his horrible
bray

---

516 *in MS. 3 DW's hand commences and runs through l. 745*
517 strike, *4*
518 Heart *3* knocks; *4*
519 Rocks *3*
520 some thing *3*
521 chear] cheer *3*
523 Twin'd *3, 4*
524 In honest truth I cannot tell *4*
525 again. *4*
526 &] and *4* crags, *4*
527 away, *4*
528 Ass *3, 4*
529 Just like . . . Shout *3* More ruefully an endless shout, *4*
530 bray. *4*

22

And down he sits beside the ass
Just under a tall alder root
If any one should come & see
~~If any one should come & see~~
That I am here they'll think quoth he
I'm helping this poor dying brute

'Tis plain quoth he as plain can be
That here has been some wicked deal-
ing
No doubt the devil in me wrought
I'm not the man who could have thought
An ass like this was worth the stealing

But now while he is thus employed
The burthen of his soul relieving
Ten thousand ugly apprehensions
Of eyes & ears the black inventions
The soul of Peter are deceiving

And closer to the ass he draws
As if into the ass he'd creep
The ass no doubt in piteous case
Just as before hangs down his face
Over the stream so clear & deep

[19v]

551 *And down he sits beside the ass*
552 *Just under a tall alder root*
553 *If any one should come & see*
{ "
{ ~~*If any one should come & see*~~
554 *That I am here they'll think quoth*
he
555 *I'm helping this poor dying brute*

556 *'Tis plain quoth he as plain can be*
557 *That here has been some wicked deal=*
=ing
558 *No doubt the devil in me wrought*
559 *I'm not the man who could have thought*
560 *An ass like this was worth the stealing*

561 *But now while he is thus employed*
562 *The burthen of his soul relieving*
563 *Ten thousand ugly apprehensions*
564 *Of eyes & ears the black inventions*
565 *The soul of Peter are deceiving*

566 *And closer to the ass he draws*
567 *As if into the ass he'd creep*
568 *The ass, no doubt in piteous case*
569 *Just as before hangs down his face*
570 *Over the stream so clear & deep*

551–555 *omitted 3; follows l. 540 in 4*
551 Ass *4*
552 root; *4*
553 &] and *4*
554 That I am here, they'll think, quoth he, *4*
555 brute. *4*
556–570 *omitted 3, 4*

What is there now in Peter's heart 73
Or what's the power of that strange sound
The moon uneasy look'd & dimmer
The broad blue heavens appear'd to glimmer
And the rocks stagger'd all around:

in
~~[illegible]~~
And now he felt but
~~[illegible]~~
~~To [illegible] the [illegible]~~
spot at once
~~[illegible] Peter's heart [illegible]~~
was in sight
~~[illegible] alteration.~~
His [illegible] must [illegible] again
~~[illegible]~~
Yet in a fit of dastard rage
He stoops the ass's neck to seize
And in the clear deep stream below
He spies an ugly sight I trow
Among the shadows of the trees
And Peter gathering heart again
Looks down the [illegible]

[20r]

531 What is there now in Peter's heart *516–520*
532 Or what's the power of that strange sound
533 The moon uneasy look'd & dimmer
534 The broad blue heavens appear'd to
glimmer
535 And the rocks stagger'd all around.

in [?in]
F
536 ~~From Peter's hand the sapling dropp'd~~ *521–525*
And now he felt but
537 ~~Twas plain that he felt small temptation~~
538 ~~To play again the ruffian's part~~
all at once
539 ~~For by this time in Peter's heart~~
was wrought
540 ~~There was a wondrous alteration.~~

~~His gather~~
His courage [?mounting on] again
[?on]
on~~ce more~~ [?]
571 *Yet in a fit of dastard rage* *526–530*
572 *He stoops the ass's neck to seize*
n
573 *A*{[?]*d* [?] *in the clear deep stream below*
574 *He spies an ugly sight I trow*
575 *Among the shadows of the trees*
(571) And Peter gathering heart again
(572) Stoops down the asses neck

---

531 heart? *4*
532 sound? *4*
533 looked *3* look'd, *4*
534 appeared *3* appear' *4*
535 staggered *3* around.] around *3*
536–540 *omitted 3*
536 dropp'd *4*
537 And now he felt but small temptation *4*
539 For all at once *4*
540 alteration.] alteration *4*
571–575 *follows long verso insertion containing ll. 513–540, 551–555, and 541–545 in MS. 4*
571–573 *copied onto opposite verso, then del 4*
571 By God I will [? ? ?] *del to* And Peter, waxing bold, once more *4* By God I will. The word scarce said, *4v*
572 He stoops *del to* Stoops down *4* Ass's *4, 4v*
573 And in the clear deep *3* When in the deep clear *4, 4v*

536–540 The wavy deletion lines were entered before MS. 3 was transcribed. An unrevised version of this stanza appears on 18v; it is canceled there and is not present in MS. 3, but is included in the long insertion on an "opposite page" in MS. 4 in a form closer to the 20r version than to the 18v version.

540/571 The intervening stanzas can be found on the two previous versos.

24 While he upholds the ass's head
What sight is that which Peter sees
Some ugly sight it is I trow
Amid the deep clear stream below
Among the shadows of the trees

Is it the shadow of the moon &c?

[20v]

(571) *While he upholds the ass's head*
(572) *What sight is that which Peter sees*
(573–574) *Some ugly sight it is I trow*
(573–574) *Amid the deep clear stream below*
(575) *Among the shadows of the trees*

(576) *Is it the shadow of the moon &c?*

Although there are significant differences, the stanza at the top of this page seems to be an alternate version of ll. 571–575, on 20r.

Is it the shadow of the moon? 25
Is it the shadow of a cloud?
Is it a gallows there pourtrayed
Is Peter of himself afraid?
Is it a coffin or a shroud

Is it a fiend that to a stake
That to a stake of red hot fire him-
red hot fire himself is tethering
Some solitary ward or cell
Where lies a damned soul in hell
Ten thousand miles from all his bre-
– thren

Is it some party in a parlour
Crammed just as they on earth were
swarming
Some sipping punch some sipping tea
But as you by their faces see
All silent, & all damn'd

[21^{r}]

Is it the shadow of the moon? *531–535*
Is it the shadow of a cloud?
Is it a gallows there pourtrayed
Is Peter of himself afraid?
Is it a coffin or a shroud

Is it a fiend that to a stake *536–540*
That to a stake of red hot fire him
[?*f*] *red hot fire himself is tethering*
Some solitary ward or cell
Where lies a damned soul in hell
Ten thousand miles from all his bre=
=thren

Is it some party in a parlour *541–545*
Crammed just as they on earth were
cramm'd
Some sipping punch some sipping tea
But as you by their faces see
All silent, & all damn'd

---

577 cloud?] cloud *3* a *over* the *3*
578 pourtray'd *3* pourtray'd? *4*
579 afraid?] afraid *3*
580 shroud? *4*
582 Of red-hot fire himself is thethering *3*, *so 4 but* red hot . . . tethering
587 Cramm'd . . . cramm'd *3*, *4*
588 punch, *3*
590 silent,] silent *3* damnd *3* damn'd. *4*

---

582 The spacing between the lines suggests that DW made the correction at the time of transcription, and that the first-written long version represented a mishearing.

Tis no such thing I do assure you
What Peter sees in the clear flood
It is no ugly apprehension
Of eyes and ears 'tis no invention
It is a thing of flesh & blood

It cannot be a water-rat
No Peter is not such a noddy
The flesh and blood which Peter sees
Among the shadows of the trees
It is a dead man's body

And Peter looks, & looks again
Just like a man whose brain is haunted
He looks, he cannot choose but look
Like one that's reading in a book
A book that is enchanted

He grasps the poor Ass by the jaws
His hands and body shake and shiver
And up & down & to & fro
The ass's head and mouth they go
Dimpling the surface of the river

[MS. 3: 14v]

591 *'Tis no such thing I do assure you* 546–550
592 *Which Peter sees in the clear flood*
593 *It is no ugly apprehension*
594 *Of eyes and ears 'tis no invention*
595 *It is a thing of flesh & blood*

596 *It cannot be a water-rat* 551–555
597 *No Peter is not such a noddy*
598 *The flesh and blood which Peter sees*
599 *Among the shadows of the trees*
600 *It is a dead man's body*

601 *And Peter looks, & looks again* 556–560
602 *Just like a man whose brain is haunted*
u}
603 *He looks, he cannot choo}se but look*
604 *Like one that's reading in a book*
605 *A book that is enchanted*

(606) *He grasps the poor Ass by the jaws*
(607) *His hands and body shake and shiver*
(608) *And up & down, & to & fro*
(609) *The ass's head and mouth they go*
(610) *Dimpling the surface of the river*

591–600 *omitted 4*
601 And] Poor *4* &] and *4*
602 Just] Even *4*
603 chuse *4*
605 enchanted. *4*

MS. 2 is missing a leaf between l. 590 and l. 606; the three missing stanzas are shown as they stand in MS. 3.

~~Sure uglier sights were never seen~~
~~By good or bad by sad or simple~~
~~Than Peter while he holds the Ass~~
~~Fasts clearly in that watry glass~~
~~Where the still moonlight waters dimple~~

Ah! well a day for Peter Bell
He will be turned to iron soon
Flesh sinew fibre bone & gristle
His hat is up, his hairs they bristle
Bristle and whiten in the noon

And see him now fast bound like iron
Head joints & hands, & lips & teeth
You'd think that he was looking at you
But no this uncouth iron statue
Is looking at the stream beneath

And now poor Peter is convinced
While while he holds the ass's head
That tis a fiend with visage wan
A livi man fiend a living man
That's lying in the river's bed

[MS. 3: 15^{r}]

611 *Sure uglier sights were never seen*
612 *By good or bad by sad or simple*
613 *Than Peter while he holds the Ass*
614 *Saw clearly in that watry glass*
615 *Where the still moonlight water* [?*s*] *dimple*

(616) *Ah! well a day for Peter Bell*
(617) *He will be turned to iron soon*
(618) *Flesh sinew, fibre, bone & gristle*
(619) *His hat is up, his hairs they bristle,*
(620) *Bristle and whiten in the moon*

(621) *And see him now fast bound like iron*
(622) *Head joints & hands, & lips & teeth*
(623) *You'd think that he was looking at you*
{*u*
(624) *But no, this* {*incouth iron statue*
(625) *Is looking at the stream beneath*

(626) *And now poor Peter is convinced*
(627) *While still he holds the ass's head*
(628) *That 'tis a fiend with visage wan*
(629) *A live man-fiend, a living man*
{*r's*
(630) *That's lying in the rive*{*r bed*

611–615 *omitted 4*

611–615 There is no room for this stanza in MS. 2 unless it was inserted on the verso of the missing leaf. It is shown in order to provide a complete record of the base text of MS. 3.

27

He grasps the poor ass by the jaws
His hands & body shake & shiver
And up & down & to & fro
mouth & nose tricks
The ass's ~~head & mouth they~~ go
Dimpling the surface of the river

Ah well a day for Peter Bell
He will be turned to iron soon
Flesh sinew, fibre, bone & gristle
His hat is up ~~his~~ hairs they bristle
Bristle & whiten in the moon

And see him now fast bound like
iron
Head, joints & hands & lips & teeth
You'd think that he was looking at
you
But no this uncouth iron statue
Is looking at ~~the~~ stream beneath

[23r]

606 *He grasps the poor ass by the jaws* 561–565
607 *His hands & body shake & shiver*
608 *And up & down & to & fro*
mouth & nostrils
609 *The ass's ~~head & mouth they~~ go*
610 *Dimpling the surface of the river*

h!
616 *A } well a day for Peter Bell* 566–570
617 *He will be turned to iron soon*
618 *Flesh sinew, fibre, bone & gristle*
619 *His hat is up, his hairs they bristle*
620 *Bristle & whiten in the moon*

621 *And see him now fast bound like* 571–575
iron
622 *Head, joints & hands & lips & teeth*
623 *You'd think that he was looking at*
you
624 *But no this uncouth iron statue*
{the
625 *Is looking at {you stream beneath*

---

606 Ass *3, 4*
607 & . . . &] and . . . and *3, 4*
608 & down, & to & *3* and down, and to and *4*
609 Ass's *4* head & mouth] head and mouth *3* mouth and nostrils *4*
610 River *4*
610/616 *MS. 3 has an extra stanza; see transcription of 15r (p. 307)*
616 Ah! *3* Ah *4*
617 turn'd *4*
618 Flesh, *4* and gristle, *4*
619 up,] up *4* bristle, *3*
620 &] and *3, 4*
622 Head, joints] Head joints *3* Head, joints, *4* hands & lips] hands, & lips *3* hands & lips, *4*
624 no, *3, 4* incouth *rev to* uncouth *3*
625 the stream *3, 4*

And now poor Peter is convinced 29
While still he holds the ass's head
That 'tis a fiend with visage wan
A live man fiend a living man
That's lying in the river's bed

He looks, he looks, he looks again
He sees a motion, hears a groan
His eyes will burst, his heart will break
He gives a loud & frightful shriek
And back he falls [illegible] dead as a stone

End of part first —

[24r]

626 *And now poor Peter is convinced* 576–580
627 *While still he holds the ass's head*
628 *That 'tis a fiend with visage wan*
629 *A live man fiend a living man*
's
630 *That's lying in the river } bed*

631 *He looks, he looks, he looks again* 581–585
632 *He sees a motion, hears a groan*
633 *His eyes will burst, his heart will*
break
t
634 *He gives a loud & frigh }ful shriek*
dead as a stone
635 *And back he falls ~~just like a~~*
stone
dead as as stone
End of Part first —

---

626 convinc'd *4*
627 Ass's *4*
629 man-fiend, *3, 4*
630 river *rev to* river's *3* River's *4* bed. *4*
634 &] and *4* frightful *3, 4*
635 just like *del to* dead as *3 (WW)* dead as *4* stone. *3, 4*
End of the first Part *3* End of the First Part *4*

[24^{v}]

(636) It was, as you belike have guessed
A dead man lying in the river
(637) Beneath the alders near the river

Good

(637) The second version here is inserted on 26^{r}, suggesting that the lines at the top of this page were written after leaf 25 was torn out. Only a stub remains of 25; midpage on the recto of the stub can be read the beginnings of what was probably a stanza: [?H] / H / De / B / Si. This stanza does not appear anywhere in the poem, despite the fact that the notation “Good” on 24^{v} may have been across from it, and may have referred to it.

31

We left poor Peter in a trance
~~We left the dead man in the river~~
~~Beneath the~~ alders near the river
The ass is by the river side
And where the feeble breezes glide
Upon the stream the moon beams
quiver

And Peter wakes, he wakes at last
He feels the glimmerings of the morn
And to stretch forth his hand he's
trying
Sure when he knows where he is
lying
He'll sink into a second swoon

He lifts his head—he sees his staff
He touches—'tis to him a treasure
To find that he is not in hell
As you'll suppose to Peter Bell
Doth give a sweet & languid plea-
=sure

[26r]

636 *We left poor Peter in a trance* 586–590
637 ~~*We left the dead man in the*~~ *river*
Beneath the alders near the river
638 *The ass is by the river side*
639 *And where the feeble breezes glide*
640 *Upon the stream the moon beams*
quiver

{*w*
641 *And Peter* {[?]*akes, he wakes at last* 591–595
642 *He feels the glimmerings of the moon*
643 *And to stretch forth his hand he's*
trying
644 *Sure when he knows where he is*
lying
645 *He'll sink into a second swoon*

646 *He lifts his head—he sees his staff* 596–600
647 *He touches—'tis to him a treasure*
648 *To find that he is not in hell*
649 *As you'll suppose to Peter Bell*
650 *Doth give a sweet & languid plea=*
=sure

MSS. 3, 4 headed Second Part
636 poor Peter *del to* our Hero *4 (MW)*
637 *as MS. 2 del to* Beneath the Alders near the river *(WW) 3, so 4 but* alders . . . River
{R
638 Ass *4* River-side *3* {river side *4*
640 moon-beams *3*
641 And Peter wakes, he wakes at last *3, 4 del to* A happy respite! but he wakes *4 (MW)*
643 he's *del to* is *4 (MW)*
644 he knows *del and restored 4 (MW)*
646 Staff *4*
647 tis *3*
649 suppose, *4*
648–649 *del to* His lot is yet where mortals dwell
Dear thought that yields *4 (MW), then del, with all but last two words of l. 650, to version on facing verso (MW):*
The recollection seems to tell
That he is yet where mortals dwell
A thought received with

There is no special heading for Part II in MS. 2, although there could have been one on the missing leaf 25.

And while upon his side he lies 33
His head upon his elbow raised
Almost you'd say as in a dream
His eyes are settling on the stream
Where he before had gazed

No dimple now disturbs the stream
In Peter's brain there is no riot
His eye upon the stream he fixes
And with the sight no terror mixes
His heart is calm & quiet

Quoth he "that is a dead man's face
Among the shadows of the trees
Those are no doubt a dead man's knees
And there you see his brass shoe-buck=
=les
And there his breeches knees"

[27r]

651 *And while upon his side he lies* 601–605
652 *His head upon his elbow raised*
653 *Almost you'd say as in a dream*
are *ing*
654 *His eyes they settle on the stream*
655 *Where he before had gazed*

656 *No dimple now disturbs the stream* 606–610
657 *In Peter's brain there is no riot*
658 *His eye upon the stream he fixes*
659 *And with the sight no terror*
mixes
660 *His heart is calm & quiet*

661 *Quoth he "that is a dead man's face* 611–615
662 *Among the shadows of the trees*
663 *Those are, no doubt a dead man's knuc=*
=kles
ou
664 *And there yu see his brass shoe-buck=*
=les
665 *And there his breeches knees"*

651–655 *canceled 4*
652 rais'd *4*
653 Almost *with* Like *written above (MW) as alt 4*
654 are settling on *3, 4*
655 gaz'd *4*
660 and quiet. *4*
661 he "that] he, "that *3* he, that *4* mans *4*
663 are,] are *3, 4*
664 you *3, 4* shoe buckles *3*
665 knees"] knees *3* knees. *4*
663–665 *del to* A harmless Body nothing worse
So better to peruse the corse
He rises on his knees *4 (MW), then entire stanza canceled, along with 666–670; on facing verso is a revision that seems to incorporate lines from both stanzas (MW):*

Quoth he that is the face of one
In his last sleep securely bound
~~Then Peter rose & forward bent~~
~~Pointing his staff~~ So gathering heart
so {plain
~~And~~ ~~Peter rose~~ ^ with {[?] intent
He
Makes ~~of~~ his staff an instrument
The rivers depth to sound

34

At this present Peter round him looks
And sees the poor & patient creature
Close to him in his uncouth way
Expressing all the joy he may
In every limb & every feature.—

[27v]

{A
676 at this friend Peter round him looks *626–630*
677 And sees the poor & patient creature
678 Close to him in his uncouth way
679 Expressing all the joy he may
680 In every limb & every feature.—

676–680 *canceled 3, omitted 4*
676 At *3* Friend *3*
680 feature.—] feature *3*

This stanza is marked for insertion following l. 675, on 28r.

And now
At last he rises from his side 35
And sits upright upon the ground
And o'er the stream he hangs his nose
And points his staff as you'd suppose
The rivers depth to sound

This sees the ass while on the grass
Close by the river's brink he lies
And strait with a transition tragic
That seems just like the touch of
magic
Up from the ground the ass doth rise
×

His meagre bones all shake with joy
And close by Peter's side he stands
While Peter o'er the river bends
The little ass his neck extends
And fondly licks his hands

[28r]

And now
666 *At last he rises from his side* *616–620*
667 *And sits upright upon the ground*
668 *And o'er the stream he hangs his nose*
669 *And points his staff as you'd suppose*
670 *The rivers depth to sound*

671 *This sees the ass while on the grass* *621–625*
672 *Close by the river's brink he lies*
673 *And strait with a transition tragic*
674 *That seems just like the touch of*
magic
675 *Up from the ground the ass doth rise*
X

681 *His meagre bones all shake with joy* *631–635*
682 *And close by Peter's side he stands*
683 *While Peter o'er the river bends*
684 *The little ass his neck extends*
685 *And fondly licks his hands*

---

666 his side *alt* the ground *4*
669 Staff, *4* suppose, *4*
670 River's *3, 4* sound. *4*
671 Ass *3, 4*
{R
672 {rivers Brink *3* River's brink *4*
673–675 like a shattered Ship uplifted
~~And strait with a transition tragic~~
~~As if he had been touched with magic~~
~~That seems just like the touch of magic~~
By [?] strong surge with motion gifted
~~Up from the ground~~ the Ass doth rise
Full suddenly *4 (rev by MW)*
674 *as MS. 2, del to* As if he had been [~~?touc~~] touched with magic *3*
675 Ass *3, 4*
684 Ass *3, 4*
685 hands] face *overwritten* hands *3* hands. *4*

675/681 The mark indicates that the stanza written on 27v is to be inserted here; there is, however, what may be another partial version on 28v.

36

Into the stream his staff he dips
Meanwhile with joy that still encreases
The ass looks on as you will guess
Close to him in his uncouth way
And with
Expresses all the joy he may
In every limb & every feature

Into the stream his staff he dips
Meanwhile with joy that still encreases
The ass looks on as you will guess
And with encreasing tenderness
You'll think he'll almost shake to pieces.

[28ᵛ]

691 Into the stream his staff he dips
with joy that still encreases
692 Meanwhile the poor and patient creature *627–630*
The ass looks on as you will guess
693 Close to him in his uncouth way
And with en
694 Expresses all the joy he may
695 In every limb & every feature

I
(691) Into the stream his staff he dips
(692) Meanwhile with joy that still encreases
(693) The ass looks on as you will guess
(694) And with encreasing tenderness
(695) You'd think he'd almost shake to pieces.

691–695 *omitted 3, 4*

691–695 This stanza was apparently drafted at the top of the page, perhaps as a revision of ll. 676–680, on 27ᵛ, then revised below, with enough differences to warrant separate line numbers; the symbol "I" seems to indicate that it is to be inserted on 29ʳ after l. 690. It does not appear in any other manuscript.

37

Such life is in the ass's eyes
Such life is in his limbs & ears
That Peter Bell if he had been
The veriest coward ever seen
Must now have thrown aside his
fears
I

With caution Peter eyes the stream
His sapling deep & deeper goes
The body is no doubt quoth he
The thing which it appears to be
It moves not, neither limbs nor cloths

The ass looks on & to his work
To Peter quietly resigned.
He touches here, he touches there
And now among the dead mans hair
His sapling Peter has entwined

[29r]

a}
Such life is in the g}*ss's eyes* 636–640
Such life is in his limbs & ears
That Peter Bell if he had been
The veriest coward ever seen
Must now have thrown aside his
fears
I

With caution Peter eyes the stream 641–645
His sapling deep & deeper goes
The body is no doubt quoth he
The thing which it appears to be
It moves not, neither limbs nor clothes

The ass looks on & to his work 646–650
Is Peter quietly resigned
He touches here, he touches there
And now among the dead mans hair
His sapling Peter has entwined

---

686 asses *rev to* ass's *3* Ass's *4*
687 &] and *4*
688 Bell, *4*
696–700 *canceled 4*
696 Stream *4*
697 The *del to* His *3 (WW)* deep, *4*
698 doubt, quoth he, *4*
700 not,] not— *4*
{A
701 {ass *3* Ass *4* on, *3, 4*
702 resign'd *4*
704 man's *3* Man's *4*
705 entwin'd *3, 4*

He pulls, he pulls & pulls again 39
And he whom the poor ass had lost
The Man who had been fair days dead
Head-foremost from the river bed
Uprises like a ghost

And Peter draws him to dry land
And lays him strait upon the grass
And Peter feels some ugly pains
Across his liver heart and reins
Just like a weavers shuttle pass

He sees the poor man's blue swoln face
And through the brain of Peter pass
Those ugly twitches fast & faster
"No doubt" quoth he, "he is the master
Of this poor miserable ass

[30^r]

He pulls, he pulls & pulls again *651–655*
And he whom the poor ass had lost
The man who had been four days dead
{rs
Head-foremost from the rive{*r-bed*
Uprises like a ghost

And Peter draws him to dry land *656–660*
And lays him strait upon the grass
And Peter feels some ugly pains
Across his liver heart and reins
Just like a weavers shuttle pass

He sees the poor man's blue swoln face *661–665*
And through the brain of Peter pass
Those ugly twitches fast & faster
"No doubt" quoth he, "he is the master
Of this poor miserable ass

---

706 He pulls, & pulls, *3* He pulls, he pulls, *4*
707 Ass *3, 4*
708 Man *4*
709 Headforemost *3* river's bed *3* River {'s} bed *4*
710 Ghost *3* ghost. *4*
711–715 *del 3, 4 and combined with following stanza*
712 *del to* And through the brain of Peter pass *3 (WW)*
713 *del to* Some ugly [-?-] twitches; fast & faster *3 (WW)*
714 liver, *4* and] & *3*
715 In quick succession pass *3*
716–720 *del 4, and recopied, combined with ll. 706–710, on previous verso (later rev by MW):*
And Peter draws to him dry Land
And through the brain of Peter pass
poignant
Some ~~ugly~~ twitches;— fast and faster
They come, quoth he, "he is the master
Of this poor miserable Ass."
716 saw] sees *3, 4* Man's *4* *entire line del to* And Peter draws him to dry Land *3 (WW), 4 then del*
717 *entire line del and rewritten (WW) 3*
718 Those *del to* Some *3 (WW), 4* twitches *rev to* twitches: *3 (WW)* twitches {:—} *4*
719 No doubt, quoth he, he *rev to* They come; quoth he, "he *3 (WW)* "No doubt," quoth he, "he *rev to* They come "he is quoth he, *4*
720 Ass. *3, 4*

714–715 On the facing verso (29^v) WW scrawled some lines of draft revision:
Which through his liver heart & reins
As quick as lightning pass

40

+ An ass so lean was never seen
By road or shed or out-door pent-
-house
If you should meet in wood or lane
An ass so lean 'twould give you pain
The sight would almost seem porten-
-tous
Then on the ass did Peter look
And all those ugly qualms encreas'd
To see him wasted to the bone
To see the meagre skeleton
Of that poor, careful beast.

and again [illegible] the meagre [illegible]

And seeing the poor meagre ass
[illegible]

[illegible] the beast [illegible]

[30^v]

(496) *An ass so lean was never seen*
(497) *By road or shed or out-door pent=*
=house
(498) *If you should meet in wood or lane*
(499) *An ass so lean 'twould give you pain*
(500) *The sight would almost seem porten=*
=tous

721 Then on the ass did Peter look *666*
722 And all those ugly pains encreas'd
723 To see him wasted to the bone
724 To the see the meagre skeleton
725 Of that poor faithful beast.

(541) And eying now the meagre beast
(541) And scanning the poor meagre ass
(547) Ive play'd with
(541) He scans the beast from limb to lim

721–725 *in base text, then canceled 3, with* out *in margin; omitted 4*
721 Ass *3*
722 encreased *3*
724 the see] see *3*
725 of *overwritten* Of *3* beast.] beast *3*

The two completed stanzas have been canceled, the first in ink, both in pencil.

(496–500) See 17^v. It seems likely that at one time the intention was to insert this stanza at the mark on 31^r, after ll. 491–495, but ll. 491–495 and 496–500 seem to have been canceled and ll. 721–725 inserted.

The incomplete final stanza relates to lines on 18^v and 31^r.

41

Then on the ass &c

from limb to limb
I've played with you an ugly game
Quoth Peter to the ass, but still
I did not mean to use you ill
You must allow you were to blame

But the poor shadow all this while
The little ass what is he doing
His joy is passed is flown
He on his knees has laid him down
As if he were his grief renewing

[31r]

491 ~~*Then on the ass did Peter look*~~ 666–670
492 ~~*And to his eye was clearly shewn*~~
493 ~~*What to that time he had not seen*~~
494 ~~*That the poor ass was guant & lean*~~
495 ~~*And almost wasted to the bone*~~

Then on the ass &c
{~~And scanning him~~ from limb to limb
546 {*He* [?*scanned*] *the ass* [? ?] 671–675
547 *I've played with you an ugly game*
~~beast~~
548 *Quoth Peter to the ass, but still*
549 *I did not mean to use you ill*
550 *You must allow you were to blame*

{shadow
726 *But the poor* {*creature all this while* 676–680
727 *The little ass what is he doing*
^ }
728 *His joy is passed* }*is flown*
729 *He on his knees has laid him down*
730 *As if he were his grief renewing*

491–495 *in base texts of 3, 4 after 485*
491–493 And then upon his sides he fell
And now to Peter's eye was shewn
What till this time he had not seen *3, so 4 but* side
494 Ass *3, 4* was] is *del to* was *4* guant *rev in pencil to* gaunt *3* &] and *4*
495 bone. *4*
546–550 *in base texts of 3 (after 725) and 4 (after 720); del 4*
546 And scanning him from limb to limb *then first three words del to* He scans the beast from *3* *(WW)* He scans the {B / beast} from limb to limb *4*
547 "I've play'd *4* game," *4*
548 Ass but *3* Ass, "but *4*
550 blame. *4*
726–730 *follows 546–550 in MSS. 3, 4*
726 But the poor *del to* The meagre *4 (MW)* shadow *3* Shadow *4* While, *4*
727 little *del to* meagre *(DW), del to* little *(WW) 3* The little Ass *del to* What seeks he now *4* *(MW)* doing? *4*
728 His joy is pass'd his joy is flown *3, so 4, then* joy is pass'd *del to* sudden fit of *(MW)*
729 has *rev to* hath *3 (WW), 4*
730 renewing. *4*

The wavy deletion lines were entered before MS. 3 was transcribed.
548 The "beast" was deleted in pencil.
Opposite the third stanza, on the facing verso, WW scrawled some lines of draft revision:

He walks with pleasure

He for four
No food, these four days
has he
tasted

An X in the lower corner of the page is in pencil.

43

That Peter on his back should mount
He's shewing all the wish he can
I'll go, I'll go if life forsake me
No doubt he to his home will take me
The cottage of this drowned man"

This said friend Peter mounts forth-with
Upon that good & faithful Ass
And strait without a moments' delay
The ass turns quietly away
Leaving the body in the grass

The little ass is strong at heart
And firm he walks & bolt upright
But well may the poor beast be wasted
~~For good these fair~~
~~For four~~ days he has not tasted
~~Of food~~ not even a single bite of food

[32r]

731 *That Peter on his back should mount* *681–685*
732 *He's shewing all the wish he can*
733 *I'll go, I'll go if life forsake me*
734 *No doubt he to his home will take*
me
735 *The cottage of this drowned man"*

736 *This said friend Peter mounts forth=* *686–690*
=with
{Ass
737 *Upon that good & faithful* {*beast*
738 *And strait without a moment's stay*
739 *The ass turns quietly away*
740 *Leaving the body in the grass*

741 *The little ass is strong at heart* *691–695*
742 *And firm he walks & bolt upright*
743 *But well may the poor beast be*
No food these four *wasted*
744 ~~*For four long*~~ *days he has not tasted*
not even
745 ~~*Of food*~~ *a single bite* of food

---

732 *rev to* He shews a wish well as he can. *4 (MW)*
733 I'll go, I'll go] "I'll go I'll go *3* {" I'll go, I'll go *4* if life forsake me *del to* whateer betide *4 (MW)*
734 *del to* He to his home my way will guide *4 (MW)*
735 Cottage *4* Man. }" *4 (MW)*
736 said, Friend *3, 4*
737 &] and *3, 4* Ass *3, 4*
738 moments *3*
739 Ass *3, 4*
739 Ass *3, 4*
740 Body *4* in] *overwritten* on *3 (WW's pencil)* on *4* grass. *4*
741–745 *canceled 4*
741 Ass *3, 4*
742 &] and *3, 4*
743 But] And *del to* But *3 (WW)* Beast *4*
744 For four long days he has not tasted *del to* No food thes four days has he tasted *3 (WW)* No food these four days he has tasted *then* he has *rev to* has he *4*
745 Of food a single bite. *del to* Not even a single bite. *3 (WW)* Not even a single bite *4*

45

Amid that green & quiet spot
He four long days & nights had pass[ed]
A sweeter meadow neer was seen
And there the ass four days had been
And never once had broke his fast
[illegible]
Across the meadow they are gone
And now are at the quarry's mouth
The little ass who is the guide
Into a thicket turns aside
And takes his way towards the south
When [illegible] the woods
But hastle among [illegible]
[illegible]
When in the silent woods they hear
A cry of lamentable sort
Though there is nothing he should stick at
Yet in the middle of the thicket
The little ass stops short

[33r]

in
746 *Amid that green & quiet spot* 696–700
{N has
747 *He four long days & {nights had pass'd*
748 *A sweeter meadow ne'er was seen*
749 *And there the ass four days had been*
s}
750 *And never once had} broke his fast*

~~But they have crossed the~~
~~meadow plain~~
751 *~~Across the meadow they~~ are gone* 701–705
in
752 *And now are at the quarry's mouth*
753 *The little ass who is the guide*
754 *Into a thicket turns aside*
755 *And takes his way towards the south*

hark among the
When ^ ~~in the lone~~
But hark among the woods they
756 ~~But hark among the rocks they hear~~ 706–710
~~hear~~
~~When in the silent woods they hear~~
757 A cry of lamentable sort
758 Though there is nothing he should
stick at
759 Yet in the middle of the thicket
760 The little ass stops short

---

746 *MH resumes transcription, MS. 3, and runs through Part 2 (l. 1040).*
746–750 *inserted in MS. 4 by DW on facing verso over what appear to be the same lines in pencil, erased*
746 Amid that green and *del to* Now learn that in this *4 (MW)*
747 He four long *del to* This beast four *4 (MW)* &] and *4* passed *3* and nights had pass'd, *4*
748 neer *3* seen, *4*
749 Ass *3, 4*
750 fast. *4*
753 Ass *3, 4*
756–760 *del 4*
756 When in the silent woods they hear *then first four words del to* But hark among the *3 (DW)* But hark! among the woods they hear *4*
757 sort *rev to* sort. *3 (DW)*
760 Ass *3, 4* short. *4*

Opposite ll. 751–752, on the facing verso, WW drafted some lines of revision:
Yet he is stout beneath his load
They have reached
And ~~now has~~ reached the Quarrys
[?]
Opposite ll. 756–757, on the verso, WW wrote:
When in the silent woods they hear
A cry of lamentable sort

47]

And Peter hears the doleful sound
And he in honest truth may say
The like came never to his ears
Though he has been full thirty years
A rover night and day

'Tis not a plover [out] of the moors
'Tis not a bittern of the fen or Ilde
Nor is it like a barking fox
Nor like a night-bird of the rocks
Or wild-cat in a woody glen

~~It does not die~~ - 'tis louder still.
The little ass who meant to climb
That lofty mountain which you see
Beneath the shadow of a tree
Is listening all this time.

[34r]

And Peter hears the doleful sound *711–715*
And he in honest truth may say
The like came never to his ears
Though he has been full thirty years
A rover night and day

out
Tis not a plover of the moors *716–720*
{n on side
Tis not a bittern of the fe{e
Nor is it like a barking fox
Nor like a night-bird of the rocks
Or wild-cat in a woody glen

~~It does not die~~—tis louder still. *721–725*
—The little ass who meant to climb
That lofty mountain which you see
Beneath the shadow of a tree
Is listening all this time.

---

761 ~~And Peter~~ hears *del to* But hark they hear *4 (MW)*

Peter {ly ig {ht
762 And ~~he in~~ honest{ ~~truth~~ may} ^ say *4 (MW's revisions)*

765 & day *3* and day. *4*

766–770 *inserted in MS. 4 by DW on facing verso; canceled 3, then marked* in *in margin and* in by all means *(WW) at top of page*

766 'Tis *3, 4*

767 'Tis *3, 4* fen] fern *over illeg erasure 3* fen, *4*

768 fox, *4*

769 Nor] Or *4* night bird *3* rocks, *4*

770 wild cat *3, 4* glen. *4*

771–775 *canceled 4*

771 The cry grows loud & louder still *3; so 4 but* &] and

772 The *3, 4* little *del to* patient *4 (MW)* Ass *3, 4*

773 see, *4*

775 time.] time *3*

---

771 WW inserted a fragment of this line on the facing verso (33v): "The cry grows loud & louder."

48

What ails you little Bess? What [illegible]

What can it be thus doleful

What make a poor heart both sobb [illegible]

And sobs the silent woods a throbbing

alas what ails you pretty Bess

+ A blooming wood-boy of the woods
And Bess I will be bold to say
If once you knew but where he is
Your heart would be as sad as his
Till you had kiss'd his tears away

[34^v]

(786) What ails you little Bess? That
[?sound]

(786) What can it be this doleful
sound
Friend
(787) That makes poor Peter look so grave
(788) And sets the silent woods athrobbing

(786) Alas what ails you pretty Bess

X
A blooming wood-boy of the woods 741–745
And Bess I will be bold to say
If once you knew but where he is
Your heart would be as sad as his
Till you had kiss'd his tears away

791–795 *in base text, then canceled 3, then marked* in *(WW); entered on facing verso 4 (DW)*
791 woods, *4*
792 And, Bess, *4*
793 If once] That if *4*
795 'Till *3* kissed *3* away. *4*

The version of l. (786) in the middle of the page may have been written before ll. 781–785 (on 35^r, facing) were canceled, and it may have been designed to connect with l. 785 through the repetition of the word "doleful."

The last stanza on this page, marked by a cross to go after l. 790, was apparently added before ll. 786–790 were canceled or after the decision was made to retain them.

49

And Peter's on the asses back
Is in the middle of the thicket
And though he's used to whistle loud
Whether alone or in a crowd
He's silent as a silent cricket.

How should it be a crazy ghost
One who must sing in doleful pain
Through a long vision to be broken
When Time shall snap the true love token
To which she sings her doleful strain

What ails you now in my pretty Bess
What is it that makes you look so grand
The is cry which sets your heart a throbbing
It is a little boy thats sobbing
Beside the entrance of a cave +

[35[r]]

And Peter's on the asses back *726–730*
Is in the middle of the thicket
And though he's used to whistle loud
Whether alone or in a croud
He's silent as a silent cricket.

Now should it be a crazy ghost *731–735*
One who must sing in doleful pain
Through a long vision to be broken
{T
When {time shall snap the true love
token
To which she sings her doleful strain

in
out
What ails you now my pretty Bess *736–740*
What ist that makes you look so grave
is
The cry which sets your heart a throbbing
lovely
It is a ~~little~~ boy thats sobbing
Beside the entrance of a cave x

---

776 Peter's *del to* Peter *3 (WW)* Peter, *4* Asses *rev to* Ass's *3* Ass's *4* *entire line del to* The Ass is startled & stops short *4 (MW)*
777 Is *del to* Right *4 (MW)*
778 us'd *4*
779 crowd *4*
780 cricket.] cricket *3, 4*
781–785 *omitted 4, canceled 3*
786–790 *canceled 4 and recopied cleanly on facing verso (DW) over scraps of WW's pencil, erased:*
What ails you now, my pretty Bess
What is't that makes you look so grave?
The cry that sets your heart a throbbing
Comes from a little Boy that's sobbing
Beside the entrance of a cave.
786 What can it be this doleful sound *4, then all but first word del to* ails you now my pretty Bess! *(last two words over WW's illeg pencil)*
787 ist] is't *3* That makes poor Peter *4, del to* What is't that makes you
788 And sets the silent woods *4, del to* The cry that sets your heart
789 It is *del to* Comes from *4* Boy *4* that's *3, 4*

785/786 The "out" is in pencil, partially overwritten by the "in" in ink.
789 The deletion and revision are in pencil.
790 The cross points to the stanza on the facing verso, to be inserted here.

Alone beside the cavern's mouth
He stands: it is a dismal place

bright
All rock with the berries ripe & red
The Child into the Cave [illegible] peeps
Up to the [illegible] mouth he peeps
Then back again he creeps
Into the cavern's mouth he peeps
Then back into the light he [illegible]
moans
And [illegible] aloud [illegible] he [illegible]
His ruddy face is [illegible] his head creeps
The tears are on his ruddy face & dread

And then his face is stained with blood
Well may he be in piteous plight
To his coat lap a bramble clings
And both his hands with the nettle stings
Are blister'd red & white
One month [illegible] the [illegible]

[35v]

(796) Alone beside the caverns mouth
(797) He stands: it is a dismal place

~~out~~

bright
(802) All ~~rich~~ with berries ripe & red
t
(803) The Child into th he Cavern peeps
h
(803) in to the cavern mouth [?]e [?] peeps
T
(804) Whe back again he creeps

(803) Into the caverns mouth he peeps
(804) Then back into the light he ~~cree~~
moans he creeps
(805) And ~~cries~~ aloud with fear & dread

(811) His ruddy face is wet with tear
(811) The tears are on his ruddy face

806 And then his face is stained with blood
807 Well may he be in piteous plight
808 To his coat lap a bramble clings
809 And both his hands with nettle stings
810 Are blister'd red & white

Once more he to the cave returns

806–810 *omitted 3, 4*

The deleted "out" below the second line evidently pertains to the stanza on the facing recto, ll. 796–800.

(803) The first version of this line is in pencil, as are the deletion and revision in the line above.

51

~~A cavern high among the hills~~
~~A rough it is a dismal place~~
With trees with rocks with ivy dark
Yet by the moonlight I can mark
The tears upon his ruddy face
He stops he looks [in / into] to right & left
On tiptoe [softly does he tread]
A branch of hawthorn's in his hand
The haws they are both ripe & red
And now towards the cave he creeps [in]
And now into its mouth he peeps
And then draws back [cries out] in fear & dread.

He is bewitched by some strange hope
~~His eye is fixed upon the cave~~
~~He~~ [And] shews a wondrous self-command
Yet though his heart be bold & staunch
The berries on the hawthorn branch
All rattle in his hand.

[36^r]

796 ~~A cavern high among the hills~~ *746–750*
{rough
797 ~~A {wild it is a dismal place~~
798 With trees with rocks with ivy dark
799 Yet by the moonlight I can mark
800 The tears upon his ruddy face

in
He stops he looks to right & left
{t
On tiptoe softly does he {cread
801 A branch of hawthorn'~~s~~ in his hand *751–755*
802 The haws they are both ripe & red
v } in
803 And now towards the ca[?]} e he creeps
804 And now into its mouth he peeps
cries out
805 And then draws back in fear & dread.

He is bewitched by some strange hope
811 ~~His eye is fix'd upon the cave~~ *756–760*
And
812 ~~He~~ shews a wondrous self-command
813 Yet though his heart be bold & staunch
814 The berries on the hawthorn branch
815 All rattle in his hand.

796–800 *omitted 3, 4*
801–805 *canceled 4, then recopied on facing verso by DW, revised there by MW:*
A branch of hawthorn'~~s~~ in his hand,
:}
All bright with berries ripe and red ,}
Into the Cavern's mouth he peeps
moon
Thence back into the ^ light ~~he~~ creeps,

What seeks he in his grief
~~And then cries out in fear~~ & dread
following this stanza in MS. 3 is a notation And sure to see him *which points to the revised first line of the next uncanceled stanza in MS. 3, ll. 826–830*
802 *original line inserted between lines, 3, then del (with note:* 2n line of next stanza*) to* All bright with berries ripe & red *(WW) adopted in 4 except* &] and
803 towards] toward *3* cave *3* Into the cavern's mouth he peeps *4*
804 And now into its *del to* Into the Cavern's *3 (WW) with alt for entire line (WW):* Thence back into the light he creeps *adopted in 4*
805 draws back *del to* cries out *3 (WW), adopted in 4* &] and *3, 4*
811–815 *canceled 3, omitted 4*
811 He is bewitch'd by some strange hope *3, 4*
812 And shews a *3*
815 hand.] hand *3*

52

And hidden [illegible]

Beneath the way now he crawls

Upon his hands & knees, and then

As [illegible]

There moon beside a frozen lake

He sobs & sobs & sobs again

Like swans which [illegible]

Poor Robin lov'd his Father well

For often by the hand he led

Sweet Robin over hill & through

And oft with his own hand, [illegible]

He [illegible]

He brought the [illegible]

He [illegible]

Sweet Robin [illegible]

sweet robin over hill & through

And oft with his own hand [illegible]

and oft [illegible]

He [illegible]

[36v]

And hidden there quite
awls
821 Beneath the ivy now he cr{eeps
822 Upon his hands & knees and then
~~at~~
823 As ~~hungry swans evenings make~~
Like swans which pressd by hunger make
824 Their moan beside a frozen lake
825 He sobs & sobs & sobs again
(823) ~~Like swans which press'd by hunger make~~

(831) Poor Robin lov'd his Father well
(832) For often by the hand he led
(833) Sweet Robin over hill & height
(834) And oft with his own hands at
night
(835) He laid him on his bed

the boy

836 He brought him playthings from the
fair
837 He told him tales—with [?nuts] him fed
838 Sweet Robin

field & height
(833) sweet robin over hill & height
(834) And oft with his own hand [?]
(834) And oft at night with his own
hand
(835) He laid him on his bed

821–825 *in base text, then canceled 3, omitted 4*
822 and] & *3*
823 Like swans when pinch'd by hunger make *3*
836–838 *stanza added by WW at foot of page in 3:*
He brought him playthings from the Fair
He told him tales with nuts he fed
Sweet Robin in the wood & he
Gave Robin many a half-penny
And many a [~~?crust~~] of bread
adopted 4, but (836) &] and *(837)* half penny *(838)* And many a crust of bread.

At the top of the page is a stanza that apparently either followed or replaced ll. 816–820 on 37r. Between drafts of ll. 831–835 and 833–835 are fragments that may first have been intended as variants of ll. 831–833 but that appear as the first three lines of a stanza that is added at the bottom of the page in MS. 3 and is present in regular sequence in MS. 4, following ll. 831–835. The phrase "the boy" just above these drafts was written here first, as a guide to revision (over erasure) of l. 829, on the facing recto.

53

~~And now [illegible] beneath the ivy~~
~~And hidden there quite out of [illegible]~~
~~With voice as plain [illegible] be~~
~~He sobs aloud [illegible] come to me~~
~~I cannot come to you~~

Ah well my pretty little Bess
To hear that miserable sound
The tears into your eyes may gather
~~The boy is~~ 'Tis Robin seeking his dead Father
His father dead & drowned

Poor Robin loved his Father well
For often by the hand he led
Sweet Robin to the & her
Gave Robin many an halfpenny
And many a crust of bread

[37r]

816 ~~And now he's close beneath the ivy~~ *761–765*
817 ~~And hidden there quite out of view~~
818 ~~With voice as plaintive as can be~~
819 ~~He sobs aloud come come to me~~
820 ~~I cannot come to you.~~

826 Ah well my pretty little Bess *766–770*
827 To hear that {miserable / [? ?] [?~~doleful~~]} sound
828 The tears into your eyes may gather
Tis Robin
829 ~~The boy is~~ seeking his dead Father
830 His father dead & drownd

816–820 *omitted 3, 4*
826 Ah! *4*
826–828 *all but last two words in 3 del by WW to:*
at this time
And sure to see ~~him [?]~~ him ~~in his quest~~
And hear him make this doleful sound
Sad thoughts round any heart
826–830 *canceled in 4 and copied, revised, on facing verso (DW):*
And sure to see him in his quest [*rev to* at this time]
And hear him make this doleful sound
Sad thoughts round any heart may gather
{The Boy / [? ?]} is seeking his dead Father—
His Father dead and drown'd.
827 miserable *3, 4*
829 The boy is seeking *3* 'Tis Robin seeking *4* father *3*
830 Father *4* &] and *4* drowned *3* drown'd. *4*

---

829 On the facing verso is a revision phrase: "the boy."

53

~~And now her [illegible] beneath the ivy~~
~~And hidden there quite out of view~~
~~With voice as plaintive as can be~~
~~He [illegible] come to me~~
~~I cannot come to you~~

Ah well my pretty little Bess
To hear that miserable sound
The tears into your eyes may gather
~~The boy is~~ is Robin seeking his dead Father
His father dead & drownd

Now Robin loved his Father well
For often by the hand he led
Sweet Robin to the [illegible] & he
Gave Robin many an half penny
And many a crust of bread

[37r continued]

Poor Robin loved his Father well *771–775*
For often by the hand he led
Sweet Robin to the & he
to him [?]
Gave Robin many a halfpenny
And many a crust of bread

831–835 *much rev in MS. 3 by WW, as follows:*
831–832 *del to:* O Bess he lov'd his Father well
For oft he he by the hand had led
833 *WW started to fill gap with* f *then del all after Robin to:*
over hill & height ^ field
834–835 *as MS. 2 but* halfpenny] half-penny *then del to:*
And oft with his own hands at night
He laid him in his bed

MS. 4 has two versions of this stanza; one in base text, canceled, has ll. 831–832 as MS. 2 but loved] lov'd *and ll. 833–835 as MS. 3 rev but* hill & height ^ field] hill and height *and* in] on *the second version of MS. 4 is written on the facing verso (continuing onto top of following verso) by DW:*

o [*rev to* O] Bess! he lov'd his Father well
For oft he by the hand had led
field and
Sweet Robin, over ~~hill and~~ ^ height
And oft, with his own hand, at night
He laid him in his bed.

this stanza is followed by He brought him &c *to lead to stanza that follows, on recto (see ll. 836–838 on 36v)*

833/834 The added words above "Robin" are in pencil.

54

[37v]

(843) Through never ending rocks & woods
(844) Inhabited by lonesome [?floods]

(841) And Robin went abrad to seek
(842) His father & through Copse & hi
(841) Hath sought all day long

Poor
846 And Robin all day long hath
sought
o}
847 His father in the wod}ds and lanes
A}
848 [?}mong the rocks behind the trees
{Now
849 {[?] creeping on his hand & knees
850 Now running on the open plains

(856) Despairing now he quits the cave
his last hopes are gone
(856) And now—for ~~he had lost all hope~~

846–850 *inserted in blank by DW on following recto, 3, and marked to go here; in regular sequence, 4*
847 Father *3, 4* woods & *3* woods and *4*
848 Among *3, 4* Rocks *3*
849 Now *3, 4* hands & *3* hands and *4*
alt version of stanza entered on facing verso, MS. 4, by MW:

he
His Father, him ^ all day long
Hath looked for through the
woods & lanes
Among the rocks behind the trees
crouch
Now crawling on his hands & knees
Now running on the open plains

55

Since five o'clock hath Robin sought
~~O'er heathy~~ hill through copse & lane
Through gipsey-scenes of rocks & woods
Toil'd day & night by mire moss flood
And wild as any place in Spain.

And hither is he come at last
When he thought such a day was gone
By this dark cave to be distress'd
Where like a bird about its nest
He flutters off and on

~~At last both~~ in distance & fear
Along the wood his road he takes
And like a little child that's lost
And thinks he's follow'd by a ghost
A wild & doleful cry he makes

[38r]

841 Since five oclock hath Robin sought 776–780
With fearful
842 ~~Oer heath & hill~~ through copse & lane
843 Through gipsey-scenes of rocks & woods
844 Soth'd day & night by murmuring floods
845 And wild as any place in Spain.

851 *And hither is he come at last* 781–785
{*rough*
852 *When he th*{*at such a day has gone*
at
853 *By this dark cave to be distress'd*
854 *Where like a bird about its nest*
855 *He flutters off and on*

856 *A*t last both in despair & fear 786–790
857 *Along the wood his road he takes*
[?in]
858 *And like a little child that's lost*
859 *And thinks he's follow'd by a ghost*
860 *A wild & doleful cry he makes*

841–845 *canceled 3, omitted 4*
841 o clock *3*
842 O'er *3*
844 Soothd *3* day and *3 over erasure, possibly* night and
845 And] as *3* Spain.] Spain *3*
851–855 *canceled 4*
851 he is *del to* is he *3 (WW)*
852 through *3, 4*
853 distressed *3*
855 & on *3* and on. *4*
856–860 *canceled 4*
856 *no eras 3, 4* both in despair *del to* in hopelessness *3 (WW), 4* &] and *4*
860 &] and *4*

845/851 The upside-down doodling between stanzas—"amen amen"—results from testing a new penpoint.

56

And towards the [illegible] whence so bri[illegible]
All through the [last] wood that such [sent]
him in faith [Comes to]
~~a few in [illegible]~~ of that for that dead
man's sake
And his poor ass from heaven or hell
Vengeance upon his head will fall
Some visitation worse than all
Which ever till this night
befell

And ever while along the wood
The ass pursues his uncouthly course
At every step the creature makes
To Peter this conviction takes
New substance & new force

[38v]

(863) And towards the cave whence robin
sent

[?dark]
(864) All through the wood that sad
lament

firm faith {f
(876) ~~a firm belief~~ that {[?] or that dead
{m
{[?]an's sake
(877) And his poor ass from heaven or hell
(878) Vengeance upon his head will fall
(879) Some visitation worse than all
(880) Which ever till this night
befell

871 And ever while along the wood
872 The ass pursues his uncouth course
873 At every step the creature makes
874 For Peter this conviction takes
875 New substance & new force

871–875 *omitted 3, 4*

57.

The ass when first he caught the noise
Stopp'd short and soon he knew it well
And towards the cave whence the sound came
~~And since directed by the sobbing~~

~~Where the ... of little Robin~~
All through the wood that sad lament
He has been carrying Peter Bell

But ~~And~~ soon as Peter saw the ass
His road all on a sudden change
And turn right upwards from the
That lamentable noise to follow
It wrought in him convictions strange

A sober and a firm belief
Is in the heart of Peter Bell
That something will to him befall
Some visitation worse than all
Which ever till this night
befell.

[39r]

861 The ass when first he caught the noise 791–795
862 Stopp'd short and soon he knew it
well
And towards the cave whence Robin sent
863 ~~And since directed by the sobbing~~
864 ~~Along the path of little Robin~~
All through the wood that sad lament
865 He has been carrying Peter Bell

{But
{[? ?]
866 ~~And~~ soon as Peter saw the ass 796–800
867 His road all on a sudden change
868 And turn right upwards from the
hollow
869 That lamentable noise to follow
870 It wrought in him conviction strange

876 A sober and a firm belief 801–805
877 Is in the heart of Peter Bell
878 That something will to him befall
{Some
879 {A visitation worse than all
880 Which ever till this night
befell.

861–865 *canceled 4*
861 Ass *3* Ass, *4*
862 short, *4* and] & *3* well *added in blank 3 (WW)*
863 And towards the cave whence Robin sent *3: so 4 but* towards *over* [?cov]
864 All through the wood that sad lament *3, 4*
866 But soon *3, 4* Ass *3, 4*
870 strange, *4*
876 and] & *3*
876–878 *del in 3 by WW to:*
A faith that for that dead Man's sake
And his poor Ass, from heaven or hell
Vengeance upon his head will fall. *adopted 4 but* Ass,] Ass *and* fall.] fall
879 Some *3, 4*
880 befell.] befel *3* befel. *4*
following l. 880 MS. 3 leaves 3-stanza gap, into which ll. 846–850 were later written (DW)

865/866 The illegible words are in pencil.

59

Meanwhile the ass in Robin's track
Is following doubtly as he may
But while he climbs the woody hill
The cry grows weak & weaker still
And now at last dies quite away.

In vain would he overtake the boy
For Robin is a very ~~He loves him with~~ a dear Delight
But finding ~~still~~ 'tis as an idle hope
Down the close pathways rugged slope
He gently turns towards the right

With Peter on his back he turns
Into a glooming grove of beech
Along the shade with footsteps true
Descending slowly till the two
The open moonlight reach.

[40r]

Meanwhile the ass in Robin's track *806–810*
st}
Is following a}outly as he may
But while he climbs the woody hill
The cry grows weake & weaker still
And now at last dies quite away.

Fain would he overtake the boy *811–815*
{ dear
For Robin is his {[?best]
~~He loves him with a dear~~Delight
tis
But finding ~~still~~ as an idle hope
Down the close pathways rugged slope
He gently turns towards the right

With Peter on his back he turns *816–820*
Into a gloomy grove of beech
sh}
Along the s}ade with footstep true
Descending slowly till the two
The open moonlight reach.

---

881 Ass *3, 4*
882 stoutly *3, 4*
884 weak & *3* weak, and *4*
wo}
886 he}uld *4* Boy *4*
887 He loves him with a *del by WW to* For Robin is his *3, adopted 4* delight *3, 4*
888 'tis an idle *3, 4*
889 pathway's *3, 4*
893 shade *3, 4* footsteps *3*
895 reach.] reach *3*

886–887 Opposite these lines, on the facing recto, WW drafted variants, one of which he adopted:

~~He fain~~
The ass would fain
For Robin is his dear delight

60

and on a that green & open
As any little [illegible] broad and
The [illegible] winds on among the
fern

And up that green & open road
As any little river broad
The [illegible] winds on among the fern

[40v]

(898) And on on that green & open
road
(899) As any little river broad
ass
(900) The ~~road~~ winds on among the
fern

(898) And up that green & open road
(899) As any little river broad
(900) The ass winds on among the fern

And there along a narrow dell 61
A fair smooth pathway you discern
An verdant and an open road
As any little river broad
Winding away among the fern.

The rocks that tower on either side
Build up a wild fantastic scene
Temples like those among the Hindoos
And mosques & spires and abbey windows
And castles all with ivy green

This smooth green path you know
Winds upwards like a straggling chain
And when you two good miles have passd
Between the rocks you come at last
Unto a high and level plain

[41r]

896 And there along a narrow dell 821–825
897 A fair smooth pathway you discern
{An verdant and an}
898 {A [? ?] and} open road
899 As any little river broad
900 Winding away among the fern.

{r
901 The rocks that tower on eithe{ir side 826–830
902 Build up a wild fantastic scene
903 Temples like those among the Hindoos
904 And mosques & spires and abbey windows
905 And castles all with ivy green

in by all means
906 This smooth-green path you know 831–835
not how
907 Winds upwards like a straggling chain
908 And when you two good miles have
pass'd
909 Between the rocks you come at last
910 Unto a high and level plain

---

896 narrow dell *3, 4*
897 discern *over illeg eras 3*
898 *no eras 3, 4* A verdant & an open road *3*
898–900 *all del (DW) to:*
And with that green and open road
As any little broad
among the fern
The Ass winds on ~~along~~ *3, adopted 4 but* [898] on *del to* with [899] As any little river broad, [900] among the fern.
900 fern.] fern *3*
following 900 a page is cut out of 3; no writing visible on stub; text resumes with l. 976
901 either *4*
904 and spires *inserted with caret 4* and] & *4*
906–910 *omitted 4*

905/906 In pencil.

[41ᵛ]

916 Poor Peter half believe that he
917 Hath bid the earth a last farew
918 The temples move; as they advance
919 The mosques & spires change
countenance
920 And look at Peter Bel

Ha}
[?]} d
(921) For that uncouth & [?doleful]
And that
He feels the stirring of

Po }
[?As]} or Peter is but half is himself
{ng
(912) For as alo{e this lonely Dell
The ass doth step [?by ste advance]
(918) As step by step the pair [?advance]

And ever as the walks
(916) *~~While Peter~~ & the ass ~~move~~ on*
along this solitary dell
(918) *As step by step the pair advance*
& towers
(919) *The mosques ~~& spires~~ change coun=*
=tenance
(920) *And look at Peter Bell*

916–920 *torn-out leaf 3;*
as the Ass pursues his way
And ~~ever as the Ass walks on~~
Along this solitary dell
As step by step he doth advance
The mosques and spires change countenance
And look at Peter Bell. *4*

---

(916) The deletion and revision of "move" are in pencil.

While Peter now is travelling on 63
Along this solitary dell
In truth I should be much inclined
To tell what's passing in his mind
If it would suit my tale as well
For [illegible] into [illegible] & [illegible]
That unintelligible cry
Hath left him high in preparation
Convinced that he or soon or late
This luckless night will meet his fate
And so he sits in expectation.

The ~~trusty~~ little ass makes no complaint
He feels not any want of strength
And slowly up the smooth green tract
He winds with Peter on his back
And to the top is come at length.
Till he has gained the top at length

[42r]

911 While Peter now is travelling on *836–840*
912 Along this solitary dell
913 In truth I should be much inclined
say
914 To tell what's passing in his mind
915 If it would suit my tale as well

O Peter Peter that strange cry
For that uncouth & doleful
out
921 That unintelligible cry *841–845*
For that
922 Hath left him high in preparation
Heaven mercy on them that strange cry
923 Convinc'd that he or soon or late
924 This luckless night will meet his fate
925 And so he sits in expectation.

~~trusty~~
926 The little ass makes no complaint *846–850*
927 He feels not any want of strength
a
928 And slowly up the smooth-green track
929 He winds with Peter on his back
930 And to the top is come at length.
Till he has gaind the top at length

911–915 *torn-out leaf 3, omitted 4*
921–930 *torn-out leaf 3*
921 unintelligle *4*
925 expectation.] expectation *4*
926 little Ass *4*
928 smooth green *4*
930 length.] length *4*

---

914 The alternate reading is in pencil.
921 The revision line beginning "O Peter" is in pencil.
921/922, 922/923 In pencil.

Now 64 Peter do I call to mind
That eventide when thou & I
Over ditch & over style [happy]
Were fellow-travellers many a mile
Near Bwallt on the banks of Wye.
Oh Peter – ~~[illegible]~~ [which couldst thou now] forget
This was of Peter thine it was
[illegible] and over the [illegible]
As it in the [illegible] walks the trusty
Its way where [illegible]

drawn onward by the breathing wind
A single leaf that [illegible] close behind
[illegible] forward [illegible] then [illegible] tore
The bottle hung back in murderers'
Was then that went afraid [illegible]
Was? that was afraid of thee
With each of us a hundred eyes

[42v]

936 Now Peter do I call to mind
937 That eventide when thou & I
hedge
938 Over ditch & over style
939 Were Fellow-travellers many
a mile
940 Near Bualth on the banks of Wye.

who could now
(936) Oh Peter—~~can I now~~ forget
(936) Thus was it Peter thus it was

(966) Right onward goes the trusty ass
walks the trusty
(967) And in the open moonlight fens
{are
(968) His way when bl{[?] as any

(973) driven onward by the breathing
wind
(974) A single leaf thats close behind

[?Thus] I was
941 I was foremost thou wert fore
942 The both hung back in murderer's
guize
943 Twas thou that wert afraid of me
944 Twas I that was afraid of thee
945 We'd each of us a hundred eyes

936–940 *torn-out leaf 3, omitted 4*
941–945 *torn-out leaf 3, omitted 4*

(966–968) These lines are in pencil except for the three words "walks the trusty," which are revisions of l. 966 on the facing recto.

65

And while together now they go
Across the open moonlight down
To say the truth they seem a pair
Come from some region of the air
Some unknown region of their own

trusty
Right onward the little ass
The ass is hopping [illegible] his [illegible]
Over the down his way he bends
Where smooth and bare as any sea
Without a plant without a tree
The level plain extends

And ever where along the [illegible] turf
They go with smooth and steady pace
You see drawn onward by the wind
A purple dancing leaf that's close behind
Following them o'er that lonely
place

[43r]

And while together now they go *851–855*
Across the open moonlight down
To say the truth they seem a pair
Come from some region of the air
Some unknown region of their own

trusty
Right onward the ~~little~~ ass *856–860*
The ass is happy in his heart
~~Over the down his way he bends~~
Where smooth and bare as any sea
Without a plant without a tree
a down
~~The~~ level ~~plain~~ extends

And ever where along the ~~down~~ turf *861-865*
{y
The{ go with smooth and steady pace
You see driven onward by the wind
single
A ~~dancing~~ leaf that's close behind
[?silent]
Following them oer that lonely
place

931–935 *torn-out leaf 3, omitted 4*
966–970 *begun at bottom of page by WW:* Right onward goes the trusty Ass *then restarted on next verso by DW, 4:*

Right onward walks the trusty Ass
And while along the Down he bends
His way, where bare as any sea,
Without a plant, without a tree
The level plain extends,

966–975 *torn-out leaf 3*
971–975 *on verso, following ll. 966–970, 4 has a version that incorporates parts of ll. 976–980; all but the last revision line, which is WW's, is in DW's hand:*

A leaf driven forward by the wind
Does with his gentle steps keep pace
wonders in his mind
And Peter ~~turns his head to find~~
thing it is which is behind
What ~~'tis which follows close behind~~
~~Following [?his ?] in that lonely place~~
~~Along that solitary place~~
Tracking them in that lonely place

Following the first stanza, a lengthy digressive address to Peter commences on 42v, running on versos over to 45v, then to 63v and 64r.
966 On the facing verso is a revision phrase: "walks the trusty."
967 The cancellation is in pencil.
970 The deletions and revisions are in pencil.
975 The alternate reading is in pencil.

66

Saint Peter, friend youre of
No — of the army I can see [the excise]
You cannot be an Officer
Youre a recruiting Serjeant
No better can you be solitary Sir

[illegible]

Ah Peter [illegible]

[illegible]

[43v]

946 Said Peter, friend you're of
[?My st] the excise
947 No—of the army I can see
{O
948 You cannot be an {officer
949 Youre a recruiting Sergeant
Sir
950 No better can you be
solitary

[?~~Thou] the~~
[?brambels]
(983) Here's not bush here not a tree
{on
(984) Yet {at my heels it follows me

what
well thou knowst that [?th]
951 Ah Peter ~~peter well thou know'st~~
What tookst to lure my secret out
952 ~~What pains thou tookst to find~~
me
out
953 Twas bullying now & now twas
crouching
Keen looks for a bards
A}
954 [?]}nd coaxing wheedling slyness
slouching
meek looks soft words
~~then~~
955 About it and about

946–950 *torn-out leaf 3, omitted 4*
951–955 *torn-out leaf 3, omitted 4*

946/947 In pencil. The "solitary" below the first stanza is an alternate for "lonely" in l. 980 of the facing stanza on 44r.

And Peter hears the ~~rustling leaf~~ stepping ~~noise~~ 67

And many a time he turns his face

Both here & there ere he can find

What tis which follows close behind

Along that ~~lonely~~ solitary place

At last he spies the wither'd leaf

And Peter is in sore distress

Where there is not a bush or tree

The very leaves they follow me

So huge hath been my wicked ness.

Along the Heathwas down they go

And to a broad-highway are come

They quit the turf and on the gravel

Upon the broad high-way they travel

A pair both sad & dumb.

[44^r]

at} stirring noise
976 And Peter hears the} ~~rustling leaf~~ *866–870*
[?suspicious]
977 And many a time he turns his face
978 Both here & there ere he can find
979 What tis which follows close behind
solitary
980 Along that lonely ^ place

981 At last he spies the wither'd leaf *871–875*
Small comfort this in his
982 And Peter is in sore distress
983 Where there is not a bush or tree
984 The very leaves they follow me
And thus
985 So huge hath been my wickedness.

[?Marking]
986 Along the   down they go *876–880*
987 And to a broad-high-way are come
988 They quit the turf and on the gravel
989 Upon the broad high-way the travel
990 A pair both sad & dumb.

976–980 *no precise equivalent 4, but see ll. 971–975*
976 the rustling leaf *3, with* rustling *over erasure; entire line del*
977 *del 3*
978 e're *3, then line del to:* And Peter turns his head to find *(WW)*
979 'tis *3*
980 that solitary place. *3*
981–985 *inserted on verso (DW) 4*
981 leaf, *4*
982 Peter is in] Peter's in a *3*   distress, *4*
983 "Where *3, 4 with quotation marks in pencil 3*   Bush *4*
984 they *del to* are *and* ing *added to* follow *3 (WW)* are following me, *4*
985 wickedness" *3, 4 with quotation marks in pencil 3*
986–990 *canceled 3, omitted 4*
986 *gap filled with illeg word in pencil, 3*
987 broad high-way *3*
988 and] & *3*
989 they travel *3*
990 dumb.] dumb *3*

---

976 The overwriting is in pencil, as is revision below the line.
980 An alternate for "lonely"—"solitary"—is written on the facing verso.
981/982 In pencil.

[44v]

{oft
& {sometime in
956 I see thee with thy snarling face
Then Peter
957 That ~~put~~ dids put on a heavy
[?sneer]
958 And toldst me of thy might & daring
[?powerful]
959 Thy subtle jabs thy [?power and]
daring
960 Tis but a traveller [?thoult find here]
[?] far below
961 ~~Yet well~~ trow ~~that~~ far below
And yet that
962 The freezing point thy courage
fell
I}
963 Yet neither of us [?]} avow
964 Was half as pale as thou art
now
965 Unhappy

(963) But we were heroes both that
night
(964) Compared with this thy present
pr[?]
(965) Unhappy

956–965 *torn-out leaf 3, omitted 4*

956/957 In pencil.

69

For Peter Bell he looks I vow
With his dull face of ashy white
Just like a creature that pertains
To some strange world of silent pains
A creature of a moonlight-night.

And now they to a lane are come
And still the little meagre ass
Moves on without a moments stop
Nor once turns round his head to crop
A bramble leaf or blade of grass

Between the hedges on they go
The dusty road is white as bone
And Peter casting down his eyes
Towards the moonlight road espies
A drop of blood upon a stone.

[45ʳ]

For Peter Bell he looks I vow *881–885*
With his dull face of ashy white
Just like a creature that pertains
To some strange world of silent pains
A creature of a moonlight-night.

And now they to a lane are come *886–890*
meek & patient
And still the little meagre ass
Moves on without a moments stop
Nor once turns round his head to crop
A bramble leaf or blade of grass

Between the hedges on they go *891–895*
The dusty road is white as bone
When
And Peter casting down his eyes
Towards the moonlight road espies
A drop of blood upon a stone.

991–995 *canceled 3, omitted 4*
995 -night.] night *3*
996 They enter now a narrow lane *del to* And now they to a Lane are come, *with* they *over illeg pencil 4*
997 Ass *3* {A
ass *4*
998 moment's *4*
999 turns] [?comes] *overwritten* turns *in pencil 3*
1000 grass. *4*
1003 When Peter *3, 4*
1005 stone.] stone *3*

70

Upon the ass hath Peter sate all night
With doubt and reverential fear
Oft deeming him as you will guess
A supernatural beast — no less —
An ass without compeer — his seat
all night

[45v]

all night
1006 Upon the ass hath Peter sate
1007 With doubt and reverential fear
1008 Oft deeming him as you will guess
1009 A supernatural beast—no less—
1010 An ass without compeer—
all night his seat

(961) Yet Peter Peter all this
while
(962) Thy pulse beat faster
than
(963) Yet either of us I [?can]
(964) Was twice the man
which thou art
(965) Traveller upon that open
d }
[?m]} own

1006–1010 *omitted 3, 4*

The second stanza of the draft is in pencil.

71

~~And so much~~

Peter has little power to move

~~Upon~~ or his sayers

~~Upon~~ this ass remain he must

They

He travels on & now & then

He sees that drop of blood again

Upon a stone or in the dust.

stake

Did Peter eer with club or ~~stone~~

Smite some poor traveller on the head

Or beat his father in a rage

And spill the blood of his old age

Or kick a child till he was dead

Did Peter ever kill his man

With fist or staff in single duel

Or stab with some inhuman wound

A soldier bleeding on the ground?

No Peter never was so cruel.

[46r]

~~And now with~~
Peter has little power to move *896–900*
[?if on] his [?seat]
~~Upon~~ the ass remain he must
They
~~He~~ travels on & now & then
He sees that drop of blood again
Upon a stone or in the dust.

stake
Did Peter eer with club or ~~stone~~ *901–905*
Smite some poor traveller on the head
Or beat his father in a rage
And spill the blood of his old age
Or kick a child till he was dead

Did Peter ever kill his man *906–910*
With fist or staff in single duel
Or stab with some inhuman wound
A soldier bleeding on the ground?
No Peter never was so cruel.

1012 Ass *3, 4*
1013 They travel on, *rev to* He travels on, *4*
1014 *pencil alt in left margin 4:* It was *(WW)*
1015 a] the *del to* a *4* dust.] dust *3, 4*
1016 e'er *4* or stake *3, 4*
1020 he] it *4*
1024 ground?] ground *4*
1025 cruel.] cruel *3*

1016 The revision seems first to have been entered in pencil, then overwritten in ink. The vertical cancellation line is in pencil.

72

He of the dead man thought I trow
Of his poor beast the faithful Ass

[46^{v}]

(1027) His very [?heart] is drooping
(1028) Touchd with the sickness
                                        of despair

(1036) He of the dead man thought & thought
(1037) Of his poor beast the faithful Ass

The drafts at the top of the page are in pencil.

73

Then why to see this drop of blood
Doth Peter look so pale and wan
Why is he in this sad despair
He knows not how the blood comes there
And Peter is a wicked man.

At length he spies a bleeding wound
Where he had struck the asses head
He sees the blood sees what it is—
A glimpse of sudden joy was his
But then it quickly fled.

He thought he could not help but think
Of that poor beast that faithful ass
And once again those ugly pains
Across his liver heart & reins
Just like a weavers shuttle pass
End of Part 2nd.

[47r]

Then why to see this drop of blood *911–915*
Doth Peter look so pale and wan
deep
Why is he in this ~~sad~~ despair
He knows not how the blood
comes there
And Peter is a wicked man.

At length he spies a bleeding wound *916–920*
Where he had struck the asses head
He sees the blood sees what it is—
A glimpse of sudden joy was his
But then it quickly fled.

He thought he could not help but think *921–925*
the dead Man & his poor
Of that poor beast that faithful ass
And once again those ugly pains
Across his liver heart & reins
Just like a weavers shuttle pass
End of Part 2nd——

1026–1030 *on back of wrapper, upside down, 3, WW has entered in ink lines that may be draft revisions of this stanza, and the opening line of another stanza:*

A Rueful sight it is for him
His countenance his heart & head
And he is shaken with
His {H / [?]eart is [?] with despair
He knows not how the blood came
there
& Peter is a wicked man
Ah well indee may you look
grave

1027 wan? *4*
1028 despair? *4*
1030 man.] man *3*
1032 asses] ass's *3* Ass's *4*
1033 blood, *3* is—] is *4*
1035 fled.] fled *3*
1036 thought— *3*
1037 Of that poor beast that faithful Ass *del by WW to* Of the dead man & his poor Ass *3* Of the dead Man, & his poor Ass *4*
1039 liver, *4* &] and *4*
1040 Just like] *del to* Swift as *3 (WW), del to* Quick as *then to* Swift as *4 (WW)* weaver's *3, 4* pass. *4*
End of Part 2d. *3* End of Part the second. *del to* End of the second Part. *4* [?Me] 7 D—11 *in pencil (WW) at bottom of p. 4*

1028 The deletion and revision are in pencil.

84 & regularly in my mind, min-
gling allusions suffused with
humour, partly to the trance
in which I have been, & partly to
the trick I have been playing
upon the Vicar. The poem
then concludes in a strain of
deep tenderness.

~~You~~

Not
You cannot be a ~~your are no~~ offen[illegible]
Your are a [illegible]
No [illegible]

Now by your [illegible]
~~[illegible]~~ Peter as I see
Not ~~[illegible]~~
Thin you are a soldiers ~~[illegible]~~

[63v]

~~Youre~~
Not
youre are no officer
(948) You cannot be an officer
(949) You ar a recruiting sergent Sir
(950) No better can you be

yo }
(946) Now by your eyes of } re of the excise
Said Peter
~~No Peter no~~
as I see
(947) Then youre a soldier ~~I can~~

The prose at the top of the page is the ending of WW's note on *To Joanna.*

[64r]

No [?no] I
(936) ~~Ah Peter peter~~ call to mind
(937) That eventide when thou & I
ditch
(938) Over ~~hedge~~ & over style
(939) Were fellows traveller many a
mile
(940) Near Bualth on the banks of
Wye
[?~~How~~] [?In]
(941) [?~~Thou~~] saw thou wert first & was
first
We both [?pressd]
(942) ~~We jour~~neyed on in Murderers
guize
(943) Twas thou that wert afraid
of me
(944) Twas I that was afraid of thee
(945) Wed each of us a hundred

87

Peter Bell
Part 3d —

I've heard of one, a gentle soul
Though given to sadness & to gloom,
And, for the fact I'll vouch, one night
It chanc'd that by a taper's light
This man was reading in his room

Reading as you or I might read
At night in any pious book
When sudden blackness overspread
The snow-white page in which he read
And made the good man round him look

walls were
The chamber ~~all~~ ~~was~~ dark all round
And to his book he turn'd again
The light had left the good man's taper
And form'd itself upon the paper
Into large letters bright & plain   x

[65r]

Peter Bell

[?P]
Bart 3d—

I've heard of one, a gentle soul 926–930
Though giv'n to sadness & to gloom,
And, for the fact Ill vouch, one night
It chanc'd that by a taper's light
This man was reading in his room

Reading as you or I might read 931–935
pious
At night in any godly book
bl c
When sudden darkness overspread
The snow-white page in which he read
And made the good man round him look

walls were
The chamber ~~all was~~ dark all round 936–940
And to his book he turn'd again
The light had left the good man's taper
And form'd itself upon the paper
Into large letters bright & plain

---

title omitted 3, 4
Part 3d. *3* Third Part *4*
1041 *the hand in MS. 3 is George Hutchinson's through l. 1200*
1041 Soul, *4*
1042 given *4* gloom,] gloom *4*
1043 I'll *3, 4*
1045 Man *4*
1047 pious *3, 4*
1048 blackness *3, 4* overspre{ad/d} *3*
1049 in] on *4*
1050 Man *4*
1051 walls were *4*
1053 Man's *4*
1055 &] and *4*

89

The godly book was in his hand
And on the page ~~as~~ more black ~~as~~ than coal
Those ghostly letters form'd a word
Which till his dying day, I've heard
Perplex'd the good mans gentle soul

The wondrous word which thus he saw
Did never from his lips depart;
But he hath said, poor gentle wight!
It brought full many a sin to light
Out of the bottom of his heart.

– Dread Spirits! thus to vex the good
How can ye with your functions jar
Disordering colour, form & stature
Let good men feel the soul of Nature
And see things as they are.

[66r]

The godly book was in his hand *941–945*
more than
And on the page ~~as~~ black ~~as~~ coal
Those ghostly letters form'd a word
o
Which till his dying day, I've heard
Perplex d the good mans gentle soul

The wondrous word which thus he saw *946–950*
Did never from his lips depart;
th
But he has said, poor gentle wight!
It brought full many a sin to light
Out of the bottom of his heart.

—Dread Spirits! thus to vex the good *951–955*
How can ye with your functions jar
Disordering colour, form & stature
Let good men feel the soul of Nature
And see things as they are.

1057 as . . . as] *del to* more . . . than *3 (WW)* more . . . than *4*
1059 till] *del to* to *first pencil, then ink 4 (WW)* day,] day *3* da{y / ve} *4*
1060 Perplex'd *3, 4* Man's *4* Soul. *4*
1062 depart;] depart *3, 4*
1063 said,] said *3* wight!] wight *3* Wight! *4*
1065 heart.] heart *3*
1066 —Dread] Dread *3, 4*
1067 jar? *4*
1068 form, *4* Stature *4*
1069 nature *3*

1059 The revision of "till" to "to" is in pencil.

91

I know you potent Spirits! well
How with the feeling and the sense
Ye play both with your foes & friends
Most fearful work for fearful ends,
And this I speak in reverence.

But might I give advice to you
Whom, in my fear, I love so well,
Fr om men of pensive virtue go
Dread Beings! and your empire show
On hearts like that of Peter Bell.

Your presence I have often felt
In darkness & the stormy night
And well I know, if need there be
Ye can put forth your agency
Beneath the sweet moonlight.

[67r]

1071 I know you potent Spirits! well *956–960*
1072 How with the feeling and the sense
1073 Ye play both with your foes & friends
1074 Most fearful work for fearful ends,
1075 And this I speak in reverence.

1076 But might I give advice to you *961–965*
1077 Whom, in my fear, I love so well,
1078 From men of pensive virtue go
1079 Dread Beings! and your empire show
1080 On hearts like that of Peter Bell.

1081 Your presence I have often felt *966–970*
1082 In darkness & the stormy night
1083 And well I know, if need there be
1084 Ye can put forth your agency
1085 Beneath the sweet moonlight.

1071 you, *4* well, *4*
1072 and] & *3*
1074 ends,] ends *3*, *4*
1075 reverence.— *3*
1077 *no commas 3*
1078 pen{s / cive} *3*
1079 beings! *3* show] shew *4*
1080 On] To *3* Bell.] Bell *3*
1082 &] and *4*
1083 know,] know *3* be, *4*
1084 Ye] *over* I *4* your] you *3*
1085 moonlight.] moonlight *3*, *4*

92

~~Only~~ How gladly would I row, dip far
thy [illegible]

But I the

I had a boat — the crescent moon
Her sister is in shape & hue
This boat, it seem'd, she lov'd me
But at the name of Peter Bell well
She left me — off she flew
Would she but take him with me now
Even as she look'd — a happy man
I mov'd to many a giddy measure.
But no — my friends —

[67v]

How
~~Rilight~~ gladly would I [?now] defer
My [?history]

But [?]

1096 I had a boat—the crescent moon
1097 Her sister is in shape & hue
1098 This boat, it seem'd, she lov'd me
me well
1099 But at the name of Peter Bell
1100 She left me—off she flew

(1101) Would she but take her with
me now
(1102) Even as she lik'd—a happy man
(1103) I mov'd to many a giddy measure
(1104) But no — my friends —

1096–1100 *omitted 3, 4*

Then, coming from the wayward world, 93
That powerful world in which ye dwell,
Come, ~~Spirits of the mood~~ Masters of the mind, and try,
To night, beneath the moonlight sky,
What may be done with Peter Bell.

Oh! would that any, friend or foe
My further labours would prevent
On me it cannot easy sit
I feel that I am all unfit
For such high argument.

I've plung'd I've danc'd with my narration
A happy and a thoughtless man
I've mov'd to many a giddy measure
But now, my friends, for your good pleasure
I'll do the best I can —

M on W

[68r]

1086 Then, coming from the wayward world, *971–975*
1087 That powerful world in which ye dwell,
~~Visions of the mind~~
1088 Come ~~Spirits of the mind,~~ and try,
Spirits of the mind
1089 Tonight, beneath the moonlight sky,
1090 What may be done with Peter Bell.

1091 Oh! would that any, friend or foe *976–980*
1092 My further labour would prevent
1093 On me it cannot easy sit
1094 I feel that I am all unfit
1095 For such high argument.

1101 I've play'd I've danc'd with my narration *981–985*
1102 A happy and a thoughtless man
1103 I've mov'd to many a giddy measure
1104 But now, my Friends, for your good pleasure
1105 I'll do the best I can. —

1086 Then,] Then *3* world,] world *3, 4*
1087 dwell,] dwell *3, 4*
1088 Come Spirits of the mind & try *3* Come, Spirits of the Mind and try *4*
1089 Tonight,] To night *3* Tonight *4* sky,] sky *3, 4*
1090 Bell.] Bell *3*
1091 foe, *4*
1092 labour] labors *del to* labor *3*
1095 argument.] argument *3*
1101 play'd, *4*
1102 man, *4 but line del to* I loiter'd long ere I began *3, 4 (both WW)*
1102–1103 *on verso in 4 in pencil WW drafted:*
I loiter'd long ere I began
I've mov'd to many a giddy measure
a blank page is now bound between this verso and the relevant recto
1104 now,] now *3* Friends,] friends *3*
1105 can.—] can *3* can . } *4*

Yet ever and anon sad thoughts 94
And woeful apprehensions gall him
And Peter in his own despite
He feels
Believes that on this very night
Some cruel judgement will befall him
While fearing in his own despite
Soon or late
By this his heart is lighter far
Of Until
For finding that he can account
So snugly for this crimson stain
His evil spirit up again
Does like an empty bucket mount
Rose before the optic nerve
And ever & anon sad thoughts
And woeful apprehensions gall him
Believing in his own despite
That soon or late this very night
Some cruel judgement will befall him
But Peter
clear
And say the best you can tis plain
That here has been some wicked dealing
No doubt the devil in me wrought
I'm not the man that could have thought
An ass like this was worth the stealing

[68v]

(1121) Yet ever and anon sad thoughts
(1122) And woeful apprhensions gall him
often
(1123) And Peter in his own despite still
He feels he
(1124) Believes that on this very night
(1125) Some cruel judgement will befall him

(1123) Still fearing in his own despite
(1124) That soon or late [?]

1111 By this his heart is lighter far *991–995*
And
1112 For ^ finding that he can account
{S
1113 {so snugly for this crimson stain *
u}
1114 His evil spirit [?]}p again
1115 Does like an empty bucket mount

(1116) Quoth Peter &c opposite page

1111–1115 *omitted 3 but in base text 4*
1112 And finding *4*
1113 So *4*
1114 up *4*
1115 mount. *4*

Yet ever and anon sad thoughts 94
And woeful apprehensions gall him
And Peter in his own despite
He feels
Believes that on this very night
Some cruel judgement will befall him
While fearing in his own deserts
soon or late
By this his heart is lighter far
And finding that he can account
So snugly for this crimson stain
His evil spirit up again
Does like an empty bucket mount
And ever & anon sad thoughts
And woeful apprehensions gall him
Believing in his own despite
That soon or late this very night
Some cruel judgement will befall him
But Peter
clear
And say the best you can 'tis plain
That here has been some wicked dealing
No doubt the devil in me wrought
I'm not the man that could have thought
An ass like this was worth the stealing

[68v continued]

1121 And ever & anon sad thoughts
1122 And woeful apprehensions gall him
1123 Believing in his own despite
1124 That soon or late this very night
1125 Some cruel judgement will befall
him

(1126) But Peter

clear
1131 *And say the best you can 'tis ~~plain~~* *1006–1010*
1132 *That here has been some wicked dealing*
1133 *No doubt the devil in me wrought*
1134 *I'm not the man that could have*
thought
1135 *An ass like this was worth the stealing*

1121–1125 *inserted by WW following l. 1225, 3; in regular sequence, same position, 4*
1121 And] Yet *3, 4* &] and *4*
1122 him. *4*
1125 judgment *4* befal *4*
1131–1135 *omitted 3; in regular sequence following l. 1130, 4*
1131 And, *4* can, *4*
1133 Devil *4*
1134 that] who *4*
1135 Ass . . . stealing. *4*

The earliest entries on the page were the two fair-copy stanzas for insertion into the base text. The other stanza, drafted at the top of the page, then copied into the space below, was marked for insertion after l. 1120, on 69r, and it is numbered accordingly here. Later the instruction was canceled, and the stanza is recopied on 74v for insertion on 75r, following l. 1225. The latter position seems to have prevailed for some time, since the stanza is inserted at that point in MS. 3 (the first line in sequence, the next three lines at the bottom of the page, and the last line vertically in the left margin) and appears at that point in regular sequence in MSS. 4, 5, and 6, being marked "out" in MS. 6.

On the facing verso (71v) WW wrote the single word "thought," possibly as an alternate to "fiend" in l. 1176.

The ass as you remember well
Is travelling now along a lane
And Peter many tricks is trying
And many anodynes applying
To ease his stomach of its pain.
By this &c Opposite page

Quoth Peter wounds will bleed I know
And blood is blood & fools have fears
But yet the beast he can't deny
That voice that dolefull cry
A ragged hem & that doleful cry
It's ~~sounds~~ it like a ~~[illegible]~~
~~[illegible]~~ still ringing in his ears
~~And [illegible]~~

But Peter is a deep logician
And hath no lack of wit mercurial
Why after all tis plain quoth he
This poor man never but for me
Could have had christian burial

And says the [illegible] you can tis clear
opposite page

95

[69r]

1106 *The ass as you remember well* *986–990*
1107 *Is travelling now along a lane*
1108 *And Peter many tricks is trying*
1109 *And many anodynes applying*
1110 *To ease his stomach of its pain*

(1111) *By this &c opposite page
1116 *Quoth Peter wounds will bleed we ~~know~~* *996–1000*
know
1117 *And blood is blood & fools have fears*
that voice that doleful cry
1118 *But yet ~~the leaf he can't deny~~*
It{D ~~still~~
1119 *~~It dogg'd him & that doleful cry~~*
He hears it like a prophecy
still ringing
,}
1120 *~~Is ringing~~} in his ears* {.—

(1121) ~~And ever and anon sad thoughts &c~~
1126 *But Peter is a deep logician* *1001–1005*
1127 *And hath no lack of wit mercurial*
1128 *Why after all 'tis plain quoth he*
1129 *This poor man never but for me*
1130 *Could have had christian burial*
(1131) And say the best you can tis clear
&c
opposite page

1106 ass] Ass *3* Ass, *4*
1110 pain] pain— *3*
1116 Peter, *4*
1117 blood, & *4*
1118 But yet that voice, that doleful cry *4*, *then* yet that voice, *del to* still he hears *4 (WW)*
1119 It [*del*] dogg'd *3* He hears it like a prophecy *4*, *then* He hears it like *del to* Heard in the wood— *(WW)*
1120 ears.— *3* Still ringing in his ears !} *4*
1128 Why, . . . all, . . . he, *4*
1129 Man *4*

97

So from his pocket Peter takes
His shining horn tobacco-box
And in a careless way as you
Or I, good Mr Swan might do
Upon the lid he knocks

There's some of you my friends perhaps
There's some of you in yawning weather
Who may have seen an ape's grin
Tis uglier far than death and sin
And all the devils together

And just as Peter struck the box—
— It might to recruit his wind
Or from some more important cause
The quiet creature made a pause
Turn'd round his head and grinn'd

[70r]

So from his pocket Peter takes 1011–1015
His shining horn tobacco-box
And in a careless way as you
Or I, good Mr Swan might do
Upon the lid he knocks

There's some of you my Friends perhaps 1016-1020
There's some of you in yawning weather
Who may have seen an asse's grin
Tis uglier far than death and sin
And all the devils together

And just as Peter struck the box— 1021–1025
—It might to recruit his wind
Or from some more important cause
The quiet creature made a pause
Turn'd round his head and grinn'd

1139 I,] I *3* Mr. *3*
1140 knocks] knocks— *3*
1141 you, *4* Friends] friends *3* Friends, *4*
'
1143 asse}s *3* Ass's *4*
1144 'Tis *4* and] & *3*
1145 together— *3* together. *4*
1146 box—] box *3*
1147 might to] *rev to* might be to *3* *(DW)* might be to *4*
1148 from] for *4*
1149 Creature *4*
{n'd
1150 grin{d *3* grinn'd. *4*

98

x

Beneath the ass's feet it pass'd
A murmur and a rumbling sound
'Twas by a ~~[illegible]~~ troop ~~group~~ of miners made
Who plied with gunpowder their trade
Some hundred fathoms underground

[70v]

X

1161 *Beneath the ass's feet it pass'd* *1036–1040*
1162 *A murmur and a rumbling sound*
~~banderew~~ troop
1163 *'Twas by a ~~group~~ of miners made*
wi
1164 *Who plied* }*th~~e~~ gunpowder their*
trade
1165 *Some hundred fathoms under-ground*

1161 asse'}s *3* Ass's *4*
1161–1162 *on facing verso in 4 is pencil draft in WW's hand:*
Just like an [?] shock it pass
Just like an earth quake did it pass
A murmuring & a rumbling sound

And like an earthquake was the sound
1163 crew *del to* Troop *3 (DW)* troup *4*
1164 pli'd *4* with *3, 4*
1165 Some *del to* a *3 (DW)* under ground *3* under ground. *4*

99

You know that Peter is resolved
His drooping spirits to repair
And thought no doubt a sight like this
To others might have come amiss
It suited Peter to a hair

And Peter grinning with a joke
His teeth in approbation shewed
When cruel blow to Peter's mirth
He heard a murmur in the earth
In the dead earth beneath the road
x Beneath &c from before x page

And I will venture to affirm
If ever any, king or cotter
Did think as sure as five is five
That he'd be swallowed up alive
T'was Peter Bell the Potter

[71r]

1151 *You know that Peter is resolved* *1026–1030*
1152 *His drooping spirits to repair*
1153 *And though no doubt a sight like this*
1154 *To others might have come amiss*
1155 *It suited Peter to a hair*

1156 *And Peter grinning with a joke* *1031–1035*
1157 *His teeth in approbation shewed*
1158 *When cruel blow to Peter's mirth*
1159 *He heard a murmur in the earth*
1160 *In the dead earth beneath the road*

(1161) X Beneath &c from opposit page
1166 *And I will venture to affirm* *1041–1045*
1167 *If ever any, king or cotter*
1168 *Did think as sure as five is five*
1169 *That he'd be swallowed up alive*
1170 *T'was Peter Bell the Potter*

1151 resolv{'d / e} *4*
1155 hair{. } *4*
1156 Peter, *4*
1157 shew'd *4*
1159 murmer *3*
1160 road. *4*
1160/1166 *in MS. 3 DW scrawled a symbol and* Beneath the road [?], *perhaps to refer to stanza ending with that phrase inserted into MS. 4 following l. 1170*
1166–1170 *canceled 3*
1167 any,] any *3*
1169 swallow'd *4*
1170 'Twas *3, 4* Bell, *4* Potter. *3, 4*
following l. 1170 a stanza is inserted in 4; in pencil (WW), on facing verso:

But still he keeps upon his seat:
The Ass moves stoutly with his load—
Peter is busy with his ears,
And now & then he thinks he hears
The murmuring noise beneath the
road

then in ink at bottom of recto WW writes:

But still he keeps upon his seat
The Ass moves stoutly with his load

continued in ink by DW at top of next verso:

Peter is busy with his ears—
And now & then he thinks he hears
A murmuring noise beneath the Road.

the first line of the inserted stanza, followed by &c, is written into MS. 3 by DW after l. 1170

101

And while the little silent ass
Requiring neither rein nor goad
Moves on beneath the moonlight skies
And the grey dust in silence lies
Upon the moonlight road

Poor Peter by an ugly fiend
So troubled more & more, quoth he
I know the truth I know it well
Through meadow-ground & rock & dell
~~A~~ the devil is following me

At this poor Peter gave a groan
And straightway from a cottage door
A little cur perhaps came barking out
Barking & making such a rout
As never cur had made before

[72ʳ]

And while the little silent ass 1046–1050
Requiring neither rein nor goad
Moves on beneath the moonlight skies
And the grey dust in silence lies
Upon the moonlight road

Poor Peter by an ugly fiend 1051–1055
Is troubled more & more, quoth he
I know the truth I know it well
Through meadow-ground & rock & dell
The
~~*A*~~ ^ *devil is following me*

At this poor Peter gave a groan 1056–1060
And straightway from a cottage-door
snappish
A little cur came barking out
Barking & making such a rout
As never cur had made before

1171–1175 *canceled in pencil and ink 4*
1171 Ass *4*
1175 road. *4*
1176 Poor] *del in pencil and ink (WW) to* And *4* fiend] *del in pencil and ink (WW) to* thought *4, picking up the word from 73ᵛ in MS. 2*
1177 &] and *4* he, *4*
1179 meadow ground *3*
1179–1180 *on the facing verso in 4 WW penciled as alt:*
Under Ground through rock & [?dell]
There s something [?]
1180 me— *3* me. *4*
1181–1185 *canceled 3, omitted 4*
1182 cottage door *3*

.103

This barking cur as you suppose
Must needs have been a joyful sight
You think no doubt it must have cut
The thread of Peters trance & put
The subterraneous devil to flight

The barking cur he might have been
A roaring lion just as well
For any good that he has wrought
For any comfort he has brought
To poor unhappy Peter Bell

doth Peter set
Upon the ass ~~back he sits~~
Like one that's riding in a swoon
Or as a ghost that cannot see
Whose face if any such there be
Is like the eyeless moon

[73r]

This barking cur as you suppose *1061–1065*
Must needs have been a joyful sight
You think no doubt it must have
cut
The thread of Peter's trance & put
The subterraneous devil to flight

The barking cur he might have been *1066–1070*
A roaring lion just as well
For any good that he has wrought
For any comfort he has brought
To poor unhappy Peter Bell

doth Peter sit
Upon the ass~~'s back he sits~~ *1071–1075*
Like one that's riding in a swoon
Or as a ghost that cannot see
Whose face if any such there be
Is like the eyeless moon

1186–1195 *canceled 3, omitted 4*
1190 subterranious *3*
1194 c{g} o{mfort od} *3*
1195 Bell— *3*
1196 Upon the Ass doth Peter sit *4*
1200 moon. *4*

[73v]

(1206) It causes pity on the patient beast

{But [?]
(1206) {A now the ass [?hath] reach a
spot
(1207) Where sheltered by
(1206) By this

105

And every twenty yards or less
Poor Peter, well may he look grim
Whether on rising ground or level
Still feels the subterraneous devil
Heave up the little ass & him

[Ass has reach'd a shot]
And now the ~~patient ass is come~~
[~~Where shelter~~ of by]
~~To where beneath~~ a mountain cove
A little chapel stands alone
With greenest ivy overgrown
And tufted with an ivy grove

[now] [just]
A building dying half away
From human thoughts & purposes
It seems both wall & roof & tower
To bow to some transforming power
And blend with the surrounding trees

[74r]

1201 *And every twenty yards or less* 1076–1080
1202 *Poor Peter, well may he look grim*
1203 *Whether on rising ground or level*
1204 *Still feels the subterraneous devil*
1205 *Heave up the little ass & him*

A}
a}ss has reach'd a spot
1206 *And now the ~~patient ass is come~~* 1081–1085
Where shelter'd by
1207 *~~To where beneath~~ ^ a mountain cove*
1208 *A little chapel stands alone*
1209 *With greenest ivy overgrown*
1210 *And tufted with an ivy grove*

now [?past]
1211 *A building dying half away* 1086–1090
1212 *From human thoughts & purposes*
1213 *It seems both wall & roof & tower*
1214 *To bow to some transforming power*
1215 *And blend with the surrounding trees*

1201 *the hand in MS. 3 is now DW's through l. 1275*
1205 Ass *3, 4* &] and *3, 4* him. *4*
1206 Ass *3* And now the Ass has reach'd a spot *4, then* And now *del in pencil to* Meanwhile the (*WW*)
1207 Where, shelter'd by *4*
1208 Chapel *3, 4*
1211 half away *omitted 4 and line left incomplete*
1212 &] and *4*
1213 seems, . . . wall, *3* & . . . &] and . . . and *4*
1215 trees. *4*

106

Though unknown not entirely
more calm though not unknown
Though calm not altogether
Even yet a whit the less sad
Yet not [illegible] though
not [illegible]

Yet ever and anon sad thoughts
And woeful apprehensions gall
Believing in his own despite
That somewhere ere this very night
Some cruel judgment will befall
him. [illegible]

[74v]

(1221) Though calmer not entirely
(1221) More calm though not entirely
(1221) Though calm not altogether

Ev'n yet
a whit the less sad
(1221) Yet not ~~the less do wretched~~ thoughts
{oubting
not d{outing

(1121) Yet ever and anon sad thoughts
(1122) And woeful apprehensions gall
him
(1123) Believing in his own despight
(1124) That soon or late this very night
(1125) Some cruel judgement will befall
him
[? ?]

107

Deep sighing as he passed along
Quoth Peter "in the Shire of Fife
'Twas just in such a place as that
Not knowing what I would be at
I married my sixth wife"

Thus Peter communed with himself
By this time he is somewhat weaned
I think from his delirious notion
That the road's giddy with commotion
Made by a subterraneous fiend
Yet ever & anon &c from [illegible]: Page
The little ass moves slowly on
And now is passing by an Inn inn
That's full of a carouzing crew
Making with curses not a few
An uproar & a drunken din

[75^r]

1216 *Deep sighing as he passed along* 1091–1095
1217 *Quoth Peter "in the Shire of Fife*
1218 *T'was just in such a place as that*
1219 *Not knowing what I would be at*
1220 *I married my sixth wife"*

1221 *Thus Peter communed with himself* 1096–1100
is
1222 *By this time he was} somewhat weand*
~~[?Ever and]~~
1223 *I think from his delirious notion*
1224 *That the road's giddy with commotion*
1225 *Made by a subterraneous fiend*

(1121) * Yet ever & anon &c from oppo: Page
1226 *The little ass moves slowly on* 1101–1105
1227 *And now is passing by an Inn*
brim
1228 *That's full of a carouzing crew*
1229 *Making with curses not a few*
1230 *An uproar & a drunken din*

1216 pass'd *4*
1217 "in] in *3, 4*
1218 'Twas *4* that, *4*
1220 wife"] wife *3*
1221 commun'd *4*
1222 he is *3, 4* wean'd *3, 4* *on facing verso, in pencil, WW wrote* hes a little *4*
1223 his] this *overwritten* his *3*
1225/1226 *ll. 1121–1125 inserted by WW 3, entered here in regular sequence 4*
1226 Ass *3, 4*
1227 inn *3; line inserted 4*
1228 That's] *del to* Brim *3 (WW)* That's full *del to* Brimfull *4 (WW)*
1230 &] and *4* dinn *3* din. *4*

BIRKBECK LIBRARY COLLEGE

109

I cannot well express the thoughts
Which Peter in those noises found
A stifling power compressed his frame
T'was just as if a darkness came
Over that dull and dreary sound

– For well did Peter know the sound
The language of those drunken joys
To him a jovial soul, I ween
But a few hours ago had been
A gladsome, & a welcome noise

But now tis plain that Peters thoughts
Have taken a far different course
What e'er he sees whate'er he hears
Gives him new sorrow or new fears
Deepens his anguish and remorse

[76r]

I cannot well express the thoughts *1106–1110*
Which Peter in those noises found
A stifling power compressed his frame
T'was just as if a darkness came
Over that dull and dreary sound

—For well did Peter know the sound *1111–1115*
The language of those drunken joys
{e
To him a jovial soul, I we{*an*
But a few hours ago had been
A gladsome, & a welcome noise

But now 'tis plain that Peters thoug= *1116–1120*
{*H* =*hts*
{*have taken a far different course*
Whate'er he sees whate'er he hears
Gives him new sorrow or new fears
Deepens his anguish and remorse

1233 compress'd *4*
1234 'Twas *3, 4*
1235 sound. *4*
{S
1238 him, *3, 4* soul,] soul *3* {soul, *4* ween *3, 4*
1240 gladsome,] gladsome *3, 4* &] and *4*
1241 now, *4* 'tis plain that] *so 4 but alt pencil (WW):* the thought of Peter's *3, 4*
1242 Have *3, 4*
1243 sees, *3*
1245 and] & *3* remorse. *4* *MS. 3 has alt line (WW):* Peter is stricken with remorse

---

1241–1243 On the facing verso (75v) WW drafted revisions, then canceled them:
But now the thoughts of Peter Bell
And ever thing he sees or hears
trouble &

111

And passing by a twisted elm
Again poor Peter thus began
Twas just by such another tree
I robbed of sixpence half penny
A Boy that led a poor blind man.

And close by such a ~~gate~~ stile as that
Did I by a most heinous murther
Destroy my good dog Ruffian he
Who gladly would have gone for me
To the world's end & further

A faith-ful beast like this poor ass
Whom I have bruised so cruelly
Just such another animal
Made by the God that made us all
And fitter far to live than I

[77r]

And passing by a twisted elm *1121–1125*
Again poor Peter thus began
'Twas just by such another tree
I robbed of sixpence half-penny
A Boy that led a poor blind man.

stile
And close by such a ~~gate~~ as that *1126–1130*
Did I by a most heinous murther
Destroy my good dog *Ruffian he*
Who gladly would have gone for me
To the world's end & further

A faithful beast like this poor ass *1131–1135*
Whom I have bruised so cruelly
Just such another animal
Made by the God that made us all
And fitter far to live than I

1249 robb'd *3, 4* halfpenny *3, 4*
1250 boy *3* man.] man *3* Man. *4*
1251 such a stile *4*
1252 I, *4*
1253 *no eras 3, 4* dog Ruffian, *3* dog, Ruffian, *4*
1255 end, & further. *4*
1256 Beast, *4* Ass *3, 4*
1257 bruis'd *4*
1259 that] who *4*
1260 I. *4*
at foot of page DW wrote An *3; on facing verso 4 WW drafted pencil variants for ll. 1256–1260:*
faithful shepherd dog had Peter
An honest Creature Ruffian was
A loving Servant and a true
Like this poor Ass for whose good deeds
And true love to the death I needs
Must ~~beat him black & blue~~
Must beat the Creature black & blue

A trusty Watchman ruffian

Like this poor Ass for whose good deeds
And true [?love to the] death he bleeds
[?Must bear my ?]

An honest Creature Ruffian was
A trusting Servant & a true
A loving
Like this poor Ass for whose good deeds
And true love to the death I needs—
Brute that I such a deed could do.

The last two stanzas have been canceled by a blunt instrument that has left large X marks indented in the paper.

113

But more than all his heart is stung
To think of one almost a child
A sweet and playful Highland Girl
As light and beauteous as a squirrel
As beauteous and as wild

A lonely house her dwelling was
A cottage in a heathy dell
And she put on her gown of green
And left her mother at sixteen
And follow'd Peter Bell.

But many good and pious thoughts
Had she and in the kirk to pray
Two long scotch miles through rain & snow
To kirk she had been us'd to go
Twice every sabbath day.

+

[78r]

But more than all his heart is stung *1136–1140*
To think of one almost a child
                                                    d}
A sweet and playful Highlang} *Girl*
As light and beauteous as a squirrel
As beauteous and as wild

A lonely house her dwelling was *1141–1145*
A cottage in a heathy dell
And she put on her gown of green
And left her mother at sixteen
And follow'd Peter Bell.

But many good and pious thoughts *1146–1150*
Had she and in the kirk to pray
                                                              {or
Two long scotch miles through rain {& snow
To Kirk she had been us'd to go
Twice every sabbath day.

1262 one, *4* Child *4*
{H {G
1263 {highland {girl *3* Highland Girl *4*
1264 and] & *3* Squirrel *3*
1265 and] & *3*
{C {i
1267 {cottage {on *4*
1269 Mother *4*
1270 followed *3* Bell.] Bell *3*
1271 and] & *3* she had *at end of line del 3*
1272 she, *4* Kirk *3, 4*
1273 Scotch *3, 4* or snow *4*
1274 used *3*
1275 Sabbath *3* day.] day *3, 4*

And when she follow'd Peter Bell 115
It was to live an honest life
For he with tongue not us'd to falter
Had pledg'd his troth before the altar
To love her as his wedded wife

A child was in her womb but soon
She droop'd and pin'd like one forlorn
From scripture she a name did borrow
Benoni or the child of sorrow
She called her babe unborn.

For she had learn'd how Peter lived
And took it in most grievous part
She to the very bone was worn
And ere that little child was born
Died of a broken heart.

[79r]

And when she follow'd Peter Bell *1151–1155*
It was to live an honest life
For he with tongue not us'd to falter
Had pledg'd his troth before the altar
{h
To love {[?]er as his wedded wife

A child was in her womb but soon *1156–1160*
She droop'd and pin'd like one forlorn
From scripture she a name did borrow
Benoni or the child of sorrow
She called her babe unborn.

For she had learn'd how Peter lived *1161–1165*
And took it in most grievous part
She to the very bone was worn
And ere that little child was born
Died of a broken heart.

1276 *George Hutchinson resumes transcription, MS. 3, through l. 1425*
1276 followed *3*
1279 alter *3*
1280 her *3, 4* wife— *3* wife. *4*
1281 Child *4*
1282 pin'd] seem'd *del to* pined *3 (?WW)*
1284 Benoni, or the Child of Sorrow *4*
1285 call'd *4* Babe *4* unborn— *3*
1286 liv'd *4*
1287 greivous *rev to* grievous *in pencil 3 (?WW)*
1288 very *inserted with caret 3 (?DW)*
1289 Child *4*
1290 heart.] heart *3*

117

And now the Spirits of the mind
Are busy with poor Peter Bell
And from the asses back he sees
I think as ugly images
As ever eye did see in hell

Close by a brake of flowering furze
He sees himself as plain as day
He sees himself, a man in figure
[illegible] like himself, nor less nor bigger
Not five yards from the broad high-way.

And stretch'd beneath the furze he sees
The Highland girl—it is no other
And hears her crying as she cried
The very moment that she died
My mother! oh! my mother!

[82r]

And now the Spirits of the mind *1166–1170*
Are busy with poor Peter Bell
And from the asse's back he sees
I think as ugly images
As ever eye did see in hell.

Close by a brake of flowering furze *1171–1175*
He sees himself as plain as day
He sees himself, a man in figure
Even [?in size]
Even
~~Just~~ ^ like himself, nor less nor bigger
Not five yards from the broad high-way.

And stretch'd beneath the furze he sees *1176–1180*
{H
The {highland girl—it is no other
'}
And hears her crying as she crie}d
The very moment that she died
My mother! oh! my mother!

1293 ass's *over eras 3* Ass's *no eras 4*
1295 hell.] hell *3, 4*
1298 himself,] himself *3*
1299 Even like *4* himself,] himself *3, 4* *second* nor *inserted with caret 3*
1300 high-way.] high-way— *3* high-way *4*
1301 Highland Girl— *4*
1303 cried *3, 4*
1305 My mother! oh! my mother!— *3* My Mother! O my Mother! *4*

Two pages appear to have been cut out of MS. 2 at this point, probably before *Peter Bell* was entered, as there is no interruption in the text.

1293 On the facing verso WW drafted the revision in pencil: "from the asses back."

119

The sweat pours down from Peter's face
So grievous is his heart's contrition
With agony his eye-balls ache
While he beholds by the furze-brake
This miserable vision.

The ass is pacing down a hill
By this he has not far to go
And now while down the slope he wends
A voice to Peter's ears ascends
From the deep woody dell below.

~~such~~ just
It is a voice ~~that~~ like a voice
Not echoed from a naked rock ~~both~~
~~Tis from that Tabernacle~~ list!
~~It comes from that low thatch'd, list~~
'Tis a pious methodist
That preaching to his pious flock

[83r]

The sweat pours down from Peter's face *1181–1185*
So grievous is his hearts contrition
With agony his eye-balls ache
While he beholds by the furze-brake
This miserable vision.

The ass is pacing down a hill *1186–1190*
By this he has not far to go
{now
And {[?hark!] while down the slope he wends
A voice to Peter's ears ascends
From the deep woody dell below.

~~*most*~~
just even
It is a voice ~~just~~ like a voice *1191–1195*
Reecho'd from a naked rock
Tis from that Tabernacle—list! [?bulk]
~~It comes from that low chapel, list!~~
It is a pious Methodist
That's preaching to his pious flock

1307 So *over eras 3* heart's *4*
1309 furze brake *4*
1310 vision— *3*
1311 Ass *4* *pencil alt above line (WW):* Meanwhile the pair *4*
1313 now *3* now, *4*
1315 steep *rev in pencil (WW) to* deep *4* below.] below— *3* below *4*
1317 Re-echoed *4*
1318 It comes from that low chapel, list *all but last word del to* Tis from that Tabernacle, *3 (WW)* 'Tis from that Tabernacle list *4*
1320 flock— *3*

Opposite l. 1311 on the facing verso is a single word in ink: "but."

121

"Repent repent, he cries aloud,
While yet ye may find mercy, strive
~~Godliness Gods of mercy, strive~~
To love ~~him then~~ the Lord with all your might
~~To him, seek him day & night~~
~~By ... with thankful ... & ... night~~
Turn to him — seek him day & night
And save your souls alive.

DOVE-COTTAGE TRUST

My friends! my brethren though you've ~~walked ...~~
Through paths of wickedness & woe
After the Babylonian harlot
And though your sins be red as scarlet
They shall be white as snow

Just as he passed the door these words
Did plainly come to Peter's ears
And they such joyful tidings were
The joy was more than he could bear
He melted into tears. —

[84r]

"Repent, repent, he cries aloud, *1196–1200*
While yet ye may find mercy, strive
~~God is a God of mercy, strive~~
the Lord
To love ~~him then~~ with all your might
~~Go to him, seek him day & night~~
~~Do that which lawful is and right~~
Turn to him—seek him day & night
And save your souls alive.

gone
My friends! my brethren though you've *1201–1205*
~~walk'd gone~~
Through paths of wickedness & woe
After the Babylonian harlot
And though your sins be red as scarlet
They shall be white as snow

Just as he pass'd the door these words *1206–1210*
Did plainly come to Peter's ears
And they such joyful tidings were
The joy was more than he could bear
He melted into tears.—
[?They are]

1321 "Repent *with quotes added 3* repent,] repent *3* repent" *4* aloud,] aloud *3*
1322 God is a God of mercy,—] *del to* While yet ye may find mercy *3 (WW)* "While yet ye may have mercy, *then* have *overwritten* find *in pencil 4 (WW)*
1323 him then] *del to* the Lord *3 (WW)* the Lord *4*
1324 Do that which is and right *then* lawful *inserted with caret by copyist, then all del to* Turn to him seek him day & night *3 (WW)* Turn to him— seek him day & nig[ ] *4*
1325 alive.] alive" *with quotes added 3* alive *4*
1326 "My *with quotes added 3* friends!] friends *3* Friends, *4* Brethren, *4*
1327 &] and *3*
1328 bab{a/o}lonian *3*
1330 snow" *3 with quotes added* snow. *4*
1335 tears— *3* tears. *4*

1335 The words below the line are in pencil.

123

Sweet tears of hope and tenderness!
And fast they fell, a plenteous shower;
His nerves his sinews seem'd to melt
Through all his iron frame was felt
A gentle a relaxing power.

Each nerve each fibre of his frame
And all the animal within
Was weak perhaps but it was mild
And gentle as an infant child
An infant that has known no sin.

But now the little patient ass
Towards a gate that's full in view
Turn'd up a narrow lane; his chest
Against the yielding gate he press'd
And quietly pass'd through.

[85r]

Sweet tears of hope and tenderness! *1211–1215*
And fast they fell, a plenteous shower;
His nerves his sinews seem'd to melt
Through all his iron frame was felt
A gentle a relaxing power.

Each nerve each fibre of his frame *1216–1220*
And all the animal within
Was weak perhaps but it was mild
And gentle as an infant child
An infant that has known no sin.

But now the little patient ass *1221–1225*
Towards a gate that's full in view
hi
Turn'd up a narrow lane; it}s chest
Against the yielding gate he press'd
And quietly pass'd through.

1336 tenderness!] tenderness *3*
1337 fell,] fell *3, 4* shower;] shower *3, 4*
1338 nerves, *4*
1339 Though] *rev to* Through *3*
1340 gentle, *3, 4* power.] power *3*
1341 nerve, *4* frame] [?heart] *overwritten* frame *3*
1343 perhaps, *3, 4*
1345 sin.] sin *3*
1346 Ass *4*
1347 thats *3*
1348 lane;] lane, *with comma in pencil 3* his *3, 4*
1349 prest *rev to* press'd *3*
1350 through— *3*
at foot of page MS. 3 has [?After] *possibly alt for* quietly

125

And up the stony lane he goes
No ghost more softly ever trod
Among the stones & pebbles he
Sets down his hoofs inaudible
As if with felt his hoofs were shod

Along the lane the little ass
Had gone two hundred yards not more
When to a lonely house he came
He turn'd aside towards the same
And stopp'd before the door

Thought Peter tis the poor Man's house
He listens—not a sound is heard
But ere you could count half a score
It chanced that at the cottage door
A little girl appear'd.—

[86^{r}]

And up the stony lane he goes *1226–1230*
No ghost more softly ever trod
Among the stones & pebbles he
Sets downs his hoofs inaudibly
As if with felt his hoofs were shod

Along the lane the little ass *1231–1235*
Had gone two hundred yards not more
When to a lonely house he came
He turn'd aside towards the same
And stopp'd before the door

Thought Peter 'tis the poor Man's house *1236–1240*
He listens—not a sound is heard
But ere you could count half a score
It chanced that at the cottage door
A little girl appear'd.—

1353 &] and *3*, *4*
1354 downs] down *3*, *4* hoofs] feet *del to* hoofs *4*
1355 shod. *4*
1356 Ass *4*
1357 yards, *4*
1360 door— *3* door. *4*
1361 Peter, *4* man's *3*
1363 But, *4*
1364 chanc'd *4*
1365 Girl *4* appear'd— *3* appear'd. *4*

127

Towards the chapel she was going
With hope that she some news might
gather
She saw the pair and with a scream
Cried out like one that's in a dream
My Father! here's my father.

The very word was plainly heard
Heard plainly by the wretched mother
Her joy was like a deep affright
And forth she ran into the light
And saw it was another.

And instantly upon the earth
Beneath the full moon shining bright
Just at the asse's feet she fell
And from the ass poor Peter Bell
Dismounts in most unhappy plight

[87r]

Towards the chapel she was going *1241–1245*
With hope that she some news might
gather
She saw the pair and with a scream
Cried out like one thats in a dream
{f
My {Father! here's my father.

The very word was plainly heard *1246–1250*
Heard plainly by the wretched mother
Her joy was like a deep affright
And forth she ran into the light
And saw it was another.

And instantly upon the earth *1251–1255*
Beneath the full moon shining bright
Just at the asse's feet she fell
And from the ass poor Peter Bell
Dismounts in most unhappy plight

1366 *del to* She to the Meeting-house was going *3 (WW) and same line entered into blank, 4*
1367 hopes] hopes *rev to* hope *4 (WW)*
1368 Pair, *4*
1369 that's *3, 4*
1370 father.] father *3* Father! *4*
1372 Mother *4*
1375 another.] another *3*
1378 ass's *3, 4*
1379 Ass *4*
{unts
1380 dismo{ut *3*

129

What could he do? the woman lay
Dead as it seemed both breath & limb
Poor Peter sadly was confused
To scenes like these he was not used
T'was altogether new to him

He raised her up & while he held
Her body propped against his knee
The woman waked & when ~~the woman~~ she spied &
The poor ass standing by her side
She moan'd most bitterly

Oh God be praised my heart's at ease
For he is dead I know it well
~~[illegible]~~
~~[illegible]~~
at this she wept a bitter flood
And in the best way that he could
His tale did Peter tell

[88r]

What could he do? the woman lay *1256–1260*
Dead as it seemed *both breath and limb*
Boor Peter sadly was confused
To scenes like these he was not used
T'was altogether new to him

He raised her up & while he held *1261–1265*
Her body propped against his knee
The } *woman* *she*
She } ^ *waked & when ~~the woman~~ spied*
The poor ass standing by her side
She moan'd most bitterly

Oh God be praised my hearts' at ease *1266–1270*
For he is dead I know it well
{~~tears~~
~~Her~~ {~~[?] fell [?with a]~~
~~*Of tears she poured a bitter flood*~~
At this she wept a bitter flood
And in the best way that he could
His tale did Peter tell

1380/1381 *a page is cut out of MS. 4, with no visible writing on stub and no interruption in text*
1381 The Woman *4*
1382 Dead, *4* seem'd *4*
1383 Poor *3, 4* confus'd *4*
1384 us'd *4*
1385 Twas *3* 'Twas *4* all together *3* him— *3* him. *4*
1386 rais'd *3, 4* up and *3* up, and *4*
1387 propp'd *4*
1388 He waked and when the woman spied *3, then all but last word del to* The Woman waked & when she *3 (WW)* The Woman wak'd & when she spied *4*
1389 Ass *4*
1391 Oh God be prais'd } ! *3* Oh! God be prais'd *4* hearts *3*
1393 Of tears she poured a bitter flood *3, then all but last two words del to* At this she wept a *(WW); 4 reads as rev 3*
1395 tell— *3* tell. *4*

1393–1394 On the facing verso WW drafted the revision:
And then she
At this she wept a bitter

He trembles he is pale as death B1
His voice is weak with perturbation
He turns aside his head he pauses
Poor Peter from a thousand causes
Is crippled sore in his narration

At last she learned how he had sped
The ass in that small meadow-ground
And that beside the river-bed
Her husband now was lying dead
That he was dead and drowned

The wretched mother looks & looks.
Upon the ass that near her stands
She sees 'tis he that 'tis the same
She calls the poor ass by his name
And wrings & wrings her hands

[89r]

s
s } is
He trembled} he ~~was~~ pale as death *1271–1275*
His voice is weak with perterbation
He turns aside his head he pauses
Poor Peter from a thousand causes
Is crippled sore in his narration

had
At last she learned how he ~~e~~spied *1276–1280*
The ass in that small meadow-ground
And that beside the river-bed
Her husband now was lying dead
That he was dead and drowned

The wretched mother looks & looks *1281–1285*
Upon the ass that near her stands
She sees 'tis he, that 'tis the same
She calls the poor Ass by his name
And wrings & wrings her hands

1396 trembled, *3* trembles, *4* was *rev to* is *3 (WW)* is *4*
e} {u
1397 pu}rt{erbation *3* perturbation *4*
1398 head, *3*, *4*
1400 narration. *4*
1401 learn'd *4* he had spied *4*
1402 Ass *4* meadow ground *3*, *4*
1403 river bed *3* River bed *4*
1404 Husband *4*
1405 drown'd *4*
1406 Mother *4* &] and *3*
1407 Ass *4*
1409 poor] *inserted with caret 3* ass *3*
1410 &] and *3*, *4*

~~he~~ my husband 133
my h[illegible]
'Oh woe is me! he was so slow
If he had died upon his bed
— He knew no sickness, knew no pain
He never will come home again
He's dead for ever dead

Beside the woman Peter stands
His heart is opening more & more
A holy sense is in his mind
He feels what he for human kind
Had never felt before

At length by Peter's arm sustained
The woman rises from the ground
Oh mercy something must be done
My little Rachael you must run
Across the meadow, by the pound

[90r]

{nd
m my husba{d
[? ?] *my husband* [? ?]
{Oh
1411 [?] *woe is me! he was so stout* *1286–1290*
1412 *If he had died upon his bed*
1413 *—He knew no sickness, knew no pain*
1414 *He never will come home again*
1415 *He's dead for ever dead*

1416 *Beside the woman Peter stands* *1291–1295*
1417 *His heart is opening more & more*
1418 *A holy sense is in his mind*
1419 *He feels what he for human kind*
1420 *Had never felt before*

1421 *At length by Peter's arm sustained* *1296–1300*
1422 *The woman rises from the ground*
1423 *Oh mercy something must be done*
1424 *My little Rachael you must run*
1425 *Across the meadow, by the pound*

1411 Oh woe is me he was so Stout *3* Oh Woe is me! he was so stout *4*
1413 sickness,] sickness *4* pain, *3*
1415 dead, . . . dead— *3* dead, . . . dead *4*
1416 Woman *4*
1417 &] and *4*
1420 before— *3* before. *4*
1421 sustain'd *3, 4*
1422 Woman *4*
1423 O mercy! *4*
1425 meadow,] meadow *3, 4* pound— *3*

At the very top of the page a line was erased, leaving no writing visible.

135

Make haste my little Rachael do
Bid ~~Matthew Jimpson~~ hither come
Ask him to lend his horse tonight
And this good man whom ~~heaven~~ God requite
Will help to bring the body home

Away goes Rachael weeping loud
An infant waked by her distress
Makes in the house a piteous cry
And Peter hears the mother sigh
Poor thing 'tis fatherless

And now does Peter feel
The heart of man's a holy thing
And Nature through a world of death
Breathes into him a second breath
Just like the breath of spring

[91r]

{*a*
1426 *Make haste my little Rach*{*eel do* 1301–1305
~~Arthur [?Arthur]~~
1427 *Bid ~~Matthew Simpson~~ hither come*
1428 *Ask him to lend his horse tonight*
God
1429 *And this good man whom ~~heaven~~*
requite
1430 *Will help to bring the body home*

1431 *Away goes Rachael weeping loud* 1306–1310
1432 *An infant waked by her distress*
1433 *Makes in the house a piteous cry*
1434 *And Peter hears the mother sigh*
1435 *Poor thing 'tis fatherless*

1436 *And now does Peter feel* 1311–1315
1437 *The heart of man's a holy thing*
1438 *And Nature through a world of death*
br}
1439 *Breathes into him a second d*}*eath*
1440 *Just like the breath of spring*

1426 *an unidentified hand completes the poem, MS. 3*
1426 haste, *4* Rachael *3* Rachael, *4*
1427 Farmer Simpson hither come *entered into blank, 4*
1428 to night *3*
1429 Man, *4* heaven] heav{n *3* God *del to* Heaven *4*
1432 Infant, wak'd *4*
1434 Mother *3, 4*
1435 Thing! *4* tis *3*
1436 And now does Peter feel *with* deeply *entered above line by WW 3* And now *with* does Peter deeply feel *entered in gap 4*
1437 The heart of mans *del to* That Mans heart is *3* The *rev to* That *and* Man's heart is a holy thing *entered in gap 4*
1438 nature *3*
1439 breath *3, 4*
1440 Just *del to* Even *3 (WW)* spring— *3; entire line entered in gap 4:* Even like the breath of spring

Upon a stone the woman sits 137
In agony of silent grief
From his own thoughts does Peter start
He longs to press her to his heart
From love that cannot give relief

At last upspringing from her seat
As with a sudden fear and dread
The ~~Woman~~ Mother through the threshold flies
And up the cottage stairs she hies
And flings herself upon the bed

And Peter turns his steps aside
Towards a shade of alder trees
And he sits down he knows not how
With his hands ~~fixed~~ pressed against his brow
And his head ~~[illegible]~~ fixed between
his knees

[92r]

Upon a stone the woman sits *1316–1320*
In agony of silent grief
From his own thoughts does Peter start
He longs to press her to his heart
From love that cannot give relief

{*up* *ing*
At last ~~sh~~e spring{s up from her seat *1321–1325*
As with a sudden fear and dread
Mother [?from]
The ~~Woman~~ through the threshold flies
And up the cottage stairs she hies
And flings herself upon the bed

And Peter turns his steps aside *1326–1330*
Towards a shade of alder trees
And he sits down he knows not how
press'd
With his hands ~~fix'd~~ against his brow
And his head ~~his head~~ fixd between
his knees

1441 Woman *4*
1446 last upspringing *3* last, upspringing *4*
1448 The woman through the threshold flies *with* woman *del to* Mother *3 (WW)* The Mother through the threshold flies *4*
1449 And up the *with no eras 3, 4* hies] *over illeg erasure 3*
1449–1450 *order of lines reversed and correct order indicated by numerals* 4 *and* 5 *entered over initial words 3*
1454 fix'd *del to* press'd *3 (DW)* press'd *4*
1455 And his head fix'd between his knees *3, 4*

In silence there does Peter sit 139
Not any sign of life he makes
As if his mind were sinking deep
Through years that have been long asleep —
-At last as from a trance he wakes.

He turn ~~eyelids~~ his head and sees the ass
Yet standing in the clear moonshine
"When shall I be as good as thou
Oh would poor beast that I had now
A heart but half as good as thine.

But hark! that doleful cry again
'Tis travelling up the woody slope
Once more while Peter hears the sound
With stifling pain his heart is bound
He feels like one that has no hope.

[93r]

In silence there does Peter sit *1331–1335*
Not any sign of life he makes
As if his mind were sinking deep
Through years that have been long asleep—
—At last as from a trance he wakes.

his head
He turn ~~he turns~~ and sees the ass *1336–1340*
Yet standing in the clear moonshine
"When shall I be as good as thou
a}
Oh would poor be }st that I had now
A heart but half as good as thine.

{ol }
But hark! that d{ool}eful cry again *1341–1345*
'Tis travelling up the woody slope
Once more while Peter hears the sound
With stifling pain his heart is bound
He feels like one that has no hope.

1459 years *inserted with caret 3* asleep—] asleep *3, 4*
1460 —At] At *3, 4* wakes.] wakes *3, 4*
1461 he turns *del to* his head *3 (DW)* his head *4* Ass *4*
1463 "When] When *3, 4* thou? *4*
1464 Oh! *3, 4* beast *3* Beast *4*
1465 thine.] thine *3, 4*
1466 hark!] hark *3, 4* doleful *3, 4* cry again] cry of *with* of *del to* again *3*
1467 'Tis] Tis *3*
1470 hope.] hope *3, 4*

Opposite ll. 1456–1457 WW wrote in pencil:

{The
{A world is now a sleepy world
A lazy world of slow belief

140

all general [illegible] all

Our hearts are [illegible]

That

[illegible]

[illegible] great [illegible]

[93v]

all genial faith all
human love
[? ? ?]
Our hearts are [~~?~~ ?]
That
[?Two]
In good [?]

It is not clear where these drafts, all in pencil, belong.

141

Tis little Robin he who sought
His father with such grief & pain
And after many perils past
Has found his way safe home at last
And now is coming up the lane

He's coming tow'rds the door, & now
He sees the ass — and nothing living
Had ever such a fit of joy
As has this little orphan boy,
For he has no misgiving.

Towards the gentle ass he springs ~~[illegible]~~
And up about his neck he climbs
In loving words he talks to him
He kisses kisses face & limb
He kisses him a thousand times.

[94r]

Tis little Robin he who sought *1346–1350*
His father with such grief & pain
And after many perils past
Has found his way safe home at last
And now is coming up the lane

He's coming tow'rds the door, & now *1351–1355*
He sees the ass—and nothing living
Had ever such a fit of joy
As has this little orphan boy,
For he has no misgiving.

springs
[?sprang]
Towards the gentle ass he ~~[?springs]~~ *1356–1360*
And up about his neck he climbs
In loving words he talks to him
He kisses kisses face & limb
He kisses him a thousand times.

1471 'Tis *4* Robin, *4*
1472 Father *4* &] and *3, 4*
1474 Has found] He finds *overwritten and del to* Has found *4*
1475 the lane] again *del to* the lane *3* the lane. *4*
1476 towards . . . door *3* towards the door, & now *written into blank 4*
1477 Ass— *4*
1479 orphan boy,] orphan boy *3* Orphan Boy *4*
1480 misgiving.] misgiving *4*
1481 Ass *4* springs *3, 4*
1482 Neck *3*
1484 kisses, kisses *4* &] and *3, 4*
1485 times.] times *3*

142

This: Peter sees where in the shade
He stood beside the cottage door
And Peter ~~the~~ Bell the ruffian wild
Sobs loud, he sobs ~~off~~ like a child,
"Oh God I can endure no more!"

Here ends my tale for in a trice
Came Mathew ~~Simpson~~ Parke with his horse
Peter set out with him strait way,
And two hours ere the break of day,
Together they brought back home the corse.

And many years did this poor ass
Whom once it was my luck to see
Not many miles from Leeming Lane
Help'd by his labour to maintain
The widow & her family.

[94v]

This Peter sees where in the shade *1361–1365*
He stood beside the cottage door
Bell
And Peter ~~he~~ the ruffian wild
even
Sobs loud, he sobs ~~just~~ like a child,
"Oh God I can endure no more."

Here ends my tale for in a trice *1366–1370*
[?Arthur]
Came Matthew Simpson with his horse
~~went back~~
Peter set out with him strait-way,
And, two hours ere the break of day,
home
Together they brought back the corse.

did}
And many years this} this poor ass *1371–1375*
Whom once it was my luck to see
{an
Not many fr miles from Leem{ing=lane
Help'd by his labour to maintain
The widow & her family.

1486 sees, *4*
1488 he *del to* Bell *3 (WW)* Bell, *4*
1489 loud,] loud *3* just *del to* even *3 (WW)* even *4* child,] child *3, 4*
1490 "Oh God! *3* "O God! *4* more."] more" *3*
1491 Tale— *4*
1492 Matthew] *del to* [?Deacon] *3; after* Came *blank line filled with* Farmer Simpson with his horse *4*
t-}
1493 strait-way,] straigh} way *3 (?WW)* straitway *4*
1494 And,] And *3* ere] in *rev to* ere *3 (?WW)* day,] day *3, 4*
{C
1495 corse.] corse *3* {corse *4*
1496 did this *3, 4* Ass *4*
1498 many miles *3, 4* Leeming lane *3* Leming Lane *4*
1499 Help'd] *del to* Help *3* Help *4*
1500 Widow *4* &] and *3, 4* family.] family *3* Family *4*

The inverted scrawl at the bottom of the page seems to repeat "thou knowest" several times; the phrase also appears at the bottom of the last page of transcription, on the inner back cover. Probably it was used to test a pen.

143

And Peter Bell who felt that night
Had been the wildest of his clan
Forsook his crimes forsook his folly
And after ten months melancholy
Became a good and honest man.

End.

First Do. 31 Stanzas
Second Do 28
First Part 58
Sec. Do 68
Third 91
Total 276 Stanzas
5
1380 lines

End

35
20
600

3 a page
88 pages

52 stanzas
3) 17.1

18 pages

40 1st part
18 pages
30
88

94

3) 88
29.1

[Inside cover]

1501 And Peter Bell who till that night *1376–1380*
1502 Had been the wildest of his clan
1503 Forsook his crimes forsook his folly
1504 And after ten month's melancholy
1505 Became a good and honest man.

End.

1502 Had been the wildest of his clan *3, 4*
1503 crimes, *4*
1504 months *3*
1505 Become *rev to* Became *4* man— *3* Man. *4*
End.] *omitted 3* The End *4*
at left foot of page, MS. 4, in pencil (?WW): 90 staz.
92
at right, in pencil (?WW): [?me 13]
[?]
on inside back wrapper of MS. 3 WW wrote in ink:
Mary Hutchinson—
Gallow-hill,
Galu-hill

---

with MS. 3 reversed, WW drafted some lines in pencil which appear to be versions of a stanza in MS. 5, ll. 596–600:

No doubt you must have [? meant]
My honest soul you must
have meant
The rouze th [? friends] in Penny gent
Quoth Peter in a heartsome tone
Those pipes of yours are clear
& shrill
My honest soul you must
And Peter in a heartsome tone
Cried out your Pipes give clear
& shrill
My honest Friend you must [?]
have meant
To rouze

Whereat in resolute mood
once more

The "End" (visible in the photograph), repeated three times across the stanza calculations, is in pencil.

143

And Peter Bell who till that night
Had been the wildest of his clan
Forsook his crimes forsook his folly
And after ten months melancholy
Became a good and honest man.

End.

First Do. 31 Stanzas
Second Do 28
First Part 58
Sec. Do 68
Third 91.
Total 276 Stanzas
5
1380 lines

End — End

End

.35
20
600

3 d part
88 Stanzas

3) 52 stanzas
17. 1

18. stanzas

40 1st hand
18. pages
30
88
94.

1 hour harvest

3) 88
29. 1

[Inside cover continued]

		{*Stanzas*		
First Pro.	*31*	[*?lines*]	35	
Second do	*28*		20	
First Part	*58*		600	
Sec. do	*68*			3d part
Third.	*91*			88 pages
Total	*276*	*Stanzas*		
	5			
	1380	*lines*	3) 52	[?stanz]
			17.1	

40	1st part	18.	~~pages~~
18.	pages	~~[?]~~	
30		3) 88	
88	—	29.1	
6			
94.	—		

On the bottom of this page are two tabulations of the length of the poem at two different stages of its composition. One tabulation, in MW's hand, is in terms of stanzas and lines; the other, in WW's hand, is in terms of pages. The latter seems to derive partly from calculations on the right side of the page, which are themselves based on a somewhat briefer tabulation, also in WW's hand, which appears inside the front cover of MS. 2:

113 stanzas 1st pt		
52 2nd		
88		
253		
5		88
		3
1265	(88 pages	264
	88) 1265	
	14	

The divisions carried out on the right of the inside back cover seem to indicate that the 18 pages for the second part and 30 pages for the third come from the 52 and 88 stanzas, respectively, tabulated on the front cover. The 40 pages allowed for the first part is, however, too much for the 113 stanzas in the front tabulation. WW seems to have calculated that 88 pages would allow for 264 stanzas. The addition of 6 pages in the calculation on the bottom left, which arrives at a total of 94 pages, may be intended to allow for the 276 stanzas in MW's tabulation, plus title pages; or it may refer to the six pages of sonnets published at the end of the first edition, which, however, with that addition still contained only 88 pages.

MS. 5 (1806–1808) and MS. 6 (1812–1818)

The last major phase in the development of *Peter Bell* is revealed in MSS. 5, 6, and 7 (DC MSS. 60, 72, and 105; see descriptions in Introduction). MSS. 5 and 6 both contain essentially two versions: an original or base text and a finished revision. MS. 5 was originally much like corrected MS. 4, but has been considerably revised, especially in the Prologue. MS. 6 was originally virtually a copy of the revised MS. 5, but was subjected to what was probably the final revision before the production of a printers' copy. MS. 7 is probably a part of that printers' copy, but only one sheet has survived. In his edition of *Benjamin the Waggoner* in this series, Paul Betz speculates that survival was owed to three corrections that made the sheet no longer acceptable as fair copy (*Waggoner*, p. 25n).

A full transcription of MS. 5 is shown here, but since much of the manuscript is fairly clean, it seemed unnecessary to present photographs of the entire MS.; facing photographs of the Prologue and Part I are offered, as well as photographs of pages from MS. 6 through the Prologue. In the transcriptions the base-text lines of MS. 5 are numbered sequentially in the left margins. When there are roughly equivalent lines in the early reading text, their numbers are given in italics in the right margin.

The *apparatus criticus* shows variants in MSS. 6 and 7 from the revised state of MS. 5. For most of the transcription, variants may be assumed to be from the only extant complete subsequent manuscript, MS. 6, and are not specifically identified as to source; in the brief area of the overlapping MS. 7, however, sources of variants are given. Unless otherwise noted, the base text is in the hand of Sara Hutchinson, revisions are in Mary Wordsworth's hand, and both the text and the revisions are in ink.

DOVE-COTTAGE TRUST

Peter Bell

Prologue

There's something in a flying horse,
There's something in a huge balloon,
But through the clouds I'll never float
Until I have a little Boat
~~In shape just~~ Whose is like the crescent moon

And now I have a little Boat
In shape ~~just like the~~ a very crescent moon;
Fast through the clouds my Boat can sail
But if perchance your faith should fail,
Look up and you shall see me soon.

The woods, my Friends, are round you roaring
The woods are roaring like a sea
The noise of danger's in your ears,

[1r] *(1)*

Peter Bell

Prologue

There's something in a flying horse, *1–13*
There's something in a huge balloon,
But through the clouds I'll never float
Until I have a little Boat
Whose is
~~In~~ shape ~~just~~ like the crescent moon.

And now I <u>have</u> a little Boat
a very
In shape ~~just like the~~ crescent moon;
Fast through the clouds my Boat can sail
But if perchance your faith should fail,
Look up and you shall see me soon.

The woods, my Friends, are round you roaring
The woods are roaring like a sea
The noise of danger's in your ears,

---

2 There's *del to* And
6 *no underlining*
10 me] us *rev to* me *(SH)*
11 roaring *del to* waving *del*
12 The woods are *del to* Rocking and sea,
11–12 *revisions drafted by WW in pencil at top of page:*
The woods my Friends are round you roaring
Rocking and roaring like a sea,
13 danger's in *eras to* danger fills *with* fills *also above line in pencil*

The lines scrawled at the top of the page in William's hand are variants of *The Waggoner,* III, 38–41: the "No not" and the lines to the right, below the title, are from *The Waggoner,* III, 30–31.

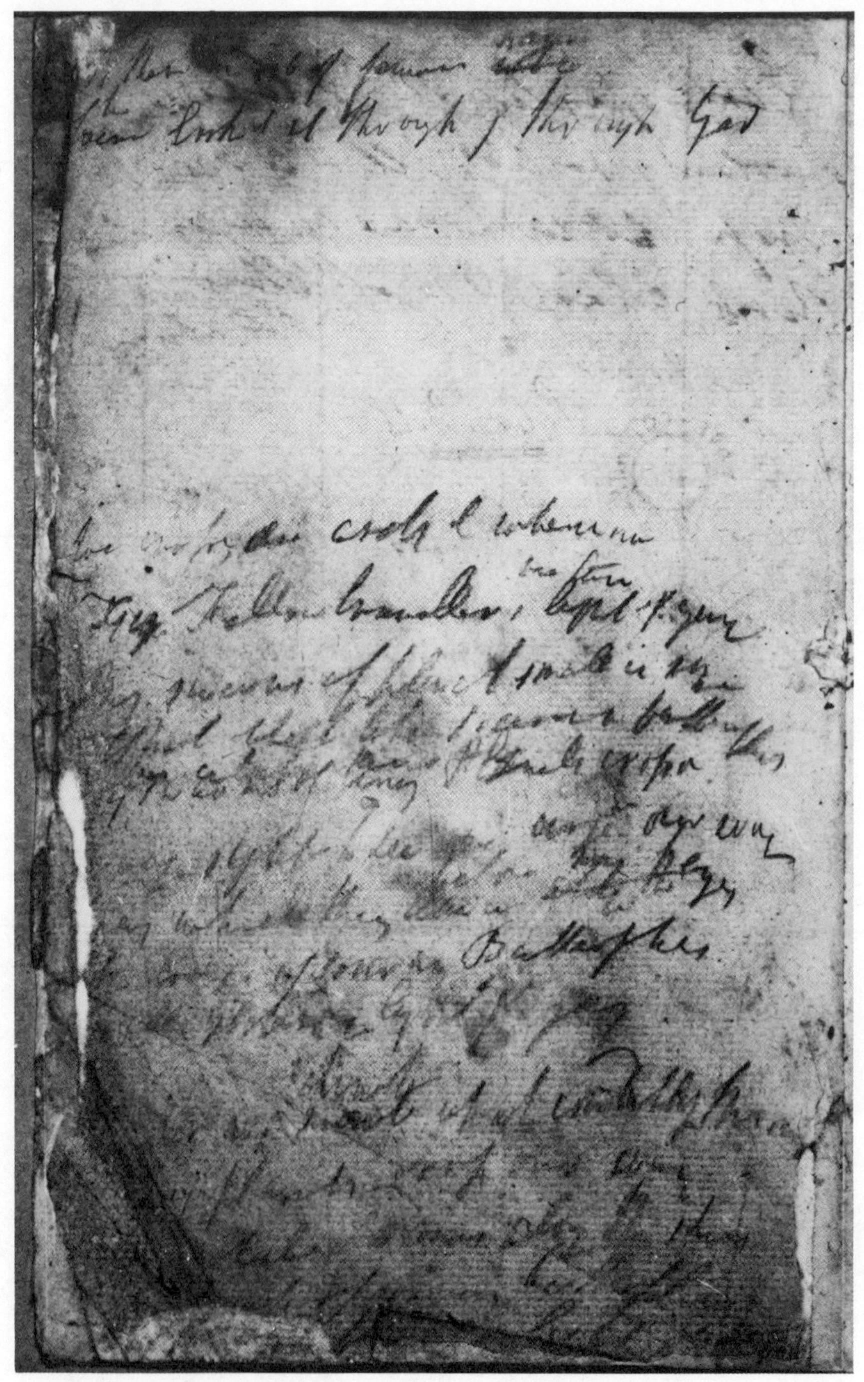

[1ᵛ]

name
Is there an orb of famous ~~note~~
he
Weve lookd it through & through God

We cross [?oer] [?crab] & wherever
{My [?we turn]
{T Fellow traveller, light [?& gay]
By swarms of planet small in size
And blest like soaring butterflies
[? ? ? ?]
if dreams of any [?] crossd

our way
[?] sight to see you [?]
before my eyes
[?] where they [?dance ?]
[? ?] of soaring Butterflies
[? ?] [?light] & gay

[?] and start up at countless throngs
[?] planets cross our way
[?] while [?showers] clog the skies
[? ?] of [?soaring] butterflies
[? ? ? ? ?]

These lines, all in pencil, appear to be either efforts at another version of ll. 36–40 (on 3ʳ) or trials toward a stanza to come between ll. 40 and 41.

(2)

And you have all a thousand fears
Both for my little Boat and me.

Meanwhile I from the helm admire
The pointed horns of my canoe
And did not pity touch my breast
To see how you are all distress'd
Till my ribs ached I'd laugh at you.

Away we go, my Boat and I,
Sure never man had such another
Whether among the winds we strive,
Or deep into the heavens we dive
We're each contented with the other.

Away we go, and what care we
For treasons, tumults and for wars
We are as calm in our delight
As is the crescent moon so bright
Among the scatter'd stars.

Up goes my Boat between the stars
Through many a breathless field of light
Through many a long blue field of ether
Leaving ten thousand stars beneath her,
Up goes my little Boat so bright.

[2r]

(2)

And you have all a thousand fears *14–35*
Both for my little Boat and me.

Meanwhile I from the helm admire
The pointed horns of my canoe
And did not pity touch my breast
To see how you are all distress'd
Till my ribs ached I'd laugh at you.

Away we go, my Boat and I,
Sure never man had such another
Whether among the winds we strive,
                                                  d
Or deep into the heavens we [?*dr*]*ive*
We're each contented with the other.

Away we go, and what care we
For treasons, tumults and for wars
We are as calm in our delight
As is the crescent moon so bright
Among the scatter'd stars.

Up goes my Boat between the stars
Through many a breathless field of light
Through many a long blue field of ether
Leaving ten thousand stars beneath her,
Up goes my little Boat so bright.

---

14 you *eras to* ye
C
17 canoe; *(SH)*
19 distress'd,
20 'Till
22 *del to* Triumphant o'er this dreadful pother *in pencil, overwritten in ink, then del by WW to* Frail Man neer sate in such another
24 dive,
25 We're *del and* each *rev to* Each is *in pencil then ink*
27 tumults, . . . wars,
30 scattered
32 light,

---

24 The miswriting "drive" is in the base text of MS. 3.

[2^{v}]

(36) The Crab, the Virgin, & the Bear
range among them all
(37) We pry into them all—Got wot

(36) Is there an orb of famous name
(?37) Weve looked it through & through

Old that
(53) ~~There~~ Andes thrusts a craggy [?spear]
c
(54) Through the grey y}louds; the Alps are there
(55) Like waters in commotion
(53) ~~That peak is Caucasus so dear~~
[? ? ? ? ?]

In the upper passages, only the inserted half line "range . . . all," is in ink; in the lower passage only the illegible final line is in pencil. What seems to be a related draft of ll. 36–37 stands at the top of 1^{v}; a further draft related to ll. 53–55 is found at the bottom of 3^{r}.

(3)

The Crab, the Virgin, & the Bear
We range among them all— God wot
~~The honest folk in Charles' Wain~~
~~Jog forward at a weary trot;~~
They're a red-headed race in Mars
Cover'd from top to toe with scars;
Such company I like it not.

The towns in Saturn are ill built
But Jove is ~~full of stately~~ towers,
The evening star is not amiss,
But what are all of them to this,
This little Earth of ours!

Then back again to our green Earth
What business had I here to roam?
The world for my remarks and me
Will not a whit the better be;
I've left my heart at home.

And there it is, the dear green Earth
And that's the ~~[illegible]~~ famous Pacific Ocean!
~~Old Caucasus thy shoulders rear~~
~~Up through that cloud! — And [illegible]~~ Thy
~~[illegible] heart's commotion!~~
~~The~~ Old Andes thrusts ~~that~~ yon craggy spear
Through the grey clouds, the Alps are there
Like waters in commotion

[3r]

(3)

(36) The Crab, the Virgin, and the Bear
(37) We range among them all— God wot
36 ~~*Those honest folk in Charles' Wain*~~
37 ~~*Jog forward at a weary trot;*~~

{'
38 *They* {*are a red-headed race in Mars*
39 *Cover'd from top to toe with scars;*
40 *Such company I like it not.*

41 *The towns in Saturn are ill built* *36–50*
i} {full of stately
42 *But Jove ha*}*s* {*very pretty bowers,*
43 *The evening star is not amiss,*
44 *But what are all of them to this,*
{E
45 *This little* {*earth of ours!*

---

spangles of the milky-way
36 ~~The Crab, the Virgin, and the Bear,~~
37 range *del to* pry *in pencil overwritten in ink* God wot *del to* have shot *in pencil and ink*
38 *del to* High oer the red-haired race of Mars *in pencil and ink*
39 Cover'd *del to* All seamed
41–45 *vertical line in margin apparently signals cancellation; extended version entered, one stanza at bottom of page, another at top of next page:*

The towns in Saturn are ill-built
{am I
But proud {I am that ~~I~~ have seen them
The Pleiads that appear to kiss
Each other in the vast abyss
With joy I sail between them

Bright Mercury resounds with mirth
Great Jove is full of stately bowers
But they & all that they contain
What are they to that tiny grain
{ darling
That {[?little] speck of ours

41 built,
42 *as MS. 5 with* rich *in pencil, del, as alt to* full
43 *as MS. 5 but* Evening Star *then pencil alt* Swift Mercury resounds with mirth *with* Great *as pencil alt to* Swift
44 this *del in pencil to* earth
45 this little Earth *del in pencil to* That darling spot

(3)

The Crab, the Virgin, & Ram, the Bear
We range among them all — Jove &c
~~The honest folk in Charles' Wain~~
~~Jog forward at a weary trot;~~
They're a redheaded race in Mars
Cover'd from top to toe with scars;
Such company I like it not.

The towns in Saturn are ill built
But Jove is ~~full of stately~~ towers,
The evening star is not amiss,
But what are all of them to this,
This little Earth of ours!

Then back again to our green Earth
What business had I here to roam?
The world for my remarks and me
Will not a whit the better be;
I've left my heart at home.

And there it is, the dear green Earth
And that's the ~~[illegible]~~ famous Pacific Ocean!
~~Old Caucasus thy shoulders rear~~
~~Up through that cloud! — And yon~~ Then
~~[illegible] forth thearts commotion!~~
~~Then~~ Old Andes thrusts ~~a~~ ~~that~~ you craggy spear
Through the grey clouds, the Alps are there
Like waters in commotion

[3r continued]

E
46 *Then back again to our green* {*earth*
47 *What business had I here to roam?*
48 *The world for my remarks and me*
49 *Will not a whit the better be;*
50 *I've left my heart at home.*

E
51 *And there it is, the dear green* {*earth*
famed
52 *And that's the ~~dear~~ Pacific Ocean!*
53 ~~Old Caucasus thy shoulders rear~~
54 ~~Up through that cloud! and am I here?~~
55 *Oh! my poor heart's commotion!*
Old ~~that~~ yon
(53) ~~There~~ Andes thrusts ~~a~~ craggy spear
(54) Through the grey clouds, the Alps are there
(55) Like waters in commotion

---

46 again to our green] to our beloved *over eras, then* our beloved *del in pencil and ink to* Earth the dear green *penciled above line by WW is* Then back to Earth [? ?]
47 *del in pencil to* Whole ages if I here should roam *in ink*
51 dear green] verdant *over eras, del in pencil to* dear green *del in pencil to* matchless *in ink*
52 And that's *del to* There spreads fam'd
53 Old Andes thrusts yon craggy spear
54 Through the grey clouds; the Alps are [?] *with last two words overwritten* appear
55 Like waters in commotion.

53–54 Erased was probably the version of MS. 4:
And that is Caucasus so dear**!**
To think that I again am here!

Yon tawny slip is Libyan sands

That silver thread the River Dnieper

~~And yonder amid Ocean's~~

And round them happy fields, like

In English gardens — I was lost then

What voice is that a voice exclaims

Was ever such a heartless loon

Unworthy you to set, and float

Through heaven with such the lovely Boat

~~[illegible]~~ the Boat that's like the crescent Moon

Unworthy you to set & float

Through heaven with such a lovely boat

A boat that's like the crescent

[3^{v}]

Yon Lybias sands
(56) ~~That~~ tawny slip is [~~?Bartas~~] waste
(57) That silver thread the River Dnieper

(58) ~~And yonder amid ocean [?]~~

(62) And round those happy fields we
span
(63) In boyish gambols—I was lost

(71) What voice is that a voice exclaims
(72) Was ever such a heartless Loon
(73) Unworthy you to sit, and float
(74) Through heaven with such a lovely Boat
(75) ~~Little [?]~~ A Boat that's like the crescent Moo

(73) Unworthy you to sit & float
(74) Through heaven with such a lovely boat
(75) A boat thats like the crescent

71–75 *see apparatus criticus to* 4^{r}

This page contains drafts toward revision of lines on 4^{r}, facing; most of the variants were inserted on 4^{r}; some are canceled in both places.

Yon tawny slip is [4] Libya's sands
That silver thread the River Dnieper
~~Then~~ And on the skirts of Ocean green
~~And there is little [illegible]~~

~~And there's the [illegible] River Dnieper;~~
And ~~yonder~~ on the skirts of
~~And [illegible] the~~ Ocean green
Is ~~that~~ a sweet Isle, of Isles the Queen;
Ye Fairies from all evil keep her!

And ~~there's~~ see, the Town where I was born,
And round these happy fields we sp[illegible]
~~And that's the house of Parson Swan!~~
In boyish gambols ~~[illegible]~~ was lost
My heart is touched ~~[illegible]~~
Where I have ~~[illegible]~~ but on this coast
~~[illegible] where I've~~ been! ~~and now~~
I feel I am a man.

Never did fifty things at once
Appear so lovely, never, never,
The woods how sweetly do they ring!
To hear the earth's ~~[illegible]~~ soft murmuring
Thus could I hang for ever.
"In, as before," [illegible]
~~Shame on you, cried my little Boat~~
~~Was ever such a heartless Loon!~~
~~In such a lovely Boat to sit,~~
~~And make no better use of it,~~
~~A Boat that's like the crescent moon.~~
What voice is that? — a voice exclaims
Was ever such a heartless Loon?
Unworthy you to sit, and flight
Through heaven, with such a lovely Boat
A Boat that's like the crescent Moon

In as before

[4r]

(4)

(56) Yon tawny slip is Lybia's sands
(57) That silver thread the River Dnieper
And}
(58) ~~There~~—}on the skirts of Ocean green
56 ~~*And there is little Tartary,*~~ *51–70*
57 ~~*And there's the famous river Dnieper,*~~
And ~~yonder~~ on the skirts of
58 ~~*And there amid*~~ ^ ~~*the*~~ *Ocean green*
a
59 *Is* ~~*that*~~ *sweet Isle; of Isles the Queen;*
60 *Ye Fairies from all evil keep her!*

see!
61 *And* ~~*there's*~~ *the Town where I was born,*
And round those happy fields we span
62 ~~*And that's the house of Parson Swan!*~~
In boyish gambols ~~for~~ I was lost
63 *My heart is touched* ~~*I must avow;*~~
Where I have but on this coast
64 ~~*Consider where I've*~~ *been!* ~~*and now*~~
65 *I feel I am a man.*

66 *Never did fifty things at once*
67 *Appear so lovely, never, never;*
68 *The woods how sweetly do they ring!*
soft
69 *To hear the earth's* ~~*sweet*~~ ^ *murmuring*
70 *Thus could I hang for ever.*

---

57 river Dnieper;
58 on the skirts of Ocean *del in pencil and ink to* yonder clothed in brightest *then* brightest *del in pencil to* lovely *del in pencil to* brightest
59 Isle, . . . queen;
61 see!] see
62 And round *rev to* Around
63 In boyish gambols—I was lost
64 been,
66 Never *alt* Ne'er
67 lovely, *del to* touching never,] never
68 woods *del in pencil and ink to* groves *then all but* ring *del to* How tunefully the forests
69 murmuring,

Yon tawny slip is (4) Lybia's sands
That silver thread the River Dnieper
And on the skirts of Ocean green

~~And there is little Tartary,~~

~~And there's the [illegible] River Dnieper;~~
~~And yonder~~ on the skirts of
~~And there amid the~~ Ocean green
Is ~~that~~ a sweet Isle, of Isles the Queen;
Ye Fairies from all evil keep her!

And ~~there~~ see! the Town where I was born,
~~And round those happy fields we span~~
~~And that's the house of Parson Swan.~~
~~In boyish gambols~~ ~~[illegible]~~ I was lost
My heart is touched ~~I must own~~
Where I have ~~[illegible]~~ but on the coast
~~consider where I've~~ been! ~~and now~~
I feel I am a man.

Never did fifty things at once
Appear so lovely, never, never;
The woods how sweetly do they ring!
To hear the earth's ~~sweet~~ soft murmuring
Thus could I hang for ever.

" on, as before, crescent
~~Shame on you! cried my little~~ Boat
~~Was ever such a heartless~~ Loon!
~~In such a lovely Boat to sit,~~
~~And make no better use of it,~~
~~A Boat that's like the crescent moon.~~

Or as before

What voice is that? — a voice exclaims
Was ever such a heartless Loon?
Unworthy you to sit, and flight
Through heaven, with such a lovely Boat
A Boat that's like the crescent Moon

[4ʳ continued]

in as before erased
71 ~~*"Shame on you"! cried my little Boat*~~
72 ~~*Was ever such a heartless Loon!*~~
73 in ~~*In such a lovely Boat to sit,*~~
as before
74 ~~*And make no better use of it,*~~
75 ~~*A Boat that's like the crescent moon.*~~
is
76 (71) What voice is th~~at~~—a voice exclaims
77 (72) Was ever such a heartless Loon?
78 (73) Unworthy you to sit, and float
79 (74) Through heav'n with such a lovely Boat
80 (75) A Boat thats like the crescent Moon

71–75 *deleted stanza in MS. 5 copied into MS. 6*
71 Shame on you! cried my little Boat *over eras*
{L
72 {loon!
73 In such a lovely *del to* Within a living
74–75 *two alt lines of pencil at top of page:*
Shame—said my [? ?] Shame
A boat more lovely than the [?crescent moon]
75 that's like *del to* more lovely than *del to* twin Sister of

---

The canceled stanza at the bottom of the page may be a version of ll. 71–75, but three lines are quite different: 76, 78, 79.

(5)

Out, out, and like a brooding hen
Beside your sooty hearth-stone cower,
Or creep along the dirt, and pick
Your way with your good walking-stick
Just three good miles an hour.

Sure in the breast of full-grown Poet
So faint a heart was ne'er before,
Come to the Poets wild delights,
I have ten thousand lovely sights,
Ten thousand sights in store.

I am a ~~pretty little~~ Barge of matchless powers
Then come, I pray you, come with me,
I want a comrade, and for you
There's nothing that I would not do,
There's nothing that you shall not see.

Come, and together we will reap
Unheard of glory and renown
Mount with me, and your darling Skiff
More daring far than Hippogriff,
Will make ~~the~~ the universe world your own.

[5^r]

(5)

Out, out, and like a brooding hen *71–85*
Beside your sooty hearth-stone cower,
G}o
{*Or*}
{*Ay creep along the dirt, and pick*
Your way with your good walking-stick
Just three good miles an hour.

Sure in the breast of full-grown Poet
So faint a heart was ne'er before,
Come to the Poet's wild delights,
I have ten thousand lovely sights,
Ten thousand sights in store.

I am a ~~*pretty little*~~ *Barge* of matchless powers
Then come, I pray you, come with me,
I want a comrade, and for you
There's nothing that I would not do,
There's nothing that you shall not see.

Come, and together we will reap
Unheard of glory and renown
Mount with me, and your darling Skiff,
More daring far than Hippogrif,
the universe
all
Will make ~~*the*~~ *world*~~*s*~~ *your own.*

---

83 dirt,] dirt
84 good *over eras (SH)*
86 Sure *del to* Neer
87 before,] before; *then line del in pencil and ink to* Fluttered so faint a heart before
88 Poets *then line del in pencil and ink to* Was it the music of the spheres
89 *del in pencil and ink to* That overpowered your mortal ears
90 *del to* Such sound shall trouble him no more *then* sound *eras to* din *and* him *overwritten* them
91 *del to* A lower range shall bound our flight *del to* These lower precincts shall suffice *del to* These nether precincts do not lack
92 Then come, I pray you, *eras to* Charms of their own then
93 *over l. 92, eras (SH)*
95 There's nothing *del to* Nought is there see.] see
96–100 *omitted*

---

83 "Go" was written first in pencil, then in ink.

[5^{v}]

[pencil underneath]

(116) Or if appearances of dread
(117) And strong disturbances please you more,
(118) These shall be given I can reveal
(119) How earth and heaven were taught
to feel
(120) The might of magic lore

[?] of worlds you [?own]

[ink over-written]

And
116 ~~Or~~ if appearances of dread
~~please~~
117 And strong disturbance tempt you more
shall
118 That voyage ~~will~~ to you reveal
(118) ~~These will be given; I can~~ reveal
given
119 How earth and Heaven are taught
to feel
120 The might of magic lore.

(126) My pretty little form of Light &c

121 Come and together we will reap
122 Transcendent glory and renown
123 Mount with me & your darling Skiff
124 Shall make us more bold than Hippogrif
125 Un[?]thought of worlds your own

(126) My pretty little Form of light

---

116 Or *over eras then last three words del to* you thirst with genuine zeal *then* genuine *del in pencil to* daring
117 *del to* Less quiet regions to explore
118 That *del to* Prompt
119 heaven
120 lore."
121–125 *omitted*

Since l. 126 appears both before and after ll. 121–125, the proper position of the stanza is uncertain; probably ll. 126–130 were once intended to follow l. 120, but ll. 121–125 were added, then canceled.

(6)

Haste! and above the Land of Snow
We'll sport amid the boreal Morning
Where thousand Forms of light are riding
Among the Stars the Stars now hiding
And now the Stars adorning

I know a deep romantic Land
A Land that's deep and far away
And fair it is as evening skies
And in the farthest heart it lies
Of deepest Africa
[illegible]
So will into the realm of Fairy
Among the lovely Shades of things
The shadowy Forms of mountains bare
And streams and bowers and ladies fair
The shades of palaces and kings."
[illegible]
"[illegible]
My pretty little Form of light,
My sweet and beautiful Canoe,
Now, though it grieves me to the heart,
I feel, I feel that we must part,
I must take leave of you.

[6r]

(6)

Haste! and above the Land of Snow *86–105*
We'll sport amid the boreal {*M* / *morning*
Where thousand Forms of Light are riding
Among the Stars, the Stars now hiding
And now the Stars adorning

I know a deep romantic Land
A Land that's deep and far away
And fair it is as evening skies
And in the farthest heart it lies
Of deepest Africa

---

101 snow *then last five words del to* let us together be taught *eras to* be taught—by me be taught *del to* above Siberean snows

102 We'll sport amid *del to illeg phrase, eras to* To mingle with *del back to* We'll sport amid

103 forms *then line del to* [?] countless lustres gliding *then illeg portion overwritten* And all her *then line del again to* Will mingle with their [*rev to* her] lustres gliding

104 hiding,

105 adorning.

106 a deep romantic *del to* the secrets of a *over illeg eras, following* the secrets of a Land *above line in pencil*

107 *del to* Where mortal [*overwritten* human] foot did never stray

108 And fair it is *del to* Fair is the Land skies,

109 farthest *del to* deepest *then line del to* And cool—though in the depth it lies

110 deepest *del to* burning Africa.

(6)

Haste! and above the Land of Snow
We'll sport amid the boreal Morning
Where thousand Forms of Light are riding
Among the Stars the Stars now hiding
And now the Stars adorning

I know a deep romantic Land
A Land that's deep and far away
And fair it is as evening skies
And in the farthest heart it lies
Of deepest Africa
~~[illegible]~~
Or we'll into the realm of Fairy
Among the lovely Shades of things
The shadowy Forms of mountains bare
And streams and bowers and ladies fair
The shades of palaces and kings."
[illegible]
~~My pretty little Form of Light,~~
~~My sweet and beautiful Canoe,~~
~~Now, though it grieves me to the heart,~~
~~I feel, I feel that we must part,~~
~~I must take leave of you.~~

[6ʳ continued]

~~Thence will we to the~~
~~world~~

111 *Or we'll into the realm of Fairy*
112 *Among the lovely Shades of things*
113 *The shadowy Forms of mountains bare*
114 *And streams and bowers and ladies fair*
115 *The shades of palaces and kings."*

And if appearances see oppos
Come & together we will reap page
{[?Transcendent]
{[? ?] or [?Innate]

126 *"My pretty little Form of Light,*
127 *My sweet and beautiful Canoe,*
128 *Now, though it grieves me to the heart,*
129 *I feel, I feel that we must part,*
130 *I must take leave of you.*

---

111 Or we'll into Faery
112 shades
144 streams, and bowers,
115 kings;
126–130 little vagrant {F {L
My ~~pretty little~~ {form of {light
gay
My ~~sweet~~ and beautiful Canoe,
Well have you played your friendly part
~~Now, though it grieves me to the heart,~~
As kindly take what from my heart
~~I feel, I feel that we must part,~~
Experience forces—then adieu
~~I must take leave of you.~~

115/126 The partly legible line partly overwritten by "Transcendent" is in pencil.

H

There was a time when all mankind
Did listen with such [illegible] their ears
Then boldly myself the trump of fame
Blown by the Poets breath proclaim
The wonders of [illegible]

* Go—but ~~the~~ world's a sleepy world
And 'tis I fear an age too late
Go ~~[illegible]~~ to seek some ~~[illegible]~~ growth
For I myself in very truth
Am ~~[illegible]~~ all unfit to be your Mate

Long have I loved what I behold
The night that calms the day that cheers
The common growth of Mother earth
Suffices me—her tears, her mirth
Her humblest mirth and tears

~~There is a Party~~ the magic ring
The dragon's wing—the magic ring
I ~~[illegible]~~ shall not covet for my dower
If I along that lowly way
With sympathetic heart may stray
And with a ~~[illegible]~~ soul of power.

H

136 There was a time when all mankind
137 Did listen with submissive ears
138 Then bodly might the trump of fame
139 Blown by the Poets breath proclaim
spheres
140 The wonders of invisible [?years]

[~~?yon~~]
146 * *Go—but ~~the~~ World's a sleepy world*
147 *And 'tis I fear an age too late*
seek wild adventurous
148 *Go ~~tempt~~ some ~~visionary~~ Youth*
149 *For I myself in very truth*
{*a*
{*u* all
150 *Am ~~o[?]n~~ unfit to be your Mate*

151 *Long have I loved what I behold*
152 *The night that calms the day that chears*
153 *The common growth of Mother earth*
154 *Suffices me—her tears, her mirth*
155 *Her humblest mirth and tears*

(181) ~~*There is a Party &c*~~
156 The dragon's wing—the magic ring
shall
157 I ~~need~~ not covet for my [?] dower
158 If I along that lowly way
159 With sympathetic heart may stray
soul
160 And with a ~~voice~~ of power.

---

137 submissive ears; *del to* a faith sincere
138 Then boldly might the trump of Fame *del to* Then Poets whereso'er their flight *del*
139 Poet's *then line del to* Rehearsed with confident delight *del*
~~such~~
{their wild career
140 The wonders of {~~the~~ ^ ~~invisible spheres~~.
138–140 *another version drafted in pencil at top of page, then overwritten in ink:*
To sage or bard in mystery versd
When Poets fearlessly rehears'd
The wonders of a wild career.
147 'tis, . . . late,
Take with you some ~~adventurous~~aspiring
wi
148 Go seek some bo ld ^ ambitious ^ youth *with first caret in pencil*

149 myself,
150 Mate.
151 lov'd
152 cheers;
153 mother
154 mirth,
155 tears.
157 I shall not covet for my dower
159 hearts *then* s *eras*

The frequent verso additions and the cancellations of stanzas make the correct numbering of lines uncertain; their order in MS. 6 has been taken as a guide. It is possible that some of the passages here numbered sequentially were not so intended, but rather that one was at the time of entry intended as a substitute for another; for example, ll. 136–140 may have been written to replace ll. 141–145, canceled, although the asterisk shows them to be ahead of that stanza.

146 Cancellation of "the" is in pencil.
147/148 The phrase "wild adventurous" is in pencil, as is the cancellation of "visionary."
156–160 Further revisions are drafted on 68r.

(7)

You are a most delightful Barge
But while your pleasure you're pursuing
Without impediment or let,
My little Barge you quite forget
What on the earth is doing.

There was a time
A time when Poets lived in clover,
What boots it now to keep the key
Of Fairy Land? for, woe is me!
Those blessed days are over.

There is a party in the Bower
Round the stone-table in my Garden,
The Squire is there and as I guess,
His little Daughter Bess,
With Harry the Church-warden.

They know not I have been so far
I see them there in number nine,
All in the Bower of Weymouth Pine
I see them, there they are!
This was the appointed day & hour

[7r]

(7)

You are a most delightful Barge *106–110*
're
But while your pleasure you p pursuing
Without impediment or let,
My little Barge you quite forget
What on the earth is doing.
♓

see opposite
Page
fond believing time !
There was a ~~time a time indeed~~ *116–120*
A time when Poets liv'd in clover;
What boots it now to keep the key
F ?
Of fairy Land for, woe is me!
Those blessed days are over.

---

131 *as MS. 5 but* Barge, *del to* Temptation lurks among your words
~~pleasure evermore,~~
these
132 But ~~while your pleasure you're~~ pursuing
while these pleasure you're ^
134 little Barge *del to* radiant Pinnace *and* quite *del*
135 Earth . . . doing:
141–145 *omitted*

135/141 The symbol points to an inserted stanza on 6v, facing.

(7)

You are a most delightful Barge
But while your pleasure you're pursuing
Without impediment or let
My little Barge you quite forget
What on the earth is doing.

There was a ~~[illegible]~~ fondly cherished time see opposite Page
A time ~~when~~ Poets lived in clover;
What boots it now to keep the key
Of Fairy Land? for, woe is me!
Those blessed days are over.

~~My [illegible] [illegible]~~ * [illegible]
~~There~~ is a party in the Bower
Round the stone-table in my Garden,
The Squire is ~~there~~ come and as I guess,
His ~~pretty~~ ruddy little Daughter Bess,
With Harry the Church-warden.

~~They were to come this very evening,~~ next
They know not I have been so far
I see them there in number nine,
All in the Bower of Weymouth Pine
I see them, there they are!
Thus was the appointed day & hour

[7^r continued]

*

(176) My shining Pinnac fare thee well
181 ~~*There is a Party in the Bower*~~ *121–130*
To
182 ~~*Round*~~ *the stone-table in my Garden,*
come
183 *The Squire is* ~~*there*~~*, and as I guess,*
ruddy
184 *His* ~~*pretty*~~ *little* ^ *Daughter Bess,*
185 *With Harry the Church-warden.*

come
meet
186 ~~*They were to come this very evening,*~~
187 *They know not I have been so far,*
188 *I see them there in number nine,*
189 *All in the Bower of Weymouth Pine*
!
190 *I see them, there they are* }
(186) This was the appointed day & hour

181–185 *much revised: original first line is canceled, original second line becomes first line, new second line is inserted, original third and fourth lines are merged in a new third line, original fifth line is canceled, and new fourth and fifth line are inserted:*

For
~~For me are homelier tasks prepared—~~
To the Stone table in my Garden
Loved haunt of many a summer hour
The Squire is come ^ ~~and, as I guess,~~
[?his]
his
~~His little ruddy~~ ^ daughter Bess,
Beside him in the cool recess
~~With Harry the Churchwarden.~~
Sits blooming like a flower.

186 This was the appointed day and hour— *del to* From all reproaches shield me heaven *del in pencil to* O shield me, shield me from reproach *in pencil overwritten in ink; pencil alt at foot of page:* With them are many more [?convened]

187 far—

188 I see them *del to* The rest are *del in pencil to* I see them *in pencil* there, nine,] nine

189 All in the Bower of *del in pencil and ink to* Beneath the spreading *with del illeg pencil below line*

---

(176), 182–183 The asterisk points to further revisions on 7^v, overleaf.

These given what more need I desire
To stir to sooth or elevate
What nobler marvels than the mind
May in ~~that~~ life's daily prospect find
May find or there create

Why wander then to fairy walks
To forests and enchantments drear
If I at home ~~may~~ ~~[illegible]~~ the might
Of one ~~[illegible]~~ and the ~~[illegible]~~ delights
Of ~~[illegible]~~ phantasy and inward fear.

~~May~~ shining Benoni ~~[illegible]~~ shall well
~~[illegible]~~ the stone ~~[illegible]~~ Table in my Garden

[illegible]
Repentance is a tender Sprite
[illegible]
Descend [illegible]
[illegible] adventurous [illegible]
Wanderers far [illegible]
And to my own delight
[illegible]

[7v]

161 These given what more need I desire
162 To stir to soothe or elevate
163 What nobler marvels than the mind
164 May in ~~that~~ lifes daily prospect find
165 May find or there create.

166 Why wander then to faery walks
167 To forests and enchantments drear
168 If I at home may see the might
a shaping Sprite strong
169 Of conscience, and the ~~dread~~ delight
shaping
170 Of [-?-] phantasy and inward fear.

{My
(176) {[?Then] shining Pinnace fare theee well
To {T
(182) ~~Round~~ the stone ~~slate~~ {table in my Garden
(183) The Squire is come and

171 A potent wand doth Sorrow wield
172 What spell so strong as guilty fear
173 Repentance is a tender Sprite
174 She dawns and smitten by her light
175 All troubles disappear

[ink over- written]
(176) ~~My Shining Pinnace fare thee well~~
176 My Shining Pinnace let us now
177 Desend from this aerial Height
178 Then take thy way adventurous Skiff
179 More daring far than Hippogrif
180 And be thy own delight
(181) For me are homelier tasks prepared

---

164 life's
166–170 *omitted*
171 sorrow *entire line written by SH over eras, possibly l. 166 entered by mistake*
172 fear?
174 *as MS. 5 but* dawns, *then entire line del to* If aught on earth have heavenly might
175 All troubles disappear. *del to* Tis lodged within her silent tear *then variants of* lodged *entered below line:* couched *del in pencil to* lodged *in pencil overwritten in ink*
176 My shining Pinnace *del to* But grant my wishes *in pencil overwritten in ink*
177 Descend . . . height.
178 advent'rous Skiff,
179 Hyppogrif,
180 delight.

171–175 Underneath the ink is a version in pencil, identical except for a dash after "dawns."

(8)

There sits the Vicar, & his Dame
~~And there's the~~ Wife of Parson Swan,
~~There sits~~
And there's my good Friend, Stephen Otter,
And, ere the light of evening fail,
To them I must relate the Tale
Of Peter Bell the Potter."

Off flew my pretty little Boat
All in a frame of indignation,
And I, as well as I was able,
On two poor legs, to my Stone-table,
Limped on with some vexation

"Oh here he is!" cried little Bess,
She saw me at the garden door
We've waited, [illegible]
"Oh here he is" cried Mrs Swan
They crowd and all about me throng
And all at once around me ran
Full nine of them, or more
[illegible]
~~[illegible]~~
[illegible]
Said I, no doubt with visage pale
And if my Friends it pleases you,
This instant without more ado
We'll have the promised Tale.

[8^r]

(8)

There sits the Vicar, & his Dame
An~~d there's the~~ Wife of Parson Swan, *131–150*
~~There sits~~
And there~~'s~~ my good Friend, Stephen Otter,
And, ere the light of evening fail,
To them I must relate the Tale
Of Peter Bell the Potter."

Off flew my pretty little Boat
All in a trance of indignation,
And I, as well as I was able,
On two poor legs, to my stone-table,
Limp'd on with some vexation

"Oh here he is!" cried little Bess,
She saw me at the garden door
We ve waited anxiously & long
"O here he is!" cried M^rs^. Swan.
They cried and all about me throng
And all at once around me ran
Full nine of them, or more.

---

191 There sit^s^ the Vicar ,} and his Dame, *with caret in pencil*
192 there's] there Friend,] Friend
193 fail,] fail
195 Potter."—
196 little *del to illeg word eras to* sparkling pretty *del and* in scorn *added to end of line*
197 All *del to* Yea *in pencil and ink* indignation;
199 *no hyphen; pencil alt entered above line:* [?bared]
200 vexation.
201 "Oh] O
202 Garden door,
203–204 "We've waited anxiously and long"
They cried, and all around me throng
205 them,] them

(8)

There sits the Vicar, & his Dame
~~And there's the~~ Wife of Parson Swan,
~~There sits~~
And there's my good Friend, Stephen Otter,
And, ere the light of evening fail,
To them I must relate the Tale
Of Peter Bell the Potter."

Off flew my pretty little Boat
All in a trance of indignation,
And I, as well as I was able,
On two poor legs, to my stone-table,
Limped on with some vexation

"Oh here he is!" cried little Bess,
She saw me at the garden door
[illegible]
"O here he is" cried Mrs Swan
[illegible]
And all at once around me ran
Full nine of them, or more
[illegible]
~~[illegible]~~
[illegible]
Sad..., no doubt with visage pale
And if my Friends it pleases you,
This instant without more ado,
We'll have the promised Tale.

[8r continued]

Resume your seats within the bower
206 ~~*"Sit down—I beg you would be seated,"*~~
I softly said
207 ~~*Said I, no doubt*~~ *with visage pale*
208 *And if, my Friends, it pleases you,*
209 This instant, without more ado,
210 *We'll have the promis'd Tale.*

206–210 *revision began with WW's pencil above stanza:*
Reproach me not your fears be still
Be thankful that we here are met
and pencil drafts at foot of page:
Resume your seats within shade
Come, Friends, & promptly shall be paid
This [?instant]
[?]
O snug within the bower ~~be~~ paid
And strait
stanza then recopied in ink by WW at top of page:
a
Repro ch me not, your fears be still—
Be thankful we again have met—
Resume your seats within the shade
My Friends, and promptly shall be paid
The well-remember'd debt

206 "Resume your seats within the Bower." *with ink alt interlined:* Reproach me not, your fears be still

207 pale,

208 And if,] And, if Friends,] Friends

209 This instant without more ado

210 promised

206/207 In pencil.

He two and thirty years or more
Had been a wild and woodland Rover
Had heard the
Had journeyed where th' Atlantic roars
On farthest Cornwall's rocky shores
And trod the cliffs of Dover.
And he had seen Caernarvon's towers
Oft had he lit his one night's fire
Beyond
And passed his bed by Severns side,
Waked by the Birds at break of day
While on the hills the vapours grey
In silent squadrons glide
From Hampshire's dreary steps
Where not a tree for miles is seen
Had carried [illegible] as [illegible]
Its [illegible] [illegible] by [illegible] [illegible]
And [illegible] [illegible] [illegible] [illegible] [illegible]
He Buffeted by storms had paced
By long [illegible] or by [illegible]
Unpeopled Charnwoods stony waste
Or sandy [illegible] Delamere

In their wood is a Travellers Hut
Renown'd for many a festive hour
There had he drank to Robin Hood
Upon the very spot where stood
That Outlaws favorite Bower.

The towers of Bedford he had [illegible]
[illegible]

[8v]

(236) He two and thirty years or more
(237) Had been a wild and homeless Rover
Had heard the
(238) Had journied where th'Atlantic roars
(239) On farthest Cornwalls rocky shores
(240) And trod the cliffs of Dover.

{T
(241) And he had seen Caernarvon's {towers
256 Oft had he lit his one night's fire
Severns
{And {Severns
257 {Had framed his bed by {Derwent Side,
258 Waked by the Birds at break of day
259 While on the hills the vapours grey
260 In silent squadrons glide

261 From Hawes his devious steps
While not a tree for miles is seen
262 Had ranged through Exmoor wide
& drear
{His
(262) {Its hospitable shade to rear
(262) And sought each strggling embraced
263 He Buffeted by storms had paced
By storms or the [?]
264 Unpeopled Charnwoods stony waste
265 Or sandy ~~del~~ Delamere

266 In Sherwood is a Traveller's Hut
267 Renown'd for many a festive hour
268 There had he drank to Robin Hood
269 Upon the very spot where stood
{Bo}
270 That Outlaws favorite {bo }wer.

(241) The Towers of Warwick he had ~~see~~
passed

(236–240) *see apparatus to 10r*
256–270 *omitted*

The additions on this page do not seem to relate to the facing recto in the customary manner, and the correct order and numbering of the lines must remain uncertain. Fragmentary variants of the first stanza may be found on 9v; the next complete stanza is written cleanly on 10v for insertion on 11r, following l. 255. The line following the first stanza on this page is the version of l. 241 used in MS. 6; it also appears on 9v and as an insertion on 10r. The last line on the page may be an alternative version of l. 241 (as numbered) or a tentative beginning of yet another stanza on Peter's wanderings.

191

And so, though somewhat out of breath,
With lips, no doubt, and visage pale,
And sore too from a slight contusion,
Did I, to cover my confusion,
Begin the promised Tale.

All by the moonlight river side
It gave three miserable groans,
"'Tis come then to a pretty pass"
Said Peter to the groaning Ass,
"But I will bang your bones!"

"My dearest Sir," ~~cried Mrs.~~ a voice exclaimed Swan,
"You've got at once into the middle,"
And little Bess with accent sweeter
Cried, "O dear Sir! but who is Peter?"
Said Harry, "'tis a downright riddle."

DOVE COTTAGE

[9[r]]

(9)

211 *And so, though somewhat out of breath,* 151–155
212 *With lips, no doubt, and visage pale,*
213 *And sore too from a slight contusion,*
214 *Did I, to cover my confusion,*
215 *Begin the promis'd Tale.*

---

216 *All by the moonlight River side* 156–165
217 *It gave three miserable groans,*
218 *"Tis [~~?~~] come then to a pretty pass"*
219 *Said Peter to the groaning Ass,*
220 *"But I will* bang your *bones."*

a voice exclaimed
221 *"My dearest Sir,"* ~~*cried Mrs. Swan,*~~
222 *"You've got at once into the middle,"*
223 *And little Bess with accent sweeter*
224 *Cried "O dear Sir! but who is Peter?"*
225 *Said Harry, " 'tis a downright riddle."*

---

211 *del by WW to* Their seats within the bower [?] *with* resum'd *entered above line*
212 *caret inserted following* doubt, *and alt phrase written by WW in pencil, overwritten in ink (once in wrong position, del):* With panting breath
213 contusion,] contusion
215 promised
215/216 *new page begins (7[v]), headed* Part First
217 groans;
218 " 'Tis come then
220 bones"
221 "My dearest Sir," a voice exclaimed, *then first four words del in pencil and ink to* Good Sir— The Vicar's *in pencil overwritten in ink*
222 "You've got *partially erased to* You rush *following pencil revision above line* middle;"
224 Cried, O
225 Harry *del in pencil and ink to* Stephen *in pencil overwritten in ink*
225/226 *two illeg pencil lines eras, the second beginning* Church[?]

---

218 Deletion by erasure.

Were
We're all left hopelessly behind;
To our infirmity [illegible]
And start from the Apennine

He had heard the wild Atlantic surges roar
On farthest Cornwall's rocky shore
And trod the cliffs of Dover
[illegible] heard he [illegible]
Had [illegible]
To the castles and halls Peter gone
To farthest Pembroke, and anon
Was found alive at Dover
To the lands end his feet had gone,
Why, no one knows — and he anon
Was found alive at Dover
And he had seen Caernarvon's towers

[9v]

~~We've~~
(228) We're all left hopelessly behind; *168–170*
(229) To our infirmity be kind
(230) And start from the beginning.

~~vex'd~~ surges
(238) Had heard the ~~deep~~ Atlantic ^ roar *177–180*
(239) On farthest Cornwall rocky shore
(240) And trod the cliffs of Dover

(256) Oft had he lit his one night's fire
(257) And framd by Severn's side

(238) To the Lands end had Peter gone
(239) To farthest Pembroke, and anon
(240) Was found alone at Dover

(238) To the Lands end his feet had gone,
(239) Why, no one knows—and he anon
(240) Was found alone at Dover

(241) And he had seen Caernarvons Towers

(10)

The Squire cried, "Sure as Paradise
Was lost to man by Adam's sinning
This leach is for us all too bold
Who Peter was let that be told
And therefore Sir, I wish you would
Begin at the beginning.
And start from the beginning
A Potter Sir, he was by trade
And becoming quite collected
And wheresoever he appear'd
Full twenty times was Peter fear'd
For once that Peter was respected.

He [illegible] more
Had [illegible] Dover
Had been in [illegible]
And he had been at Dover
And trod the cliffs of
In Kent, Sir, and at Dover.
And he had seen Caernarvon's towers
And he had been at Nottingham,
And well he knew the Spire of Sarum,
And he had been where Lincoln Bell,
To Shepherds in the distant Dell
Rings out his loud alarum.

[10^r]

(10)

226 *The Squire cried, "Sure as Paradise* 166–185

Man

227 *Was lost to ~~us~~ by Adam's sinning*

This leap is for us all too bold

228 ~~*We all are wandering in a wood,*~~

Who Peter was let that be told

229 ~~*And therefore Sir, I wish you would*~~

230 ~~*Begin at the beginning.*~~

And start from the beginning

231 *A Potter Sir, he was by trade*
232 *Said I becoming quite collected*
233 *And wheresoever he appear'd*
234 *Full twenty times was Peter fear'd*
235 *For once that Peter was respected*

236 *He two and thirty years or more*
237 *Had been a wild and woodland Rover*

heard the Atlantic surges roar
in }

238 *Had ~~been [?at]} farthest Pembroke~~, Sir,*

~~At Falmouth and Winchester~~

239 ~~*And he had been at Exeter*~~

And trod the cliffs of

240 ~~*In Kent, Sir, and at*~~ *Dover.*

And he had seen Caérnarvon's towers

241 ~~*And he had been at Nottingham,*~~
242 *And well he knew the Spire of Sarum,*
243 *And he had been where Lincoln Bell,*
244 *To Shepherds in the distant Dell*
245 *Rings out his loud alarum.*

---

226 "sure
227 sinning,
228 bold;
230 beginning"
231 Sir,] Sir
232 I, . . . collected,
233 appeared
235 respected.
237 rover;
238 Had heard the Atlantic surges roar
239 On farthest Cornwall's rocky shore,
240 Cliffs of Dover:
241 Caernarvon's Towers
242 Sarum,] Sarum
244 To Shepherds in the distant Dell, *del to* Flings oer the fens [*with* s *eras*] its ponderous knell *ink over pencil*
245 Rings out his [*eras to* its] loud alarum. *del to* Its far renouned *ink over pencil*

If hard he let his only nightly fire
That framed his bed by Derwent's side
Waked by the birds at break of day
While on the hills the vapours grey
In silent squadrons glide

[10v]

Oft had he lit his one night's fire
And framed his bed by Derwents side
Waked by the birds at break of day
While on the hills the vapours grey
In silent squadrons glide

(11)

At Doncaster, at York, and Leeds,
And merry Carlisle had he been,
And all along the Lowlands fair
All through the bonny Shire of Ayr
And far as Aberdeen.

And he had been at Inverness,
And Peter by the mountain rills
Had danced his rounds with Highland Lasses
And he had lain beside his Asses
On lofty Cheviot Hills

And he had trudg'd thro' Yorkshire Dales
Among the rocks and winding Scars
Where deep and low the hamlets lie
Beneath their little patch of sky
And little lot of stars

And all along the indented winding Coast,
Bespatter'd by the salt sea foam
Where'er a knot of houses lay,
On headland or in hollow bay,
Sure never man like him did roam

DOVE COTTAGE TRUST

[11^r]

(11)

246 *At Doncaster, at York, and* Leeds, 186–205
247 *And merry Carlisle had he been,*
248 *And all along the Lowlands fair*
249 *All through the bonny Shire of Ayr*
250 *And far as Aberdeen.*

251 *And he had been at Inverness,*
252 *And Peter by the mountain rills*
253 *Had danced his round~~s~~ with Highland Lasses*
254 *And he had lain beside his Asses*
255 *On lofty Cheviot Hills*
*

271 *And he had trudg'd thro' Yorkshire Dales*
272 *Among the rocks and winding Scars*
~~mouldering~~
273 *Where deep and low the hamlets lie*
274 *Beneath their little patch of sky*
275 *And little plot of stars.*

indented
276 *And all along the winding Coast,*
277 *Bespatter'd by the salt-sea foam*
278 *Where'er a knot of houses lay,*
279 *On headland or in hollow bay,*
280 *Sure never man like him did roam.*

---

249 shire
250 And] As *rev to* And
254 *over l. 255 eras (SH)*
271 through
272 Scars;
273 Hamlets
274 sky,
275 stars:
276 indented coast,
277 Bespattered . . . foam,
278 Houses
279 bay—

---

246 Erased was probably the reading of MS. 4: "Brou**gh**."
272 The "mouldering" in the margin may have been an alternate for "winding."

(12)

As well might Peter in the Fleet
Have been fast bound, a begging debtor
He travell'd here, he travell'd there;
But ~~Peter never~~ was a hair
~~In~~ heart or head the better
[Interlined: not the value of; Was]

He rov'd among the vales and streams,
In the green wood and hollow dell;
They were his dwellings night and day
But Nature ne'er could find the way
Into the heart of Peter Bell

In vain through every changeful year
Did Nature lead him as before;
A primrose by a River's brim
A yellow Primrose was to him
And it was nothing more.

Small change it made in Peter's heart
To see his gentle pannier'd train
With more than vernal pleasure feeding
Where'er the tender grass was leading
It's earliest green along the lane

[12r]

(12)

As well might Peter in the Fleet 206–225
Have been fast bound, a begging debtor
He travell'd here, he travell'd there;
not the value of
But Peter never was ^ a hair
Was
~~In~~ ^ heart or head the better

He rov'd among the vales and streams,
In the green-wood and hollow dell,
They were his dwellings night and day
But Nature ne'er could find the way
Into the heart of Peter Bell

In vain through every changeful year
Did Nature lead him as before;
A primrose by a River's brim
A yellow Primrose was to him
And it was nothing more.

Small change it made in Peter's heart
To see his gentle pannier'd train
With more than vernal pleasure feeding
Where'er the tender grass was leading
It's earliest green along the lane

---

282 debtor;
283 travelled . . . travelled there,
284 But not the value of a hair
285 better.
287 green wood
288 day,
289 way, *then comma eras*
290 Bell.
291 year,
293 Primrose river's
297 panniered
300 lane.

284–285 The revisions are MW's.

(13)

In vain through water earth and air
The soul of happy sound was spread
When Peter on some April morn
Beneath the broom or budding thorn
Made the warm earth his lazy bed.

At noon when by the forest's edge
He lay beneath the branches high
The soft blue sky did never melt
Into his heart, he never felt
The witchery of the soft blue sky

On a fair prospect some have look'd
And felt as I have heard them say
As if the moving time had been
A thing as stedfast as the scene
On which they gazed themselves away.

With Peter Bell, I need not tell
That this had never been the case
He was a Carl as wild and rude
And ever hue and cry pursued,
As ever ran a felon's race.

[13r]

(13)

In vain through water earth and air *226–245*
The soul of happy sound was spread
When Peter on some April morn
Beneath the broom or *budding thorn*
Made the warm earth his lazy bed.

At noon when by the forest's edge
He lay beneath the branches high
The soft blue sky did never melt
Into his heart, he never felt
The witchery of the soft blue sky

On a fair prospect some have look'd
And felt as I have heard them say
As if the moving time had been
A thing as stedfast as the scene
On which they gaz'ed themselves away.

With Peter Bell, I need not tell
That this had never been the case
{*C*
He was a {*carl as wild and rude*
And ever hue and cry pursued,
As ever ran a felon's race.

---

302 spread,
303 morn,
304 thorn,
310 the *over illeg eras (SH)* sky.
315 gaz'd
317 case;

(14)

Of all that lead a lawless life,
Of all that love their lawless lives,
In city or in village small
He was the wildest far of all,
He had a dozen wedded wives.

"Nay start not! wedded wives & twelve!
But how one Wife could e'er come near him
In simple truth I cannot tell,
But I must say of Peter Bell
To see him, was to fear him.

Though Nature could not touch his heart
By lovely forms and silent weather
And tender sounds, yet you might see
At once that Peter Bell and she
Had often been together.

A savage wildness round him hung
As of a Dweller out of doors,
In his whole figure and his mien
A savage character was seen
Of mountains and of dreary moors.

[14r]

(14)

Of all that lead a lawless life, 246–250
Of all that love their lawless lives,
In city or in village small
He was the wildest far of all,
He had a dozen wedded Wives.

Nay start not! wedded Wives—& twelve! 256–270
{W
But how one {*wife could e'er come near him*
In simple truth I cannot tell.
For}
But} *I must say of Peter Bell*
To see him, was to fear him.

Though Nature could not touch his heart
and
By lovely forms ~~or~~ silent weather
And tender sounds, yet you might see
At once that Peter Bell and she
Had often been together.

A savage wildness round him hung
{D
As of a {*dweller out of doors,*
In his whole figure and his mien
A savage character was seen
Of mountains and of dreary moors.

---

323 or in *over* village *eras (SH)*
324 all—
325 wives. *rev to* Wives.
326 &] and
327 wife
328 tell.] tell
329 I must say *del to* be it said
330 him,] him
334 She
339 seen,

326–330 Erased was probably the stanza as it stood in MS. 4:
"O monster"! cried the Parson's **Lady**
"Poor fellow"! echo'd **Ste**phen O**tt**er,
"Po**or Fellow**! say you!" "Mistress **Swan,**
I do assure you su**ch** a man
Was Peter Bell the Potter

331/332 In pencil, as is the deletion.

(15)

To all the unshap'd half human thoughts
Which solitary Nature feeds
Mid summer storms or winter's ice
Had Peter join'd whatever vice
The cruel city breeds.

His face was keen as is the wind
That cuts along the hawthorn fence
Of courage you saw little there
But in its stead a medly air
Of cunning and of impudence

He had a dark and sidelong walk
And long and slouching was his gait
Beneath his looks so bare and bold
You might perceive, his spirit cold
Was playing with some inward bait.

His forehead wrinkled was and furr'd
A work one half of which was done
By thinking of his whens and hows,
And half by knitting of his brows
Beneath the glaring sun.

[15r]

(15)

To all the unshap'd half human thoughts *271–290*
Which solitary Nature feeds
or
Mid summer storms [*?and*] *winter's ice*
Had Peter join'd whatever vice
The cruel city breeds.

His face was keen as is the wind
That cuts along the hawthorn fence
Of courage you saw little there
But in it's stead a medly air
Of cunning and of impudence

He had a dark and sidelong walk
And long and slouching was his gait
*Be*neath *his looks so bare and bold*
You might perceive, his spirit cold
Was playing with some inward bait.

His forehead wrinkled was and furr'd
A work one half of which was done
By thinking of his whens and hows,
And half by knitting *of his brows*
Beneath the glaring sun.

---

341 the' half-human
342 feeds,
343 'Mid
350 impudence.
355 bait.] bait
356 furr'ed

---

353 Erased was probably the reading of MS. 4: "tween."
359 Erased was probably the reading of MS. 4: "wrinkling."

(16)

There was a hardness in his cheeks
There was a hardness in his eye,
As if the Man had fix'd his face,
In many a solitary place
Against the wind and open sky.

One night, and now my little Bess!
We've reach'd at last the promis'd Tale,
One beautiful November night
When full the moon was shining bright
Upon the rapid River Swale.

Along the Rivers winding Banks
Peter was travelling all alone,
Whither to buy or sell, or led
By pleasure running in his head,
To me was never known.

[16r]

(16)

There was a hardness in his cheeks 291–305
There was a hardness in his eye,
As if the Man had fix'd his face,
In many a solitary place
{nd o} {en
Against the wind ~~tha~~{*t ~~swee~~*}*p*{*s ~~the~~ sky.*

One night, and now my little Bess!
We've reach'd at last the promis'd Tale,
One beautiful November night
When full the moon was shining bright
2 1
Upon the rapid River Swale.

Along the Rivers winding *Banks*
Peter was travelling all alone,
Whether to buy or sell, or led
By pleasure running in his head,
To me was never known.

---

361 cheeks, *with* s *del in pencil*
365/366 *no space left, but short rule marks division between sections*
366 Night,
367 Tale,] Tale
368 night,
369 full the moon] the full moon
371 River's

369/370 The numbers, revising the phrase, are in pencil.
371 Erased was probably the revised reading of MS. 4: "It chanc'd that by the River's."

(17)

He trudg'd along through copse and brake,
He trudg'd along o'er hill and dale;
Nor for the moon cared he a tittle,
And for the stars he cared as little
And for the murmuring River Swale

Quoth Peter "here's a nearer cut,
'Twill save a mile as sure as day;"
He took the path, the path did lead
Across a green and open mead
And a tall wood before him lay.

And Peter to the wood is come,
And with the path his way he weaves
He whistles, & may yet be heard,
Though he is buried, like a bird,
Among the boughs and leaves.

But quickly Peter's mood is changed,
And on he drives with cheeks that burn
In downright fury and in wrath,
There's little sign that Peter's path
Will to the road return.

[17^r]

(17)

He trudg'd along through copse and brake, *316–335*
He trudg'd along o'er hill and dale;
Nor for the moon cared he a tittle,
And for the stars he cared as little
And for the murmuring River Swale

Quoth Peter "here's a nearer cut,
'Twill save a mile as sure as day;"
He took the path, the path did lead
Across a green and open mead
And a tall wood before him lay.

And Peter to the wood is come;
And with the path his way he weaves
He whistles, & may yet be heard,
Though he is buried, like a bird,
Among the boughs and leaves.

But quickly Peter's mood is changed,
And on he drives with cheeks that burn
{In {in
{*With downright fury and* {*with wrath,*
There's little sign that Peter's path
Will to the road return.

---

378 car'd
379 car'd
380 Swale.
381–385 *as MS. 5, del to:*
But chancing to espy a path
That promised to cut short the way
As many a wiser man hath done
He left a trusty guide for one
That might his steps betray
entered in pencil (erased) at top of page, then interlined in ink
386–390 *all revisions entered in pencil, overwritten in ink*
386 *as MS. 5, del to* To a thick wood he soon is brought
387 And with the path *del to* Where chearfully weaves,
388 He whistles and *del to* And whistling loud
389 he is *del to* often
390 Among *del to* Darkling
394 that Peter's *partially del in pencil and ink, partially eras to* the treacherous *entered above stanza in pencil, interlined in ink*

387–392 The hand is MW's; erased was probably the version of MS. 4:
And **there** he is, in w**hole** cart **loads**
Upheaping curse**s** on them **all,**
Commissioners both **great and sma**ll
Who made those **elbows in the roads**.

For while he drives amo**ng the** bou**ghs**
With **head** and **hands—and**

[17v]

daunt
woulds Thou ~~turn~~ me Den
(401) What ~~am I stoppd~~ Thou griesly ~~Jaws~~ 341–344
~~Den~~
(402) Back must must when Ive come

(403) Stretch as thou wilt thy gloomy jaws
on} n}
(404) I'll [?]} on, d}or do I care two straws

(18)

The path grows dim and dimmer still
Now up now down his way he wends
With all the sail that he can carry
Till he is brought to an old Quarry
And there the pathway ends.
What am I left [illegible]
~~What [illegible] again, my constant~~, — ho!
~~And, think you~~ must I when I've come so far!
You stretch a pair of gloomy jaws
But I'm your Man, nor care two straws
For lantern or for star.

And so where on the huge rough stones
The black and massy shadows lay
And through the dark and through the cold
And through the yawning fissures old
Did Peter boldly press his way

Right through the Quarry — and behold!
A scene of soft and lovely hue
Where blue and grey and tender green
Together made as sweet a scene
As ever human eye did view.

[18r]

(18)

396 *The path grows dim and dimmer still* *336–355*
397 *Now up now down his way he wends*
398 *With all the sail that he can carry*
399 *'Till he is brought to an old Quarry*
400 *And there the pathway ends.*

What am I stopp'd thou griesly Den
old Grimface !
401 *What back again* my Antient,— *No.*
must I !
402 *Back, ~~think you~~, when I've come so far* }
403 *You stretch a pair of gloomy jaws*
404 *But I'm your Man, nor care two straws*
405 *For lantern or for star* ~~[?]~~.

{re
406 *And so whe*{*n on the huge rough stones*
407 *The black and massy shadows lay*
408 *And through the dark and through the cold*
409 *And through the yawning fissures old*
410 *Did Peter boldly press his way*

411 *Right through the Quarry—and behold!*
412 *A scene of soft and lovely hue*
413 *Where blue and grey and tender green*
414 *Together made as sweet a scene*
415 *As ever human eye did view.*

---

396 dim,
397 his way *del to* the rover *in pencil and ink*
399 'Till] Till
401 "What! wouldst thou daunt me grizly Den
402 Back must I when I've come so far? *over l. 403 eras (SH), then* when I've *del to* having
403 Stretch as thou wilt thy gloomy jaws *over l. 404 eras (SH), then* Stretch as *del to* Gape as *(with* Yawn *entered in margin in pencil, uncanceled) del in turn to* Stretch as *and* thy *del to* with *del in pencil*
404 I'll on, nor do I care two straws *then* do I care *del to* would I give
405 star."
408 cold,
409 old,

400/401 The phrase "old Grimface" is in pencil, as is the deletion of "my Antient," which WW apparently wrote into a gap left in the text.

(19)

Beneath the clear blue sky you saw
A little green plot of meadow-ground
But oh! far rather name it not,
Call it of earth a small green plot
With rocks encompass'd round.

The Swale flow'd under the grey rocks;
But he flow'd quiet and unseen
You need a strong and stormy gale
To bring the noises of the Swale
To that green spot so calm and green.

Now you'll suppose that Peter Bell
Felt small temptation here to tarry,
And so it was, but I must add
His heart was not a little glad
That he was out of the old Quarry.

And is there no one dwelling here?
No hermit with his beads and glass?
And does no little Cottage look
Upon this green and silent nook?
Does no one live near this green grass?

[19r]

(19)

Beneath the clear blue sky you saw *356–375*
field
A little plot of meadow-ground
But oh! far rather name it not,
Call it of earth a small green plot
With rocks encompass'd round.

The Swale flow'd under the grey rocks;
But he flow'd quiet and unseen
You need a strong and stormy gale
To bring the noises of the Swale
To that green spot so calm and green.

Now you'll suppose that Peter Bell
Felt small temptation there to tarry,
And so it was, but I must add
His heart was not a little glad
That he was out of the old Quarry.

And is there no one dwelling here?
?}
No hermit with his beads and glass }
or
{A {C
{*and does no little* {*cottage look*
Upon this green and silent nook?
Does no one live near this green grass?

---

416 you] he
417 field meadow ground
422 unseen;
424 Swale,
425 green.] green!
427 tarry;
431 dwelling *started over illeg eras (SH)*
432 Hermit
433 And
434 green *del to* soft

416/417 In pencil.
432/433 The "or" is in pencil.

(20)

Across that deep and quiet spot
Is Peter driving through the grass
And now he is among the trees,
When turning round his head he sees
A solitary Ass.

"No doubt, I'm founder'd in these woods,
For once" quoth he "I will be wise,
~~Upon my faith~~ With better speed I'll back again
And not to make my journey vain
I'll take the Ass likewise.

Off Peter hied— and at his side
Lo where beneath the bright moon beam
The Ass is standing on the bed
Of that green meadow with his head
Over the silent stream.

"A pretty beast! though we'll allow
Not quite so ~~[illegible]~~ plump as he might be
My honest Friend, with such a platter
You should have been a little fatter
But come Sir, come with me"

[20r]

(20)

Across that deep and quiet spot *376–395*
{*P*
Is {*peter driving through the grass*
And now he is among the trees,
When turning round his head he sees
A solitary Ass.

"No doubt, I'm founder'd in these woods,
For once," quoth he "I will be wise,
With better speed
~~*Upon my faith*~~ *I'll back again*
And not to make my journey vain
I'll take the Ass likewise.

Off Peter hied—and at his side
Lo where beneath the bright moonbeam
The Ass is standing on the bed
{*en*
Of that gre{[?] *meadow with his head*
Over the silent stream.

"A pretty beast! though we'll allow
plump
Not quite so ~~*fat*~~ *as he might be*
My honest Friend, with such a platter
You should have been a little fatter
But come Sir, come with me"

---

437 grass;
438 he is] he's [?] *eras to* he is *(SH)*
441 foundere'd woods,] woods
442 quothe he,
444 not . . . journey *del to* lest the journey should prove *following pencil version at top of page*

{yon
Will {is ~~beast~~ my lawful prize"
445 ~~I'll~~ take {th{e Ass ~~likewise.~~
with Will *in ink over pencil,* Ass *eras, then restored, and* beast *eras and draft version penciled at top of page:* Will take this beast, my lawful prize
446–450 *marked* out
447 Lo! moon-beam
449 meadow,
451 *as MS. 5 but* Beast! *then all del to* Of Peter hied—"A pretty Beast *with second* f *added to* Of *in pencil*
452 Not quite *del to* Though not be;
455 me."

---

443 On 19v, facing, WW experimented with revisions:
By the same road
With ~~my~~ better speed
451/452 In pencil. The deletion in l. 452 is by erasure.

There's nothing to be seen but woods,
And rocks that spread a hoary gleam,
And this ~~poor Oak~~ one Beast which ~~o'er~~ [?] the bed
Of the green meadow hangs his head
Over the silent stream.

Close to the

[20v]

*

461 There's nothing to be seen but woods, *401–405*
462 And rocks that spread a hoary gleam,
one Beast from
463 And this ~~poor Ass~~ which ~~near~~ the bed
464 Of the green meadow hangs his head
465 Over the silent stream.

(466) Close to the

461–465 *in regular sequence, MS. 6*
461 woods,] woods *pencil alt above line* Nothing around is seen
462 gleam,] gleam
463 which] that

462/463 The "near" was deleted and the "from" added in pencil; the asterisk, which corresponds to an asterisk on 21r, facing, is also in pencil.

The fragmentary last line apparently indicates further the position of the insertion.

(21)

But first, doth Peter deem it fit
To spy about him far and near
There's not a single house in sight,
No woodman's hut no cottage light
* Peter you need not fear

Close to the River stands the Ass
His head is with a halter bound
Now Peter's purpose did not alter
And so at once he seized the halter
And would have turn'd him round

He pull'd—the creature did not move,
Upon his back then Peter leapt,
And stoutly with his heels he plied
The little Ass on either side,
But still the Ass his station kept.

Quoth Peter "you're a beast of mettle
I see you'll suit me to an ace;"
out And now the Ass through his left eye
On Peter turn'd most quietly
Look'd quietly in his face

[21r]

(21)

456 *But first, doth Peter deem it fit* 396–400
457 *To spy about him far and near*
458 *There's not a single house in sight,*
459 *No woodman's hut no cottage light*
460 * *Peter you need not fear*

466 *Close to the River stands the Ass* 406–420
467 *His head is with a halter bound*
468 *Now Peter's purpose did not alter*
{'
469 *And so at once he seiz{ed the halter*
470 *And would have turn'd him round*

471 *He pull'd—the creature did not move,*
472 *Upon his back then Peter leapt,*
{*tou*
473 *And s{hortly with his heels he plied*
474 *The little Ass on either side,*
475 *But still the Ass his station kept.*

476 *Quoth Peter "You're a beast of mettle*
suit
477 *I see you'll ^ me to an ace;"*
478 out *And now the Ass through his left eye*
479 *On Peter turn'd most quietly*
480 *Look'd quietly in his face*

---

457 near;
459 hut, light—
466–470 *full transcription may be helpful (deletion of l. 468 is in pencil):*
~~And in that posture as he stands~~
~~Close to the River stands the Ass,~~
His head is with a halter bound;
The halter seizing Peter leapt
~~Now Peter's purpose did not alter~~
{Upon 's}
{Ass the Asses} back ~~& would~~ & plied
~~And so at once he seized the halter~~
With ready heel the Creature's side
~~And would have turn'd him round~~.
But still the Ass his station kept
471–475 *marked* out
471 move,] move
474 Ass *alt* [?he's] *eras above line* side;
476–480 *omitted*

476–480 The X canceling the stanza is in pencil.

(22)

What's this" cries Peter, brandishing
A new peel'd sapling, white as cream;
The Ass knew well what Peter said
But as before hung down his head
Over the silent stream.

Then Peter gave another jerk
A jirk that from a dungeon floor
Would have pull'd up an iron ring;
But still the heavy-headed Thing
Stood just as he had stood before

Quoth Peter leaping from the Ass,
There is some plot against me laid;
Once more the little meadow ground
And all the hoary cliffs around
He cautiously survey'd.

All, all is silent, rocks and woods
All all is silent far and near;
Only the Ass with motion dull
Upon the pivot of his skull
Turns round his long left ear.

~~All~~ Is still & silent, far & near

[22r]

(22)

What's this" cried Peter, brandishing *421–425*
A new peel'd sapling, white as cream;
knew well
The Ass [?well knew]} what Peter said
But as before hung down his head
Over the silent stream.

Then Peter gave another jirk *431–440*
A jirk that from a dungeon floor
Would have pull'd up an iron ring;
But still the heavy-headed Thing
Stood just as he had stood before

Quoth Peter leaping from the Ass,
There is some plot against me laid;
Once more the little meadow-ground
And all the hoary cliffs around
He cautiously survey'd.

All, all is silent, rocks and woods *446–450*
All all is silent far and near;
Only the Ass with motion dull
Upon the pivot of his skull
Turns round his long left ear.

~~All~~
(497) Is still & silent far & near

---

481 "What's this," Peter,] Peter
482 peeled sapling,] sapling cream,
483 said;
484 hung down] he hung
486 another *del to* sudden jirk,
490 before.
491 the Ass, *del to* his seat
495 surveyed.] surveyed
497 All, all is *over* [?Is still ?] *(SH)*

---

497 SH probably miscopied, then erased, l. 498.

[22v]

(506) Ill cure you of these desperate tricks
(507) His staff then Peter lifted high
{ d
(508) And making from the asses hi{[?]e
(509) The hair and glittering dust fly wide
smote right
(510) He ~~beat~~ ~~most~~ lustily

(511) And soon the little harmless beast
(512) Gently as if to take his ease

[pencil underneath]
(506) Ill cure you of these desperate tricks
(507) His staff then Peter lifted high

*

(506–526) A Witch is playing in my sight
(507–527) Her desperate tricks—but what care I?
And
(508) ~~So~~ making from the Asses hide
(509) The hair and glittering dust fly wide
smote lustily
(510) He beat most ~~furiously.~~
right lustily

(531) O mercy for the Beast!—at last

X
506 Ill cure you of these desperate tricks
~~Quoth Peter~~, and with action slow
507 ~~And with deliberate motion slow~~
~~And with deliberate acti~~
508 His staff high raising, in the pride
509 Of skill, upon the Asses ~~side~~ hide
sturdy
510 He dealt a ~~lusty~~ blow.

(511) More followed of like sort—and soon
(512) The Ass, as if to take his ease

506–510 "I'll cure you of these desperate tricks!"
And with deliberate action slow
high-
His staff ~~up~~raising, in the pride
Of skill, upon the Asse's hide
He dealt a sturdy blow
revision by erasure (SH)

This verso was used to draft a stanza whose final version appears uncanceled toward the bottom of the page, marked by an X that indicates that it was to be inserted after l. 505 on 23r, facing. The version canceled in the middle of the page provides the first two lines for a version of ll. 526–530, inserted on 23r. The large zero at the bottom of the page, in the right margin, corresponds to another on 24r, opposite ll. 511–512.

(508) The "And" is in pencil, as is the deletion.

510 The deletion and the revisions are all in pencil.

(28)

Thought Peter, what can mean all this?
There is some ugly witchcraft here:
Once more the Ass with motion dull
Upon the pivot of his skull
Turn'd round his long left ear.
A Witch is plunging in my sight
Her desperately he spoke but what care I
Yet Peter struck of this proud boast
For a brief while his courage lost
Then [illegible]
Oh mercy for the beast
[illegible] at last
4 His sides did heave his belly stirr'd
He gave a groan, and then another
Of that which went before the brother,
And then he gave a third

All by the moonlight River side
He gave three miserable groans;
"'Tis come then to a pretty pass."
Said Peter to the groaning Ass,
"But I will bang your bones" 5

But Peter [illegible]

[23r]

(23)

501 *Thought Peter, what can* mean *all this?* 451–455
502 *There is some ugly witchcraft here:*
503 *Once more the Ass with motion dull*
504 *Upon the pivot of his skull*
505 *Turn'd round his long left ear.* X

* A Witch is playing in my sight
526 ~~*Cried Peter, "you'll be wise I hope*~~ 466–480
Her desperate tricks but what care I
527 ~~*Before we're both five minute's older"*~~
Yet Peter spite of this proud boast
528 ~~*Upon the Ass the sapling rings*~~
For a brief while his courage lost
529 ~~*Each blow the arm of Peter stings*~~
Then beat most lustily
530 ~~*Up to the elbow and the shoulder.*~~

---

502 There is *del and* some *capitalized* must be *inserted before* here:
526–530 (*marked* out):
Up! up! quoth Peter, you'll be wise
Before we're both five minutes older
[? ?] rung
Upon the Ass the sapling ~~rings~~
[—?—] Peters arm with pain is stung
~~Each blow the arm of Peter stings~~
~~High as~~
~~Stings to the elbow and~~ the shoulder:
And vibrates to ^
illegible eras line of pencil below stanza; alt below second line in pencil

---

The proper numbering of lines on this and adjacent pages is uncertain; the order indicated by the numerals inserted in margins of 22v, 23r, 23v, and 24r has been followed, as it is the order of MS. 6. Possibly the original order of lines in MS. 5 was 501–505, 526–540, 511–515, 541–545 (the order of MS. 4); ll. 506–510 and 516–525 are probably later additions.

(23)

Thought Peter, what can mean all this?
There is some ugly witchcraft here:
Once more the Ass with motion dull
Upon the pivot of his skull
Turn'd round his long left ear.
+A Witch is plugging in my sight
[illegible] desperate tricks but what care I
Yet Peter shook of this proud boast
For a brief while his courage lost
Then [illegible] most [illegible]
Oh never for the beast
[illegible] at last
His sides did heave his belly stirr'd
He gave a groan and then another
Of that which went before the brother
And then he gave a third

All by the moonlight River side
He gave three miserable groans;
"'Tis come then to a pretty pass."
Said Peter to the groaning Ass,
"But I will hang your bones"

But Peter [illegible]

[23r continued]

Oh mercy for the beast—
531 *~~At last, poor patient Thing!~~ at last*
532 4 *His sides did heave his belly stirr'd*
533 *He gave a groan and then another*
534 *Of that which went before the brother,*
535 *And then he gave a third*

in

536 *All by the moonlight River side*
537 *He gave three miserable groans;*
538 *"'Tis come then to a pretty pass,"*
539 *Said Peter to the groaning Ass,*
540 *"But I will bang your bones"* 5

(541) And Peter halts to gather breath

531–532 Upon the Beast the sapling rings—
—~~at length~~ }
~~O! mercy for the Beast!~~ }
Heaved his lank sides his limbs they
~~His sides did heave his body~~ stirr'd
535 third,
538 "'Tis] "Tis

The bottom line on the page is in pencil.

And then upon his side he fell
And by the river's brink did lie
And as he lay like one that mourn'd,
The patient Beast on Peter turned
His shining hazel eye
'Twas but one mild & sorrowful look
And straitway, silent, without fear,
In agony sorrow not in dread,
He turn'd the eyeball in his head
Towards the stream so deep and clear.

Up! Up! quoth Peter, you'll be wise
Before we're both five minutes older
Upon the Ass the sapling rings
Each blow the arm of Peter stings
Stings to the elbow and the shoulder
O mercy for the Beast [illegible]
And Peter halts to gather breath
He halts and to his eye [illegible]

[23v]

* 3
516 And then upon his side he fell
517 And by the rivers-brink did lie
518 And as he lay like one that mourn'd,
Beast
519 The patient ~~Ass~~ on Peter turn'd
520 His shining hazel eye

mild reproachful
521 Twas but one ~~look, one patient~~ look
522 And straitway, silent, without fear,
In very sorrow
523 ~~For twas in sorrow~~ not in dread,
524 He turn'd the eyeball in his head
525 Towards the stream so deep and clear.

(526) Up! Up! quoth Peter, you'll be wise *466–470*
(527) Before we're both five minutes older
(528) Upon the Ass the sapling rings
(529) Each blow the arm of Peter stings
(530) Stings to the elbow and the shoulder
4

(531) O mercy for the Beast at [?last]

[ink over pencil] O mercy for the beast at last

(541) And Peter halts to gather breath
(542) He halts and to his eye was shewn

---

517 river's brink lie;
520 eye:
521 'Twas look;
522 *del to* A glance more tender than severe *following pencil draft at top of page*
523 *as MS. 5, then* In very *del to* And straight in *and comma inserted after* sorrow
525 stream so *del to* river
526–530 *see apparatus criticus to 23r*

522/523 In pencil, overwritten in ink.

(24)

And now the little harmless Beast
Gently as if to take his ease
In quiet uncomplaining mood
Upon the spot where he had stood
Dropp'd gently down upon his knees

And Peter halts to gather breath
~~And then upon his side he fell~~
Until to his eyes was fully shewn
~~And now to Peter was shewn~~
What ~~all this time he had not~~ seen
How gaunt was the poor Ass and lean,
Yea wasted to a skeleton!

With legs stretch'd out and stiff he lay
No word of kind commiseration
Fell at the sight from Peter's tongue,
With hard contempt his heart was wrung,
With hatred and vexation.

The meagre beast lay still as death
And Peter's lips with fury quiver,
Quoth he "you little mulish dog"
Quoth he, I'll fling you like a log
Head foremost down the River

Until to his was fully shewn
What he before in part had seen

[24r]

at wh (24)
this
At Which
511 *And now the little harmless Beast* 481–485
512 *Gently as if to take his ease*
513 0 *In quiet uncomplaining mood*
514 *Upon the spot where he had stood*
515 *Dropp'd gently down upon his knees.* 3

* And Peter halts to gather breath
541 5 ~~*And then upon his side he fell*~~
And to his eye was fully shewn
542 *And* ~~*now to Peter's eye was shewn*~~
he before in part h seen
ill
543 *What t* ~~*o this time he had not seen*~~

,
544 *How gaunt was the poor Ass and lean*
Yea wasted to a skeleton !
545 *And* ~~*almost wasted to the bone*~~

546 *With legs stretch'd out and stiff he lay*
547 *No word of kind commiseration*
548 *Fell at the sight from Peter's tongue,*
549 *With hard contempt his heart was wrung,*
550 *With hatred and vexation.*

551 *The meagre beast lay still as death* 491–495
552 *And Peter's lips with fury quiver,*
553 *Quoth he "you little mulish dog"*
554 *Quoth he, "I'll fling you like a log*
555 *Head foremost down the River*
(542) And to his was fully shewn
(543) What he before in part had seen

---

511 More follow'd of like sort—and soon
512 Gently] The Ass
515 Dropt
541–545 And Peter halts to gather breath,
now full clearly was it
And ~~to his eye was fully~~ ^ shewn,
What he before in part had seen
,
How gaunt was the poor Ass and lean
Yea wasted to a skeleton!
(revision of l. 542 drafted in pencil at foot of page and between lines; comma inserted in l. 544 is in pencil)
549 wrung,] wrung
554 Quoth he, *del and* you *rev to* your carcase

Wordsworth's drafts at the top and bottom of the page are in pencil.

The zero in the margin, opposite the first stanza, refers to a draft of ll. 511–512 at the bottom of 22v, the 3 to a similar notation at the top of 23v, and the 5 to 23r; see note to 23r.

544 Erased was probably the reading of MS. 4 (with "gaunt" uncertain): "**That the** poor **Ass** was **gaunt**."

(25)

By God I will"—The word scarce said,
As stretched upon his side he lay,
To all the echoes South and North
And East and West the Ass sent forth
A loud and clamorous bray

This outcry on the heart of Peter
Seems like a note of joy to strike;
Joy on the heart of Peter knocks
But in the echo of the rocks
Was something Peter did not like;

Whether to cheer his coward heart,
Or that he felt a wicked chain
Twined round him like a magic spell
In honest truth I cannot tell,
But to the work he fell again

Among the rocks and winding crags
Among the mountains far away
Once more the Ass did lengthen out
More ruefully an endless shout
The long dry see-saw of his horrible bray!

[25r]

(25)

By God I will .} *"—The word scarce said,* 496–515
As stretched upon his side he lay,
To all the echoes South and North
And East and {W *west the Ass sent forth*
A loud and clamorous bray

This outcry on the heart of Peter
Seems like a note of joy to strike;
Joy on the heart of Peter knocks
But in the echo of the rocks
Was something Peter did not like:

Whether to chear his coward heart,
Or that he felt a wicked chain
Twine'd round him like a magic spell
In honest truth I cannot tell,
But to the work he fell again

Among the rocks and winding crags
Among the mountains far away
Once more the Ass did lengthen out
More ruefully an endless shout
The long dry see-saw of his horrible bray. !}

---

556 By God I will"—the word scarce said, *del to* An impious Oath confirmed the threat *in ink, drafted in pencil below stanza*
557 As . . . side *del to* But while upon the ground *in ink, drafted in pencil below stanza*
558 North,
559 West,
560 clamourous *del to* piteous *in pencil and ink* bray.
565 like.
566 heart *del to* breast
567 wicked *del to* dragging *del in pencil to* ruthless *in pencil and ink, then alt entered from pencil drafts at foot of page to follow first three words:* could not break the chain
568 like a magic spell *del first to illeg phrase, then to* with demoniac sway *then to* by demoniac power *(in pencil and ink)* or [?struck] *inserted after* him *then alt version of line entered above:* In this serene & silent hour *at some stage* better *was entered in margin in pencil*
569 In honest truth *del first to illeg phrase, del by erasure to* To drag him on *del to* And force him on I cannot *del* tell, *del to* say
570 But to *del to* To *and* blind *inserted before* work fell *del to* turned again] again.
575 his] her *rev to* his *(SH)* bray. *rev to* bray!

---

557 WW penciled "the ground" on the facing verso, probably as an alternate for "his side."
574 An illegible letter, probably a "d," was erased.

(26)

What is there now in Peter's heart?
Or what's the power of that strange sound?
The moon uneasy look'd and dimmer,
The broad blue heavens appear'd to glimmer,
And the rocks stagger'd all around.

From Peter's hand the sapling dropp'd
And now he felt but small temptation
To play again the ruffian's part;
For all at once in Peter's heart
Was wrought a wondrous alteration.

And down he sits beside the Ass
Close under a tall alder root
"If any one should come and see
That I am here they'll think" quoth he,
"I'm helping this poor dying Brute."

He scans the Ass from limb to limb
And Peter now uplifts his eyes.
Steady the moon doth look and clear
And like themselves the rocks appear
And quiet are the skies.

[26r]

(26)

What is there now in Peter's heart? *516–525*
Or what's the power of that strange sound?
The moon uneasy look'd and dimmer,
The broad blue heavens appear'd to glimmer,
And the rocks stagger'd all around.

From Peter's hand the sapling dropp'd
And now he felt but small temptation
To play again the ruffian's part;
For all at once in Peter's heart
Was wrought a wondrous alteration.

And down he sits beside the Ass
{*Close*
{*Just under a tall alder root*
"If any one should come and see
That I am here they'll think" quoth he,
{*B* ”}
"I'm helping this poor dying {*brute*}

He scans the Ass from limb to limb
And Peter now uplifts his eyes
Steady the moon doth look and clear
And like themselves the rocks appear
And quiet are the skies.

---

577 what's *del to* whence power *del to* might that *del to* this
581–585 *marked* out *in margin; the stanza is coalesced with the next one by revisions in ll. 586–587*
586–587 *del to:*
From Peters hand the sapling droppd
Threat had he none to execute
589 think," *over illeg eras (SH)*
590 Brute"
591 to limb;

(27)

And Peter in a heartsome tone
Cries out "Your pipes are clear and shrill
So as a rare peal no doubt you might
[illegible]
Now, let another [illegible]
To rouze your friends by Pennygent,
And far as Pendle hill.

Whereat in resolute mood once more
He stoops the Ass's neck to seize
When in the deep clear stream below
He spies an ugly sight, I trow,
Among the shadows of the trees

moon's resplendent face
Is it the shadow of the moon?
Is it the shadow of a cloud?
Is it a gallows there pourtray'd?—
Is Peter of himself afraid?
Is it a coffin or a shroud?

Is it a fiend that to a stake
Of red-hot fire himself is tethering?
Some solitary ward or cell
Where lies a damned soul in hell
Ten thousand miles from all his brethren?

[27r]

(27)

And Peter in a heartsome tone
Cries out "Your pipes are clear and shrill,
Twas a rare peal no doubt you meant
~~*'Twas a rare peal! no doubt you meant*~~
~~*Now, let another peal be sent*~~ {e
To rouze your Friends by Pennyg{ant,
And far as Pendle hill.

Whereat in resolute mood once more 526–540
He stoops the Ass's neck to seize
When in the deep clear stream below
He spies an ugly sight, I trow,
Among the shadows of the trees.

moons resplendent face
Is it the shadow of the moon?
Is it the shadow of a cloud?
Is it a gallows there pourtray'd? —
Is Peter of himself afraid?
Is it a coffin or a shroud?

{*F*
Is it a {*fiend that to a stake*
Of red-hot fire himself is tethering?
Some solitary ward or cell
Where lies a damned soul in hell
Ten thousand miles from all his brethen?

596–600 *marked* Q. out
597 "your shrill,] shrill
598 'Twas peal,
600 Hill!"
601 Whereat,
603 *eras to* Ill [*rev to* Foul] purpose quickly put to flight
604 *eras to* For in the pool an ugly [*rev to* a startling] sight
605 *eras to* Beneath the shadowy trees *then* Meets him *prefixed*
606 Is it the moon's distorted face? *with* distorted *over illeg eras and illeg pencil word above*
607 *as MS. 5, eras to* The ghost-like image of a cloud
608 a *over eras, corr according to pencil* a *in margin* pourtray'd?
611–615 *as Ms. 5 but* cell, *(613)* Hell *(614) and* brethren? *(615), then entire stanza del to:*
A grisly Idol hewn in stone
'
Or Imp from Witche}s lap let fall
Or a gay ring of shining Fairies
their
Such as pursue ^ brisk vagaries
In sylvan bower or haunted Hall

The vertical line alongside the first stanza is in pencil.

598 On the facing verso, 26v, WW penciled a line of draft: "Twas a rare peal, no doubt you [?meant]."

599–600 Pen y ghent and Pendle Hill are notable peaks in the Pennines: Pen y ghent (2231 feet), in the West Riding of Yorkshire, is about 16 miles north of Pendle Hill (1831 feet), in Lancashire. Wordsworth refers to both peaks in *The White Doe* (l. 1175). De Selincourt calls attention to *The Ballad of Flodden Field*: "From Penigent to Pendle Hill" (*PW*, III, 555).

(28)

Is it some party in a parlour
Cramm'd just as they on earth were cramm'd
Some sipping punch some sipping tea
But as you by their faces see
All silent and all damned.

Poor Peter looks and looks again
Even like a man whose brain is haunted
He looks he cannot chuse but look
Like one thats reading in a book
A book that is enchanted.

He grasps the poor Ass by the jaws
His hands and body shake and shiver,
And up and down, and to and fro,
The Ass's mouth and nostrils go
Dimpling the surface of the River

Ah! well-a-day for Peter Bell!
He will be turn'd to iron soon
out Flesh, sinew, fibre, bone and gristle
His hat is up his hairs they bristle
Bristle and whiten in the moon.

[28r]

(28)

Is it some party in a parlour *541–545*
Cramm'd just as they on earth were cramm'd
Some sipping punch some sipping tea
But as you by their faces see
All silent and all damned.

Poor Peter looks and looks again *556–570*
Even like a man whose brain is haunted
He looks he cannot chuse but look
Like one that's reading in a book
A book that is enchanted

He grasps the poor Ass by the jaws
His hands and body shake and shiver,
And up and down, and to and fro,
The Ass's mouth and nostrils go
Dimpling the surface of the River

Ah! well-a-day for Peter Bell!
He will be turn'd to iron soon
out *Flesh, sinew, fibre, bone and gristle*
His hat is up his hairs they bristle
Bristle and whiten in the moon.

---

616 parlour,
617 cramm'd,
618 punch, . . . tea,
619 But, as *over* by *eras (SH)* see,
621 Poor Peter looks, and looks again; *del to* A throbbing heart hath Peter Bell *then last four words del to* pulse the gazer hath
622 *as MS. 5 but* haunted; *then all del to* Puzzled he was, and now is daunted
623 looks, . . . look,
624 that's reading in *del to* ~~intend~~ intent upon book,
625 enchanted.
626–630 *marked* out
626 jaws;
627 His hands and body *del to* That seems like him to *entered below line, then eras and entered above* shiver;
628 And *eras to* For
630 River.
631–635 *a version is written between the lines over a canceled version of ll. 641–645 which follows ll. 626–630:*

~~And now poor Peter is convinc'd,~~
Ah! well-a-day for Peter Bell
~~While still he grasps the Ass's head,~~
He will be turned to iron soon
~~That underneath that leafy shade,~~
Meet statue for the Court of Fear!
~~A grizly {W water-fiend is laid~~
His hat is up, and every hair
~~Within the River's bed.~~
Bristles, and whitens in the moon.

(29)

And see him now fast bound like iron,
Head, joints, and hands & lips & teeth!
You'd think that he was looking at you,
But no; this uncouth iron Statue
Is looking at the stream beneath.

And now poor Peter is convinc'd
While still he holds the Ass's head
That 'tis a fiend with visage wan,
A live Man-fiend, a living Man
That's lying in the River's bed

He looks, he ~~looks~~ ponders, he looks again,
He sees a motion, hears a groan,
His eyes will burst, his heart will break,
He gives a loud and ~~frightful~~ shriek,
And back he falls, ~~dead~~ as a stone!
a senseless

[29r]

(29)

And see him now fast bound like iron, 571–585
Head, joints, and hands & lips & teeth !}
out *You'd think that he was looking at you,*
But no, :} *this uncouth iron* {S *statue*
Is looking at the stream beneath.

And now poor Peter is convinc'd
grasps
While still he holds the Ass's head
That 'tis a fiend, with visage wan,
A live {M *man-fiend, a living* {M *man,*
That's lying in the River's bed.

ponders
He looks, he ~~looks, he~~ looks again,
He sees a motion, hears a groan,
His eyes will burst, his heart will break,
He gives a loud and f{*rightful* *earful shriek,*
And back he falls, ~~dead~~ as a stone !}
as senseless as

636–640 *omitted*
641–645 *see apparatus criticus to 28r*
646 ponders, again;
647 groan;
648 break;
649 back he falls, as senseless as a stone! *del to* drops a senseless weight as if his life were flown *following pencil draft below stanza*

---

642 The revision is in pencil, overwritten in ink; the symbol points to revision on 28v, facing.
643–645 On the facing verso, 28v, WW drafted revisions:

[?~~glimmering~~]
That underneath that ~~leafy~~ shade
{aid
A griesly Water fiend is l{ying
Within the rivers bed

[30r]

(30)

Second Part

651 *We left poor Peter in a trance* 586–590
652 *Beneath the alders, near the river,*
653 *The Ass is by the river side*
654 *And where the feeble breezes glide,*
655 *Upon the stream the moonbeams quiver*

656 *And Peter wakes, he wakes at last;* 591–595
657 *He feels the glimmerings of the moon*
658 *And to stretch forth his hands is trying;*
659 *Sure when he knows where he is lying*
660 *He'll sink into a second swoon.*

661 *He lifts his head—he sees his staff* 596–600
662 *He touches—'tis to him a treasure;*
663 *To find that he is not in hell,*
664 *As you'll suppose to Peter Bell*
665 *Doth give a sweet and languid pleasure*

666 *And while upon his side he lies,* 601–605
667 *His head upon his elbow rais'd,*
668 *Almost, you'd say, as in a dream*

[30v]

(678) A harmless body—no thing worse
[?The] the
(679) See the whole figure of the corse
(680) Head, trunk, feet, hands, and knees
A[?] off then Peter {rose
(681) ~~Then~~, from his side ~~did Peter~~ {rise
^
(681) From off his side then Peter rose

650/651 *new page headed* Part Second *followed by short rule*
651 Poor Peter *del to* our Hero Trance
652 Alders, . . . River,
655 quiver] glitter *eras to* quiver *(SH)*
656 And Peter wakes,] And Peter wakes *del to* A happy respite—but *over illeg pencil draft* at last; *del*
657 He] And *with alt* He *in pencil* glimmering moon,
659 Sure, . . . lying,
661 head,— . . . staff;
663 *as MS. 5, del to* The [*del to* Faint] recollection seems to tell
664 *as MS. 5, del to* That he is yet where mortals dwell
665 Doth give a sweet and *del to* A thought received with pleasure.
666–670 *marked* out

---

653 Erased, following "river," was doubtless "'s," as in earlier manuscripts.

[31r]

(31)

669 *His eyes are settling on the stream*
670 *Where he before had gaze'd*

671 *No dimple now disturbs the stream,* *606–610*
672 *In Peter's brain there is no riot;*
673 *His eye upon the stream he fixes,*
674 *And with the sight no terror mixes:*
675 *His heart is calm and quiet.*

676 *Quoth he "that is a dead man's face* *611–615*
677 *Among the shadows of the trees,*
~~With his clothes on the man is lying~~
678 ~~*Those are no doubt a dead man's knuckles*~~
His clothes are on; tis past denying
679 ~~*And there you see his brass shoe buckles,*~~
That a dead body there is lying,
naked
680 ~~*And there his breeches knees*~~
Face, feet, and hands and knees.

---

669 stream,
670 gaz'd.
671 *as MS. 5 but* stream; *del to* And now upon his elbow raised
672 *as MS. 5 but* riot *del to* Becoming less & less perplexed
673–675 *as MS. 5, del to:*
Forward he leans in placid mood
With heart as quiet as the flood
On which his eye is fixed *then all del by WW to:*
Skyward he looks—to rock—and wood
And then upon the placid flood
His wandering eye is fix'd
676–680 Thought he that is the face of one
~~Quoth~~ he, ~~"that is a dead man's face~~
In his last sleep securely bound
~~Among the shadows of the trees,~~
Of this assured }
[? ?] trunk } with plain intent
~~A harmless body—nothing worse,~~
He makes his staff an instrument
~~whole~~
~~I see the~~ ^ ~~figure of the Corse.~~
The rivers depth to sound
~~Head, trunk, feet, hands, and knees.~~ *then rewritten at top of page (over two words of illeg pencil) but (678)* So fau }fa ltering not in this intent *and (680)* river's

---

676–680 Drafts toward revision are on 30v, facing.

~~Then from his side himself he rais'd~~
681 ~~*At last he rises from his side*~~ *616–620*
682 *And s{ae / its} upright upon the ground,*
head} he bent
683 *And o'er the stream ~~he hangs~~ his nose}*
with plain
684 *And points his staff ~~as you'd suppose~~* intent
685 *The river's depth to sound.*

686 *This sees the Ass, while on the grass* *621–625*
687 *Close by the river's brink he lies*
688 *And straight with a transition tragic*
689 *As if he had been touch'd with magic*
690 *Up from the ground the Ass doth rise.*

[32r]

(32)

691 *His meagre bones all shake with joy,* *631–635*
692 *And close by Peter's side he stands:*
693 *While Peter o'er the River bends*
694 *The little Ass his neck extends*
695 *And fondly licks his hands*

681–685 *marked out*
681 From off his side then Peter rose
686–690 *much revised:*

~~Lo!~~ Now
~~When~~ sh
~~And~~ ^ like a tempest-~~b~~attered Bark
~~This sees the Ass, while on the grass~~
That overwhelmed & prostrate lies
~~Close by the river's brink he lies~~
~~like a shattered ship uplifted~~
~~And straight with a transition tragic~~
~~By a strong surge with motion gifted~~
~~Or rather as if touch'd by magic~~
~~Full suddenly~~
~~Up from the ground the Ass doth rise.~~
And in a moment to the verge
Is lifted of a foaming surge
Full suddenly the Ass doth rise

687 *revision drafted in pencil by WW at foot of page:* That overwhelmed & prostrate lies
690 *second half line deleted in pencil*
691 meagre *del to* staring
695 hands.] hands

Such life is in the Ass's eyes *636–640*
Such life is in his limbs and ears
That Peter Bell if he had been
The veriest coward ever seen
Must now have thrown aside his fears

But 'tis not {*by* / *in*} *the Ass's eyes*
Or Ass's ears that he's protected
There is a weakness in his heart
{Which / That} may not readily depart,
Peter in spirit is dejected

With caution Peter eyes the stream, *641–645*
His sapling deep and deeper goes,
The body is, no doubt, quoth he
The thing which it appears to be
It moves not neither limbs nor clothes.

The Ass looks on and to his work *646–650*
Is Peter quietly resigned,

[33r]

(*33*)

He touches here, he touches there,
And now among the dead Man's hair
His sapling Peter has entwin'd

He pulls, and ~~*pulls*~~ ^*looks*^*, and pulls again* *651–655*
And he whom the poor Ass had lost,
The Man who had been four days dead,

---

696 eyes,
697 ears;
700 now *del to* soon fears.
701–705 *marked* out
702 that he's] he is *corr by overwriting to* that he's *(SH)*
704 That may not readily depart—
705 dejected.
706–710 *marked* out
710 not,
712 resign'd,
714 man's
715 entwin'd.
716 again,

---

716 WW wrote on the facing verso "and looks & pulls a."

Head foremost from the river's bed
Uprises like a ghost.

And Peter draws him to dry land 656
And through the brain of Peter pass 662–665
Some ugly twitches fast and faster,
No doubt *quoth he, "he is the master,*
Of this poor miserable Ass

He scans the beast from limb to limb 671–675
"I've play'd with you an ugly game"
Quoth Peter to the Ass, "but still
I did not mean to use you ill,
You must allow you were to blame.

But the poor Shadow all the {*is*} *while* 676–680
The little Ass what is he doing?
His joy is pass'd, his joy is flown,

[34^r]

(*34*)

He on his knees hath laid him down,
As if he were his grief renewing.

That Peter on his back should mount 681–685
He's shewing all the wish *he can*
"I'll go, I'll go if life forsake me,
No doubt he to his home will take me
The Cottage of the {*is*} *drowned Man"*

---

719 River's
720 Ghost.
723 ugly *del to* poignant *in pencil, overwritten in ink*
724 "No doubt," quoth he, he is the Master
725 Ass."
726–730 *marked* out
729 use] do
730 blame."
731 But the poor *del to* The meagre th{is/e} *as MS. 5 (SH)*
732 The little Ass *del to* What seeks he now
733 joy is pass'd, his *del to* sudden fit of
734 down,] down
737 He's shewing all the wish *del to* He shews a wish well as can,
738 go] go, if life forsake me— *del to* whateer betide
739 *as MS. 5, del to* He to his home my way will guide
740 man."

---

724 The erased reading is probably that of revised MS. 4: "**They** come."

This said friend Peter mounts forthwith *686–690*
Upon that good and faithful Ass,
And straight~~way~~ without a moment's stay
The Ass turns quietly away
{*B*
Leaving the {*body on the grass.*

The little Ass is strong at heart, *691–695*
And firm he walks, and bolt upright;
But well may the poor Beast be wasted
No food these four days has he tasted,
Not even a single bite.

Amid that green and quiet spot, *696–700*
He four long days and nights had pass'd,
A sweeter meadow ne'er was seen,

[35r]

(35)

And there the Ass four days had been
And never once had broke his fast.

Across the meadow they are gone, *701–705*
And now are at the quarry's mouth;
The little Ass who is the guide

---

741 said, friend *del to* uttered *in pencil, overwritten in ink*
742 that good and faithful Ass; *del to* the pleased & thankful Ass *partly in pencil, overwritten in ink*
743 straight *del to* then
744 Ass turns quietly *del to* earnest creature turn'd *partly first drafted in pencil*
746–750 *marked* out
747 upright,
751 Amid that green and *del to* Now learn that in this *then entire line del to* Intent upon his faithful watch *drafted first in pencil*
752 He four long *del to* This beast four *then* this *rev in pencil to* The night's
755 And *del to* Nor never *eras to* ever had broke *del to* did break *(WW)* *all revisions drafted first in pencil*
756 *as MS. 5, del to* Yet firm his step & stout his heart *in ink over pencil; pencil draft for revision at page foot but* &] and
757 And now are at *del to* The mead is crossed Quarry's *revision drafted at page foot in pencil*
758 *As MS. 5, del in pencil to* Is reached but there the trusty guide *in ink; pencil draft for revision at page foot but* reach'd,

---

743 Deletion by erasure.

Into a thicket turns aside,
And takes his way towards the {*S*/*south.*

But hark! among the woods they hear 706–710
A cry of lamentable sort;
Though there is nothing he should stick at
Yet in the middle of the thicket
The little Ass stops short.

And Peter hears the doleful sound 711–715
And he in honest truth may say
The like came never to his ears
Though he has been full thirty years
A rover night and day.

'Tis not a plover of the moors, 716–720
'Tis not a bittern of the fen,
Nor is it like a barking fox,
Nor like a night-bird of the rocks
Or wild cat in a woody glen.

[36r]

(36)

The cry grows loud and louder still 721–725
The little Ass who meant to climb
That lofty mountain which you see,
Beneath the shadow of a tree
Is listening all this time.

761–765 *marked* out
761 hear] fear
766 And Peter hears *del to* But hark! they *then all but* doleful sound; *del and eras, following pencil draft, to* When hark a burst of
767 he *del to* Peter in *del in pencil* honest truth may *rev to* honestly might
770 and] and and
773 is it like *del to* can it be
774 like a *del and* of *del to* chambered in
775 Or *rev to* Nor wild-cat
776–780 *marked* out
776 still;

781 *And Peter on the Ass's back* 726–730
782 *Is in the middle of the thicket*
783 *And, though he's used to whistle loud,*
784 *Whether alone or in a crowd*
785 *He's silent as a silent cricket.*

786 *What ails you now my pretty Bess?* 736–740
787 *Ah well indeed may you look grave*
788 *The cry which sets your heart a throbbing,*
789 *Comes from a little Boy that's sobbing*
790 *Beside the entrance of a cave.*

791 *A blooming Wood-boy of the woods,* 741–745
792 *And Bess I will be bold to say*
793 *If once you knew but where he is*
794 *Your heart would be as sad as his*
795 *'Till you had kiss'd his tears away*

[36ᵛ]

(806) He loved his gentle Father well
(807) Oft by the hand that Father led
(808) Sweet Robin over field & height
(809) And oft with his own hands at night
(810) He laid him in his bed

(811) He brought him Play things from the {F / fair}
(812) He told him tales, with nuts he fed
(813) Sweet Robin in the woody bowers
(814) And help'd him oft to gather flowers
(815) And wove rush-bonnets for his head

---

781 *del to* The Ass is startled and stops short
782 Is *del to* Right *first by WW in ink* thicket;
783 though he's used *del to* Peter wont
784 crowd,
785 He's *eras to* Is cricket.—
{W tremble & ~~sad &~~
787 ~~Ah!~~ {well ~~indeed~~ may you ^ look ^ grave
788 *rev and del to* This cry that rings along the wood
789 *del to* This cry that floats adown the flood
790 Beside *del to* Comes from
791 *del to* I see a blooming-Wood-boy there
792 Bess I will be bold *del to* if I had the power
793 *del to* How sorrowful the Wanderer is
795 away.

These are clean copies of stanzas on 37ʳ, facing, which are revised, then canceled there in ink and marked "in" in pencil.

[37^{r}]

(37)

796 *A branch of hawthorn's in his hand,* 751–755
797 *All bright with berries ripe and red*
798 *Into the caverns mouth he peeps*
799 *Thence back into the light he creeps,*
800 *And then cries out in fear and dread*

801 *And sure to see him at this time*
802 *And hear him make this dolorous sound* 767–770
803 *Sad thoughts round any heart may gather,*
804 *The Boy is seeking his dead Father*
805 *His Father dead and drown'd*

He loved his gentle father well
806 ~~*O Bess! he lov'd his Father well,*~~ 771–773
Oft by the hand that Father led
807 ~~*For oft he by the hand had led*~~
in
808 ~~*Sweet Robin over field and height*~~
809 ~~*And oft with his own hands at night*~~
810 ~~*Had laid him in his bed.*~~

811 ~~*He brought him playthings from the Fair*~~
812 ~~*He told him tales, with nuts he fed*~~
in woody bowers
813 ~~*Sweet Robin in the wood, and he*~~ 773–775
And [?] oft to gather [—?—][?]
814 ~~*Gave Robin many a halfpenny*~~
815 ~~*And many a crust of bread*~~
And wove rush bonnets for his head

---

796 *del to* Holding a hawthorn branch in hand
797 red;
798 cavern's
799 he *del and* light *rev to* moon-light
800 What seeks the boy ~~in grief~~ the silent dead
~~And then cries out in fear~~ ^ ~~and dread.~~ *with last phrase drafted below line by WW in pencil*

801–815 *marked* out
805 drown'd.
806 lov'd Father
808–810 *as MS. 5 (37^{r}) before deletion, but (810)* Had] He *as MS. 5, 36^{v}*
811–815 *as MS. 5, 36^{v}, but (811)* play-things *(812)* tales; *(815)* rush bonnets . . . head.

The vertical line in the left margin, as well as the "in" against each of the last two stanzas, is in pencil.

[38r]

(38)

816 *And Robin all day long hath sought* 776

road
{By {p {& { th }rough}
817 {~~*His*~~ {~~*Fath*~~{*er* {~~*[?in}?the]*~~} ~~*woods and lanes,*~~

His Father through the woods & lanes

818 *Among the rocks, behind the trees,*
819 *Now creeping on his hands and knees*
{*s.*
820 *Now running on the open plain*{

821 *And hither is he come at last,* 781–785
822 *When he through such a day has gone,*
823 *By this dark cave to be distress'd*
824 *Where like a bird about it's nest.*
825 *He flutters off and on*

---

816 *probably as MS. 5 but eras to illeg line, eras again to* The orphan child his Father seeks *del in turn to* His Father—him doth he require *with dash in pencil*

817 *probably as MS. 5, rev, but eras to illeg line, eras again to* Whom he all day with fruitless pains *then* all day *del to* hath sought

818 *probably as MS. 5, rev, but eras to illeg line, eras again to* Hath sought among the rocks & trees *del in turn to* Among the rocks behind the trees

821 is he] he is

824 *probably as MS. 5, eras to* Like a poor Bird her plundered nest

825 *as MS. 5, eras to* Hovering around with dolorous moan

825/826 *extra stanza drafted by WW in pencil at top of next verso:*

Of that intense & piercing cry
listening
This [?] Ass [?] rightly dwell
As sage Astronomers can see
[?] [?in heavens bright] [?]
[?] *with fourth line recast on facing recto:* And Heavens bright canopy *then entire stanza written by MW at bottom of previous recto:*

Of that intense & piercing cry
The listening Ass doth rightly spell
Wild as it is he there can read
~~As sage Astronomers can see~~
Some intermingled notes that plead
~~Meanings in heaven's bright canopy~~
With touches irristible
~~To no one else perceptible~~

---

817 The "s" on woods and the "s" on lanes were deleted by erasure before the line was canceled, converting it to "By path & road through wood and lane." WW penciled on the facing verso: "His father in the woods & lanes."

At last in hopelessness and fear 786–790
Along the wood his road he takes
And like a little Child that's lost
And thinks he's follow'd by a ghost
A wild and doleful cry he makes

The Ass when first he caught the noise 791–795
Stopp'd short and soon he knew it well
And towards the cave whence Robin sent
All through the wood that sad lament
He hath been carrying Peter Bell

[39r]

(39)

But soon as Peter saw the Ass 796–800
His road all on a sudden change
And turn right upwards through the hollow
That lamentable noise to follow
It wrought in him conviction strange.

A faith that for that dead Man's sake 801–805
And his poor Ass, from heaven or hell
Vengeance upon his head will fall,
Some visitation worse than all
Which ever till this night befell.

826–835 *marked* out
830 makes.
832 Stopt short,
833 cave,
834 lament,
836 But $\left\{\begin{matrix}\text{soon}\\\text{Peter}\end{matrix}\right\}$ $\left\{\begin{matrix}\text{But}\\\text{as}\end{matrix}\right\}$ ‸ Peter ‸ $\left\{\begin{matrix}\text{!— when he}\\\text{‸}\end{matrix}\right\}$ saw the Ass *with illeg pencil above line (and with* soon *in SH's hand)*
837 *as MS. 5 but* change, *then del to* Not only stop but turn & change *with possibly related pencil traces below stanza*
838 *as MS. 5, then all but first two words del to* with $\left\{\begin{matrix}\text{unremitt}\\\text{[?]}\end{matrix}\right\}$ing pace *all del to* The cherished tenor of his pace
839 follow *del to* chase
840 conviction] commotion *del to* conviction
841 *second* that *del in pencil to* the *overwritten* the *in ink*
842 his *rev to* this *and last five words del to illeg half line; both original reading and revision eras to* Slave from heaven or hell
845 befel.

Meanwhile the Ass in Robin's track 806–810
Is following stoutly as he may
But while he climbs the woody hill,
The cry grows weak and weaker still
And now at last dies quite away

Fain would he overtake the Boy 811–815
For Robin is his dear delight
But finding 'tis an idle hope
Down the close pathway's rugged slope,
He gently turns towards the right;

[40r]

(40)

With Peter on his back he turns 816–820
Into a gloomy grove of beech
Along the shade, with footstep~~s~~ true
Descending slowly till the two
The open moonlight reach.

And there along a narrow dell 821–825
A fair smooth pathway you discern,
{*length of*
A{*nd with that green and open road,*
As any little river broad
Winding away *between the fern*

The rocks that tower on either side 826–830
Build up a wild fantastic scene,
Temples like those among the Hindoos,
And mosques, & spires, & Abbey windows
And castles all with ivy green.

---

846 in Robin's track, *del to* to gain his end
847 following *del to* striving may,
850 dies quite away] it dies away.
851–855 *marked* out
851 Boy,
852 delight,
855 right.
856 With Peter on his back he *del to* So with his freight the Creature
858 shade,] shade footsteps
859 'till
865 fern.
868 these *rev to* those
869 & . . . &] and . . . and abbey

---

858 Deletion by erasure.
865 Erased was probably the reading of MS. 4: **"The Ass** winds on."

And while the Ass pursues his way,
Along this solitary dell 837
As ste~~e~~p by ste~~e~~p he doth advance
The mosques & spires change countenance
And look at Peter Bell.

[41r]

(41)

That unintelligible Cry 841–845
Hath left him high in preparation
Convinc'd that He or soon or late
This luckless night will meet his fate
And so he sits in expectation.

The smooth green pathway in and out
Winds upwards like a straggling chain
And when two toilsome *miles ~~h~~ave pass'd*
Up through the rocks it leads *at last*
Unto a high and open plain

The little Ass makes no complaint 846–850
He feels not any want of strength
And slowly up the smooth green track
He winds with Peter on his back
Till he hath gain'd the top at length

Right onward steers the trusty Beast 856–860
Over the Down his way he bends

---

873 step by step he doth *del to* silently his steps
874 &] and
876 cry
881 smooth green *del to* verdant
883 have] are
885 Unto] Into plain.
886–890 *marked* out *and marked with vertical pencil and ink lines*
886 complaint,
887 strength;
888 smooth *del to* st *revision left unfinished* -grown *inserted after* green
889 winds,
890 'Till . . . length.
891 *as MS. 5 but* Beast, *del to* The strenuous animal hath gain'd *then last two words eras to* hath clomb *at top of page WW scrawled pencil drafts:* The strenuous animal [?proceed]
892 *probably as MS. 5, eras to* The height & now his way descends *del to* With the green path & now he wends

---

873 Deletion by erasure.
883 Erased was probably the reading of MS. 2: "you two **good**." The "h" in "have" is deleted by erasure, presumably to revise the reading to "are."
884 Erased was probably the reading of MS. 2: "you come."

Where smooth and bare as any sea
Without a plant without a tree
The level plain extends

[42r]

(42)

And ever where along the turf *861–865*
They go with smooth and steady pace
You see driven onward by the wind
A dancing leaf that's close behind
Following them o'er that lonely place

And Peter hears that stirring noise *866–870*
And many a time he turns *his face*
Both here and there ere he can find
What 'tis that follows close behind
Along that solitary place

---

893 smooth and bare as any sea *del to* quiet as the smoothest sea *then* quiet *del to* placid *then all del to* shining like the smoothest sea

894 Without a plant, without a tree, *del to* In undisturbed immensity

895 The *rev to* That extends.

896–900 *much revised:*

But they urge their way
~~And~~ ever where ~~along the turf~~

In presence of that lonely waste
~~urge their way with~~
~~They go~~ ^ ~~with smooth and steady pace~~

A rustling leaf is close behind
{~~D~~ ~~sportive~~
~~You see~~ {~~driven onward by the~~ ^ ~~wind~~

Light play-thing for the sportive wind
[?~~thats dancing~~]
A ~~dancing~~ leaf ^ ~~that's close behind~~

Far fetched & fondly chased
{e
~~Along th{at solitary place.~~

deletion above l. 899 is by erasure; a vertical line alongside left margin may signal intention to cancel the stanza and replace it with one inserted below, at foot of page, over illeg pencil drafts:

How blank! but whence that rustling sound
Which}
That } all too long the pair hath chased
A dancing leaf is close behind—
Light play-thing for the sportive wind
Upon that solitary waste

901–905 *omitted; probably replaced by the stanza above, which partly telescopes ll. 896–905*

At last he 'spies the wither'd leaf, 871–875
And Peter's in sore distress
"Where there is not a bush or tree
{*th* {*y*
The very Leaves {*are* {*following me*
So huge hath been my wickedness.

And now they to a lane are come 886–890
And still the little meagre Ass
Moves on without a moment's stop
Nor once turns round his head to crop
A bramble leaf or blade of grass.

[43r]

(44)

{*on*
Between the hedges {*as they go* 891–895
The dusty road is white as bone,
When Peter casting down his eyes
Towards the moonlight road espies
A drop of blood upon a stone.

---

906 At last *del to* When Peter spies leaf,
907 And Peter is in sore *del to* It yields no cure to his distress—
—}
908 }"Where
909 they follow me,
910 wickedness!"
911 And now they to a lane *del to* To a close lane they now
912 *as MS. 5, eras and del to* Where as before the enduring Ass
n
914 rou d *(SH)*
916 on *overwritten* as
917–920 *much revised:*

white dust sleeps upon the lane
~~The dusty road is white as bone;~~
^
And Peter ever & anon ~~down looking~~
~~When Peter casting down his eyes~~
Down looking sees upon a stone
~~Toward the moonlight road espies~~
Or in the dust, a crimson stain
~~A drop of blood upon a stone.~~

deletion of down looking *by erasure*

---

907 Deletion by erasure, perhaps of the MS. 3 reading, "a."
909 Deletion by erasure.
The page number appears to be a mistake; there is no p. 43, but no text is missing.

921 *Peter has little power to move* *896–900*
922 *Upon the Ass remain he must,*
923 *He travels on, and now and then*
924 *He sees that drop of blood again*
925 *Upon a stone, or in the dust.*

926 *Did Peter e'er with club or staff* *901–905*
927 *Smite some poor traveller on the head?*
928 *Or beat his Father in a rage*
929 *And spill the blood of his old age*
930 *Or kick a child till he was dead?*

931 *Did Peter ever kill his man* *906–910*
f
932 *With fist or staf in single duel?*
933 *Or stab with some inhuman wound*
934 *A Soldier bleeding on the ground,*
935 *No, Peter never was so cruel*

[44^r]

(45)

936 *Then why to see this drop of blood* *911–915*
937 *Does Peter look so pale and wan?*
938 *Why is he in this sad despair?*
~~sees~~
939 *He knows not how the blood comes there*
940 *And Peter is a wicked man*

921–935 *marked* out
923 on,] on
925 stone,] stone
926 e'er] ere
927 Traveller
Or beat his Father
928 Did Peter [?] in a rage *(SH)*
931 man,
932 duel;
934 ground—
935 cruel.
936–950 *stanzas equivalent to these lines appear on one of the two surviving leaves of MS. 7, numbered 40*
936 Then why to see this *del to* A stain as of a *MS. 6* A stain—as of a *MS. 7*
937 Did Peter look so pale *del to* By moonlight made more faint *MS. 6* By moonlight made more faint wan— *MS. 7*
938 *del to* Ah! why this comfortless despair *MS. 6, then* Ah *apparently converted to* Ha *the reading of MS. 7*
939 there, *MS. 7*
940 wicked] wicked *del to* Godless *MS. 6* wicked *del to illeg word, which is eras and* wicked *reinstated MS. 7* Man. *MSS. 6, 7*

---

939 The word "sees" is added and deleted in pencil.

At length he spies a bleeding wound *916–920*
d
Where he hath struck the Ass's head,
sees
He sees the blood, knows ^ what it is,
A glimpse of sudden joy is his
But then it quickly fled

He thought he could not help but think *921–925*
Of the dead *Man and his poor Ass*
And once again those ugly pains
Across his liver heart and reins
Swift as a weaver's shuttle pass

[45ʳ]

(46)

Third Part

I've heard of one, a gentle Soul, *926–930*
Though given to sadness and to gloom
, *,*
And for the fact I'll vouch one night
It chanc'd that by a taper's light
This Man was reading in his room.

---

941 wound, *MS. 7*
942 head; *MSS. 6, 7*
943 knows *MSS. 6, 7* is,— *MS. 7*
944 is] is *del to* was *in pencil, overwritten in ink MS. 6* was *MS. 7* his, *MS. 7*
945 fled. *MS. 6* fled; *MS. 7*
946 *MS. 6 probably as MS. 5, then partly rev and both revision and original line eras to* Of him whom sudden death had seized *the reading of MS. 7, except* seized] siezed
947 *MS. 6 as MS. 5 except* Ass; *then all but last word del to illeg line, eras to* He thought, and of his faithful *then* his *overwritten* the *in pencil* He thought,—and of his faithful Ass! *MS. 7*
948 ugly *del to* darting *MS. 6, the reading of MS. 7*
949 Across his liver, heart, and reins, *MS. 6, del to* As meteors shoot through heaven's wide plains *the reading of MS. 7, except* plains,
950 Swift as a weaver's shuttle, *del to* Pass through his bosom & *MS. 6, the reading of MS. 7 except* bosom—and pass. *rev to* repass. *MS. 6* repass! *MS. 7*
951–965 *stanzas equivalent to these lines appear on the second of the two surviving pages of MS. 7, numbered 41; all punct in MS. 7 not in MS. 6 appears to be added*
Third Part] Part Third *MSS. 6, 7*
952 gloom; *MSS. 6, 7*
953 And,] *so MS. 6* And *MS. 7* I'll *rev by eras to* will *MSS. 6, 7*
955 room; *MS. 7*

---

943 The caret and the revision are in pencil.
947 Under the erasure is perhaps a miswriting, "poor."

956 *Reading as you or I might read,* 931–935
957 *At night in any pious book*
958 *When sudden blackness overspread*
959 *The snow-white page on which he read*
960 *And made the good Man round him look*

961 *The chamber walls were dark all round* 936–940
962 *And to his book he turn'd again*
963 *— The light had left the good Man's taper*
964 *And form'd itself upon the paper*
965 *Into large letters bright and plain*

[46r]

(47)

966 *The godly Book was in his hand* 941–945
967 *And on the page more black than coal*
968 *Those ghostly letters form'd a word*
969 *Which to his dying day, I've heard,*
970 *Perplex'd the good Man's gentle soul*

971 *The wondrous word which thus he saw* 946–950
972 *Did never from his lips depart*
th
973 *But he has} said, poor gentle Wight!*
974 *It brought full many a sin to light*
975 *Out of the bottom of his heart.*

---

956 Reading . . . read,] Reading, . . . read *MS. 7*
957 book, *MS. 7*
958 blackness] darkness *rev to* blackness *MS. 7*
959 read, *MS. 7*
{M
960 {man *MS. 7* look. *MSS. 6, 7*
961 round; *MS. 6* round,— *MS. 7*
962 again; *MS. 7*
963 taper, *MS. 7*
964 paper, *MS. 7*
965 letters— *MS. 7* plain. *MS. 6* plain! *over eras MS. 7*
968 *as MS. 5, then partly rev, then revision eras and line del to* Appeared, set forth in strange array
969 *del to* A word which to his dying day
970 Soul.
971 wondrous *del to* ghostly he saw *del to* was framed
972 depart;
975 Out of *del to* From out *in pencil overwritten in ink, then* Out of *restored in pencil, overwritten in ink*

Dread Spirits! thus to vex the good 951–955
How can Ye with your functions jar?
{*st*
Disordering colour, form, and {*feature,*
Let good men feel the soul of nature,
And see things as they are;

I know you potent Spirits! well 956–960
How with the feeling and the sense
Ye play both with your foes and friends
Most fearful work for fearful ends,
And this I speak in reverence

[47r]

(*48*)

But might I give advice to you 961–965
Whom in my fear I love so well,
From men of pensive virtue go,
Dread Beings, and your empire shew
On hearts like that of Peter Bell!

Your presence I have often felt 966–970
In darkness and the stormy night;
And well I know if need there be
{e
Y{*ou can put forth your agency*
Beneath the sweet moonlight.

Then coming from the wayward world 971–975
That powerful world in which ye dwell
Come, Spirits of the mind! and try
Tonight beneath the moonlight sky
What may be done with Peter Bell.

---

976 thus to vex *del to* to torment
977 *del to* Why wander from your course so far
983 play,
984 work. ends,] ends
985 reverence.
986 you,
990 Bell.
994 You *eras to* Yo *evidently for* Ye
995 *del to* When earth is calm & heaven is bright
996 world,
997 dwell,
998 Mind!
999 To-night

---

994 Revision in pencil.

Oh! would that any friend or foe *976–980*
My further labour would prevent!
Aw'd am I when I think of it;
I fe{e/ll that I am all unfit
For such high argument.

[48r]

(*49*)

I've play'd, I've danc'd with my narration, *981–985*
I loiter'd long ere I began
I've mov'd to many a giddy measure
But now, my Friends, with your good pleasure
I'll do the best I can.

The Ass, as you remember well, *986–990*
Is travelling now along a lane,
And Peter many tricks is trying,
And many anodynes applying
To ease his stomach of it's pain.

By this his heart is lighter far, *991–995*
And finding that he can account
So snugly for that crimson stain
His evil Spirit up again
Does like an empty bucket mount

Quoth Peter wounds will bleed we know *996–1000*
And blood is blood and fools have fears

1001 O! any, . . . foe,
1003 *del to* Kind listeners that around me sit
1006 *second* I've *overwritten* and danc'd,
1007 began;
1008 I've moved *eras to* Moving *then line del to* Ye waited then on my good pleasure
1009 *as MS. 5 but* pleasure, *then del to* [?] your indulgence still yould measure *then rev in pencil to* Pour out indulgence still in measure
1010 *del to* As liberal as ye can
1011 The Ass, as *del to* Our Travellers
1012 now along a *del to* through a sheltered *then* travelling *del to* thridding *then all but last word in line del to* Are thridding a sequestered lane;
1014 applying,
1015 stomach] conscience *over eras*
1016 far;
1018 snugly] clearly *over eras*
1019 spir{i}t *(SH)*
1020 Bucket mount.
1021–1025 *marked* out
1021 Peter, "wounds
1022 is blood, . . . fears—"

1023 *But yet the leaf, he can't deny,*
{;
1024 *Dogg'd him*{ *and still that doleful cry*
1025 *Is ringing in his ears.*

[48v]

1031 * And say the best you can, tis plain *1006–1010*
th}
1032 That here has } been some wicked dealing,
1033 No doubt the Devil in me wrought,
1034 I'm not the Man who could have thought
{A
1035 An {ass like this was worth the stealing.

[49r]

(50)

1026 *But Peter is a deep logician* *1001–1005*
1027 *And hath no lack of wit mercurial*
1028 *"Why after all 'tis plain," quoth he*
1029 *"This poor Man never but for me*
1030 *Could have had christian burial"*
*

1030/1031 *false start by SH without leaving stanza space:* And
1031 "And . . . 'tis
1032 dealing;
1033 wrought—
1035 An] And *eras to* An stealing.] stealing
1026 But *del to* And
1027 *as MS. 5 but* mercurial; *then* And hath no lack of *del to* Stored plenteously with *del in pencil to* Who hath no lack of *in pencil and ink*
1028 Why after all 'tis plain *del to* Blood drops, leaves rustle, yet he,
1029 man
1030 burial."

1031 The asterisk apparently indicates that this stanza (inserted on facing verso in MS. 2, omitted in MS. 3, present in regular sequence in MSS. 4 and 6) is to be inserted following l. 1030 on 49r.

So from his pocket Peter takes *1011–1015*
His shining horn Tobacco box,
And in a careless way, as you
Or I, good Mr Swan, might do
Upon the lid he knocks.

There's some of you, my Friends, perhaps *1016–1020*
There's some of you in yawning weather
{*a*
Who may have seen {*An Ass's grin;*
'Tis uglier far than death and sin,
And all the devils together.

And just as Peter struck the box, *1021–1025*
It might be to recruit his wind
Or for some more important cause
The quiet creature made a pause
Turn'd round his head and grinn'd

1038 light and *inserted after* a *and* as you *del*
1039 I, good Mr Swan,] any of our friends *over eras, probably the reading of MS. 5, then line del to* As men who with their purpose play
1041–1045 *marked* out
1041 There's some of you, my Friends *del to* Of those who hear me now *del in ink and pencil*
1044 sin,] sin
1046–1050 *much revised, canceled with pencil* X, *and rewritten at bottom of page:*

them whose voice can stop
Let ~~such as can detain~~ ^ the clouds
Whose cunning eye can see the wind
~~The quiet Creature instantly~~
~~And just as Peter struck the box,~~
~~Or solve the motions of the~~
~~It might be to recruit his ^ wind~~,
a
Tell to ~~the~~ curious world the cause
~~Or for some more important cause~~
~~Did make an unexpected~~
~~The quiet creature made~~ a pause
~~Why the poor Ass here made~~ ^
~~Turn'd round his head and grinn'd~~.

Let them whose voice can stop the clouds
Whose cunning eye can see the wind
Tell to a curious world the cause
Why making here a sudden pause
The Ass turned round his head & grinn'd

[50r]

(51)

1051 *You know that Peter is resolv'd* 1026–1030
1052 *His drooping spirits to repair*
1053 *And though no doubt, a sight like this*
1054 *To others might have come amiss*
1055 *It suited Peter to a hair.*

1056 *And Peter, grinning with a joke,* 1031–1035
1057 *His teeth in approbation shew'd*
1058 *When, cruel blow to Peter's mirth!*
1059 *He heard a murmur in the earth,*
1060 *In the dead earth beneath the road.*

1061 *Beneath the Ass's feet it pass'd* 1036–1040
1062 *A murmur and a rumbling sound,*
1063 *'Twas by a troop of miners made*
1064 *Who plied with gunpowder their trade*
Some twenty
1065 *A score of fathoms underground.*

1051–1055 *much revised:*

Apalling process—I have marked
~~You know that Peter is resolved~~
The like on heath—in lonely wood
~~His drooping spirits to repair,~~
verily have seldom met
And ^ ~~though no doubt a sight like this~~
A spectacle more hideous—yet
~~To others might have come amiss,~~
present mood
It suited Peter{'s} ~~to a hair~~.{—}

1053 *final revision is drafted in pencil at top of page*
1055 *the final dash is in pencil*
1056 *as MS. 5 but* Peter,] Peter *then* with a joke *del to* in his turn *then* Peter *del and* —his teeth *added at end of line in pencil, overwritten in ink*
1057 His teeth *del and* in approbation *del to* he in jocose defiance, *then* he *capitalized* shew'd—
1058 cruel blow to Peter's *del to* to confound his spiteful
1059 He *del to* Was *then* Was heard *del in pencil,* a *capitalized in ink, and* pent with *inserted after* murmur *in pencil, overwritten in ink* earth.] earth
1061 Beneath *del to* Under *then entire line del to* Rolled audibly—it swept along *drafted first in pencil between stanzas;* in *del, in margin*
1062 murmur and *del and overwritten to* muffled noise— *drafted first in pencil above line*
1064 Who plied *del to* Plying
1065 Some twenty *no period*

1065 Erased was probably the reading of MSS. 3 and 4: "**hundred**." Revision above the line is in pencil.

1066 *And I will venture to affirm* 1041–1045

{,
1067 *If ever any{ King or Cotter,*
1068 *Did think, as sure as five is five*
1069 *That he'd be swallow'd up alive*
1070 *'Twas Peter Bell the Potter.*

1071 A faintness overspreads his heart
1072 out Giddy his head his frame doth shiver
1073 And oft the road appears to rise
stir
1074 In waves and ~~dance~~ before his eyes
1075 With motion like a rapid River

[50v]

{if
(1071) He quakes, {as in the stirring air
(1072) A lightsome birch tree bend & shiver
~~and~~ Anon—the road
(1073) The broad high way appears to rise
dance
(1074) In waves, and ~~flows~~ before his eye
(1075) With motion like a rapid river

{A
(1074) {T sickness overspread his heart
runs round
His head ~~turns [?ro]~~
(1072) Giddy his head, his frame doth shiver
(1071) By slow degrees do Peters fears
(1072) Abate yet still

1066–1070 *much revised:*

{read
Small cause of d{ire effect—for surely
~~that~~
~~when he heard ^ rumbling sound~~
~~And I will venture to affirm~~
mortal
—}
If ever ~~any~~} King or Potter
~~Ceased inwardly with fate to strive~~
~~Did think, as sure as five is five~~
{Believed
{[? ?] that earth was charged to quake
~~That he'd~~ be swallow'd up alive
And yawn, for his unworthy sake
'Twas Peter Bell the Potter.

1066 *final version drafted in pencil at top of following recto*
1069–1070 *revisions drafted in pencil at top of page*
1071–1075 *omitted*

1067 The first comma was added, or reinforced, in pencil.
1071–1075 The stanza was canceled.

so [?]
{~~So~~ {[?pallid]
{[?] black so {[?pale], [? ?]
{Yet now}
{And [?]} and then ~~he sho~~ok with fear

[51r]

(52)

1076 ~~*But still he keeps upon his seat,*~~
1077 ~~*The Ass moves slowly with his load*~~
1078 ~~*Peter is busy with his ears*~~
1079 ~~*And now and then he thinks he hears*~~
1080 ~~*A murmuring noise beneath the road.*~~

1081 ~~*And Peter by an ugly fancy*~~ *1051–1055*
1082 ~~*Is troubled more and more; thought he*~~
1083 ~~*I know the truth, I know it well,*~~
1084 ~~*Through meadow ground, and rock & dell*~~
1085 ~~*A devil is following me.*~~

1086 *Upon the Ass's back he sits* *1071–1075*
1087 *Like one that's riding in a swoon,*
Blank
1088 ~~*Or*~~ *as a ghost that cannot see*
1089 *Whose face if any such there be,*
1090 *Is like the eyeless moon*

1091 ~~*And every twenty yards or less*~~ *1076–1080*
1092 ~~*Poor Peter well may he look grim*~~
1093 ~~*Whether on rising ground or level*~~
1094 ~~*Still feels the subteraneous devil*~~
1095 ~~*Heave up the little Ass and him*~~

1076–1085 *omitted*

1086–1090 *marked with vertical line in margin as though for deletion, then line eras and* in *entered in margin; much revised:*

But as an oak in breathless air
~~Upon the Ass's back he sits~~
Will stand though to the center hewn
~~Like one that's riding in a swoon,~~
Or as the weakest things if frost
~~Blank as a ghost that cannot see~~
Have stiffened them maintain their post
~~Whose face, if any such there be,~~
So he beneath the gazing moon
~~Is like the eyeless moon.~~

1090 *revision drafted in pencil below line*

1091–1095 *omitted*

(1076) ~~But still he keeps upon his [?seat]~~
(1077) ~~The Ass moves slowly with his load~~

[52r]

(53)

~~*Meanwhile*~~
1096 *And now the Ass hath reach'd a spot* 1081–1085
1097 *Where, underneath a shelter'd cove,*
1098 *A little Chapel stands alone,*
1099 *With greenest ivy overgrown,*
1100 *And tufted with an ivy grove* .}

Dying insensibly away
{*all*
1101 ~~*A building dying*~~ {~~[?] *away*~~ 1086–1090
1102 *From human thoughts and purposes*
{~~*The*~~ *Building*
1103 {*It seems* ~~*both*~~ *wall and roof and tower*
1104 *To bow to some transforming power*
1105 *And blend with the surrounding* trees.

1106 *Deep sighing as he pass'd along* 1091–1095
1107 *Quoth Peter "in the Shire of Fife*
1108 *'Twas just in such a place as that,*
1109 *Not knowing what I would be at*
{*W*
1110 *I married my sixth* {*wife*

1111 ~~*Thus Peter communed with himself,*~~ 1096–1100
1112 ~~*By this time he is somewhat wean'd*~~
1113 ~~*I think, from his delirious notion*~~
1114 ~~*That the Road's giddy with commotion*~~
1115 ~~*Made by a subteraneous fiend*~~

1096 and *del to* But Ass hath *del to* Pair have
~~sheltering~~
1097 Where ~~underneath a shallow cove,~~
sheltered by a rocky cove *revisions apparently drafted first in pencil*
1099 overgrown,] overgrown
1103 The Building seems, wall roof and tower
1106 along,
1107 Peter,
1108 *del to* Mid such a ruin, following still
1109 *as MS. 5 but* at, *then del to* From Land to Land a lawless will
1110 Wife.
1111–1115 *omitted; l. 1111 becomes first line of following stanza*

[53^{r}]

(54)

Thus Peter communed with himself
~~*Yet ever and anon, sad thoughts*~~
While
~~*And*~~ *woeful apprehensions gall him;*
Believing in his own despite
That soon or late this very night
Some cruel judgement will befal him.

The little Ass moves slowly on *1101–1105*
And now is passing by an Inn
Brim-full of a carouzing Crew
Making with curses not a few
An uproar and a drunken din

I cannot well express the thought *1106–1110*
Which Peter in those noises found,
A stifling power compress'd his frame
'Twas just as if a darkness came
Over that dull and dreary sound

— For well did Peter know the sound: *1111–1115*
The language of those drunken joys
To him, a jovial Soul I ween,
But a few hours ago had been
A gladsome and a welcome noise.

[53^{v}]

(1146) And headlong from a bridge like this
(1147) ~~I flung it was a heinous murther~~

(1147) Just heaven it was a heinous murther—
(1148) I flung my good dog Ruffian he

1116–1120 *marked* out
1121 little *del to* heedless *(following* The heedless *in pencil on preceding page) rev by erasure and overwriting to* unheeding on,
1123 Crew,
1125 din.
1127 found;
1128 frame,
1129 'Twas just *del* as *rev to* As a *del to* confusing
1130 sound.
1131 —For] For sound—

On 53^{v} WW appears to have drafted versions of ll. 1146–1148 before he entered them on 54^{r}.

[54r]

(55)

But now 'tis plain that Peter's thoughts *1116–1120*
Have taken a far different course
Whate'er he sees, whate'er he hears
Gives him new sorrow or new fears
Deepens his anguish and remorse

And passing by a twisted Elm, *1121–1125*
Again poor Peter thus began
Beneath the boughs of such a
~~*"'Twas just by such*~~ *another Tree*
in scorn of Charity
I robb'd ~~*of sixpence halfpenny*~~
A Boy that led a poor blind Man."

And headlong from a bridge like this
Just heavn it was a heinous Murther.
[?stile]
G}
And ~~*close by such a g*~~ ~~*ate as that*~~ *1126–1130*
~~*Did I by a most heinous mur*~~*ther*
I flung
~~*Destroy*~~ *my good Dog Ruffian, he*
Who gladly would have gone for me
To the world's end and further

A faithful Beast like this poor Ass *1131–1135*
Whom I have bruis'd so cruelly
~~an unoffending~~
~~*Just such another*~~ *animal,*
in *Made by the God who made us all,*
And fitter far to live than I."

1136–1155 *omitted, but one stanza is added at foot of page, much revised:*
turned adrift into the past
~~Now all is changed & turned adrift~~
Dire phantoms meets he in his course
~~Into the past; he feels its force~~
Like planet-stricken Men of yore
He trembles smitten to the core
By strong compunction & remorse

1146 The doubtful reading is in pencil.

[55r]

(56)

But more than all his heart is stung 1136–1140
To think of one, almost a {*C* / *child,*}
A sweet and playful Highland Girl
As light and beauteous as a Squirrel,
As beauteous, and as wild.

A lonely House her dwelling was, 1141–1145
A Cottage in a heathy Dell
And she put on her gown of green
And left her mother at sixteen
And follow'd Peter Bell.

But many good & pious thoughts 1146–1150
Had she; and in the Kirk to pray
Two long Scotch miles through rain {*or* / *and snow*}
To Kirk she had been used to go
Thrice every sabbath day.

And when she followe'd Peter Bell 1151–1155
It was to live an honest life
For he with tongue not used to falter
Had pledg'd his troth before the altar
To love her as his wedded {*W* / *wife.*}

1159 squirrel,
1160 beauteous,] beauteous
1162 Dell;
1164 Mother
1165 followed
1166 &] and
r
1167 p ay *(SH)*
1170 Thrice *del to* Twice Sabbath Day.
1171 follow'd Bell,
1175 Wife.] wife

[56r]

(57)

A Child was in her womb, but soon *1156–1160*
She droop'd and pin'd like one forlorn;
From Scripture she a name did borrow;
Benoni, or the Child of Sorrow
She call'd her babe unborn.

For she had learn'd how Peter liv'd *1161–1165*
And took it in most grievous part
She to the very bone was worn,
And ere that little Child was born
Died of a broken heart.

And now the Spirits of the Mind *1166–1170*
Are busy with poor Peter Bell,
And from the Ass's back he sees
I think as ugly images
As ever eye did see in hell.

Close by a brake of flowering furze *1171–1175*
He sees himself as plain as day
He sees himself a Man in figure
~~His very~~
~~*Just like him*~~*self, nor less nor bigger,*
His very self
Not five yards from the broad high-way

1176 child was in her womb, *del to* mother's hope is her's
1177 pined
1178 borrow,
1179 child of Sorrow,
1181 learnt . . . lived
1182 part;
1187 Bell;
1188 *del to* Distraction reigns in soul & sense
1189 ugly *eras to* hideous *then line del to* And Reason falls in impotence
1190 *del to* From her accustomed pinnacle
1192 *del to* Above it shivering Aspens play
1193 himself a Man in figure *del to* an insubstantial creature
1194 nor less nor bigger, *del to* in form and f{ea / [?ix]}ture
1195 five] four

1194 "His very" above the line is in pencil; both deleting lines are in ink.

[57r]

(58)

1196 *And stretch'd beneath the furze he sees* 1176–1180
1197 *The Highland Girl — it is no other;*
1198 *And hears her crying as she cried*
1199 *The very moment that she died*
1200 *My Mother! oh! My Mother!*

1201 *The sweat pours down from Peter's face* 1181–1185
1202 *So grievous is his heart's contrition,*
1203 *With agony his eye-balls ache*
1204 *While he beholds by the furze brake*
1205 *This miserable vision.*

1206 *The Ass is pacing down a hill,* 1186–1190
1207 *By this he has not far to go*
1208 *And now while down the slope he wends*
1209 *A voice to Peter's ears ascends*
1210 *From the deep woody dell below*

1211 *The voice he hears is like a voice* 1191–1195
1212 *Re-echoed from a naked Rock*
1213 *'Tis from that Tabernacle—List!*
Within,
1214 *It is a pious Methodist*
Is
1215 *That's preaching to his pious flock.*

1196 stretched
1197 other:
1198 cried,
1199 died,
1200 *second* My] my
1201 face,
1203 eyeballs
1206 The Ass is pacing down a hill; *del to* Calm is the well-deserving Brute *in pencil, then ink*
1207 By this he has not far to go; *del to* His peace has no offence betrayed *in pencil, then ink; then* has *rev to* hath *in pencil*
1208 And *del to* But
1210 From the deep woody dell below. *del to* From out a *alt pencil draft at bottom of page, then to* Resounding from a woody glade *drafted first in pencil at bottom of page; alt pencil draft between stanzas:* [?Sinking down through]
1211 The voice he hears is like a *del to* Though clamourous as a hunter's
1214 Within, a pious Methodist *then* pious *del to* fervent *in pencil, overwritten in ink*
1215 Is preaching to his pious Flock. *then* pious *del to* daunted *then* daunted *del in pencil to* no heedless

---

1206 Erased was perhaps the word "the."
1214–1215 Revision was drafted by WW on facing verso:
Within, a pious Methodist
Is preaching

[58r]

(59)

"Repent, repent" he cries aloud *1196–1200*
While yet ye may find mercy—strive
To love the Lord with all your might
Turn to him, seek him, day and night
And save your souls alive.

My Friends, my Brethren, though you've gone *1201–1205*
Through paths of wickedness and woe
After the Babylonian harlot,
And though your sins be red as scarlet
They shall be white as snow."

Just as he pass'd the door, these words *1206–1210*
Did plainly come to Peter's ears
And they such joyful tidings were
The joy was more than he could bear
He melted into tears

Sweet tears of hope and tenderness, *1211–1215*
And fast they fell, a plenteous shower,

1215/1216 *at top of page appears a stanza in pencil, overwritten in ink, and canceled (a similar stanza appears in 1819, but before the equivalent of MS. 5, ll. 1241–1245); question mark probably indicates uncertainty about the fate of the stanza:*

? Who washed his poor disciple's feet?
Upon as Ass who deigned to ride
Entering the proud Jerusalem
In lowly meekness by a stream
Of shouting People deified

1216 repent," . . . aloud,
1217 "While
1218 "To . . . might,
1219 "Turn
1220 "And
1221 "My Friends, my Brethren, *del to* On him repose— *in pencil overwritten in ink, then del to* Repent repent *(WW) and* you've *rev by WW to* you have
1222 "Through
1223 "After . . . Harlot,
1224 "And . . . scarlet,
1225 "They
1226 Just *del to* Even *in pencil*
1227 ears;
1230 tears.
1232 fell,] fell

His nerves his sinews seem'd to melt;
frame
Through all his iron ~~heart~~ ^ was felt
A gentle a relaxing power.

[59^r]

(60)

Each nerve, each fibre of his frame *1216–1220*
And all the animal within
Was weak, perhaps; but it was mild
And gentle as an infant Child,
An infant that has known no sin

But now the little patient Ass, *1221–1225*
Towards a gate that's full in view
Turn'd up a narrow lane: his chest
Against the yielding gate he press'd
And quietly pass'd through.

And up the stony lane he goes; *1226–1230*
No ghost more softly ever trod,
Among the stones and pebbles, he
Sets down his hoofs inaudibly,
As if with felt his {hoofs / feet} were shod.

Along the lane the little Ass *1231–1235*
Had gone two hundred yards, not more,
When to a lonely House he came;
He turn'd aside towards the same
And stopp'd {b / fefore} the door.

1234 felt,
1235 power!
1236 Each nerve *del and* each *capitalized;* grew weak *added to line, after* frame, *with comma eras*
1237 And *del to* Weak within,
1238 Was weak perhaps; but it was *del to* But in its powerlessness grew *then* power *del to* help
1239 child,
1240 sin.
1241 And *del to* But little patient *del to* persevering
1242 that's full in *del to* in open
1249 inaudibly,] inaudibly
1251 little *del to* trusty
1253 house

1234 Revision, including caret, in pencil.

[60r]

(61)

Thought Peter, 'tis the poor Man's House, 1236–1240
He listens — not a sound is heard;
you
But ere ~~he~~ could count half a score,
{*d*
It chance{*th that at the cottage door*
{*G*
A little {*girl appeared*

She to the Meeting-house was going, 1241–1245
With hope that she some news might gather,
She saw the Pair, and with a scream
Cried out like one that's in a dream,
"My Father! here's my Father!"

The very word was plainly heard, 1246–1250
Heard plainly by the wretched Mother,
Her joy was like a deep affright,

1256 House,] house *overwritten* home
1258 *del to* Save one, the trickling household rill *then* one *del to* from
1259 *as MS. 5 but* Cottage *then all del to* But stepping oer the Cottage sill
1260 A little girl appeared. *then* Forthwith *inserted with caret and* A *overwritten* a
1261–1265 *much revised, partly in pencil overwritten in ink, then rewritten at top of page:*

bound
She to the Meeting-house is ~~going~~,
In tidings there to
~~With~~ hope ~~that she~~ some ~~news might~~ gather,
~~O never issued from a dream~~
~~She~~ No glimpse it is no doubtful gleam
~~And ^ saw the Pair and with a scream~~
[?] the Pair &
{S [~~? ?~~]
~~As oft~~ {she saw & ~~uttered~~ with a scream
~~Cried out, ^ like one that's in a dream~~,
~~Such outcry such a thrilling scream~~
~~Cried out~~ ^ "My Father! here's my Father!"

She to the Meeting-house is bound
In hope some tidings there to gather
No glimpse it is no doubtful gleam
& uttered
She saw ~~the Pair &~~ with a scream
~~Cried out~~ my father! here's my father!

r{ush'd / an} rushed

And forth she ^ ~~*came*~~ *into the light,*
And saw it was another.

And instantly upon the earth 1251–1255
Beneath the full moon shining bright
Just at the Ass's feet she fell,
And from the Ass poor Peter Bell
Dismounts in most unhappy plight.

[61r]

(62)

What could he do? The Woman lay 1256–1260
Dead as it seem'd both breath and limb
Poor Peter sadly was confus'd
To sights like these he was not used,
'Twas altogether new to him

He rais'd her up ~~*up*~~, *and while he held* 1261–1265
Her bog{d}y propp'd against his knee
The {W}woman wak'd and when she 'spied
The poor Ass standing by her side
She wept most bitterly.

"Oh! God be praised! my heart's at ease 1266–1270
For he is dead I know it well"
At this she wept a bitter flood
And in the best way that he could
His Tale did Peter tell.

1270 another!—
1274 And from the Ass poor *del to* At the same instant *then* instant *del to* moment
1277 *del to* Breathless & motionless—the mind
1278 Poor *del to* Of
1279 *del to* But though to such demands unused
1280 *as MS. 5 but* him. *del to* His wishes were humane & kind. *del to* He shrunk not from the task assign'd *in ink over* [?the task] *in pencil, del to* And helpless almost as the Blind,
1282 prop'd his *over* [?other] *erased (SH)*
1283 waked
1285 wept *del to* moaned

1281 Deletion in pencil.

He trembles, he is pale as death 1271–1275
His voice is weak with perturbation,
He turns aside his head— he pauses
Poor Peter from a thousand causes
Is crippled sore in his narration

[62r]

(63)

At last she learn'd how he espied 1276–1280
The Ass in that small meadow-ground
And that beside the River's bed
Her Husband now was lying dead,
That he was dead and drowne'd.

The wretched Mother looks, and looks 1281–1285
Upon the Ass that near her stands
She sees 'tis he, that 'tis the same,
She calls the poor Ass by his name
And wrings, and wrings, her hands

"O woe is me! he was so stout— 1286–1290
If he had died upon his bed
— He knew no sickness, knew no pain
He never will come home again
He's dead——for ever dead."

Beside the Woman Peter stands, 1291–1295
His heart is opening more and more

1291 death;
1292 perturbation;
1295 narration.
1296 last *del to* length She
1297 meadow-ground;
1298 beside the River's bed *del to* her Husband now lay dead
1299 *as MS. 5, then* [?] *inserted before* Husband *and* was lying *del to* lay *then entire line del to* Beside that luckless River's bed
1300 *as MS. 5 but* drowned. *then all del to illeg line, eras to* In which he had been drowned
1301 *del to* A piercing look the Sufferer cast
1302 Ass *del to* Beast stands;
1304 name,
1305 hands.
1306 woe is me! *del to* wretched loss— he was so stout— *del to illeg phrase, eras to* untimely stroke
1308 no sickness, knew no *del to* not one forwarning *partly in pencil eras and overwritten in ink* pain,
1310 He's *rev by erasure to* —Is dead."] dead!"
1312 and more;

A holy sense is in his mind
He feels what he for human kind
Had never felt before

[63r]

(64)

At length, by Peter's arm sustain'd, 1296–1300
{W
The {woman rises from the ground,
"O mercy! something must be done
My little Rachael you must run
Across the meadow by the pound

Make haste my little Rachael do, 1301–1305
Bid Farmer Simpson hither come
Ask him to lend his horse tonight,
And this good Man, whom heaven requite,
Will help to bring the Body home."

Away goes Rachael weeping loud 1306–1310
{I
An {infant wak'd by her distress
Makes in the House a piteous cry,
And Peter hears the Mother sigh
"Poor Thing! 'tis fatherless."

And now does Peter deeply feel 1311–1315
That Man's heart is a holy Thing
And Nature thro' a world of death
Breathes into him a second breath
Even like the breath of Spring.

1313 is in *del to* pervades
1315 before.
1316 length,] length sustained,
1317 Woman *with* oma *over eras (SH)*
1318 "O] Oh done,
1320 *as MS. 5 but* pound, *del to* Some willing neighbour must be found
1321 haste, . . . Rachael,
1322 *as MS. 5 but* come; *del to* The first you meet with bid him come
1326 loud—
1328 house
1330 Poor Thing! 'tis *del to* "Seven are they & all Fatherless!
1331 does *del to* is deeply *del to* taught to
1332 Thing;
1333 through
1335 Even like *del to* More searching than

[64r]

(65)

Upon a stone the Woman sits *1316–1320*
In agony of silent grief
From his own thoughts does Peter start;
He longs to press her to his heart
From love that cannot give relief.

At last upspringing from her seat *1321–1325*
As with a sudden fear and dread
The Mother through the threshold flies
And up the cottage stairs she hies
And flings herself upon the bed.

And Peter turns his steps aside *1326–1330*
Towards a shade of alder trees,
And he sits down he knows not how
With his hands press'd against his brow
And his head fix'd between his knees.

In silence there does Peter sit, *1331–1335*
Not any sign of life he makes
As if his mind were sinking deep
Through years that had been long asleep
At last as from a trance he wakes.

1337 grief *del to* woe
1338 does] did
1340 From love that cannot find relief. *del to* In pitying loves wild overflow *then reinstated with* stet
1341 *del to* Short time she sate, disturb'd & rous'd
1342 with *del to* from *del to* by fear and *del to* stroke of *in pencil overwritten in ink*
1344 Cottage
1345 flings herself upon the bed. *del to* to the pillow gives her burning head *following pencil draft between stanzas*
1347 Towards *del to* Into Alder *del to* darksome
1348 And *del to* Where
1350 his head fix'd between his *del to* resting on his tremulous *following pencil draft below stanza*
1351 sit;
1351–1352 *rewritten at top of page (WW):*
There selfinvolvd does Peter sit
Untill no sign of life he makes
1352 Not any *del to* And now no *in pencil overwritten in ink, then canceled* makes,
1354 had *rev by erasure to* have asleep—

[65r]

(66)

1356 *He turns his head and sees the Ass* 1336–1340
1357 *Yet standing in the clear moonshine,*
1358 *"When shall I be as good as thou?*
1359 *Oh! would poor Beast, that I had now*
1360 *A heart but half as good as thine"*

1361 *But hark! that doleful cry again!* 1341–1345
1362 *'Tis travelling up the woody slope;*
s
1363 *Once more while Peter heard the sound*
1364 *With stifling pain his heart is bound,*
1365 *He feels like one that has no hope.*

w o
1366 *'Tis little Robin, he h~~as~~ sought* 1346–1350
1367 *His Father with such grief and pain*
1368 *And after many perils past*
1369 *Has found his way safe home at last*
1370 *And now is coming up the lane.*

1357 moonshine;
1360 thine."
1361–1365 *much revised, then canceled*
1361 cry *del to* voice *with pencil alt above line:* a doleful cry that you
1362 *del to* If hope he had it kills his hope
Tis the
1363 *as MS. 5 but* sound, *then del to* [?] renewal of the cry
1364 *del to* That smote him like a prophesy
1365 *del to* Heard under Heaven's cerulean cope *following pencil draft at top of page*
1361–1365 *after revision, rewritten at bottom of page over illeg pencil, then both versions marked out*
~~That weeping voice that stifling cry~~
~~Now~~ travelling up yon grassy slope
'Tis
That unintelligible cry
That startling, dismal prophesy
Heard under heavens cerulian cope
1366–1370 *much revised; some revisions eras and final readings drafted in pencil at top and bottom of page*
1366 'Tis little Robin, he who sought *del (with* 'Tis *del in pencil) to* He comes who deviously hath sought *then* He comes *del to* But He—
[~~?~~]
through the lonesome woods
1367 His Father with such grief ~~and pain~~ *with illeg word eras*
1368 *del to* Hath sought proclaiming to the ear
1369 *del to* Of night, his inward grief & fear
He comes escaped from fields & floods;
1370 ~~And now is coming up the lane~~

1366 Deletion by erasure.

1371 *He's coming towards the door, and now* *1351–1355*
1372 *He sees the Ass — and nothing living*
1373 *Had ever such a fit of joy*
1374 *As had this little Orphan Boy* {,}
1375 *For he has no misgiving.*

[66r]

(67)

1376 *Towards the gentle Ass he springs* *1356–1360*
1377 *And up about his neck he climbs;*
1378 *In loving words he talks to him,*
1379 *He kisses* {,} *kisses face and limb,*
1380 *He kisses him a thousand times.*

1381 *This Peter sees, while in the shade* *1361–1365*
1382 *He stood beside the Cottage door*
1383 *And Peter Bell, the Ruffian wild*
1384 *Sobs loud, he sobs even like a Child,*
1385 *O God! I can endure no more"*

1386 *—Here ends my Tale: for in a* [?*trice*] *1366–1370*
1387 *Came Farmer Simpson with his horse*
1388 *Peter* {*w* / *se*}{*nt* / *t*} {*forth* / *out*} *with him straightway*
1389 *And two hours ere the break of d*[ ]
1390 *Tog*[ ]*her they brought back the corse*

1391 [ ]*d many years did this poor Ass* *1371–1375*
1392 [ ]*m once it was my luck to see*

1371 He's *eras to* Is coming *del to* drawing *alt line entered by WW:* With anxious hope is drawing near
1376 springs,
1378 him,] him
1382 door;
1385 "Oh! God I can endure no more."
1386 a trice
1387 *as MS. 5 but* horse; *then name following* Farmer *totally erased, then* Came Farmer *del to* Arrived a neighbour
1388 *del to illeg line, eras, and original restored by overwriting, but* straitway
1389 ~~And two hours~~ ^ ere ~~the~~ break of day ~~They hasten~~ {A / and} with due care
1390 Together . . . Corse.
1391 And Ass,
1392 Whom

The page is badly torn, resulting in gaps in the readings.

{l
Not ma[]y m[ ]s from Leming-{Lane
Help by his labour to ma[]ntain
The Widow and her Family.

[67r]

(68)

And Peter Bell, wh[ ]till th[ ]night 1376–1380
Had been the wildest of his Clan,
Forsook his crimes, f[]rsook his folly,
And after ten months melancholy
Became a good and honest Man

[68r]

(156) The dragon's wing the
I need not covet
(157) ~~These never wishd I~~
If I along
(158) ~~Be mine~~ along that [?]
(159) With sympathetic heart
(160) And with a soul of [?]

(161) These given what [?more]
Of wonder [?nove]
Wh
~~What more or~~ [?]
~~And solemn~~ [?]
(164) May in lifes [?]
(165) May fi[ ]d

A spirit
~~The~~[ ][?stron]
[?]
[?]
[?]
{If
{To there be [ ][?]

1393 Not many miles from *del to* Cropping the shrubs of Leming Lane
1394 maintain
1396 And Peter Bell, who, till that night,
1397 Clan,] Clan
1398 forsook *del to* repressed
1399 melancholy,
1400 Man.

67r is badly torn, resulting in gaps in the readings.
68r is badly torn, resulting in gaps in the readings. This fragment seems to be a draft of ll. 156–165; see 6v and 7v.

DOVE COTTAGE TRUST

Peter Bell

Prologue

There's something in a flying horse,
~~Theres~~ And something in a huge balloon,
But through the clouds I'll never float
Until I have a little Boat
Whose shape is like the crescent moon.

And now I have a little Boat
In shape a very crescent moon;
Fast through the clouds my Boat can sail
But if perchance your faith should fail,
Look up and you shall see me soon.

The woods, my Friends, are round you roaring
Rocking and roaring like a sea,
The noise of danger fills your ears,
And ye have all a thousand fears
Both for my little Boat and me.

Meanwhile I from the helm admire
The pointed horns of my Canoe;
And did not pity touch my breast
To see how you are all distress'd,
'Till my ribs ached I'd laugh at you.

Away we go, my Boat and I,
Frail man ne'er sate in such another
Whether among the winds we strive,
Or deep into the heavens we dive,
Each is contented with the other.

Away we go, and what care we
For treasons, tumults, and for wars,
We are as calm in our delight
As is the crescent moon so bright
Among the scattered stars.

Up goes ~~my Boat between~~ the stars
Through many a breathless field of light,
Through many a long blue field of ether
Leaving ten thousand stars beneath her,
Up goes my little Boat so bright.

spangles of the milky-way
~~The Crab the Virgin, and the Bear,~~
We ~~cross~~ among them all ~~&c~~ have shot
High o'er the red-haired race of Mars
~~Who've a red headed race in stars~~
All seamed
~~Covered~~ from top to toe with scars;
Such company I like it not.
The towns in Saturn are ill-built
But proud around that I have seen them
The Pleiads that appear to kiss
Each other in the vast abyss
With joy I sail between them

Bright Mercury resounds with mirth
Great Jove is full of stately bowers
But they & all that they contain
What are they to that tiny green
That darling speck of ours
The towns in Saturn are ill built,
But Jove is full of stately bowers,
The Evening Star is not amiss,
But what are all of them to this, earth
This little Earth of ours!

Then back to Earth the dear green Earth
Whole ages if I should roam
What business had I here to roam!
The world for my remarks and me
Will not a whit the better be;
I've left my heart at home.

And there it is, the matchless earth,
There spreads the fam'd Pacific Ocean!
Old Andes thrusts yon craggy spear
Through the grey clouds; the Alps appear
Like waters in commotion.

Yon tawny slip is Lybia's sands
That silver thread the river Dnieper;
And {yonder clothed in ~~brightest~~} ~~on the Skirts of Ocean~~ green
Is a sweet Isle, of Isles the queen;
Ye Fairies from all evil keep her!

And see the Town where I was born,
~~An~~ Around those happy fields we span
In boyish gambols — I was lost
Where I have been, but on this coast
I feel I am a man.

{Ne'er} Never did fifty things at once
Appear so ~~lovely~~ {touching} never never;
{~~groves~~ How tunefully the forests} ~~The Woods [illegible] [illegible] [illegible]~~ ring
To hear the earth's soft murmuring,
Thus could I hang for ever.

Shame on you! cried my little Boat
Was ever such a heartless Loon!
{Within a living} ~~In such a lovely~~ Boat to sit
And make no better use of it,
A Boat {twin Sister of} ~~that is like~~ the crescent moon.

Out, out, and like a brooding hen
Beside your sooty hearth-stone cower,
Go creep along the dirt and pick
Your way with your good walking-stick
Just three good miles an hour.

Ne'er
~~Love~~ in the breast of full-grown Poet
Fluttered so faint a heart before—
~~So faint a heart was neer before~~
Was it the music of the spheres
~~Come to the [illegible] delight~~
That overpowered your mortal ears
~~Have ten thousand lovely sight~~
Such din shall trouble them no more
~~Ten thousand sights in store.~~
These nether precincts do not lack
Charms of their own—then come with me,
I want a comrade, and for you
There's nothing that I would not do,
Nought is
There's ~~nothing~~ that you shall not see

above Siberian snows

Haste! and ... of snow

Will sport amid

~~Will sport among the boreal Morning~~

Will mingle with their lustres flying

Among the Stars, the Stars now hiding,

And now the Stars adorning.

I know the secrets of a Land

Where human foot did never stray

Fair is the Land as evening skies,

And cool though in the depth it lies

Of burning Africa.

Or we'll into the realm of Faery

Among the lovely shades of things

The shadowy forms of mountains bare

And streams, and bowers, and ladies fair

The shades of palaces and kings;

~~you thirst with~~ desiring ~~generous~~ zeal
Or if ~~appearances of dread~~
Less quiet regions to explore
~~And strong disturbance thrust you more~~
~~that~~ Prompt voyage shall to you reveal
How earth and heaven are taught to feel
The might of magic lore."

little vagrant
My ~~pretty little~~ Form of Light,
gay
My ~~sweet~~ and beautiful Canoe
Well have you played your friendly part
~~Now, though it grieves me to the heart,~~
As kindly take what from my heart
~~Sped, sped that we must part,~~
Experience forces—then adieu
~~I must take leave of you.~~

Temptation lurks among your words,
~~You are a most delightful Barge,~~
~~pleasure~~ ~~you~~ ~~rove,~~
But ~~while~~ ~~that~~ pleasure ~~you're~~ pursuing
whiles these pleasure you're—
Without impediment or let,
radiant Pinnace
My ~~little~~ Barge, you ~~quite~~ forget
What on the Earth is doing:

To sage or bard in mystery vers'd
When Poets fearlessly rehears'd
The wonders of a wild career.

There was a time when all mankind
Did listen with a faith sincere
~~Then Poets where~~ ~~on their flight~~
~~Then boldly might the trump of Fame~~
~~Rehearsed with confident delight~~
~~Blown by the Poets breath proclaim~~
The wonders of ~~their~~ wild career

Go – but the World's a sleepy world
And 'tis, I fear an age too late,
Take with ~~you some adventurous~~ aspiring
~~[illegible]~~ ambitious youth
For I myself, in very truth
Am all unfit to be your Mate.

Long have I lov'd what I behold
The night that calms the day that cheers;
The common growth of mother earth
Suffices me – her tears, her mirth,
Her humblest mirth and tears.

The dragon's wing—the magic ring
I shall not covet for my dower
If I along that lowly way
With sympathetic heart may stray
And with a soul of power.

These given what more need I desire
To stir to soothe or elevate
What nobler marvels than the mind
May in life's daily prospect find
May find or there create.

A potent wand doth sorrow wield:
What spell so strong as guilty fear!
Repentance is a tender Sprite
If aught on earth have heavenly might
Like dreams, and written by her light
Tis [illegible] within her silent tear
All troubles disappear.
~~quenched~~
lodged

But grant my wishes
~~My shining Pinnace~~ let us now
Descend from this aerial height.
Then take thy way adventrous Skiff,
More daring far than Hyppogrif,
And be thy own delight.

To
~~For me are homelier tasks prepared~~

To the stone table in my Garden
Loved haunt of many a summer hour
The Squire is come ~~and as I guess~~,
his the
~~His little ruddy~~ daughter Bess,
Beside him in the cool recess
~~With them the Churchwarden.~~
Sits blooming like a flower.
O shield me, shield me from reproach
~~This was the appointed day and hour~~
From all reproaches shield me heaven
They know not I have been so far—
~~I'm wretched~~ see th
~~I see them~~ there in number nine
Beneath the spreading
~~All in the Bower of~~ Weymouth Pine
~~I see them~~
I see them, there they are!

There sits the Vicar, and his Dame,
And there my good Friend Stephen Otter,
And, ere the light of evening fail
To them I must relate the Tale
Of Peter Bell the Potter."—

Off flew my ~~pretty~~ ~~little~~ sparkling Boat in scorn
Yea ~~All~~ in a trance of indignation;
And I, as well as I was able,
On two poor legs, to ~~my~~ brown stone table,
Limp'd on with some vexation.

O here he is!" cried little Bess,
She saw me at the Garden door,
"We've waited anxiously and long"
They cried, and all around me throng
Full nine of them or more.

Reproach me not. your fears be still
Be thankful we again have met—
Resume your seats within the Bower
My friends, and promptly shall be given

"Resume your seats within the Bower"
Reproach me not, your fears be still
I softly said with visage pale,

And, if my Friends it pleases you,
This instant without more ado
We'll have the promised Tale.

They resumed their seats within the bower,
And I though somewhat out of breath,
With panting breath
With lips, no doubt, and visage pale,
And sore too from a slight contusion
Did I, to cover my confusion,
Begin the promised Tale.

Appendixes

Appendix I

Andrew Jones: Reading Text and Transcriptions

Although *Peter Bell* did not get into the *Lyrical Ballads,* where it may at one time have been intended to go (see Introduction), a thirty-five-line poem called *Andrew Jones,* written in the *Peter Bell* stanza, was published in the second edition (1800). It reappeared in all subsequent editions of *Lyrical Ballads* and in Wordsworth's 1815 collected edition; it was dropped out of all the editions from 1820 to 1849–50.

The connection of *Andrew Jones* with *Peter Bell* seems obvious from the versification and the similarity of the story line to an incident in Peter's history (see 1799 reading text, ll. 1123–1125). Decisive evidence is available in manuscript versions in the Alfoxden Notebook (DC MS. 14) and what used to be called MS. Verse 18A (DC MS. 16—see *Chronology: EY,* pp. 321–322), both of which give the name of the central character as Peter, not Andrew.

This appendix presents the *Lyrical Ballads* (1800) version and a transcription of the lines as they appear in the Alfoxden Notebook. Variant readings from MS. 16 are included in an *apparatus criticus* to the Alfoxden transcription, which begins with five lines not in MS. 16. The published version has an introduction and conclusion apparently designed to give the incident sufficient independence to separate it from *Peter Bell*; it is therefore ten lines longer than the manuscript version—otherwise the differences are not significant. The 1800 version has been collated with the versions in *Lyrical Ballads* of 1802 and 1805 and in the 1815 collected edition.

The entire passage in the Alfoxden Notebook is written closely, without divisions between stanzas. It is in Wordsworth's hand and appears to be a swift fair copy. The passage begins after a horizontal line drawn about one-quarter of the way down the page, and it ends with a line drawn across the page overleaf, followed by a single line of verse:

> The echoes beat the rocks as if with wings

followed by another line drawn across the page.

ANDREW JONES.

I hate that Andrew Jones: he'll breed
His children up to waste and pillage.
I wish the press-gang or the drum
With its tantara sound would come,
And sweep him from the village!

I said not this, because he loves
Through the long day to swear and tipple;
But for the poor dear sake of one
To whom a foul deed he had done,
A friendless Man, a travelling Cripple!

For this poor crawling helpless wretch
Some Horseman who was passing by,
A penny on the ground had thrown;
But the poor Cripple was alone
And could not stoop—no help was nigh.

Inch-thick the dust lay on the ground
For it had long been droughty weather:
So with his staff the Cripple wrought
Among the dust till he had brought
The halfpennies together.

It chanc'd that Andrew pass'd that way
Just at the time; and there he found
The Cripple in the mid-day heat
Standing alone, and at his feet
He saw the penny on the ground.

---

1 "I *1802, 1805*
2 "His *1802* pillage: *1815*
3 "I *1802* press-gang, *1815*
4 "With *1802* sound, *1802, 1805* come,] come *1802, 1805* Would, with its rattling music, come— *1815*
5 "And *1802* village!" *1802, 1805* village. *1815*
10 Man] man *1815* Cripple. *1802–1815*
12 Horseman, *1815* by,] by *1802, 1805*
14 alone, *1805, 1815*
16 ground, *1802–1815*
19 dust, *1815*
21 chanced *1805, 1815* passed *1805, 1815*

He stoop'd and took the penny up:
And when the Cripple nearer drew,
Quoth Andrew, "Under half-a-crown,
What a man finds is all his own,
And so, my Friend, good day to you."

And *hence* I said, that Andrew's boys
Will all be train'd to waste and pillage;
And wish'd the press-gang, or the drum
With its tantara sound, would come
And sweep him from the village!

---

26 stoop'd] stopp'd *1800, corrected in errata* stooped *1805, 1815*
28 "*Under half-a-crown, 1815, in italics*
29 "What *1802* *entire line in italics 1815 with* own,] *own;*
30 "And *1802* friend, *1802–1815, but entire line in italics 1815*
31 said] say *1815*
32 trained *1805, 1815*
33 wished *1805, 1815* press-gang,] press-gang *1815*
34 Would, with its rattling music, come— *1815*
35 village. *1815*

[23r]

And now he sees a shallow stream
Across the highway fret and ripple
And he bethinks him then of one
To whom a foul deed he had done
A helpless man a travelling cripple
For this poor crawling helpless wretch
It chanced some traveller passing by
A penny on the ground had thrown
But the poor cripple was alone
And could not stoop no help was nigh
Inch-thick the dust lay on the ground
For it had long been droughty weather
So with his staff the cripple wrought
Among the dust till he had brought
The halfpennies together—
It chanced that Peter passed that way
Just at the time & there he found
The cripple in the mid-day heat
Standing alone and at his feet
He saw the penny on the ground

[23v]

He stooped and took the penny up
And when the cripple nearer drew
Quoth Peter under half a crown
What a man finds is all his own
And so my friend good day to you—

1–5 *not present in MS. 16, from which pages have been cut just before the surviving text of Andrew Jones begins in DW's neat fair copy*

10 stoop, *MS. 16*

11 lies *rev to* lay *MS. 16*

15 together—] together *MS. 16*

17 time, *MS. 16*

19 alone, & *MS. 16*

20/21 *two words in pencil* (WW) *probably overflow revision from facing verso, now removed*: To [?smile] *MS. 16*

21 and] & *MS. 16* Penny *MS. 16*

23 *in left margin, one illeg word in pencil* (WW), *MS. 16* "under *MS. 16*

25 And so, my Friend good day to you" *MS. 16*

25/ *two words in pencil in left margin, MS. 16* (WW): steps [?severe] *illeg line in pencil across bottom of page, MS. 16*

Appendix II

"I love upon a stormy night": Transcription

Following Dorothy Wordsworth's copy of the conclusion of *Andrew Jones* (see Appendix I) on 89r of DC MS. 16, there appears in her hand on 89v and 90r the only known version of "I love upon a stormy night." Like *Andrew Jones*, this forty-five-line passage is written in the *Peter Bell* stanza. The proximity to *Andrew Jones* and the stanzaic form prompted de Selincourt's comment accompanying the first publication of the passage in 1944: "This poem . . . was probably written at the same time as *Peter Bell*, and is, perhaps, a rejected first draft of its Prologue, or an overflow from it" (*PW*, II, 531). It is also possible that the passage was part of the beginning of the third section of *Peter Bell*.

This appendix presents a transcription "I love upon a stormy night" as Dorothy wrote it into DC MS. 16.

[MS. 16, 89v]

I love upon a stormy night
To hear those fits of slender song
Which through the woods and open plains
Among the clouds or in the rains
The loud winds bear along

Then do I love to stand alone
By some huge rock or tree defended
To stand like one that's blind and catch
Of those small strains the last faint snatch
For human ears intended

But sweeter when the moon shines bright
And the clear sky in calm blue weather
With rocks and woods and with the green
Of a small meadow makes a scene
Of earth and heaven together

But sweeter then when you could hear
Almost could hear a falling feather
To listen to that music small
Prolonged through many a madrigal
For half an hour together

[MS. 16, 90r]

But you will say how can this be?
I'll tell you for the truth I know
Above the ocean's foaming~~s~~ waves
Through hollow woods and gloomy caves
A thousand beings come and go

I've heard them many and many a time
A thing you'll say that's past cconceiving
Over the green and open lands
And o'er the bare and yellow sands
Their airy dances weaving

'Tis not for one like me to tell
Their shape their colour and their size
But they are thin and very spare
Beings far thinner than the air
And happier than the summer flies

And often too by lake or grove
Have I beheld from time to time
A troop of tiny spirits fair

All glistening like the moonlight air
Or sparkles in the frosty rime

And I have seen in glade or bower
Sweet shapes upon the moonlight ground
Some here as little fairies small
Some there as human beings tall
All dancing round and round

827
WOR
PET

CLASS MARK | STOCK No.
YHK, W8
Y. C7
Wor

AUTHOR/HEADING
WORDSWORTH, W.

BIRKBECK COLLEGE
19 0737140 0

BIRKBECK COLLEGE
Malet Street, London WC1E 7HX
071-631 6239
If not previously recalled for another reader, this book should be returned or renewed before the latest date stamped below.

22-5-95
1999
16 APR 1999